Tchaikovsky
THROUGH OTHERS' EYES

Russian Music Studies
Malcolm Hamrick Brown, founding editor

Tchaikovsky
THROUGH OTHERS' EYES

Compiled, Edited and with an
Introduction by

ALEXANDER POZNANSKY

Translations from Russian by

RALPH C. BURR, JR. & ROBERT BIRD

INDIANA UNIVERSITY PRESS
Bloomington & Indianapolis

This book is a publication of

Indiana University Press
601 North Morton Street
Bloomington, Indiana 47404-3797 USA

http://www.indiana.edu/~iupress

Telephone orders 800-842-6796
Fax orders 812-855-7931
Orders by email iuporder@indiana.edu

Manufactured in the United States of America

Library of Congress Cataloging-in-Publication Data

Tchaikovsky through others' eyes / compiled, edited and with an introduction by
Alexander Poznansky; translations from Russian by Ralph C. Burr, Jr. and Robert Bird.
p.   cm. — (Russian music stidies)
Includes bibliographical references and index.
ISBN 0-253-33545-0 (cl. : alk. paper)
1. Tchaikovsky, Peter Ilich, 1840–1893. 2. Composers—Russia—Biography.
I. Poznansky, Alexander.   II. Series: Russian music studies (Bloomington, Ind.)
ML410.C4T38 1999
780'.92—dc21

[B]   98-45509
                                              MN

1 2 3 4 5 04 03 02 01 00 99

CONTENTS

ACKNOWLEDGMENTS

I would like to thank the New York Foundation for the Arts, whose financial support made the research and writing of this book possible. The work was financed in part by a grant from the International Research and Exchanges Board, with funds provided by the U.S. Department of State (Title VIII program) and the National Endowment for the Humanities. None of these organizations is responsible for the views expressed herein.

Among the individual scholars, friends, and colleagues who have contributed to this project in many ways, I would begin by thanking the late Lowry Nelson for his enthusiasm and practical help. I owe a personal and professional debt to Vasily Rudich, who contributed criticisms, comments, and insights at every stage of the work. My special thanks go to Robert Bird and Ralph C. Burr, Jr., for their major contribution in translating the Russian texts into English, to Masayuki Yasuhara for his invaluable assistance during one of my recent archival trips to Russia, and to the late Leonard Forman, who helped me in locating many obscure Tchaikovsky memoirs and photographs.

I feel particularly grateful to Joanna and Daniel Rose for their generous material and moral support.

For their hospitality and unfailing interest in my work I am further indebted to my Russian colleagues Galina Belonovich, Polina Vaidman, and Lyudmila Shapovalova, all of the Tchaikovsky Archive and House Museum at Klin, who provided me with an opportunity to examine the composer's papers; to Irina Medvedeva of the Glinka State Central Museum of Musical Culture in Moscow; to Lyudmila Korabelnikova of the Institute of Art in Moscow; to Anatoly Altshuller of the Institute of the History of Arts in St. Petersburg and especially, to Valery Sokolov, an independent scholar, who through his diligent documentary research and commitment has recently succeeded in changing much in our understanding of Tchaikovsky.

Also I want to express my thanks to the friendly staff of the Helsinki University Library, the Russian National Library, the Archive of the Russian Federation, the Russian State Archive of Literature and Art in Moscow, and the Yale University Sterling Memorial Library.

My special gratitude goes to Jeffrey S. Ankrom, Malcolm Hamrick Brown, and Roberta L. Diehl for their editorial help.

I deeply appreciate considerable help by Brett Langston, who compiled the index and generously shared with me his fine knowledge of Tchaikovsky's work.

I owe the completion of this book to my wife Elena and son Philip, whose love and patience never cease to provide me with confidence and inspiration.

ALEXANDER POZNANSKY
HAMDEN, CONNECTICUT

Note on Transliteration, Names, and Dates

In transliterating Russian titles and names in bibliographical references I have used the Library of Congress system. Russian names in the main body of the text are spelled so that the sound of the Russian variant is preserved without an eccentric appearance: Pyotr instead of Petr, Alexander instead of Aleksandr, Poplavsky instead of Poplavskii. Russian patronimics have been dropped in most cases, with the exception of members of Russian royalty and Pyotr Ilyich Tchaikovsky. In order not to confuse the Western reader, Russian diminutives are changed to the person's full name. Dates in the book are Old Style, which was twelve days behind the Western calendar in the nineteenth century. For references to Tchaikovsky's stays abroad, both the Old and New Styles are given.

INTRODUCTION

When Pyotr Ilyich Tchaikovsky died unexpectedly of cholera on 25 October 1893 in St. Petersburg, nobody could have anticipated the manner in which his personality would be perceived throughout the next century. Today, when Tchaikovsky's place as the most popular composer in the world after Mozart has been assured and the basic facts of his life are known to many music lovers from a number of biographies, his personality still remains shrouded in misstatements and misconceptions.

In the West, he has often been referred to as a "crazy genius" or, stereotypically, as a "mad gay Russian," and his music—by extension—has been decried as sentimental or decadent. In contrast, the official line in the Soviet Union, starting with 1940, strove for the unqualified glorification of Tchaikovsky as both artist and human being by suppressing all material deemed ideologically suspect, including references to the composer's private life.

Both Western and Soviet attitudes have facilitated the spread of sensational rumors about his allegedly enforced suicide in consequence of some murky drama, a legend that has even found its way into otherwise respectable studies. Not a single shred of concrete evidence exists to support these allegations. A careful analysis of the available material as regards the circumstances of his fatal illness rules out any possibility of foul play and of a subsequent cover-up. Furthermore, the very picture of the great composer as a tormented soul is incompatible with contemporary documentation about his character and the facts of his biography.[1] Since little new and unbiased documentary material on Tchaikovsky is being published in the West or even in today's Russia, it is imperative to make available more information about him in order to elucidate the realities of his life and combat the wild speculations of some Tchaikovsky biographers.

The present book does not propose to provide a full range of contemporary responses to Tchaikovsky's music. An English translation of critical pieces from the period concerning Tchaikovsky's music would indeed be a valuable contribution, since it would tellingly reveal the dynamics of the composer's public reception, but this would comprise an altogether different project that perhaps should be taken up in the near future. The purpose of the present effort is to concentrate on Tchaikovsky's personality, to explore its many dimensions and those aspects which so far have either remained unknown or have been suppressed by his earlier biographers.

In the Soviet Union several collections of memoirs about Tchaikovsky have been published, but the texts presented there were selected from a biased perspective and, furthermore, carefully censored.[2] Most of the material which has recently become available in English was derived from this source.[3] The present volume is intended to fill a long-existing gap, and to bring into scholarly circulation many reminiscences of Tchaikovsky by his contemporaries which hitherto have remained either obscure, uncollected, or altogether unpublished.

Approached either as documentary evidence or literary genre, memoirs often create difficulties for interpreters. A historian or biographer working with this kind of material must be continuously aware that it stands somewhere between fiction and nonfiction. As nonfiction, a memoir is supposed to deal with facts, but the very nature—emotional and psychological—of reminiscence causes it to exhibit a tendency toward literary forms and techniques characteristic of a work of fiction. On the other hand, the very ambiguity of memoiristic discourse provides us with a spectrum of insights into a subject, going beyond a mere establishment of what actually happened in the past.

For the historian of private lives—that is, the biographer—getting beyond birth certificates and wills is the major goal, and one is lucky if one has available a good archive of correspondence, diaries, and contemporary publications. None of this, however, can replace the avenues of research opened up by the recollections of those who personally knew the subject.

The study of memoirs has to proceed, on the one hand, as the comparative analysis of texts with regard to the fact or fiction presented by a memoirist. On the other hand, it also demands a psychological inquiry that takes into account the personalities and the idiosyncrasies of both memoirist and subject.

Memoirs differ from official documents in their unfixedness, since the subject appears in a different light in each new recollection, and in their partiality, insofar as the character of the memoirist invariably leaves an indelible imprint of him- or herself. Likewise, memoirs differ from testimony, i.e., a fixed recording of an immediate experience (e.g., in a letter or diary entry), since they are distinguished by a distance in time, by their being re-created in retrospect, and, consequently, by the risk of past events being distorted, whether intentionally or not.

One must not seek dates, names, and even definite facts of the subject's life in biographical recollections. Unless there are substantial grounds to suspect fraud or a cover-up, a document leaves no doubt as to the veracity of what it records. This is not always the case with memoirs. One is entirely dependent on each individual memoirist, not only in terms of his or her subjectivity, sympathies, and bias, but also with respect to his or her strength of memory, willingness to verify reported information, and an entire gamut of psychological characteristics. One trap into which memoirists often fall is reporting an episode borrowed from the reminiscences of others as if it were first-hand experience.

The value of memoirs lies not so much in the concrete evidence they afford, but rather in the multifaceted portrayal of their subject. Here, despite the disagreements obtaining between various accounts, the reader is bound to appreciate elements of both psychological and artistic truth. Even if endowed with the purest intention of objectivity and superior powers of observation, authors of memoirs are bound to diverge in their perception even of individual episodes; consider the number of witnesses in court who never provide exactly the same information of the event they are supposed to have witnessed at first hand.

At the same time, in any collection of reminiscences about a given individual, one always discovers an unmistakable agreement on basic personality traits—and it cannot be otherwise. Two metaphors illustrate the tension between factual disparity and basic consensus: the resultant force in physics; or, perhaps more to the point, a symphony, which counterpoints a multitude of voices but harmonizes them within the unity of the work as a whole.

It is on the aspects and quality of those individual voices that the authenticity of our knowledge and impressions depends. What counts is, in the first place, the time when the memoirist embarked on writing his or her reminiscences—that is to say, the stretch of time between the date in question and the date of composition. A sole reliance on memory can be deceptive, especially in the matter of dates, places, and personal names. This also pertains to the degree of the memoirist's participation in the events described and his or her intimacy with the subject—authors often tend to exaggerate one or both of these factors.

Next, one should be capable of discriminating between memoirists' use of personal material and their reliance on other sources, a matter which is not always easy to resolve. Last but not least, it is imperative to expose both fantasies and omissions caused by individual bias on the part of authors who were family members, friends, or enemies of the subject, not only those arising from conscious strategies, but also those of a spontaneous origin, caused by factors ranging from ignorance to self-deception. In the final analysis, the pitfalls one encounters in ascertaining the truth about someone else's life are essentially the same as those which we encounter in our daily existence and which help us to determine introspectively whether we are self-aware or self-deluded.

Memoirs, as a source of exciting information about private lives, never cease to generate considerable attention on the part of the general public. Tchaikovsky the reader was no exception. Herman Laroche, a music critic and his close friend, recalls that the composer's greatest passion after music was "memoir literature—the sort of history in which the fates of government and society disappear behind the depiction of personality, behind the elaborate detail of someone's psychology and everyday life."[4]

Concerning the life of Pyotr Ilyich Tchaikovsky our source material is indeed abundant. The main stages of his public and professional career are easily established or verified with the help of contemporary official documents, which include his prodigious correspondence and surviving diaries. As regards the corpus of memoirs written by his family, friends, and acquaintances, it is both voluminous and heterogeneous, so that it calls for careful judgment in selection and interpretation. Ideally, each case must take into account what may be called the shaping or the literary ambition of the memoir as a whole, in other words, the ruling hypotheses, theories, or intents that motivated the authors to share their memories with the rest of the world.

The majority of the extant texts offer a glowing picture of the composer, elaborating (sometimes almost ecstatically) on his modesty, benevolence, generosity, and so forth, which is not surprising given Tchaikovsky's considerable charisma and his status as a celebrity. Still, one should observe that several authors—none of them belonging to his close circle—emphasize the composer's less attractive features, such as misogyny, irritability, and egotism. As far as the numerous anecdotes about him found in reminiscences are concerned, they must be taken with some caution: in the first place, this is a habitual device used to enliven the narrative. Further, one expects to hear anecdotes about any famous person. Finally, often one and the same anecdote recurs in several texts, the authors of which could by no means have witnessed the actual episode they report.

Perhaps the subtlest temptation for the interpreter is to accept, against all caveats, a dramatically narrated event that may contravene probability. Thus, for instance, the well-publicized story, told by Nikolay Kashkin allegedly from Tchaikovsky's own words, that the latter attempted suicide in 1877 by entering the Moskva River in order to contract pneumonia, not only fails to be supported by any other evidence but flatly contradicts the composer's basic pattern of behavior, which was to flee and hide at moments of hardship, and not to court death by Russian roulette.

In some cases this penchant for drama results in the distortion beyond credibility of otherwise known events, as, for instance, in the reminiscences of the Hungarian violinist Leopold Auer, when he recalls Tchaikovsky's momentous marriage to Antonina Milyukova and writes that the latter "had fallen in love with him and, despairing of attracting his attention, went to his house one evening and knelt before him pale and haggard, saying that she had come to die beside him, since without him life meant nothing to her. She then drew a revolver, and pressing it against her heart, prepared to pull the trigger. Tchaikovsky, much alarmed, and eager to avert a tragedy in his quiet home, wrested the revolver from the young girl's hands, sought to calm her agitation and, in order to soothe and reassure her, went so far as to promise to marry her. Like the true gentleman he was he kept his word, and this hasty and ill-starred marriage took place not long afterward."[5] Besides the fact that the Conservatory student Antonina Milyukova did fall in love with Tchaikovsky and finally married him in July 1877, nothing in this story corresponds to reality.

Other authors apparently tried to adjust their memories of the composer to their own psychological needs and prejudices. Thus, the pianist Alexander Siloti, who knew Tchaikovsky quite well for many years, claims that "everybody knew" of Tchaikovsky's homosexuality and "about his sufferings from it." "His continuous urge for solitude, his reserve, his secretiveness... we used to explain by this pathological abnormality of his. Thereby we pitied and loved him even more."[6] There is little doubt that the composer's sexual orientation was common knowledge, but one cannot help asking how Siloti would have known about Tchaikovsky's "sufferings" from it if the composer, according to all available documentation and with the exception of the brief period before his marriage, always insisted on the opposite. Finally, it is imperative to identify sheer fiction based, at best, on hearsay, a category of memoiristic storytelling to which the whole theory of Tchaikovsky's enforced suicide undoubtedly belongs.

The present volume is a first critical edition in English of reminiscences about Tchaikovsky the man. The memoirs, diary entries, and interviews written and conducted by his contemporaries—friends, relatives, fellow musicians, journalists, and state officials—focus on him as both public and private figure: student of the School of Jurisprudence, Conservatory professor, generous promoter of talent, loving brother and uncle, conductor, philanthropist, intrepid traveler, and friend to many individuals over the entire range of Russian society, from servants to members of the Imperial family. These texts provide multiple insights into little-known facets of Tchaikovsky's character, his foibles and manners, politics and tastes, prejudices and preferences, including ones of a sexual nature, so that the reader may appreciate the richness of the artist's nature, which ultimately could not but affect the nature of his art.

Ten chapters offer over fifty entries of varying lengths. I have allowed some editorial intervention by including only those parts of the lengthier texts which deal directly with Tchaikovsky and his environment, as well as by omitting a few repetitive passages. In contrast to all previous endeavors, I have deliberately presented some narratives unfavorable to the composer, such as those by Alexander Rubets, Mariya Gurye, Alexandra Sokolova, and Leonid Sabaneyev.

Among the least known texts I would note the uniquely informative diary of Tchaikovsky's one-time servant Nazar Litrov, written in 1890 during the composer's work on *The Queen of Spades*; entries from the diary of Grand Duke Konstantin Konstantinovich concerning his first meeting with the composer in 1880; and selections from Modest Tchaikovsky's *Autobiography*, which illuminate the composer's early years.

Considerable attention is paid to Tchaikovsky's marriage and death, since new materials from Russian archives throw additional light on these central and controversial episodes from his life. The memoirs of Tchaikovsky's wife Antonina and of Vladimir Nápravník, son of Eduard Nápravník, the conductor of the Imperial Opera, are published here in English for the first time. Nápravník's memoir, never published in any language, is devoted to his encounters with Tchaikovsky in St. Petersburg in October 1893.

The reader will also find many new and exciting stories concerning the composer in memoirs which have hitherto been completely unknown in the English-speaking world, written by his friends: the actor Konstantin de Lazari, the architect Ivan Klimenko, the musician Vasily Korganov, manager of the office of Imperial Theaters Vladimir Pogozhev, and the pianist Vasily Sapelnikov.

Special attention is also drawn to 1892 interviews with Tchaikovsky from the Russian press, which contain many valuable observations concerning Tchaikovsky's relations with his contemporaries. These interviews have also never been published in English.

The primary intent of this book is to provide new and stimulating material for scholarly biographical treatment. The scope and constraints of the volume made it perforce impossible to handle each selection with the same methodological rigor. Each chapter is prefaced with a statement on facts from the composer's life, given chronologically, and brief comments on the authors and the character of their memoirs.[7]

The notes provide the relevant bibliography and, whenever possible, identify individuals and artifacts. They are limited to those matters which are not self-explanatory and which bear directly on the subject of the narrative. The desired effect is to create a dynamic portrayal of the composer seen from the perspectives of very different people. In other words, instead of the mosaic of the earlier similar collections, I have attempted to achieve a kind of polyphony, interweaving old and new voices in order to relate the remarkable story of the great man.

Knowing the life and personality of any artist helps to enrich our perception of that artist's work, allowing us to respond in a more complex way both to

the emotional and psychological problems encountered by the creative genius
and to their aesthetic resolution. In Tchaikovsky's case this bears on the peculiar
emotional poignancy of his music, which has either been extolled or berated,
but which has never received a proper explication. Rethinking this matter may
help us to reconsider certain musicological clichés regarding Tchaikovsky, and
perhaps even his place in the cultural Pantheon, together with the relevance of
his work to our present-day concerns.

Tchaikovsky
THROUGH OTHERS' EYES

I

The Schoolboy
(1840–1863)

The following recollections focus on the three least documented periods of Tchaikovsky's life: his childhood, school years, and the time immediately following his graduation from the School of Jurisprudence. The future composer spent his earliest years with his family in the Urals, and later in St. Petersburg, up to the time when he began to study music seriously at the St. Petersburg Conservatory.

Pyotr Ilyich Tchaikovsky was born on 25 April/7 May 1840 at Votkinsk, in Viatka Province, which is located in the Urals 600 miles east of Moscow. He was the second son of Ilya Petrovich Tchaikovsky, a mining engineer and manager of the Kamsko-Votkinsk ironworks, and Alexandra Andreyevna Tchaikovsky (née Assier).[1]

On his father's side, Tchaikovsky's origin may be traced to the Ukrainian village Nikolaevka in the Poltava region. His great-grandfather was an eighteenth-century Ukrainian Cossack named Fyodor Chaika. Later the family name was changed to Chaikovskii, which is usually spelled in English according to the French transliteration, Tchaikovsky.

At first Chaika's son Pyotr studied in a seminary in Kiev, but he later received medical training in St. Petersburg. From 1770 to 1777 he served as a physician's assistant in the army. Eventually, he found himself in the Ural region and there, in 1776, married Anastasiya Posokhova. In 1785 he was included (as a member of the landless gentry) in the register of nobility instituted by Catherine the Great. He resigned from his medical service and ended his life as city governor of Glazov in Viatka Province. Pyotr Tchaikovsky had nine children, one of whom was the composer's father Ilya (1795–1880). After graduating from the College of Mines in St. Petersburg with a silver medal, he held several teaching and administrative posts, some of the latter in the northeast of Russia.

In 1837 Ilya became a factory manager in Votkinsk. This city was famous for its ironworks, which had been founded in 1758, and by 1820 it could boast the first hearth furnace in all Russia. As manager of the ironworks Ilya Tchaikovsky enjoyed broad authority within the Ekaterinburg region—from governing local factories to repealing the decisions of local courts. Ten years earlier, in 1827, he had married Mariya Kaiser, who died in 1830, leaving him with a daughter, Zinaida.[2]

Tchaikovsky's mother, Alexandra (1812–1854), was the younger daughter of Andrey Assier (1790–1832), who was descended from a French émigré family. According to the version preferred by Tchaikovsky himself, the d'Assiers were Protestants who left France after the revocation of the Edict of Nantes in 1685; another, more reliable version maintains that the d'Assiers left in the wake of the French Revolution in 1789. At first Michel d'Assier lived with his family in German lands. Around 1795 they moved to Russia and, by an oath of allegiance, officially became subjects of the Imperial Crown. Michel's son Andrey, "owing to his social connections and excellent knowledge of almost every European language, came to occupy a distinguished position within the bureaucracy" in St. Petersburg, where he served in the Customs Department.[3] He received government honors and was twice married. From his first marriage to Ekaterina Popova he had four children, including Alexandra, the composer's mother. After the divorce of her parents and the death of her mother in 1816, Alexandra was placed in the so-called Patriotic Institute, the government sponsored school for orphaned girls from noble families, where she received a fine education. In 1833 she met Ilya Tchaikovsky and married him.[4]

Apart from his stepsister Zinaida (1829–1878) and elder brother Nikolay (1838–1911), after Pyotr's birth in 1840 the Tchaikovskys would have a daughter, Alexandra (1841–1891), and three more sons: Ippolit (1843–1927), and the fraternal twins Anatoly (1850–1915) and Modest (1850–1916).

Tchaikovsky was never close to Zinaida, nor was he particularly intimate with his older brother Nikolay, who followed in the steps of their father as a mining engineer, or with the younger one, Ippolit, who became a naval officer. But he dearly loved his sister Alexandra (or Sasha), and his youngest brothers, the twins Modest and Anatoly, always enjoyed his particular affection. Later in life Anatoly made a prominent career in law, rising eventually to the rank of privy councilor and senator, while Modest became a playwright and educator, as well as the biographer of his famous brother Pyotr.

Tchaikovsky's earliest musical impressions came from the family's orchestrion, with its excerpts from Mozart, Rossini, Bellini, and Donizetti. In September 1844, he made his first documented attempt at composition—"Our Mama in Petersburg," a song written together with Alexandra. Pyotr became deeply attached to his French governess, Fanny Dürbach, and he also developed a friendship with the son of a neighbor, Venedikt Alekseyev. At the end of 1845 he began taking piano lessons with one Mariya Palchikova and became familiar with the mazurkas of Chopin. Tchaikovsky later recalled, "In my boyhood I had an inclination for music. I was only five years old when I began my studies with a lady, and soon I began to play upon the piano Kalkbrenner's 'Le Fou' and other fashionable pieces of the day. I believe I used to surprise my friends in the Ural district with my virtuosity."[5]

In 1848 Ilya Tchaikovsky resigned his post and the family moved first to Moscow and later, in the expectation of a new appointment, to St. Petersburg. In St. Petersburg, Pyotr and Nikolay were placed in the private Schmelling School, where Pyotr resumed piano lessons. But the appointment in the capital did not materialize, and in May 1849 the family had to return to the Urals where Ilya Tchaikovsky was appointed manager of an ironworks in another city, Alapaevsk, some 300 miles to the east of Votkinsk. This did not prevent the composer's mother from returning with him to the capital the following autumn so that he could enroll in the preparatory class of the Imperial School of Jurisprudence.[6] On this occasion Pyotr saw Mikhail Glinka's *A Life for the Tsar* [*Zhizn' za Tsaria*] at the Alexandrinsky Theater, which made a lasting impression on him.

During the next couple of years Tchaikovsky's parents moved back and forth between the Urals and St. Petersburg, finally settling in the capital in 1852. By this time Pyotr had successfully passed his entrance exam for the School of Jurisprudence, where he participated in the school choir under the direction of distinguished Russian choirmaster Gavriil Lomakin (1812–1885).[7] Tchaikovsky later remembered, "My voice was a splendid soprano and for several years in succession I took the first line in the trio which on these occasions was sung by the three boys at the altar at the beginning and end of [the Liturgy]."[8]

Tchaikovsky's mother's sudden death from cholera on 14 June 1854 was a traumatic event for Pyotr, then a young adolescent. Later that year the Tchaikovsky family chose to live together with the family of Ilya's brother Pyotr (1789–1871), a retired general, in a large apartment on Vasilyevsky Island, an arrangement that lasted for three years. After Ilya's eldest daughter Zinaida married Evgeny Olkhovsky and left the capital to live in the Urals, Alexandra, now fifteen years old and newly graduated from school, ended up in charge of the household and of the twins.

Tchaikovsky spent the years 1850–1859 as a boarding student at the School of Jurisprudence. "I remained there nine years, and did not do much in music in that time," Tchaikovsky observed thirty years later.

> There was a musical library, a piano room, and a teacher; but he simply gave indifferent technical instruction—a sort of fashionable instruction for the young nobles in the school. My parents did not see anything more in me than a future office-holder. At the age of seventeen I made the acquaintance of an Italian singing teacher named [Luigi] Piccioli. He was the first person who took an interest in my musical inclinations, and he gained great influence over me. My father was finally obliged to give me

some scope for the development of my taste, and before I had reached my eighteenth birthday he was good enough to put me under Rudolph Kündinger, a piano teacher. Kündinger was a native of Nuremberg, and had settled in St. Petersburg. He was a fine pianist and thorough musician. I took lessons from him every Sunday, and made rapid progress in piano playing. Kündinger took me to concerts where I heard plenty of classical music and my fashionable prejudice against it began to disappear. At last, one fine day, I heard Mozart's 'Don Giovanni.' It came as a revelation to me. I cannot express the delight which seized me.[9]

At that time Tchaikovsky also made his first attempts at composition, among which were an opera, *Hyperbole* (lost), a waltz for piano, and his first published work, the song "Mezza notte."

His stay at the School of Jurisprudence must have enhanced Tchaikovsky's innate homosexual sensibilities. This institution, like any boarding school, was never distinguished by high morals of any sort, a fact well known to contemporaries: the school, for instance, could boast an obscene homosexual song composed by its students, and it also produced a number of prominent homosexuals. Of his schoolmates, two loomed large in his life of that period— Alexey Apukhtin (1841–1893), a future poet of renown, and Sergey Kireyev (1845–1888?), arguably the most passionate of all Tchaikovsky's attachments.[10] Outside the school he forged a close relationship with his cousin Anna Tchaikovsky (later Merkling), the daughter of his uncle Pyotr.

In the autumn of 1858 Tchaikovsky's father was named to the coveted directorship of the Technological Institute in St. Petersburg, and his family moved to the director's large apartments. At the end of 1860 Tchaikovsky's sister Alexandra moved away from the family after marrying Lev Davydov, a well-to-do landowner; the couple settled at his family estate, Kamenka, in Ukraine. A few years later Ilya Tchaikovsky married for a third time, taking as his wife Elizaveta (or Lizaveta) Lipport, who had already been taking care of his household for several years.

A month after his graduation on 13 May 1859, Tchaikovsky began working as a clerk in the Ministry of Justice. Although he remained there for four years, he quickly found the job ill-suited to his abilities. At the same time, he entered the capital's social and cultural milieu as a young man about town, spending much of his energies in the pursuit of pleasure, engaging in affairs and amorous adventures with members of his set, until the threat of homosexual scandal, according to the account of his brother Modest (following in this chapter), sobered him up.[11]

In the summer of 1861, Tchaikovsky traveled abroad for the first time as secretary and interpreter for a family friend, Vasily Pisarev. In the course of this trip he visited Berlin, Hamburg, Antwerp, Brussels, London, and Paris.

In the autumn Tchaikovsky's life took an unexpected turn: he began attending Nikolay Zaremba's class in thoroughbass offered by the Russian Musical Society, which had recently been founded by Grand Duchess Elena Pavlovna and Anton Rubinstein with the purpose of promoting professional music education in Russia. Much later Tchaikovsky himself explained this turn of events to an American reporter:

> Yet, after leaving the School [of Jurisprudence] I was still only a fairly accomplished dilettante. I often had the desire to compose, but I did little. I spent two years as an undersecretary in the Ministry of Justice, went into society and to the theatres a good deal, but did not push forward in music. In 1861 I became acquainted with a young officer who had a great reverence for music. He had been a student of Zaremba's courses in musical theory. This officer expressed himself as not a little astonished at my improvisation on a theme which he gave me. He became convinced that I was a musician and that it was my duty to make music my earnest and continued study. He introduced me to Zaremba, who accepted me as a student and advised me to leave my office and devote myself to music.[12]

When the St. Petersburg Conservatory was opened on 8 September 1862, Tchaikovsky was among its first students. Herman Laroche, the future music critic and composer, also enrolled in the same year, and the two soon became friends. Tchaikovsky studied harmony and form with Nikolay Zaremba and orchestration and composition with Anton Rubinstein.

Having decided to devote his life to music, Tchaikovsky resigned from the Ministry of Justice on 11 April 1863. This decision coincided with the onset of financial hardships for his father Ilya, who by this time had retired from the directorship of the Technological Institute. To support himself, Tchaikovsky began giving private lessons in piano and music theory to students recommended to him by Anton Rubinstein.

The first part of the chapter consists of the reminiscences of Tchaikovsky's French governess Fanny Dürbach (1822–1901) and Tchaikovsky's younger brother Ippolit. Fanny Dürbach's account combines excerpts both from her letters to Modest and Pyotr and from Modest's records of his later conversations with her.[13]

Fanny Dürbach was governess in the Tchaikovsky home from November 1844 until September 1948, when the family left Votkinsk. A gifted teacher, she had a marked influence on Tchaikovsky's early development. Although he was only eight years old when he parted with Fanny, he never forgot her, occasionally corresponded with her, and in December 1892 he visited his former governess at her home in Montbéliard, a small town in eastern France.[14] He later wrote to Modest that his impression from this visit was "extraordinarily powerful, strange, and magical."[15] To his surprise, Fanny had preserved all of his childhood letters and exercise books. In 1894 Modest also visited Fanny and recorded her recollections of those early years.[16] One must observe, however, that, written decades after the events described, her narrative sentimentalizes past experiences and is fraught with customary clichés on the theme of a "golden childhood." Consequently, it should be treated with some caution.

The composer's younger brother Ippolit was a major-general in the Russian Navy and, from 1919 until his death eight years later, served as curator of the Tchaikovsky House Museum at Klin. In 1913 he published extensive memoirs about his life in the navy that mention his famous brother Pyotr only in passing, at the beginning of his narrative where he touches briefly on his family.[17] The Tchaikovsky archives have preserved his brief unpublished notes concerning the death of their mother; they also contain some observations on Tchaikovsky's personal traits, intended to help his younger brother Modest write the composer's biography.[18] The narrative in this chapter combines recollections from both sources. This is a valuable document owing to its vivid description of the eleven-year-old Ippolit's reaction to his mother's death, which also must shed some light on Pyotr's feelings at the same time.

The second part of the chapter offers the recollections of Tchaikovsky's classmates and schoolmates from the School of Jurisprudence: Fyodor Maslov, Ivan Turchaninov, Vladimir Gerard, and Alexander Mikhailov, as well as those of his piano teacher Rudolph Kündinger. All these memoirs, with the exception of Mikhailov's, were recorded by Modest Tchaikovsky as he conducted research for his biography of his older brother.[19]

Fyodor Maslov (1840–1915) was one of Tchaikovsky's closest friends during their first years at the school and as fellow clerks at the Ministry of Justice. He later became chairman of the Moscow Appellate Board. In his memoirs Maslov brings out many interesting facts, among them Tchaikovsky's first unsuccessful attempt at conducting the school choir. It can hardly be doubted that Maslov played some role in developing the future composer's "special friendships" within the walls of the school. His own intimate relationship with his schoolmate Vladimir Taneyev is well documented.

Ivan Turchaninov (1839–1910), in addition to being in the same class as Tchaikovsky, also belonged for a period of time to the future composer's close circle of friends, which makes him a reliable source even for details. By contrast, Alexander Mikhailov (1842–1899) was merely a fellow student at the school, one who most likely saw the young Tchaikovsky only from a distance, which did not, however, prevent him from producing a colorful, if brief, sketch of Tchaikovsky's behavior and appearance.

Vladimir Gerard (1839–1903), another classmate and fellow clerk at the Ministry of Justice, later became a prominent lawyer and public activist. Gerard was particularly close to Tchaikovsky during the last year of their senior course, which is attested by several photographs taken of them together in the year of their graduation and shortly thereafter. There exists a group photograph of the twentieth graduating class, where Tchaikovsky and Gerard are seated together in the first row and make the impression of a couple in clear and close physical contact with one another: Gerard is pressed up against Tchaikovsky, tenderly holding his hand.[20] Other evidence exists suggesting that, after their graduation, Gerard continued to belong to the homosexual milieu that gathered around Apukhtin. His memoirs stress quite ostentatiously Tchaikovsky's interest in the opposite sex, which is not surprising given the societal conventions of the time.

Rudolph Kündinger (1832–1913), a German pianist, moved to Russia in 1850, where he became a piano teacher and later a professor at the St. Petersburg Conservatory. At the request of Tchaikovsky's father he gave private lessons to Tchaikovsky while the future composer was a student at the School of Jurisprudence. His brief recollections shed additional light on Tchaikovsky's musical development and on the status of a professional musician in Russian society of the period. Surprisingly enough, Kündinger evidently failed to appreciate the youthful Tchaikovsky's talent.

Modest Tchaikovsky was also a graduate of the School of Jurisprudence. Eventually, he would became Tchaikovsky's closest friend and confidant, although their relationship was by no means simple, and on occasion fraught with mutual frustration. Modest made a moderately successful career as a tutor for a deaf-mute pupil, Nikolay Konradi. A minor playwright and a translator of Shakespeare, he was also the author of the librettos for his brother's operas *The Queen of Spades [Pikovaia dama]* and *Iolanta*. After the composer's death, he devoted himself to establishing the Tchaikovsky Museum at Klin.[21] In 1902 Modest published his monumental three-volume *Life of Pyotr Ilych Tchaikovsky (Zhizn' Petra Il'icha Chaikovskogo)*, available in English only in an abridged one-volume edition compiled by Rosa Newmarch in 1906. This biography has made available many excerpts from the composer's letters, the memoirs of his friends and relatives, and Modest's own reminiscences, all of which are interwoven with the biographer's narrative.

Even with the publication in 1981 of all Tchaikovsky's known correspondence in his *Complete Works (Polnoe sobranie sochinenii: Literaturnye proizvedeniia i perepiska)*, Modest's biography continues to be a valuable source owing to its inherent literary merits and to its generous quotations from Modest's own recollections and from recollections which he compiled from various people, and which are not otherwise available in print. However, Modest's narrative suffers from a conflict between two tendencies—the memoiristic and the documentary—which is never resolved. Furthermore, his purpose, clearly and consistently carried out, was to idealize and romanticize the figure of Tchaikovsky and present all his actions in the best possible light. Since it would have been very difficult to mention the composer's unorthodox sexual preferences at the end of the last century, this led naturally to the exclusion of anything that might have dealt directly with Tchaikovsky's homosexuality (a predilection that Modest shared), even to the point of expurgating his correspondence and, most likely, tampering with the original letters. Some evidence suggests that Modest may have done this reluctantly, at the insistence of his other relatives and in accordance with contemporary social conventions.[22] Nevertheless, however obliquely, in his biography Modest still left us many glaring hints and indications of Tchaikovsky's interest in the same sex.

Modest recognized that, at the time when his biography was published, it was impossible to delve into some of the more intimate aspects of his brother's and his own experiences. This accounts for the fact that, around 1905, Modest undertook to write an unofficial *Autobiography,* the text of which was apparently not intended to see the light of day during its author's lifetime.[23] Although it was left unfinished (it ends with Modest still in the graduating class of the School of Jurisprudence), this account is remarkable in its candid confession of homosexual sensibilities, and it fills in a few gaps concerning his brother's adolescence and early youth.

Published here are the most important excerpts bearing directly on the composer from the text of Modest's still unpublished *Autobiography.* Some parts of the *Autobiography* were published in 1962, but the most revealing facts Modest tells about his older brother have never been published before.[24]

In order to fill in Modest's description of his brother's lifestyle between the latter's graduation from the School of Jurisprudence and his matriculation at the Conservatory in St. Petersburg, I have also added a curious anecdote from the recollections of Arkady Raich, a socialite and minor journalist, who was at the time well acquainted with Tchaikovsky's immediate milieu.[25]

Fanny Dürbach

The journey from Petersburg [to Votkinsk] with Mrs. Tchaikovsky and [her elder son] Nikolay took about three weeks, and during this time we became so close that by the time we approached the [ironworks] factory we were quite friendly. The kindness and attentiveness of Mrs. Tchaikovsky and the good looks, even beauty, of Nikolay warmed me to my traveling companions, while the latter's good manners were a guarantee the task before me would not be difficult. But still I was very nervous. Everything would be fine if on arriving I had only to deal with Mrs. Tchaikovsky and her son, but shortly I would be finding myself among completely unfamiliar people and living conditions.

Therefore, the nearer we drew to our journey's end, the more anxious and agitated I became. But when we finally arrived at the house, it took a mere moment for all my fears to vanish without a trace. A crowd of people came running out to greet us, there were delighted embraces and kisses all round, and in this group of people it was hard to distinguish relatives from servants. A sincere, lively joy made everyone equal; everyone welcomed the return of the mistress of the house with the same affection and warmth. Mr. Tchaikovsky came up to me and, without a word, embraced me and kissed me like a daughter. This easy and patriarchal manner immediately reassured me and put me in the position almost of a member of the family. I had not simply arrived but seemed also, like Mrs. Tchaikovsky and her son, to have "returned home." The next morning I took up my lessons without the slightest apprehension or fear for the future.[26]

I soon had a very diligent little class. We had our rules, and each of the children strove to get the best mark without any envy among them. The one who did best during the week was awarded a red ribbon on Sunday. Besides Mlle Amable Tastu's *L'Education maternelle,* we also had Miss Edgeworth's *L'Education familière* in several volumes.[27] For natural history we had a small illustrated copy of Buffon.[28] For reading, there were the tales of Guizot, Father Schmidt, and my own class books, which I also used.[29] One volume, a particular favorite of ours, which we used to read and retell on Saturday evenings, was Michel Masson's *Les Enfants célèbres.* . . .[30]

As far as textbooks are concerned, we also had the geography and atlas of Meissas and Michelot, which at the time served us well, though now they have long since been replaced by others in the schools, and more than once, I believe.[31] For German language we followed [Johann] Ahn's method, which has now vanished as well.[32] When Pierre was here he said to me, "You should know that I've not forgotten my German," and we talked together for a while. "You now speak better than I," I said to him. "Do you like the language?" "I like them [i.e., Germans]," he answered. He liked Germans, but also Englishmen. In general he was fond of everyone. . . . It was impossible to know him and not feel the tenderest affection for him. . . .

We [my charges and I] lived entirely apart from the adults; we joined them only for meals. Not only our lessons but also our amusements were our own. We spent evenings before a holiday reading or talking in our rooms upstairs. In the summer we had a carriage at our disposal, and we made excursions to the lovely environs of Votkinsk. On weekdays, from six o'clock in the morning, all our time was strictly ordered, and the program was carried out punctually. Since the free time when children could do what they wanted was very limited, I insisted that they spend it in physical exercise, and for this reason I was always having altercations with Pierre, who after class was strongly drawn to the piano. Although he always obeyed readily and enjoyed running and romping about with the others, he always had to be told to do so. Left to his own devices, he would more willingly turn to music or else start reading or composing verses. . . .

After lessons or long improvising at the piano he always came to me nervous and distressed. One time the Tchaikovskys had guests, and the whole evening was spent in musical entertainment. Because of the holiday the children had joined the adults. Pierre was at first very lively and merry, but toward the end of the evening he became so tired that he went upstairs earlier than usual. When I went into the nursery some time later, he was not yet asleep but was crying agitatedly with glistening eyes. When I asked what was the matter, he answered: "Oh, this music, this music!" But there was no music to be heard at that moment. "Save me from it! It's here, here," said the boy, sobbing and pointing to his head, "it never leaves me in peace!"[33]

The child's exceptional charm was apparent in nothing in particular and in absolutely everything that he did. In class no one could have been more diligent and quick, while at recreation time no one invented more amusing games; when we read for entertainment no one listened more attentively, and at twilight on the eve of a holiday, when I would gather my charges about me and have them each by turns tell some story, no one was more charmingly inventive. I shall never forget those wonderful times in our life together. In daily converse with him everybody loved him, because they felt how much he himself loved everybody. His sensitivity knew no bounds, so one had to treat him very carefully. The slightest trifle could hurt or offend him. He was a child of glass. When he was scolded or reprimanded (punishing him was out of the question), what other children turn a deaf ear to, he took very much to heart, and the slightest increase in severity so upset him that it became quite terrible. Once, while scolding both brothers for a poorly done exercise, I mentioned that I pitied their father who worked so hard to make money for his children's education, while they were too ungrateful to appreciate this and treated their lessons and responsibilities carelessly. Nikolay heard me out and later that day was running and playing as happily as ever with a group of his friends, but Pierre remained pensive all day, and in the evening, as he was going to bed, when I myself had already forgotten the reprimand I had given that morning, he suddenly burst into sobs and began saying how much he loved his father and how unfair it was to accuse him of ingratitude toward him. One could not help loving him, because he loved everybody. The weak and unfortunate had no more ardent defender than he. Once he heard that someone was preparing to drown a kitten. Finding out who the monster was who was contemplating such a dreadful act of villainy, he went off and successfully petitioned for mercy. Then he raced home, burst into his father's study, where his father was meeting with some business associates, and, thinking there could not possibly be any topic of conversation in the house other than the kitten, triumphantly reassured them, reporting the joyous news of the "rescue."

Not long before the Tchaikovsky family left Votkinsk, a certain Romanov [an employee of the factory] came to work there. His son, Nikolay, was for a few months one of my pupils. He enjoyed teaching his new playmates games he had brought from Petersburg. Though an excellent student, his favorite pastime was wrestling and sparring. Mrs. Tchaikovsky, who desired the children to be well behaved even during playtime, strictly forbade these contests, but one day while I was giving Alexandra and Ippolit their lessons I was very surprised and distressed when Carolina (the younger children's nanny) arrived from the garden very upset to tell me that Nikolay and Venedikt were wrestling fiercely and that the contest was nearly becoming a fight, with neither of them listening to her, and Venedikt, in particular, refusing to stop fighting. I was especially surprised by this, because Venedikt was normally very sensible and obedient for his age. Carolina had just left when my boys returned. [Tchaikovsky's cousin] Lidiya was at the piano. Without saying a word, my pupils sat down on the sofa opposite our class bench. "It pains me greatly," I began, "that I cannot trust you and work with the younger children in peace. You, Venedikt, for your disobedience go tell the coachmen to hitch up the carriage and take you home." No sooner had I uttered these words than I immediately regretted it. The poor child burst into tears. Then Pierre stood up and said: "Mlle Fanny, you forget that Venedikt has no mother and that, since you are taking her place, you don't have the right to send an orphan away." "So, Pierre, my pupils can misbehave and I have no right to punish them?" "Punish him with the same punishment as you do us, and don't think up something special. We are all three guilty and should all be punished alike." Venedikt could only say: "Forgive me." Nikolay also. And I was all the more willing to forgive them since even by sending Venedikt home for one day I would have violated the rights granted me by Mrs. Tchaikovsky. . . .

One time during recreation Pierre sat studying an atlas. Coming to a map of Europe, he suddenly began covering Russia with kisses and then pretended to spit on all rest of the world. I stopped him and started to explain that it was shameful to have such an attitude toward beings who prayed the Lord's Prayer just as he did, that scorning his neighbors for not being Russian was bad, that this meant he was spitting on me as well, since I was not Russian. "You're wrong to scold me," answered Pierre. "Didn't you notice that I covered France with my hand? . . . "

Poor Pierre felt very lonely when [after leaving Votkinsk] he had to study by himself. In the absence of Nikolay, his friend [Venedikt], and myself, he sought consolation in music. He himself wrote me of this: "I try as much as possible not to leave the piano, it is a comfort to me." I do not forget that he was an artist by birth, but he was as much a poet as musician. I write this because I do not want the child I loved so much to be misjudged. . . .

Rereading his papers not long time ago, I found on a page he had written when he must have been no more than eight years old: "For what purpose did He create me, this all-powerful God?" How many mature people have perhaps never asked themselves this question, and here he was asking it while still a child! . . .

I have never seen such beautiful sunsets as in Russia, when the sky was filled with such amazingly vivid colors; I especially loved the quiet, mild evenings in late summer. The boats of the fisherman drifted in the pond, smooth as a mirror, in which the sun was reflected. From the balcony we listened to their sweet and melancholy songs—they alone broke the silence of those wonderful nights. [Pierre] must remember them; none of [the children] wanted to go to bed then.

Ippolit Tchaikovsky

Our apartment [during the summer of 1854] was on Solyanoy Lane. As soon as our mother's malicious disease (cholera) was discovered, the four younger children, myself included, were sent to the apartment of our Aunt El[izaveta] Schobert, who was then living on Vasilyevsky Island, on the Second Line, in the Schiele house.[34]

When it was clear that Mama was near death, someone, I don't recall who, but I think it was Aunt Elizaveta, arrived from Solyanoy Lane, and they discussed which of the children to take to receive our mother's blessing. I remember they took Alexandra and Pyotr. My brother Nikolay and the two babies [Modest and Anatoly] stayed at the Schiele house.

I was in anguish at the sight of Nikolay's grief. Just as I was, without my hat which they had hidden from me on purpose, I set off at a run toward Solyanoy Lane. I was eleven years old at the time. With no clear idea how Petersburg was laid out, I asked passersby how to get there. Many people, seeing how upset I was, took notice of me, and, when asked where I was rushing to, I would explain, not without some posturing, that I was in a hurry to see my mother who was dying, and thus I evoked considerable sympathy.

I reached the gates of our house just as Pyotr and Alexandra were coming out, and they told me that it was all over. I was taken back home without being allowed to go up to the apartment.[35]

After our mother's funeral, our father also came to live temporarily in the home of our aunt, and soon, from the heavy loss he had suffered and a cold, he too took to his bed. There were days when his life was in serious danger. . . . Always kind and enormously loving by nature, our father worshipped his children, and thus was greatly distressed by the doctor's prohibition against letting the children in to see him for fear of disturbing his already weakened condition.

Fyodor Maslov

Pyotr Ilyich was a favorite not only of his fellow students, but also of the administration. No one else enjoyed such widespread appeal. Starting with his graceful appearance, everything about him was attractive and placed him in a quite exceptional position.

When we entered the seventh form, Pyotr Ilyich was particularly friendly with [Fyodor] Belyavsky, but I soon replaced the latter.[36] During the second semester of the seventh form and the first semester of the sixth we were almost inseparable. With the move to the sixth form we were joined by Apukhtin, who came from my province. Things continued in this way until the end of 1853, when a rift occurred. I had fallen ill and spent some time in the infirmary. When I got out, I was very surprised to see that Tchaikovsky was no longer my deskmate. He was sitting with his new friend Apukhtin. A quarrel ensued. We former friends stopped speaking to one another. In the fifth form we made up, and until the end of the [junior] course, and later for the rest of our lives, we remained quite friendly, though we never regained our original intimacy. But with Apukhtin I was never friends again.

With respect to music, Pyotr Ilyich, of course, stood head and shoulders above his fellow students, but he found in them no serious sympathy for his vocation. We were merely amused by the musical tricks he used to perform, such as guessing keys and playing the piano with the keyboard covered by a towel.

From the day he entered the school he sang in the choir, and for the first three years he was one of the second trebles, where he sang the lead part. They needed him there because this was where they put the trebles with poor voices and ears. Having to sing alongside these comrades who were singing out of tune was torture for him. In the seventh and sixth forms Pyotr Ilyich sang in the "You have entered, O Master" *["Ispolaeti despota"]* trio at the archbishop's service on St. Catherine's Day, then later, in the fifth form, "Let my prayer arise" *["Da ispravitsia"]*, though now as an alto rather than a treble. The precentor was always a student of the first form. This was essential because the precentor's duties were more than just musical. It was his job to assemble everyone for choir practice, which for the older students required the authority of someone senior in years and position at the school. But in the 1853/54 school year, there was no musician good enough in the senior course to be precentor, and a student of the junior course, Gamaley, was appointed to the position.[37] In 1856/ 57 he was followed by Khristianovich (brother of the composer),[38] in 1857/58 by [Pyotr] Yurenev, and in the autumn of 1858 by Tchaikovsky.[39] Pyotr Ilyich remained precentor only a short time, no more than two months, because he demonstrated neither the skill nor the inclination to take command, and Seletsky, who started out as his assistant, replaced him.[40]

Pyotr Ilyich began to smoke very early on, though his most intimate friends were not smokers.

In daily life he was notable for his disorderliness and untidiness. He pinched nearly the whole of his father's library for his friends, but then he himself never bothered to return other people's books that he had borrowed. In 1869 in Moscow at the home of the new conservatory professor, who no longer had anything to do with jurisprudence, I found juridical works still "overdue" from the time of his stay at the school, including, among others, three copies of Stoyanovsky's handbook of criminal proceedings.

Pyotr Ilych was always without his textbooks and would beg his friends for theirs, but his own desk was, as it were, public property, and anyone who wished could rummage around in it. In the senior course Pyotr Ilyich and I prepared for our exams together. We chose the Summer Garden for our study spot, and so as not to lug our notes and textbooks about with us we hid them in the hollow trunk of one of the linden trees, covered over with boards. When the exams were over I removed my papers from the tree. But Pyotr Ilyich constantly forgot to do this, and his school books may well to this day be rotting away inside one of Peter the Great's seedlings.

Pyotr Ilyich was keen on literature and took an active part in the *School Herald [Uchilichshnyi vestnik]*, the journal published and edited in the fifth form by Apukhtin and Ertel.[41] It was he who penned the remarkably simple and incisive "History of Literature in Our Class."

In his last years at school Tchaikovsky kept a diary titled *Everything,* where he poured out all his innermost secrets, yet he was so trusting and naive that he never locked it away, but left it in his desk where his and other people's books and writing pads were all heaped together.[42]

[During his years at the Ministry of Justice] the aristocratic side of his personality, in the sense of a refined and perceptive sensibility, showed in his striving to reach the heights of society in the figurative and literal sense of the word, and also in the profound distaste he felt for the spirit then reigning among the military. His attraction to everything beautiful and lovely to look at showed, among other things, in his concern with his appearance. Being poor, he could not dress elegantly, and this caused him much pain.

Ivan Turchaninov

There was something undeniably special about Tchaikovsky that set him apart from the crowd of other boys and made our hearts go out to him. Kindness, gentleness, responsiveness, and a sort of insouciance with respect to himself were from early on distinctive features of his character. Even the stern and savage Rutenberg showed a special sympathy for him.[43]

We first met in the preparatory class, during Tchaikovsky's second year there, so that I did not witness his extraordinary longing for his parents. We were always on friendly terms and maintained the best of relations during our time at the school. The outward reason for our closer friendship was that, beginning in 1856, we both spent our holidays on Vasilyevsky Island and therefore would make trips there and back together. The period of our friendliest relations was while we were preparing for examinations in the senior course. Then we would take turns staying at each other's home, and I became quite at home in the Tchaikovsky household.

After graduation from the school our ways parted and we rarely saw each other. I visited Pyotr Ilyich for the first time after graduation when he was already at the Conservatory and living with his father on the corner of Leshtukov Lane. There, in Pyotr Ilyich's small, poorly furnished room, I once met a young man with whom he apparently studied—this was Laroche. I also visited the apartment at the Technological Institute.

Like most of our fellow students, I took little interest in Pyotr Ilyich's musical talent. No one at the school ever foresaw his future fame, but I remember how the future composer at that time used to dream that someday an opera of his would be presented on the stage, and I promised to be at the first performance. This came to pass, though at a performance not of *Oprichnik* but of *Vakula the Smith [Kuznets Vakula]*. I went backstage to show that I had kept my promise, and I had the pleasure of meeting and embracing the composer, who was then glowing with satisfaction and happiness.

Alexander Mikhailov

Always pensive, preoccupied with something or other, with a slight but charming smile and girlishly pretty, [Tchaikovsky] would appear among us in his little jacket with the sleeves rolled up and spend hours on end at the piano in the music room. He played magnificently. . . . Tchaikovsky showed the clear beginnings of a solid musician.

Vladimir Gerard

His gentleness and tact in his relationships with all his fellow students made Pyotr Ilyich everybody's darling. I do not remember him ever having any serious quarrel or enmity with anyone. During our first years at the school we were more or less strangers to one another. In the final forms of the junior course, however, we were already beginning to grow closer; for a time we shared the same desk. Our real friendship took off in the senior course, and in particular in the first form. At this time I kept a diary in which I would pour out my enthusiastic feeling of first love for a certain lady and, I recall, at the same time, thank fate for granting me, alongside this love, such an ideal friendship.

Besides an inexplicable mutual sympathy, we were bound together by a love of the theater. One time Pyotr Ilyich took me to a performance of [Rossini's] *Guillaume Tell* at the Italian Opera. Tamberlik, De Bassini, and Bernardi sang.[44] The impression was so powerful that from that day on I became a passionate lover of opera and often attended performances together with my friend. Moreover, we both loved French theater, which was generally in vogue among the students of the school. At that time the Mikhailovsky Theater (before its renovation) had a balcony of fifty-two seats. We were not allowed to sit in the regular theater seats, and it might happen, especially at benefit recitals by favorite performers, that all fifty-two places in the balcony were occupied by students of the school.

Although Pyotr Ilyich's fame as a musician was eclipsed by the fame of the poet Apukhtin, in whom we saw a future Pushkin, his talent nevertheless attracted attention, but none of his fellow students ever had an inkling of the future composer's fame. I remember clearly how after choir practice in the White Hall, when Lomakin had left, Pyotr Ilyich would sit down at the harmonium and improvise on themes suggested to him. One could give him any melody, and he would play endless variations on it. For the most part, the themes for these improvisations came from the new operas we had just heard.

As a student, Pyotr Ilyich was capable, but only moderately diligent and very absent-minded, and later, as a civil servant, he failed to distinguish himself in either a good or bad sense.[45]

Both of us loved social affairs. I recall how, for the sake of meeting the pretty sister of one of our schoolmates, we both went to some length to get invitations to a ball at the Zalivkina boarding school, and how our efforts were crowned by success and we both danced zealously.[46]

Through Pyotr Ilyich I was welcomed into his family, though compared with others of his friends I visited more rarely, because during my last two years at the school I became terribly keen on billiards and spent a great deal of time at Wolf's (a restaurant near the Police Bridge).

The general spirit of the students of the school differed significantly from that of today. A tendency to dandyism began to appear only toward the end of our stay at school. At that time, even in the senior class only two of our classmates had their own uniforms, and they were often mocked by the others for their foppery. The rest all made do with conventional uniforms. On the whole, our attitudes and interests were very serious. We were all mad about literature, and therefore most of us regarded almost with contempt any attempts to compete in elegance with the Lyceum students.[47]

Rudolph Kündinger

I arrived in Russia as a young man of eighteen and first made a name for myself with a performance of Litolf's piano concerto at one of the university concerts.[48] On this occasion it happened that the orchestra, which was made up primarily of amateurs with only a small number of real musicians, was for some reason unable to play, and I had to perform the concerto without an orchestra. I managed to win the sympathy of the audience, and at once I began receiving offers from all sides for employment as a music teacher.

I[lya] Tchaikovsky engaged me to give lessons to his son Pyotr, a student at the School of Jurisprudence. From 1855 till 1858 our lessons were interrupted only during the summer months, and my pupil made good progress, though not such as to spark in me any particular hopes for him. When Ilya Petrovich asked me whether it would be worthwhile for his son to dedicate himself wholly to a musical career, I replied in the negative, first of all because I did not see in Pyotr Ilyich the talent that subsequently came to light and, second, because I knew from my own experience how difficult the position of a "musician" was at that time in Russia. We were looked down upon in society and treated with condescension, nor was there any serious appreciation or understanding [of music as a profession]. A[nton] Rubinstein was already playing nearly as well as during the most brilliant period of his career, but until his tour abroad he was held in slight esteem in Russia. I heard him for the first time in the early 1850s in Bernard's shop.[49] The occasion made a staggering impression on me, yet those around me remained cool to his playing.

If I could have foreseen whom that law student would turn into, I would have kept a journal of my lessons with him, but, unfortunately, I have to say that I never had the slightest inkling of the sort of musician I was dealing with, and therefore I have only a very vague recollection of the details of my pupil's musical development. To be sure, his abilities were striking: a remarkably keen ear, a memory, an excellent hand, but this was not enough to cause me to foresee in him even a splendid performer, much less a composer. There was nothing surprising in this: I have met many young men with these same talents, both before and after Tchaikovsky. The only thing that somewhat caught my attention was his improvising—in this, one did indeed get a faint sense of something rather out of the ordinary. In addition, I was sometimes struck by his flair for harmony. He still had little acquaintance with music theory, but several times when I showed him my compositions he gave me advice concerning harmony that was for the most part quite sensible. . . .

For a certain time, on my recommendation, Pyotr Ilyich took lessons in music theory from [my] brother August, now deceased. How long this lasted, I cannot say, but, in any event, it was no more than a season. Why these lessons ceased, I also do not recall.[50]

I held my lessons with him once a week, on Sundays. In terms of virtuosity, the progress made during the three years of my lessons was not significant, most likely because Tchaikovsky had no time to practice properly. Very often we would finish our lesson by playing something for four hands, after [which] I would stay to have lunch with the Tchaikovsky family (I remember a great number of young ladies there), and then he and I would go to the university concerts, which were then the sole refuge for music-lovers. The low level of musical requirements at that time is clear from the fact that these better symphonic concerts took place with no rehearsal.

In 1858, owing to changed circumstances, Tchaikovsky's father was no longer able to pay me for lessons, and I completely lost sight of my pupil, whom I always remembered quite clearly and fondly as a most charming young man in whom I did not foresee the renowned future composer.[51]

Arkady Raich

I knew Apukhtin in his early youth, when he was in the upper forms of the School of Jurisprudence, at the beginning of the 1860s. At that time Apukhtin was a small, thin, blond youth with light blue eyes and a scrofulous aspect. No one of course, could then have imagined that this skinny boy would change over the years into the hulk that he later became. . . .

On graduating from the school, Apukhtin, like all his classmates, joined the staff of the Ministry of Justice. But the civil service, a serious attitude toward it and a career clearly held little interest for the young poet. To all appearance, his young fancy, under the influence, perhaps, of his encouragement at the school, continued unwittingly to harbor an image of Pushkin and his stormy youth. He mingled wholeheartedly with Petersburg's gilded youth and shared the passions of their frenzied nights. And the pranks were endless. Two of these come to mind. One summer evening Petersburg's *beau monde*, promenading along Elagin Island and watching the setting sun, caught sight of a most eccentric amazon in a fantastic costume surrounded by brilliant young cavalrymen. The cavalcade galloped past once, twice, and many of his acquaintances finally and not without surprise recognized the mysterious amazon to be Apukhtin.

Then another: During the 1860s the Italian singer [Emma] Lagrua was singing in Petersburg, where she was enormously popular.[52] But the crowning role in her repertoire was [Bellini's] *Norma*, and especially Norma's aria "Casta diva," which music lovers claimed she performed like no one else. One evening when *Norma* was scheduled at the Bolshoy Theater, Lagrua was unable to go on due to illness, and the performance was postponed. Later that evening at Lagrua's apartment on Nevsky Prospect, in the former Demidov house, the bell suddenly rang, and the housemaid informed her ailing mistress that two gentlemen were at the door, insisting that they see her on an urgent matter. Lagrua assumed them to be officials or doctors from the directorship come to verify her illness. She ordered them let in. In walked Apukhtin with a friend [Tchaikovsky] and announced to the singer that they were provincial landown-ers who had come especially from Orel for one day to hear Lagrua in *Norma*, and that they had to return to Orel immediately following the performance.[53] His pronouncement was quite categorical, with Apukhtin adding that they were not going to leave until Lagrua sang "Casta diva" for them. They could not return to Orel without hearing her! And Lagrua, who at first laughed aloud at the audacity of these odd fellows, demurred, but ended, hoarse though she was, by sitting at the piano and singing "Casta diva" for them.

Modest Tchaikovsky

My first memory of Pyotr is this: evening, a shaded lamp, Papa there with us, something vague having to do with our sister Alexandra—she has arrived or is expected from *Annenschule*—and he [Pyotr] is nearby in the room, sick, and I am so glad that he is home and not at school. Also connected with this is some very foggy image of Pyotr's pale skinny little schoolfriend, Apukhtin. I find him unpleasant, but Pyotr likes him, so we must like him as well. I do not know whether Mama is still alive or not.

Then we are living with the family of Uncle Pyotr Petrovich [Tchaikovsky] on the Cadet Line in the Osterlov house. It is Sunday. The smell of pies fills the air. After breakfast Pyotr has his piano lessons with Kündinger. This is a bore because it takes him away from us. He is much less good-looking than our brother Nikolay. Nikolay has beautiful clean hands, Pyotr not especially, and his nails are bitten down; Nikolay is always elegant, his hair neatly combed, Pyotr always has messy hair, and everything about him is untidy, but I want to be just like him, I love everything about him, both the good and the bad. . . . Pyotr likes to take tea at Aunt Elizaveta's [Schobert], and I want to like it too. . . . Our female cousins and aunts find Apukhtin offensive, but this is because they do not know what Pyotr and I know, that beneath that ugliness and sharp way of saying unpleasant things lie certain treasures. Pyotr's room has a faint odor of tobacco and something else, and I am sad that mine does not have the same. . . . On rare occasions he consents to tell us about his childhood, remembering the Votkinsk factory and Alapaevsk, and sometimes he plays with us for a bit. . . .

He emanated such *joie de vivre,* such an incessant hymn of joy, that like the foolish sounds of a spring bird, his foolish jokes were colored by his charm. Thus, calling me over to him, he would make me say: "Pita, Pita-pitatura, Pita, Pito. . . Pite. . . Petu. . . Petrusha!"—and after this would let me kiss him, and nothing seemed so witty and charming as this.

When he agreed to "torment" us [i.e., Modest and his twin brother Anatoly], he did not condescend, but actually had fun himself, and this made his participation in the game very entertaining for us. He would improvise and create things and thus amuse himself as well. His games were unlike anything else, and everything proceeded from his strange and enchanting nature. . . . No one ever criticized him. On the contrary, he knew how to make the unacceptable permissible. Not only that, even something ludicrous in a pejorative sense became charming when he did it. Thus, he had a passion for imitating female dancers; I too loved to do this, but those around me, both adults and peers, made fun of me and scornfully called it an affectation. . . . Pyotr would do this openly, and in the evenings near the dacha, in the ditch separating the New Place from the English Park, he would give full-scale performances that everyone applauded and no one saw as unsuitable for a boy, and his friends in fact took part in them with pleasure.[54]

In this period [1861] I see Pyotr for the first time in the reception room of the preparatory class. He has just arrived from Paris and has come to visit us, elegant, very handsome now, bringing caramels from Faye. This winter he seems to me, as before, very busy and carried away with amateur theatricals. I remember him in the company of Apukhtin, the Imperial hussar Prince Pyotr Meshchersky, Adamov, Slatvinsky, and Tevyashev, constantly telling of performances in homes unknown to me or rehearsing for them at our home.[55] He was great friends at this time with our cousin Lidiya's husband, Nikolay Olkhovsky.

Olkhovsky was a very talented, witty, and amusing fellow with a fierce love of the theater who managed to be both a serious businessman and a specialist (he was a mining engineer). As such, he received a commission to study financial affairs in Paris. It was there, when Pyotr, having abandoned his traveling companion Pisarev, found himself alone, that the two cousins, who had hitherto been rather indifferent to one another, became close. Throughout the winter, they were constantly reminiscing about their adventures in Paris. Their mania for amateur theatricals brought them even closer. Nikolay Olkhovsky was the director for their little troupe, in which my cousin Amaliya Schobert played the major female roles, while the men included all the friends of Pyotr mentioned above.[56] I remember Pyotr in the play *Gentlelady—Peasant Woman [Baryshnia—krestianka]*, where in the second act he played the secondary role of the landowner and amused everyone with his mimed mosquito-catching, and in *Woe from a Tender Heart [Beda ot nezhnogo serdtsa]*, where he performed the part of the young man, which was considered the "crowning role" in his repertoire.[57] Either I did not see him or do not remember him in other roles. In any case, even my biased eye could not set him apart from the other performers. But I had quite a different attitude about his dramatic talent and knowledge. Not only did I melt with ecstasy when he gave recitations, imitating Ristori, but I also learned from him the "art of rhythmical movement and gesture."[58] He explained to me in detail the difference between the poses of Lagrua (mainly in *Norma*), Ristori, and other actresses, showing where the differences lay, and for a long time his theory of rhythmical movement was for me a standard of theatrical art. The torso invariably had to rest on one leg, as in a statue of Praxiteles, the movement of the arms always fluid and like a statue in every transition—the hand must not be held with the fingers all together or with the fifth finger sticking out, as most Russian singers do, but with the fingers separated from one another so that the fourth finger alone falls slightly and easily below the others. Whether pointing to a door or pointing out guilt, the forefinger should not be on the same plane as the rest of the hand, but invariably form an angle with it, and so on. In ballet, he cited fluidity and the absence of sharp, mincing movements as the chief virtues and, dancing himself, would show me what this consisted of; but, never managing to coax these qualities from me, he laughingly called me Savrenskaya (a third rate female dancer from the Russian Opera), while calling himself Ferraris, because of the fluidity and classicism of his movements.[59] In any event, it seemed to me then that his theatrical interests were more important than his musical ones, which I saw manifested when, recounting the story and stage action, he played and sang for me Mozart's *Don Giovanni*, which he did many times.[60] When our Aunt Ekaterina came to visit us, she would join him in her old lady's voice, but with traces of excellent training, and this was a real occasion for me.[61] Besides *Don Giovanni*, Pyotr often sang and played "Mi mania la voce" from Rossini's *Moïse* and several numbers from [Weber's] *Der Frei-schütz*. Later, when the courses with Zaremba started, Pyotr's musical friends began coming around, and he and they would play four-hand versions of Beethoven's symphonies. Of his partners I can name only Baronetsky, also a graduate of the School of Jurisprudence. I vaguely remember a concert in one of the halls of the Technological Institute to benefit a female student, a certain Siluyanova, where Pyotr and van Ark played on two pianos (or four-handed, I don't remember).[62] In this same concert he gave a solo performance of a polonaise by Weber—his favorite virtuoso piece. I recall that he was offended that the audience gave him little applause, though in his heart of hearts he was equally unimpressed by his performance. Then, as the [music] classes at the Mikhailovsky Palace continued, the pieces Pyotr chose to play became increasingly incomprehensible to me, until finally he began spending hour after hour playing something quite dreadful—the fugues of Bach. He tried in vain to get me to take an interest in them, advising me to follow the repetition of the first theme, but, while I recognized this fact, still I could see nothing good about it, and I began to take less and less pleasure in sitting next to Pyotr at the piano. It pained me not to understand what he understood and to feel that there was an area in which we would always be strangers. . . . During this period Pyotr often improvised at the piano, in particular, as I recall, in the early evening; never at anyone's request, and for the most part avoiding an audience. And if there happened to be people listening and they complimented him, he replied sharply: "It's not worth anything. . . it's nothing much. . . ." When I asked him why he never wrote these improvisations down, Pyotr answered: "Such trifles aren't meant to be written down."

During the summer of 1862, Pyotr spent almost no time at the Golov dacha, coming only for holidays.[63] None of the family or servants had remained at the Technological Institute, and it was impossible for him to live completely alone, so he took up residence with one of his new friends, Vladimir Tevyashev, on Mokhovaya Street. I know that the apartment was on the ground floor, because he would tell of how he used to return home through the window. This was the summer of his most zealous service at the Ministry.

From the autumn of 1862 on, there was no longer any question of amateur theatricals or society acquaintances. Music swallowed up everything. People teased him for letting his hair grow long, were confused and critical and disappointed at his resolution. Laroche made his appearance. I recall how surprised I was to see this near-child (he was seventeen, but looked even younger), whom Pyotr saw as one of the most intelligent and learned of people. Pyotr seemed completely new to me. He was tender with Papa, stayed at home, began increasingly to neglect his appearance, labored assiduously, and paid attention to the needs of Anatoly and me, and he started to care about such things as formerly were incompatible with the image of a brilliant rake. His tender endearments, the utter absence of any talk about theatricals or balls—all of it surprised and moved us and made us happy. . . .

At the Technological Institute his room was located one floor down from our apartment and was for me a sort of sacred place. On his writing table lay some stones he had brought back as souvenirs from Imatra [the waterfalls in Finland], where he had once traveled. . . . Later on, this and a pilgrimage he made by foot to the Sergiyev Monastery in 1858 were two events he always recounted with enthusiasm. . . .

A portrait of Sergey Kireyev stood on Tchaikovsky's desk. . . . This was the strongest, most durable and purest amorous infatuation of his entire life. It comprised all the charms, all the sufferings, all the depth and force of a love both luminous and sublime. This was the courtly "service to the Lady," without the slightest sensual design or intention. Anyone who doubts the beauty and high poetry of this cult should be pointed to the finest passages of Tchaikovsky's musical oeuvre: the middle portion of *Romeo and Juliet, The Tempest [Buria]*, *Francesca*, Tatyana's letter [from *Eugene Onegin*], which could never have been "invented" without having first been experienced, and he would never experience in later life so powerful, lasting and torturous an emotion. . . . They shared their feelings for a period of ten years.[64] Side by side with this Kireyev cult, Pyotr experienced many involvements of a different character, yielding to them unrestrainedly, and with the full fervor of his passionate and sensuous nature. Women were never the object of these infatuations; physically, they aroused in him only indifference.[65]

[At that time] it never occurred to me that the delight that blazed up at the sight of the beauty of a boy or young man, the mad desire to kiss his hand, to serve him, to feel ecstatic anguish at the contemplation of his form and languid pain from the thought that this was impossible—that any of this had anything in common with such filth. I was a thousand miles away from seeing in Pyotr's adoration of Sergey Kireyev anything akin to these dirty things [the matter of sexual relationships] we had been told about [at the age of eight, together with Anatoly, by one of their peers].

Even had I thought to question it, Pyotr's openness in expressing his love, and everyone's recognition of it as something quite normal, would have quelled my doubts. Starting with Papa, everyone talked about Sergey Kireyev, and when Pyotr befriended a certain Sadovnikov, a student at the Technological Institute, seeing in him a resemblence to Kireyev, Sadovnikov became a part of our family, visiting us during holidays, since he was an orphan, and joining me and Anatoly as a playmate.

Following Pyotr's example with Sadovnikov, everyone else in the family, starting with Aunt Elizaveta, found favorites of their own who were invited by turns to our home. Aunt Elizaveta, our sister, and our cousins treated this situation half-jokingly, but not me. . . .

[On one occasion some patrons at St. Petersburg's restaurant Chautemps] were defamed throughout the city as "bougres" [from French bougre; cf. English bugger]. . . .[66] Among the "Chautempsians" were Pyotr and Apukhtin, and they forever acquired reputations as "bougres." . . . The Chautemps affair had a significant effect [on Pyotr]. It was the first time he had to confront the cruel injustice of people who felt indignation and contempt for what should, at the very worst, have evoked in a reasonable and clear-thinking person a feeling of pity for an irremediable natural defect. Of course, just as nothing else in the world could change Pyotr's inclinations, neither did the Chautemps scandal, but he became more circumspect in his amorous adventures and, nursing a feeling of resentment, began to avoid society, where his reputation might do harm to his self-esteem, instead seeking interests outside of the beau monde. I also believe that while he recognized the injustice this condemnation of what is beyond human power to rectify, at the same time society's cruel attitude toward homosexuality affected to some extent Pyotr's critical attitude toward himself. Despite his inner protestations, he could not help succumbing to the influence of the general detestation of this very defect, and, after looking at himself through the eyes of those merciless and unjust judges, he felt an equal lack of mercy in regard to his own infatuations and reached a point of such despair, such dissatisfaction with himself, that the young rake and socialite was transformed into a tender son and brother, the poor civil servant into a fine musician. . . .

In our absence (during the summer holiday [in 1863]) [Tchaikovsky's stepmother] Elizaveta Lipport moved us out of the Technological Institute and set us up in an apartment on Zagorodnyi Avenue, on the corner of Leshtukov Lane, in the Fyodorov house. Everything I found in Petersburg I liked. I do not remember the slightest sense of loss for the spaciousness of the director's apartment at the Technological Institute. It was so warm and cozy in our six rooms! During this time, our brother Nikolay lived with us, and therefore it was very crowded on Saturdays, when we spent the night at home. But it seems to me now that there was not a cozier and happier period in my life than these two years spent in the Fyodorov house. If one recalls how comfortable and warm our family was in the Schiele house [at Elizaveta Schobert's] after Papa's ruin, it would appear that the periods of greatest need and poverty were almost the best, since now Papa was again in a critical position, being obliged to spend half of the two thousand rubles of his annual pension to pay off his debts. How [our stepmother] Elizaveta contrived to do it, I do not know, but I know that none of us went hungry or suffered any privations in that first year. One means of economy, by the way, was to send Papa off to stay with one of his daughters for the summer. So in 1864 he headed to the home of our sister Zinaida in the Urals, Pyotr was bundled off to [his society friend] Prince Golitsyn, and we [the twins, Modest and Anatoly] were sent to stay with Uncle Pyotr in Merekyul, near Narva.

That autumn in Petersburg we resumed our semi-bachelor existence in the Fyodorov house (for our stepmother, as before, lived apart). Like the previous year, I felt the glow of an ineffable hominess and the warm relations among everyone living there, despite our impoverished situation and, at times, near indigence. There were days when our poor stepmother Elizaveta did not know how to feed us. . . . But about the fact that we could not even afford a meal in a Greek eating house, or that for the two days before the blessed day when the pension arrived we had to live on fish and willow grouse, that Elizaveta was forced to make her own dresses out of old curtains or Pyotr went about in a threadbare jacket and wore rags instead of linen—at all this we just laughed. Only our dear old father, planning to go off to our sister Zinaida's for an entire year in order to pay off his debts, did not laugh.

Having renounced his sociable pleasures, Pyotr, apart from visits to his closest friends and to the theater, was for a time keen on games of domino-lotto at the Nobles Club. Besides these diversions, Pyotr kept on Mondays a *jour fixe* at the home of a certain Khristianovich, where a very interesting company used to gather.[67] There he met Gorbunov, a storyteller, the actor Vasilyev, and several men of letters whose names, unfortunately, I cannot now recall, except for Nekrasov and Shcherbina.[68] Add to this the "five-kopeckers," that is, the little restaurants where one could get a tolerable meal for five, ten, fifteen, or twenty kopecks and where Pyotr went "carousing" with Laroche, and we have accounted for all his amusements. During this period one could see in Pyotr an ever-growing estrangement from his former friends. He spoke with scorn of their emptiness and little by little abandoned them completely. . . .

One evening as Anatoly and I were taking a coach back to the School [of Jurisprudence], he grimly told me about a "horrible thing" he had learned just that day: "There exist debased persons called 'bougres' who do not engage in sexual relations with women, but only with boys, and—o woe!—Pyotr is one of them!" I forgot that I was returning to the school, that there was no holiday that week and that the next day off would not be till Saturday; I forgot every trouble and was filled with inexpressible joy. A heavy weight fell from my shoulders. I was not a freak, I was not alone in my strange desires! I might find sympathy not merely with the pitiful pariahs among my classmates, but also with Pyotr! I might fall in love and feel no shame, since Pyotr would understand me. "I am also a bougre!" I blurted out involuntarily. I remember Anatoly's indignation at this outburst, his reproach that I was blindly imitating Pyotr, that I was immoral and a freak. I cared not a whit! Pyotr was like me. Pyotr could understand me. What did the rest of it matter? It was then too that I realized that Apukhtin, Prince Shakhovskoy, Adamov were also "bougres," and it became clear to me why I had always felt a vague sympathy for these men.[69]

With this discovery everything changed. Mankind was now divided into "us" and "them." Seeing among the former not only Pyotr but also such men of outstanding intelligence and talent as Apukhtin and such charming, kind, and elegant men as Shakhovskoy, Golitsyn, and Adamov, and having heard that the heir apparent Nikolay Aleksandrovich, the very embodiment of majesty and beauty, was also "one of us," my earlier contempt for my freakish tastes was replaced with self-satisfaction and pride at belonging to the "chosen. . . ."[70] Not daring to touch upon this subject with Pyotr or any other adult, I played the confidant with other novices such as myself among the "bougres." . . . Some time later, relying on Pyotr's authoritative example, I had the courage to speak openly [in school] about my own abnormal inclinations. . . .

Let me note here a strange phenomenon, that while Pyotr talked willingly about his school days, about his early childhood, and later about the Moscow Conservatory, he almost never shared with us his impressions of the Petersburg Conservatory while he was there and never recalled it after he graduated, so that for me there is no patch in his life more obscure than those three years he spent as a conservatory student.

II

The Music Student
(1863–1865)

Tchaikovsky spent almost three years at the St. Petersburg Conservatory. In addition to harmony, strict counterpoint, composition, and instrumentation—and despite having been excused from the compulsory piano class—he also decided to study flute and organ.

The leading spirits of the Conservatory from its beginning were Nikolay Zaremba and Anton Rubinstein. Despite Tchaikovsky's enthusiasm for learning, he considered Zaremba a merely average instructor, whose dislike of Mozart and Glinka greatly disappointed him, and whose admiration for Beethoven and Mendelssohn the future composer found unbearable.

There is no doubt that the main attraction of the newly founded Conservatory for Tchaikovsky was from the beginning its director, Anton Rubinstein, who seems to have had the power to stimulate his student's innate abilities, so that Tchaikovsky soon threw off the last traces of dilettantism in pursuit of his goal to become a good composer.

Tchaikovsky never worked so hard as in those years: he faithfully fulfilled his technical assignments and instrumental studies, and tried to master the art of conducting. Always in the company of his new friend Herman Laroche, a fellow student at the Conservatory and, later on, the first critic to champion Tchaikovsky's music, he attended concerts and operas. Together the two friends made many important connections in St. Petersburg music circles, including Alexander Serov, an ideological opponent of Rubinstein, but the composer of the opera *Judith* [*Iudif'*], which Tchaikovsky admired.

During the summer of 1863, Tchaikovsky stayed at Apukhtin's estate in Pavlodar. The next summer he spent at the home of his society friend Prince Alexey Golitsyn near Kharkov. Here he composed his overture *The Storm* [*Groza*] to the Alexander Ostrovsky play (which was later the source of Leoš Janáček's opera *Kátá Kabanová*). Tchaikovsky also sketched out a program for this descriptive concert overture. Upon completing the music, Tchaikovsky sent it to Herman Laroche with instructions to pass it along to Rubinstein. For Tchaikovsky the idea of taking the overture to Rubinstein was still uncomfortable: his adoration for his eminent teacher was mixed with fear. This was just as well, for it was the hapless Laroche who received the full force of Rubinstein's anger. Here was not the expected classical exercise, but a remarkably powerful work, a mature attempt at dramatic program music (after the programmatic overtures of Henry Litolff), scored for orchestra with some instruments "forbidden" to mere students, such as the harp, cor anglais, and tuba. It even incorporated a Russian folk song.[1]

Tchaikovsky was not discouraged by what was to be the first of many such incidents with Rubinstein. Theirs was always an uneasy relationship. Nevertheless, in the summer of 1865, Tchaikovsky found himself fulfilling a promise to Rubinstein to translate for conservatory students the much-needed textbook *Traité général d'instrumentation* by the eminent Belgian theorist François Auguste Gevaert, which had appeared in 1863. This task did not spoil Tchaikovsky's happy vacation spent with his younger brothers Anatoly and Modest on the estate of their brother-in-law Lev Davydov at Kamenka, near Kiev in Ukraine. Rubinstein proved to be quite pleased with the completed translation.

While at Kamenka Tchaikovsky paid close attention to Ukrainian folk songs, gathering material for use in future compositions. Soon after his return to St. Petersburg he learned that Johann Strauss the younger had conducted Tchaikovsky's own "Characteristic Dances" *[Kharakternye tantsy]* for orchestra, composed earlier that year, at a concert in Pavlovsk in late August 1865. The young composer was delighted. It was the first public performance of any of his works.[2]

On 27 November 1865, Tchaikovsky made his debut as a conductor, directing the Conservatory orchestra in a performance of his Overture in F. Four weeks earlier his String Quartet Movement in B flat was played by a quartet of his fellow students, including the violist Vasily Bessel.

The Conservatory's graduation concert on 29 December 1865 included a performance of Tchaikovsky's ambitious cantata on the text of Schiller's ode *An die Freude* (which Beethoven used in the Finale of his Ninth Symphony).[3] According to Tchaikovsky's first biographer, his brother Modest, the young composer absented himself because of his fear of the public examination, much to Rubinstein's annoyance. But the examination commission's records, preserved in the archives of the Conservatory, insist that "all students were present."[4] Still, Rubinstein threatened to withhold Tchaikovsky's diploma and refused to countenance public performance of the cantata unless it was revised.

A number of musical celebrities who were present at the concert, among them Serov and Cui, also disliked it. The final report on Tchaikovsky was, however, very favorable and two days later he was graduated from the Conservatory. But it appears that Tchaikovsky's diploma was withheld by Anton

Rubinstein after all: the extant copy is dated 30 March 1870. His grades were reported as: theory and instrumentation—excellent; organ—good; piano—very good; conducting—satisfactory. To Tchaikovsky's surprise, he also received the silver medal, which happened to be the highest student award at the Conservatory, since the gold medal was not offered at that time.

Tchaikovsky's years at St. Petersburg Conservatory were well described by his classmate and friend Herman Laroche in the recollections published by Modest Tchaikovsky in his biography of the composer, known to English-speaking readers in the translation by Rosa Newmarch.[5] For new and more varied perspectives on these key formative years, I have included here other memoirs about Tchaikovsky as a music student, by his relatives, classmates, and friends, together with Laroche's own less familiar recollections. Most of this material was published almost a century ago in obscure Russian magazines and newspapers and only selective excerpts were included in the standard Soviet collections of memoirs. Soviet editors were determined to preserve the canonical image of the great composer and systematically expunged details of his private life. But Tchaikovsky's personal tastes and private vicissitudes quite naturally played a central role in his life.

In order to understand the complexity of Tchaikovsky's attitudes toward Anton Rubinstein, which prevailed right up to the former's death, it is instructive to take into account a little-known portion of Modest's personal recollections, found at the beginning of this chapter.[6]

There is no doubt that Tchaikovsky felt an adoration for Anton Rubinstein that bordered on real love. This sentiment survived much harsh criticism and seeming unkindness on the part of Rubinstein.[7] It was an unrequited love. Until well into middle age Tchaikovsky would have valued Rubinstein's praise above all, but he never fully received it. Rubinstein's coolness toward him as a composer Tchaikovsky always attributed to their radical differences in musical temperament, but the problem may have had more to do with Rubinstein's professional jealousy or even his homophobic attitudes. Rubinstein was nevertheless the dedicatee of Tchaikovsky's Six Pieces for Piano, op. 21 (1873), the *Impromptu* (1889), and the chorus "A Greeting to Anton Rubinstein on the occasion of the Golden Jubilee of His Artistic Career" (1889).

The memoirs of Vasily Bessel (1843–1907) are less personal and deal mostly with musical and social events at the Conservatory, but they contribute many valuable details.[8] Bessel was Tchaikovsky's classmate at the St. Petersburg Conservatory, and later the founder and joint owner of an important music publishing house in the Russian capital. In fact, Bessel was one of the first to publish Tchaikovsky's works. When the composer later moved to the Jurgenson brothers' publishing firm, Bessel became incensed and turned quite unpleasant in his communications with Tchaikovsky, especially in regard to the renewal of the copyright for the opera *The Oprichnik*.

The single most valuable source of information about Tchaikovsky's years at the St. Petersburg Conservatory remains Herman Laroche (1845–1904), who studied there with Tchaikovsky from 1862 to 1865. He became one of the composer's closest friends and the most supportive and encouraging critic of his music. Tchaikovsky dedicated three works to Laroche: the piano piece based on the Russian folk song "By the river, by the bridge" *["Vozle rechki, vozle mosta"]* (1862; lost); the song "Accept but once" *["Poimi khot' raz"]*, op. 16, no. 3 (1872); and the *Thème originel et variations*, op. 19, no. 6 (1873).

In addition to Laroche's account as it was included by Modest in *The Life of Pyotr Ilyich Tchaikovsky*, Laroche also left additional reminiscences about the composer from their years together at the St. Petersburg Conservatory. These were published in the newspaper *Novosti i birzhevaia gazeta* in 1893 and in the magazine *Severnyi vestnik* in 1894.[9] These much less well known reminiscences are included in this chapter to provide supplemental information on Tchaikovsky's personality, tastes, talents, and daily life.

Ivan Klimenko (1841–1914), an architect and railroad official who also became Tchaikovsky's close friend, left a short but vivid description of his first meeting with the composer and Laroche at Serov's house in St. Petersburg.[10] Later chapters include further excerpts from Klimenko's memoirs.

Adelaida Spasskaya (1848–?) was a pianist who later organized and taught music classes in Vilno (now Vilnius, the capital of Lithuania). From 1863 to 1864 she was one of Tchaikovsky's classmates at the Conservatory. In 1899 she recreated the atmosphere of the first professional music school in Russia in her reminiscences about its teachers and students, which were published in the *Russkaia muzykal'naia gazeta*.[11] Here, Tchaikovsky is seen from the unusual point of view of a woman student and classmate.

Another classmate of Tchaikovsky was Alexander Rubets, a music theorist and collector of Ukrainian folk songs, later a professor at the St. Petersburg Conservatory. In 1912, he published his recollections of the first years of the St. Petersburg Conservatory in the Russian daily *Novoe vremia*.[12] Again, one encounters Tchaikovsky portrayed from a distance, by another student, not a close friend, who observed the future composer with a mixture of bewilderment, curiosity, and respect. These reminiscences preserve valuable information about some of Tchaikovsky's early musical compositions, subsequently lost. Rubets's memoir appeared twelve years after Modest Tchaikovsky's first comprehensive biography of his brother, and it is obvious that Rubets had read the latter and even paraphrased a few lines of its narrative.

Modest Tchaikovsky

In the same year in which my brother began to study with Zaremba, in 1861 (or perhaps the previous year—I cannot remember for certain), he took Anatoly and myself to an amateur performance in aid of some charity, given in the house of Prince Beloselsky. Anton Rubinstein, already at the height of his fame, was among the audience. Pyotr Ilyich pointed him out to me for the first time, and I still remember the excitement, rapture, and reverence with which the prospective pupil gazed on his future teacher. He forgot the play entirely, his eyes following his "divinity" with the rapt gaze of a lover for the unattainable object of his fancy. During the intervals he stood as near to him as possible, straining to catch the sound of his voice and envying the fortunate mortals who ventured to shake hands with him.

This feeling (I might almost say "infatuation" had it not been rooted in a full appreciation of Rubinstein's worth as a man and an artist) lasted virtually to the end of Tchaikovsky's life. Outwardly he remained ever "in love" with Rubinstein, even though—as is always the case in love affairs—there were periods of coolness, jealousy, and irritation, which invariably gave place, in turn, to a fresh access of that sentiment which so impressed me in Prince Beloselsky's reception room. In Rubinstein's presence Tchaikovsky became quite diffident, lost his head, and seemed to regard him as a superior being. When once at a supper given during the pianist's jubilee, someone, in an indelicate and unseemly way, suggested that Rubinstein and Tchaikovsky drink to each other "as brothers," not only was the latter embarrassed and indignant, but, in his reply to the toast, he protested hotly, saying that his tongue would never consent to address the great artist in the second person singular—that it would be entirely against the spirit of their relationship. He would be happy if Rubinstein were to address him by the familiar "thou," but, for his part, the more ceremonious form better expressed the pupil's sense of reverence for his teacher, the man's for the embodiment of his ideal. These were not empty words. Rubinstein had been the first to give the musical novice an example of the untiring devotion and disinterested spirit that animates the life of the true artist. It was in this sense that Tchaikovsky was the pupil of Rubinstein, far more so than in the matter of orchestration and composition. With his innate gifts and thirst for knowledge, Pyotr Ilyich could have gotten the same instruction from any other teacher. It was in Rubinstein's character as an energetic, irreproachably pureminded and inspired artist, as a man who never compromised his conscience, who all his life detested every manner of humbug and the successes of vulgarity, as an indefatigable worker, that he left the deepest traces upon Tchaikovsky's artistic career.

Vasily Bessel

In those days (1859), when the study of music, that is, the piano, with a good teacher (almost always a foreigner) was a great luxury in St. Petersburg, when it was obligatory in Russia to know a foreign language (German) in order to study music theory, since those who taught what was then an obscure scholarly subject were almost exclusively foreigners (Gunke, Decker, Stiehl)[13]—in that sad period in Russian music history there arose in Petersburg, from the ruins of the "Symphonic Society" (that is, on the foundations of its altered charter), the Russian Musical Society, which set about immediately to offer various music courses, including "courses in the theory of musical composition." For the latter the new Society managed to enlist the highly respected lyceum teacher Nikolay Zaremba (a disciple of the famous Berlin professor A. B. Marx),[14] a very well educated and resolute man, deeply devoted to the art of music, and a splendid lecturer. As soon as these "courses in the theory of musical composition" were announced, several individuals from various levels of society signed up for them; among them were the present author (already a violinist by occupation) and a clerk at the Ministry of Justice, Pyotr Ilyich Tchaikovsky; two later well-known musicians who also attended these courses were the pianists Ivan Rybasov and Gustav Kross, both long since dead.[15] At first, almost no one attending the courses was close to or friendly with Tchaikovsky, who was extremely sensitive, reserved, and even shy; the only person he talked with was an acquaintance of his who had signed up for the courses at the same time he did, the officer Mosolov.[16] During the first winter, the new courses were held in a private apartment, and later on the lower floor of a side wing of the Mikhailovsky Palace, where lived the eminent patroness of the Russian Musical Society and of the "future conservatory," the Grand Duchess Elena Pavlovna.

In 1862, on 8 September, the day of the celebration of Russia's thousandth anniversary, the Petersburg Conservatory was inaugurated. From among all Zaremba's former students, only Kross, Rybasov, Tchaikovsky, and I entered the Conservatory. (Of course, several other individuals from elsewhere also entered the first-year class.) The first two, both pianists, and the present author, a violinist—all three of us "instrumentalists"— registered for two specialties each, while Tchaikovsky, although he was also a fine pianist, registered for a single specialty, the theory of composition; thus, Tchaikovsky was in all our music theory and orchestration classes together with us. It was in this period that I first became good friends with my likable, kind, and openhearted fellow student Pyotr Ilyich Tchaikovsky. During the more than three years we were students together, we spent a great deal of time together, engaging in entertaining, always interesting and witty conversation, meeting not only within the walls of the Conservatory (at that time located along the Moika, on the corner of Demidov Lane), where we spent several hours nearly every day (and some evenings), but also during our spare time, in an intimate circle of friends. One quite casual circumstance brought me still closer to Tchaikovsky: Pyotr Ilyich asked me, as a student in Professor Wieniawski's class,[17] to give violin lessons to his brother Anatoly (who was then still studying at the School of Jurisprudence) in the apartment of his father, at that time director of the Technological Institute.

At the Conservatory, Tchaikovsky very soon (within half a year) was excused from the "required" classes in piano with Professor Otton Gerke, his former teacher at the School of Jurisprudence.[18] In 1863, the director of the Conservatory, its never-to-be-forgotten founder Anton Rubinstein, established (at his own expense) twenty scholarships for free instruction in wind instruments, with the object of creating a student orchestra as quickly as possible. Among those who took advantage of this opportunity was Pyotr Ilyich, who began studying the flute. His progress was so rapid that when the orchestra was formed a year or a year and a half later he was already able to occupy with honor the position of first flutist. It is very likely that, apart from Tchaikovsky's extraordinary natural abilities, his rapid progress also owed a great deal to his friendship with one of the most likable professors at the Conservatory—the flutist Cesare Ciardi.[19] I shall always remember the rehearsals of the Conservatory orchestra, under the direction of the founder himself, Anton Rubinstein, and with the participation of several later prominent musical figures. (The pianist Viktor Tolstov, now a Conservatory professor, played clarinet, Herman Laroche played kettledrums, Ludvig Gomilius, now professor of organ at our Conservatory, played cello, among others.)[20] There can be no doubt that this extensive study of the flute proved very useful to Tchaikovsky later on: many of our brilliant composer's scores clearly show a deep knowledge of this favorite instrument of his.

The class in practical composition and orchestration at the Conservatory was taught by Rubinstein himself. His wonderfully distinctive manner of expression and his remarkable (even then) experience as a composer made his lectures endlessly fascinating; to miss even one of them was considered by every student to be, as it were, a misfortune, an irretrievable loss. Tchaikovsky's work at first differed little from that of the other students, but he soon began to show signs of his unique gifts; the symphonic Allegro he wrote for his final examination revealed at once his outstanding talent as a composer. There can be no denying that Tchaikovsky's compositions exhibit something of the influence of his teacher Rubinstein, in particular with regard to his clarity of form and the great sonority in his orchestration. During his time at the Conservatory, from the moment orchestral scores first became comprehensible to him, Pyotr Ilyich could inevitably be found in the cramped Conservatory library (housed in the half-lit kitchen of the Conservatory building), sitting on an uncomfortable chair, reading scores.

Soon, however, his intensified study of music forced Tchaikovsky to give up his duties at the Ministry of Justice, and, in this way, the question of a change of career was settled once and for all. At the start, Pyotr Ilyich found himself in a very difficult material position; he had to take odd jobs as an accompanist for Professor Ciardi (when he performed in concert) and sometimes for other musicians and singers.

While still studying at the Conservatory, Tchaikovsky was offered a job as a teaching assistant in the (required) harmony class; then, following graduation (in December 1865), he was invited, in the autumn of 1866, to become a professor at the Conservatory that was being opened in Moscow.

Herman Laroche

I met him in September 1862, early in the morning, in the little room of the Demidov house (on the corner of Demidov Lane and the Moika River) where the newly opened Conservatory was located. Here in this little room, from eight to nine in the morning, Anton Gerke, at that time one of the three or four finest pianists in Petersburg, taught piano to three "theorists" and one bassoonist. This was the "required piano class," that is, for students who wished to devote themselves to composition, who in this case were Tchaikovsky, myself, and Porfiry Konev, later a piano teacher at the Moscow Consevatory, who died several years ago.[21] The bassoonist was a young Pole named Ogonowski, who soon dropped out of sight.

The days rapidly grew shorter, and by the end of the year, we were having our lessons by candlelight. Since Tchaikovsky and I were both excused from this class in January as playing "quite well enough for theory students" (the Conservatory's resources were then meager and expenses were reduced as far as possible), my recollection of our studies together, and of our earliest musical discussions and debates, is inextricably linked with an image of dark autumn mornings in St. Petersburg, and of a particularly fresh and cheerful frame of mind combined with a slight edginess from having to get up unusually early.

It is hard to say why Pyotr Ilyich had been assigned to this class: he not only already played "quite well enough for a theory student," but in fact could perform pieces of the utmost difficulty with assurance, even brilliantly. At the time, I found his playing rather too coarse for my taste, somewhat lacking in warmth and emotion—precisely the opposite of what the modern reader is most likely to imagine. It is very possible that I might in some sense find the same to be true today. The fact is that Pyotr Ilyich feared sentimentality like the plague and, in consequence of this, deplored excessive emphasis in piano playing and sneered at the expression "play with feeling." And if he disliked the phrase, he was even less fond of the manner of playing that the phrase denoted; the musical emotion that lived in him was held in check by a certain chasteness, and out of fear of vulgarity he might well run to the opposite extreme.

Be that as it may, he played not like a composer (in 1862 he was not yet a composer in any real sense), but like a true pianist. For a long time I kept a program (perhaps it still exists today in somebody's possession), elegantly printed on thick paper, from a musical matinee or evening at which Pyotr Ilyich and Karl van Ark, now a professor at the Petersburg Conservatory, performed Max Bruch's F-sharp Minor Fantasy for two pianos.[22] This was the only time during the period of our acquaintance that he played in public, though I believe that there had been other occasions before this.

Besides being an amateur pianist, he was also an amateur singer. He had a slender, to my ear very pleasant baritone, with an unusual purity and precision of intonation: sometimes as a prank I would accompany him in "Là ci darem la mano" in A-flat major or B-flat major, while forcing him to sing in A major, and never once did he go off key.[23] It is worth noting that he was very fond of Italian coloratura singing. He himself could vocalize cleanly and fluently; perhaps for this reason he delighted, though half-jokingly, in adorning his repertoire with such works as arias and duets from [Rossini's] *Semiramide* and *Otello*, and so on. He was, by the way, enormously fond of Rossini during this period; something of this attraction remained with him throughout his life.

Since we were in different classes, we saw each other relatively little at the Conservatory itself; but we were inseparable at concerts of the Musical Society and at rehearsals, we attended the opera and the ballet together, we played piano duets and had long conversations. . . .

Perhaps I am deluding myself, but it seems to me that the Tchaikovsky of the 1860s and the Tchaikovsky of the 1880s were two different persons. Tchaikovsky at twenty-two . . . was a young man about town, clean-shaven in spite of the then already universal fashion, and dressed somewhat carelessly in clothes from an expensive tailor but not quite new, with charmingly simple and, as I thought at the time, rather cold manners; he had countless acquaintances, and when we strolled together along Nevsky there was no end to the greetings and bows. By and large, though not exclusively, it was the elegant people who greeted him. Of foreign languages, he knew French and a little Italian; he used to make a particular show of his ignorance of German, saying, for example: *Er ist an der Sehnsucht gestorben* [He died of yearning] when he wanted to say He died of consumption *[Schwindsucht]*, or *Was dieser Mensch für ein Geheimnis hat!* [What a secret this man has!] (instead of: what a memory *[Gedächtnis]* this man has!), or *Ich habe grosse Gelegenheit zu schlafen* [I have a great opportunity to sleep] (intending: I have a great need to sleep), which invariably delighted any Germans who happened to be with him. His knowledge of music was limited, to say the least, but for a young man of twenty-two who had decided to devote himself specifically to composition, it was dreadfully insufficient: he played the piano splendidly and had taken a course in harmony according to Marx, or according to the lectures of Professor Zaremba, which amounts to the same thing. You would have to search long and hard in the history of music before finding an example of a prominent composer who began so phenomenally late. Of course, his knowledge grew rapidly. Of the other traits I have mentioned, his carelessness about his appearance developed almost as rapidly, so that in 1866 and 1867 his colleagues at the Moscow Conservatory, who themselves were far from dandies, used to nag him and poke fun at his untidiness. He enjoyed excellent health, but was extraordinarily fearful of death, fearful even of anything that so much as hinted at death; in his presence one had to avoid using such words as "coffin," "grave," and "funeral"; one of his greatest griefs in Moscow consisted in the fact that the entrance to his apartment building (which, owing to the circumstances, he could not change) was located next door to an undertaker's. I might also add that Pyotr Ilyich—who in the 1880s was a tireless walker—in those early years, and for a long while afterward, was quite incapable of going anywhere on foot and would call a cab to go even the shortest distances; if I said just now that I used to stroll with him along Nevsky, this was the typical exception for a resident of Petersburg: even people who cannot walk at all, walk along Nevsky. This was especially true in the 1860s, when people used to stroll aimlessly along its wide sidewalk, to and fro. . . .

I cannot remember all the many things that, in Tchaikovsky's own view, he "could not" or "could in no way" do. If we are to take him at his word, he was "quite incapable" of conducting. I should note that we theory students were expected to conduct in the orchestra class, and Tchaikovsky, the only one of us who showed any promise as a composer, was no exception; but this experience did nothing to reassure him. . . .

The reader will no doubt be surprised to learn that another of the subjects that were "quite beyond him" in 1863 and 1864 was the composition of pieces for piano and strings, of songs, and even of piano pieces in general. Though he had to write a great deal of this sort of thing at the Conservatory, as exercises for the composition class, he did it grudgingly. In this case, however, the ice broke rather early, since by the summer of 1867 he had already written his first piano pieces and had them published; followed shortly thereafter by his first six songs, of which two or three were very well liked, and one ("None but the lonely heart" ["Net, tol'ko tot, kto znal"]) became quite famous. He retained rather longer his antipathy (shared by many modern composers) toward the sound of the piano combined with stringed instruments. . . .

At one time he played the flute fairly well. He studied with the famous Ciardi and chose the instrument when Anton Rubinstein suddenly decided to slap together a student orchestra at the Conservatory. I remember a student evening attended by Clara Schumann[24] at which Pyotr Ilyich and three other students (among them the future well-known soloist Pugny)[25] played a quartet for four flutes by Kuhlau.[26] I need not add that he abandoned the flute as soon as he was no longer needed, that is, as soon as another student was found to take his place in the orchestra.

He also had talents about which I knew only by hearsay. Thus, in his youth, for example, he quite often took part in amateur theatricals. During the time I knew him there were no such instances, as far as I know; still, I can believe he had a gift for the dramatic, particularly the comic, stage, as he possessed remarkable powers of observation and sometimes would imitate mutual acquaintances to perfection.

A passion for the theater—that is, for attending the theater—was one trait that was almost equally strong in both the young and the mature Tchaikovsky. In his youth, quite in keeping with the prevailing inclinations and habits of society of the time, he loved most of all the Italian Opera and the Mikhailovsky Theater,[27] then the Alexandrinsky Theater and the ballet. Like an imitation Eugene Onegin, he spoke about ballet in the manner of an expert, and with the greatest contempt for the "vulgar public" who attend performances merely for the pleasure of ogling naked ballerinas. . . .

He did not have any serious poetic talent, nor did he cherish any illusions on that score. His aspirations, it seems, never went beyond the composition of vaudeville pieces; on a few occasions he told me that, if he wished, he could write a vaudeville sketch no worse and no better than anyone else. Though he never did write any vaudevilles, he did improvise verses quite often, chiefly comic verses, sometimes with complex and foppish rhythms. This talent was mainly of use to him in translating librettos. As is well known, he translated Da Ponte's *Le nozze di Figaro,* even performing the painstaking and quite useless task of fitting a Russian text to the *recitativo secco,* while it would have been more in the spirit of both the Russian language and the Russian Opera to follow the example of the French and the Germans and replace the recitative with spoken dialogue, which, of course, would have been rendered in prose. Be that as it may, he was very proud of his translation and very upset when a different one was performed at the Petersburg Conservatory four years later.

I cannot indulge in my recollections of Tchaikovsky without mentioning something here about his literary abilities and pursuits. Literature occupied a far greater place in his life than in that of the usual educated person: it was, after music, his chief and most important interest. The pictorial arts did not interest him at all. He would attend exhibitions, like everyone else, but he never ran around to museums or galleries and, as if mocking his own ignorance, used to say that in the whole of the Imperial Hermitage he recognized only the hall of Russian painting. There is no doubt that his love of literature was influenced by his early friendship with Apukhtin, but the chief reason for it, in my view, was the fact that he himself was to a considerable degree a born man of letters, even quite apart from his talent as a maker of rhymes, which in his case never led to any poetic output. When his letters are published, or a portion of them (which is bound to come about sooner or later), people will discover that this man, who lived in a world of chords and rhythms, wrote more clearly, precisely, logically, and elegantly than the majority of our professional men of letters today. . . .

But as much as he loved literature in general, he ignored musical literature and even found critical discussions about music tiresome. I know of only one exception: Otto Jahn's book on Mozart, which for several years never left his desk and whose margins were covered with his various *boutades*, expressions of sympathy, and so on.[28] The reason for this was not so much the classical qualities of the work, which has very few equals among biographies, as the simple fact that it was the best book about Mozart, who constituted Tchaikovsky's ideal of a musician and of an artist in general. The slightest detail concerning this genius was filled with significance for him, but this curiosity in no way spilled over into the history of music in general, and I have rarely seen an artist for whom the history of his art held so little attraction. . . . His real passion was for memoir literature—the sort of history in which the fates of government and society disappear behind the depiction of a personality, behind the elaborate detail of someone's psychology and everyday life. . . .

Neither in his youth nor in his later years did he ever, so far as I could see, exhibit any trait that revealed his legal training. Quite apart from the fact that he never expressed the slightest interest in the social or political sciences, . . . there was nothing at all in his manner or his cast of mind which might reveal him to have been a student of law. If, through some error in judgment or weakness of will, he had decided in 1861–1862 to do what everyone at that time wanted and advised him to do—that is, to remain at his job in the Ministry of Justice, where he was doing quite well—he would most likely have become one of the unhappiest people in the world. To have been obliged to devote himself constantly to a pursuit in which he had no serious or heartfelt interest—the common lot of the vast majority of people—would have been for him a slow torture, precisely because there would have existed for him another pursuit, one he longed to follow with all the force of his energetic nature but which would have been pushed into the background by his hated civil service duties.

As a beginning music theory student, he decided to abandon the civil service and become a "professional musician." That Tchaikovsky should have styled himself thus is especially remarkable in that this was still a rarity in Russia at that time. There have probably always, in every age, been people with a vocation for music; but to devote oneself entirely to music in the sense of making a living from one's art was, in the generation preceding our own, only possible, it seemed, in two cases: by working in the Imperial theaters or by giving piano lessons. Music composition was out of the question. Neither Glinka nor Dargomyzhsky nor Rubinstein had lived or could have lived on the income made from composing. To write music "on the side" was considered not only not a dishonorable occupation for a member of the Russian gentry, but, on the contrary, one of the essential trappings associated with a certain level of culture. Pyotr Ilyich himself once said to me jokingly that in Russia, "every person with even the slightest drop of noble blood has written at least one song." At the same time, it was understood that the nobleman would have some other occupation; the only exception was made for those who possessed a sufficient number of serfs to be able to live prosperously without having to work. In the subsequent generation, when serfdom no longer existed and composers had begun to appear—only a handful, but still more frequent than before—they found, thanks to the opening of the conservatories, new work as professors of music theory. But in 1862 there was only one conservatory and no one yet foresaw the founding of any others. Even now, things have changed little on the whole: that is to say, a Russian composer living on the income from his compositions is as rare today as he was then.

I remember clearly that throughout the 1860s, and especially during the years we were students together, I was pessimistic about his determination to be a composer. "Did Liszt or Rubinstein achieve their worldwide fame through their compositions? Aren't all the places in the composer market long since filled? Can a newcomer's ambition guarantee him anything other than endless privations, disappointments, and humiliations? Isn't it a thousand times better to work in a department or to earn a living doing translations from English, and to satisfy your artistic impulses by improvising at the piano in the evening or, at most, doing an occasional bit of composing, but letting it, with desperate pride, remain in manuscript?" In saying this, I had in mind the popular success of Verdi, Flotow, and Offenbach, but I knew that Tchaikovsky would never take this route. Then too, to be sure, there was Richard Wagner, there was the modest but unquestionable posthumous success of Schumann, but it seemed to me that these were exceptions that proved the rule.

I turned out to be a poor prophet, but there are clear extenuating circumstances for my error. The success that would ultimately justify the bold hopes of the young composer, as he started out, was entirely unprecedented in Russia.

Besides, he seemed almost deliberately to narrow his chances for success by depriving himself beforehand of those meager resources on which someone in his position could count. While he played the piano, if not like a virtuoso, then at least like an excellent amateur, Tchaikovsky began from the very moment he entered the Conservatory to neglect this gift of his and, as often happens, he gradually started playing worse. Thus he neglected even the last salvation of many composers, namely, the ability to play some instrument and so as performers to propagandize their own compositions. We must not forget that he took up conducting only some six years before his death, and in his youth (as I have already mentioned) feared the stage like death. He gave up his job, he gave up the piano, he showed no pretensions to conducting, he did not foresee that he would be offered a professorship at the Moscow Conservatory—in short, he burned all his bridges and determined to make a career by musical composition alone.

No one could have been further than he from vainglory or in general from any unpleasant displays of conceit. But in his heart of hearts, his belief in his own destiny must have been colossal. When he handed in his resignation, none of his friends or acquaintances detected the slightest trace of agitation or uneasiness in him. I am certain that he did not hide such feelings, but was simply altogether free of them.

While he enjoyed room and board, and so on, in his father's home, he found himself entirely without pocket money and therefore decided to take on a few private pupils recommended to him by Anton Rubinstein. Some of these lessons were in piano, some in music theory. He took on only a very small number of hours, so as not to lose any of the time which, from 1863 on, and especially after 1864—that is, after he entered the class in "free composition"—had become so precious to him. Rubinstein used to give enormous assignments, which, as far as I know, Tchaikovsky's classmates never even attempted to complete in their entirety; only he alone (if I may allow myself to use a French turn of phrase) "took them *au sérieux*" and, indeed, he would spend Monday through Thursday or Thursday through Monday orchestrating, for example, an entire vocal scene with recitative and aria or an entire large chorus. During this period in his life he would sometimes sit up all night working on an exercise, completing it only by breakfast or just in time for class. Such "turning night into day" was indicative of his urgency and the enormity of the exercise; on the whole it did not accord with the habits of Pyotr Ilyich, who gave up working at night very early on and never afterward resorted to this method. For what it may be worth, I might add that whenever he went to bed late or not at all, he never, the following morning, made up the sleep he had lost, but invariably rose at his usual time, between eight and nine o'clock. Likewise, he never slept during the day under any circumstances, except, if I am not mistaken, during the short period in Moscow and also, much later, when he had to conduct in the evening. Thus, during his final two years as a student at the Conservatory he worked with extreme intensity, but I do not find that this intensity told on his health or his frame of mind. Of course, he found encouragement and support in the knowledge of his inner success, the sight of the horizon opening up before him: in his four and a half years of study he had succeeded in transforming himself completely, from a musical infant he had become an adult, and along with a technical proficiency he had acquired a familiarity with classical music, which before the Conservatory he had known only slightly.

Ivan Klimenko

One Tuesday evening at Serov's home I found two new faces who immediately captivated me: one was very young, extraordinarily affable, well-mannered, infinitely modest, and somehow peculiarly handsome; the other was almost a boy, with a face that reminded me of an inferior bust of Schiller I had at home, straight Liszt-like hair, and such a leanness in his face that he unwittingly resembled that Englishman in Heine who was so thin that he had no front—only a profile. Of course, the first [was Tchaikovsky], and the second, [Herman] Laroche. The latter talked a great deal and very interestingly, told jokes and played the piano, and was, so to speak, the life of the party, the more so as Serov expressed his own delight and by his conversation gave the young man an opportunity to shine. All the while Tchaikovsky's face showed genuine pleasure at the success Herman was having. From that memorable evening we took a liking to one another, which increased with each new encounter and eventually grew into a most sincere attachment. . . .

He and Laroche made an amazing four-hand pair; they knew one another so well and had such an intuitive sense of one another as they performed that the resulting duet was exquisite. Once I was afforded enormous pleasure by such a duet when, coming to see me one evening . . . and discovering that I had [Glinka's] *A Life for the Tsar* for four hands, they played the entire opera from start to finish without skipping a thing. They played with sincere youthful ardor and passion, and the whole thing turned out marvelously well. However, at one point Herman faltered and only on the third or fourth try did he manage to get back on track. This was in the third act where the Poles enter Susanin's hut. At this spot in the four-hand transcription several measures occur where the bass part (Laroche) goes in 6/4 time, while in the primo (Pyotr) the upper line is in 6/4, and the lower in 4/4. Laroche's part is uncommonly simple and easy, but Pyotr's part, owing to the divergence of accents in the left and right hands, is on the contrary very difficult. Precisely because Pyotr accented both his lines with unusual accuracy, Herman was quite unable to execute his simple accents, which were not synchronized with Pyotr's line in 4/4, and so he stumbled two or three times, marveling at his partner's skill and irritated at his own inability.

Several times other people had told me that Herman and Pyotr were so deeply in tune with each other that they could quite freely improvise four-hand duets; I did not believe this until I had occasion to witness it for myself: one time (upon my word, I am not lying) they improvised in my presence a four-hand overture in the style of Rossini; this was at the same time amazing and incredibly funny, so that I was both stupefied and rolling on the floor with laughter.

Adelaida Spasskaya

Our wonderfully learned, eloquent, and engaging professor, and later director of the Conservatory, Nikolay Zaremba, perceived Tchaikovsky's outstanding talent from the start, treating and working with him with particular care. I did not take classes together with Tchaikovsky, since he was in the junior group, having started a year later than I. . . .[29] For the opening of the Conservatory they wanted to combine us all into one general class, and so we in the senior group were held back to the extent possible through various details and repetitions, during which time the junior group caught up with us by accelerating and intensifying their lessons. Thus, when the Conservatory opened, we found ourselves on the same level in terms of our knowledge of music theory and could continue the course together. . . . At the Conservatory our studies assumed a still broader scope; we studied strict counterpoint, orchestration, and practical composition—the latter two subjects being taught by Anton Rubinstein. At one of his very first lectures Rubinstein assigned us the task of writing sample pieces for a small number of instruments (which had been gone over in the lectures). I believe it was a string quartet with the use of a drum. One of the students wrote his pieces with no separations, and many assignments turned out to contain errors contrary to the rules of harmony. Rubinstein grew very angry and, since everyone who had gone through [the Russian Musical Society's courses in music theory] had been admitted [into Conservatory] with no examination, he arranged a special examination for the entire class. As I now recall, we were all to assemble in the evening after classes were finished for this examination. Nikolay Zaremba arrived for the examination very agitated, and we were all handed various melodies and chorales to harmonize. On the basis of this examination some students were transferred to the lower course. . . .

Anton Rubinstein's lectures, which later evolved simply into discussions about orchestration and practical composition, have always remained my fondest memory, both of that highly artistic teacher and of Tchaikovsky, his gifted pupil at the time. These were the most interesting and most substantive discussions, with analyses and critical remarks about every detail, every trifling manifestation of some peculiarity or intention of a composer, none of which escaped the attention of the professor and his students. Demanding fairly elaborate exercises in practical composition from his students, Rubinstein would then pick these apart, as they say, bit by bit. Few students were able, with their other special studies, to satisfy his strict requirements. Tchaikovsky was an exception, being an expert in musical composition, and also because of his outstanding talent. He almost always came up with interesting compositions for the exercises assigned on various programs. I recall how Rubinstein, after going over a fairly large number of instruments with us, including the harp, had us write and orchestrate, employing the harp, the fountain scene from [Pushkin's] *Boris Godunov.* No one, of course, wrote anything worthwhile. Only Tchaikovsky fulfilled this task brilliantly. Later, many students gradually began to leave off attending these lecture-discussions, and often only Tchaikovsky and I would show up for them. I rarely presented any compositions of my own, but I showed up unfailingly to listen to Rubinstein's fascinating remarks about Tchaikovsky's compositions, which constituted an enormous pleasure for me. I never missed a single opportunity to attend a lecture and critique of Tchaikovsky's unfolding talent. Often, arriving for class and finding no one there but Tchaikovsky and one or two other students, Rubinstein would take Tchaikovsky's composition, look it over where he stood, and, notebook in hand, proceed out into the hall and begin to walk up and down, accompanied by the few students. I remember even now our interesting parades through the hall: Rubinstein in the middle, Tchaikovsky and I, and sometimes someone else as well, on either side, listening to and devouring every word, every remark that might be worth its weight in gold. Often our little procession would come to a halt in front of the piano, and Rubinstein would play those passages in the composition where he had pointed out particular features or which had evoked comment or needed changes. No one witnessing our walks would have thought they were lectures, indeed the most interesting, most useful of lectures, which, perhaps, significantly contributed to the development of the brilliant composer that Tchaikovsky would become. Nikolay Zaremba also spent a great deal of time talking with Tchaikovsky, discussing his vocation with him. When Tchaikovsky made up his mind to leave the civil service and devote himself entirely to music, I remember a great conference with Zaremba on this matter. . . .

During this period, student musical evenings were instituted at the Conservatory, and a student chorus and orchestra were formed, the first rehearsals for which were comical to the point of absurdity. It required all of Rubinstein's energy, patience, and stamina to reconcile this large heterogeneous group, which had never played together before, into something decent. His zealous assistant in this task was Tchaikovsky. Tchaikovsky accompanied the chorus on piano and sometimes rehearsed with the fledgling orchestra, in which he took the part of drummer, being able to keep the sometimes straying musicians on the right track with his steady rhythm.

Choral singing held a particular attraction for Tchaikovsky. Often, in the class on counterpoint, where, though a woman, I had ended up in the men's class since my area of specialty was the theory of composition, Tchaikovsky would ask the professor whether the examples might be sung rather than played, and we all gladly divided up into the necessary four parts, with me, of course, singing soprano, and, even though I did not possess a remarkable voice, still I contributed, with a reliable tone and a musical sense, to an interesting recreation of some old choral style or other medieval composition of the time of Palestrina or other classical composers of the Dutch period. The alto part was sung by one of the male students (Ermolayev), who possessed a high tenor voice. All this would have been comical had it not been so musical, and performed with such heart and conscientiousness.

As was his nature, Tchaikovsky always held himself aloof and never showed signs of friendship with anyone. During Zaremba's lectures in counterpoint and compositional form, we listened studiously and wrote down everything the professor said; Tchaikovsky alone never took notes nor even, I believe, carried pencil and paper with him. I can see him thus even now, sitting by himself with his arms folded across his chest, following seriously and attentively the professor's every word, gravely pondering the examples cited, and often interrupting the professor to ask some question which elucidated in still greater detail the already detailed lecture.

We had a great deal of freedom. Questions were often brought up or objections raised, and sometimes the lectures would turn into fascinating discussions of tremendous benefit to us all. Tchaikovsky's class assignments were always interesting, worked out down to the tiniest detail, and bore the mark of remarkable talent. I can say frankly that it was always a pleasure for me to listen to the professor play his assignments, which differed so noticeably from everyone else's in their originality and distinctive character. At Zaremba's suggestion, we Conservatory students were to attend all rehearsals and concerts without fail. Rubinstein even demanded that we sit in the orchestra itself, mainly during rehearsals, listening carefully to the particular features and effects of each individual instrument, while later he would draw our attention to these features in the orchestration class. For our study of counterpoint, we were assigned to attend the Lutheran church in order to listen closely to the performance of the chorales, about which we would often report and make comments. In all these places Tchaikovsky could almost always be found with Laroche, to whom he was closer than the others, although the latter was the class behind him. They could always be found at orchestra rehearsals with score in hand or, if none was available, with the piano arrangement of whatever was being performed. They were both fervent admirers of Glinka, whose compositions they always listened to, score in hand. After he learned that I had many scores of compositions by Glinka, Dargomyzhsky, Beethoven, Mendelssohn, and other exemplary composers, Tchaikovsky called on me several times to borrow these scores for study. Some of them were returned to me through Laroche long after our graduation from the Conservatory, in the Moscow period of Tchaikovsky's teaching career.

Alexander Rubets

Among those who enrolled in the first year of the Conservatory's existence, Pyotr Tchaikovsky and Herman Laroche stood out the most in terms of their abilities and prior training. . . . [Tchaikovsky] loved music, but as a mere dilettante, nothing more. His knowledge was extremely superficial, though I believe he had begun taking lessons in theory with Zaremba or someone else. He had a negligent attitude toward his civil service work, and being of a light-hearted nature, he lived a more or less frivolous and rakish life. He was enormously fond of strolling along Morskaya Street or Nevsky Prospect or through the Summer Garden at certain times, in the company of his friends and acquaintances, of whom he had many. In general, he was very fond of society during this period, and since by birth he belonged to a fairly prominent administrative circle—his father was a mining engineer and later director of the Technological Institute—and had received his education at a privileged school, he had no lack of society acquaintances.

But finally there came a sudden change of heart. He became fed up with the dissipated life, and when they began offering preparatory music classes at the Mikhailovsky Palace, he was one of the first to enroll in them, while still working at the Ministry [of Justice]. When I arrived at the Conservatory in the early days of its existence, I found Tchaikovsky already there, in the class ahead of me. His undoubted abilities, which had always been apparent, had compelled him to devote himself exclusively to music. He had a bent for improvising at the piano. His success in theory, which he studied with Zaremba, spurred him on. In the classes at the Mikhailovsky Palace, that is from 1861 to 1862, he had studied A. B. Marx's theory of harmony, and then, in his first year at the Conservatory (1862–1863), Bellermann's system of strict counterpoint and church harmony.[30] By September 1863, he found himself in the so-called form class (also with Zaremba) and, at the same time, in the newly offered orchestration class, which was taught by Rubinstein.

Once Laroche was drawn to Tchaikovsky, they quickly took a liking for one another, and a close friendship developed between them which reached the point of something like schoolboy worship: they would send notes to one another, even during class. Laroche suggested to Tchaikovsky that they spend some time studying Russian literature and literature in general—of which Tchaikovsky, oddly enough, had a poor knowledge at that time—as well as the study of versification. They began working with hexameters, Alexandrine verse, iambics, trochees, and other verse forms. They became so carried away by this that even in their free time between classes, standing by some window and drumming their fingers against the pane, they would rhythmically beat out ponderous hexameters, falling into a quarrel whenever one of them made a mistake.

As both far surpassed the rest of their classmates in their education, they naturally established a certain authority among them, apart from their musical abilities, which were clearly evident even then. They thus enjoyed a popularity which the others could in no way count on for themselves. They stood head and shoulders above their woefully ill-informed classmates, to whose aid they would willingly come, explaining not only the theoretical lessons assigned by Zaremba, but in general anything the others did not understand. They never ventured to make fun of the lack of preparation and knowledge of those who came to them. Save that sometimes, after two or three explanations which nonetheless proved in vain, Tchaikovsky, with an ironic smile, would say: "My dear fellow, just think about your assignment a bit. Take some musical examples and try to figure out what's being said there. Perhaps then the venerable Zaremba won't seem so terrifying to you."

Rubinstein, despite the fact that he was busy from morning till night, assigned the theory students special classes from six to nine in the evening. During these classes he would read a poem aloud, and the students then and there had to come up with a musical setting for one or more voices, as each judged best. They had to compose a draft, and the next day the work was to be handed in, already finished and recopied. These after-dinner studies enthralled the young people, women and men alike. Everybody worked willingly and executed their music with enthusiasm. Rubinstein would then correct it. As I recall now, some of the themes assigned were "A Prayer" ["Molitva"] by Lermontov, "Dance of the Flowers" ["Khorovod tsvetov"], "Bells" ["Kolokol'chiki"], and so on.

Sometimes he varied the method, making the students improvise in the form of one of the first three types of rondo, a largo, an Andante cantabile, a quick march with trio, a polonaise or a minuet. In this way, by practicing various forms of composition, we mastered them.

Rubinstein's lectures were enormously beneficial. It cannot be said that he possessed a gift for words. He knew several languages, but spoke all of them rather incorrectly. He never minced words or sought well-rounded phrases, in contrast with Zaremba, whose speech was notable for its fluency and orderliness. I even think that Rubinstein arrived for class with nothing prepared and did not know himself five minutes before the start of class what he was going to discuss. Nevertheless, his lectures and lessons were filled with inspiration, and when he illustrated an explanation by playing at the piano, it was a general delight: his explanation then took on a magical character. We were terribly pleased whenever he praised our experiments in composition. . . .

In expounding theoretical views, Rubinstein, as I have said, was the opposite of Zaremba. On the whole, he conducted his lectures and our composition exercises with him in a practical fashion, never on paper; rather, when he discovered errors in our assignments or did not like something, he would at once sit down at the piano and begin improvising animatedly, saying that the chords and harmonies we had used in this place or that were unclear or did not fit the goal of the piece. At the same time, he would always add: "It seems to me that what I am now playing for you is precisely what you yourself meant at heart to express." We would agree, delighted at his inspired emendations. Occasionally he might exclaim, "Good, well done!" and clap the author of the composition in question on the shoulder. He always spoke of the danger of timidity, advising us never to linger over a difficult passage, to skip it and go on, to get in the habit of writing in draft, with allusions to this or that form, and to avoid resorting to the piano. With such improvisation, if one abandoned inspiration, a composition would inevitably move slowly and indeed nothing would come of it. He demanded every composition—from the smallest to the largest—in several versions and in various tonalities; the form of a song or rondo—in different tempos, slow and fast, rondos with trio, marches, polonaises, waltzes, funeral marches with two trios, minuets, scherzos, folk dances of every possible nation—was written in a broad and comprehensive development of musical exposition. Sometimes he gave rapturous praise to the elegance of compositional forms which represented some novelty in rhythmics. He gave his lessons in a hall adjacent to Zaremba's classroom.

I remember how once he burst into the latter's class with a shining face and, grabbing his arm, said: "Come with me, I'll show you a trial composition by Tchaikovsky." Zaremba was about to refuse, saying that he would be leaving his discussion barely started. "Don't worry, I'll let you come straight back once you've heard Tchaikovsky's exercise." About fifteen of us in all gladly trooped into the hall, where we found just two students, Tchaikovsky and Kross.

Rubinstein told Laroche to play the notes on the third line. Tchaikovsky had been assigned the task of setting [Vasily] Zhukovsky's "Nocturnal Parade" [Nochnoi parad] to music. I could not restrain myself and mentioned that Glinka had already written such a song. Rubinstein shrugged his shoulders and replied: "So what? Glinka wrote his music, and Tchaikovsky has written his. Any poem can be set to music by various composers, without worrying about those who went before." Tchaikovsky's piece turned out to be not a song but an entire complex portrait, having nothing in common with Glinka's work. The accompaniment for each stanza was varied and intricate. Laroche declared enthusiastically that he was struck both by the conception of the piece and by the truth of its music, which corresponded perfectly to Zhukovsky's poem. We applauded the composer heartily, and Rubinstein, after thanking Zaremba on behalf of his student, said: "Well, now, Nikolay, go finish your lesson."

Tchaikovsky had written the piece quickly, in just two days.

From that day, Laroche and Tchaikovsky grew especially close, and they were united by friendship for the rest of their lives, though with a few interruptions. After class, I nonetheless went over to Laroche and expressed my bewilderment at setting to music a text already used by Glinka. Who does not know the music of this beautiful "Nocturnal Parade"! It echoes in the ears of every singer. Another time Rubinstein had Tchaikovsky write music for the Fountain Scene from Pushkin's *Boris Godunov*. This turned out to be quite a substantial composition and was fully orchestrated. Perhaps the score for this scene is preserved among the composer's papers; for the present it is not to be found in the catalogue of his works. It was, I remember, both soaring and inspired, despite its Italianisms. This latter work is, in any event, more important than "Nocturnal Parade," which apparently Tchaikovsky later destroyed. . . .

Rubinstein was both fond and proud of Tchaikovsky, pushing him forward and looking after him in every way possible. He was especially insistent in requiring Tchaikovsky to write down quickly, without the aid of a piano, all the compositions assigned to him without improvising on that instrument beforehand. He always said that a composition is like a simple letter: first you have to think about what you want to write, then set your thoughts down on paper. By carrying out Rubinstein's advice, Tchaikovsky trained himself to write quickly, in draft, and only when he had made a preliminary sketch to try it on the piano. I believe he retained this practice for the rest of his life. . . . When giving his advice Rubinstein added, however, that while he demanded speed in composition, still he considered it essential for the completed work to remain without fail in one's briefcase for a time and not be launched immediately. One must sit on it for while, then make corrections, and only then consider it finished. All the mistakes and weak aspects of the composition will then become perfectly clear to the composer's eye.

I do not know whether Rubinstein himself observed the rules he recommended to his students. His critics, as we know, have always pointed to the hurriedness of his works and his insufficient self-appraisal of them. As far as I know, Rubinstein believed, and was convinced, that everything in his compositions was impeccable and in its place. Therefore, like Tchaikovsky later, he usually sent his works to the printer almost as soon as they issued forth from his pen, forgetting his own aphorism about the necessity of putting them in a briefcase for a time. For this reason, he and Tchaikovsky share a great similarity in their technical methods.

Even while a student at the Conservatory, Tchaikovsky could be considered a cosmopolitan. He recognized no nationality in art nor the particular musical constitution of any nation. He did not care about national character or about what sort of plot was proposed to him and where the action took place—in Finland, Poland, or some other country. I was never able to agree with such a view and several times quarreled with him on this subject. I pointed out to him that anyone who speaks a foreign language badly provokes an involuntary feeling of annoyance in his interlocutor: you stop listening attentively and end up by walking away from him. The same thing must be experienced by people who are familiar with the peculiarities of character and thought of this or that nationality; music written by a foreigner that is uncharacteristic of his own people will strike them as repellent or unattractive or will say nothing to them. They will condemn the composer of a piece or an opera that includes, let us say, Polish or Spanish or other melodies which the composer himself cannot thoroughly grasp and whose meaning he fails to understand. Tchaikovsky would always respond heatedly that all that was unimportant, that the important thing was to express emotion, which must be the same in all people regardless of different nationalities. In a word, he, like Rubinstein, did not recognize nationality in music.

Since he was easily offended, after such conversations he would usually avoid me for some time, angry that I had dared to contradict him.

III

The Conservatory Professor
(1866–1876)

In September 1865, Anton Rubinstein's brother Nikolay offered Tchaikovsky the post of professor of classes in harmony sponsored by the Moscow branch of the Russian Musical Society, which would shortly become the Moscow Conservatory under the directorship of Nikolay Rubinstein. Tchaikovsky moved to Moscow on 5 January 1866. Nikolay Rubinstein welcomed him, not only providing him with accommodations in a part of his apartment, but also introducing him to his circle of friends, which included writers, musicians, and publishers. Tchaikovsky found teaching rather a strain, but Nikolay Rubinstein's constant enthusiasm and encouragement were to have a bracing effect on him. At a concert on 4 March 1866, Rubinstein conducted Tchaikovsky's Overture in F Major to great acclaim, which helped the composer to have faith in his own potential. He began to work on his First symphony, but found this not an easy matter: he was unable to sleep and suffered from headaches and depression.

At the end of November, his First symphony, *Winter Daydreams [Zimnie grezy]*, op. 13, was complete. Nikolay Rubinstein had offered to give the work its first performance, but Tchaikovsky refused because he wanted first to hear the opinions of Zaremba and Anton Rubinstein from St. Petersburg. Apparently they did not like the symphony, and its first performance did not take place until February 1868, with Nikolay Rubinstein conducting. In March 1867 Tchaikovsky started to work on an opera, *The Voyevoda*, with a libretto by the well-known Russian playwright Alexander Ostrovsky. Tchaikovsky lost the libretto and, despite Ostrovsky's efforts to reconstruct it, their collaboration ended in failure. Tchaikovsky himself completed the libretto on Ostrovsky's plot.[1]

Tchaikovsky spent the summer of 1867 in Finland and Estonia, where he composed a set of piano pieces, "Souvenir de Hapsal" *["Vospominanie o Gapsale"]*, op. 2. After returning to Moscow, he continued to work on his opera, and in February 1868 he was invited to conduct some portions from it at a charity concert. Music from *The Voyevoda* was well received, even by the "Mighty Handful," a group of nationalist composers who were making their presence known in Russian composition at that time. Later that spring Tchaikovsky went to St. Petersburg, where he met members of the Mighty Handful personally and also visited the composer Alexander Dargomyzhsky. In January of 1868 he became friendly with the self-appointed leader of the Mighty Handful, Mily Balakirev, whom he sent a score of his new tone poem *Fatum*. Balakirev did not like it.

The premiere of *The Voyevoda* took place at the Bolshoy Theater on 30 January 1869. Despite initial success, interest in the opera soon evaporated, and it was withdrawn from the repertoire after only five performances. Two weeks after the premiere Nikolay Rubinstein conducted the first performance of the symphonic poem *Fatum*. Public reaction was favorable, but again this success was short-lived. After Balakirev's harsh criticism of its St. Petersburg performance, Tchaikovsky refused to allow the work to be published and, a few years later, destroyed the score. It was reconstructed after his death on the basis of some discovered orchestral parts. The same fate befell his opera, *The Voyevoda*, from which Tchaikovsky decided to retain only the overture, one chorus, an entr'acte, and the dances.

Struggling for recognition, the young composer started work on another opera, this time based on a Russian translation of Fouqué's famous story "Undine."[2] On 6 August 1869 he submitted the finished opera to the Opera Directorate of the Imperial Theaters. Two years later the work was formally rejected and, like its predecessor, consigned to the flames by the composer himself. He saved only four pieces from it which were used later in the Symphony No. 2, the ballet *Swan Lake [Lebedinoe ozero]* and the incidental music to Ostrovsky's play *The Snow Maiden [Snegurochka]*.

In the autumn of 1869 Tchaikovsky met in Moscow with Balakirev, who encouraged the composer to begin a new tone poem based on Shakespeare's tragedy *Romeo and Juliet*. The Russian obsession with love and death, themes that permeate the story of the young lovers from Verona, almost immediately fired Tchaikovsky's imagination. After many revisions and modifications were made at Balakirev's suggestion, *Romeo and Juliet* was heard for the first time at a concert in Moscow on 4 March 1870, conducted by Nikolay Rubinstein. Tchaikovsky himself held a very high opinion of *Romeo and Juliet* to the end of his life.

It is ironic that the tragic situation so well presented by Tchaikovsky in his tone poem had real-life implications. About the same time, he was involved in a passionate love affair with a student at the Moscow Conservatory, Eduard Sack, which ended in Sack's suicide on 2 November 1873. Fourteen years after the young man's death, Tchaikovsky wrote in his diary: "It seems to me that I have never loved anyone so strongly as him . . . and his memory is sacred to me!"[3]

Tchaikovsky's relationships with young men were starting to cause talk in Moscow musical circles, but despite this he continued to pursue his love affairs. He rushed off to join one young man, Vladimir Shilovsky, a wealthy and talented student, after the latter fell seriously ill in Paris in 1870, and the two traveled together for some time following Shilovsky's recovery.

On 16 March 1871 a concert at Moscow's Hall of Nobility witnessed a successful performance of the young composer's First String Quartet, as well as a few of his piano pieces and songs.

In the autumn of 1871, Tchaikovsky finally engaged a small apartment of his own, furnished with a sofa, a few chairs, and two pictures, one a portrait of Anton Rubinstein, the other of Louis XVII, the dauphin who died in the aftermath of the French Revolution and whom Tchaikovsky had adored from childhood. He also took on a manservant, Mikhail Sofronov (soon to be replaced by the latter's younger brother Alexey), a peasant boy from the Klin region near Moscow. About this time, Tchaikovsky began to supplement his small income as a Conservatory professor by writing music criticism for the Moscow newspaper *Russkie vedomosti*.

In May 1872 he finished another opera, *The Oprichnik,* and, while staying at Kamenka during the summer, he began work on his Second Symphony, later dubbed the "Little Russian."[4] The new symphony was received enthusiastically in February 1873. Encouraged, Tchaikovsky proceeded to his next project, incidental music for Ostrovsky's play *The Snow Maiden [Snegorochka]*. After another vacation in Europe, he spent almost the whole of August at Shilovsky's estate Usovo, near Kiev, where he sketched out a new symphonic fantasia, *The Tempest [Buria]*, based on Shakespeare's play. *The Tempest* was a great success at its first performance in Moscow in early December.

On 12 April 1874 *The Oprichnik* was first performed at the Maryinsky Theater in St. Petersburg. Despite some initial success, the opera did not overwhelm the composer's critics. César Cui attacked the music as "barren of ideas" and "without a single outstanding passage or a single happy inspiration."[5] Tchaikovsky found himself agreeing: "*The Oprichnik* torments me," he confided to his cousin Anna Merkling.[6] The failure of the opera spoiled his journey to Italy, where he went right after the premiere in his capacity as music critic. He returned to Russia seized by an intense desire to prove to himself and others that he was capable of better things. By mid-June, while staying at Nizy, the estate of his society friend Nikolay Kondratyev, he started another new opera, this time to a libretto based on Nikolay Gogol's story "Christmas Eve" [*"Noch' pered Rozhdestvom"*].

A few years earlier, the music patron Grand Duchess Elena Pavlovna had commissioned a libretto for an opera based on Gogol's tale from the poet Yakov

Polonsky. It had originally been intended for Alexander Serov, but the latter had died in 1871 without commencing the project. The Grand Duchess decided to offer a prize in Serov's memory for the best setting of the libretto. Upon her own death in 1873, responsibility for the competition passed to the Russian Musical Society. Having learned that Balakirev, Anton Rubinstein, and Rimsky-Korsakov were not competing, and under the impression that the closing date for entry was 1 August 1874, Tchaikovsky finished his new opera within a month, only to discover that he would be obliged to wait a full year for the decision. Although Tchaikovsky eventually won first prize, the setting did not impress the public and the opera *Vakula the Smith [Kuznets Vakula]* was abandoned. Nine years later, the composer radically revised it under the new title, *The Slippers [Cherevichki]*. In 1895 the same story became the subject for Rimsky-Korsakov's opera *Christmas Eve*.

In November 1874 Tchaikovsky began working on a piano concerto, a draft of which he had completed by 24 December, when he played it for Nikolay Rubinstein. Three years later he described Rubinstein's reaction on that occasion in a letter to Mrs. von Meck: "I patiently played the concerto to the end: it was greeted with silence. I got up and asked, 'What do you think of it?' Suddenly a torrent of words gushed from Rubinstein's lips, getting louder and fiercer every minute until he sounded like a thundering Jupiter. According to him my concerto was no good at all, impossible to play, with many awkward passages. . . so poorly composed that it would be impossible to correct them. The composition was vulgar, and I had stolen bits from here, there, and everywhere. . . . I was not only astonished but offended by this scene." Stunned, the composer left the room without a word. Presently Rubinstein came to Tchaikovsky and seeing how upset he was, tried to soften the blow by saying that if Tchaikovsky agreed to revise the piece, he would introduce it at one of his concerts. "I shall not alter a single note," answered Tchaikovsky, "I shall publish the work precisely as it stands!"[7]

The concerto was indeed published exactly as it stood, but Tchaikovsky did eventually make alterations, particularly to the piano part. He decided to dedicate it not to his student at the Moscow Conservatory, the future composer Sergey Taneyev, as he had originally intended, but to the famous German pianist Hans von Bülow, whom Tchaikovsky had heard in recital at the Bolshoy Theater the previous March. Bülow, highly flattered by the dedication, gave the first successful performance of the B-flat Minor Concerto in Boston 13/25 October 1875. On 1 November Tchaikovsky attended the concerto's premiere in St. Petersburg. Despite excellent forces—the pianist was Tchaikovsky's old school friend, Gustav Kross, and the conductor Eduard Nápravník—the reviews were almost all unfavorable. When, later that autumn, Taneyev performed the "impossible" work at a concert of the Russian Musical Society in Moscow with Nikolay Rubinstein conducting, the concerto was proclaimed an instant success.

Tchaikovsky spent the summer of 1875 with his sister's family at Kamenka, his brother-in-law's estate in Ukraine. Here, Tchaikovsky composed his Third Symphony, this time in five movements, two of them in dance style. The symphony has since been nicknamed *"The Polish,"* for no more reason than the marking *tempo di polacca* of the finale. Performed for the first time on 7 November with Nikolay Rubinstein conducting, the symphony gained almost immediate acclaim.

In August, Tchaikovsky began work on the first of his famed trilogy of ballets, *Swan Lake,* which was commissioned by the Imperial Theaters in Moscow. Throughout the winter months the work progressed steadily and was finished by 10 April 1876. Meanwhile he also accepted a commission from the editor of *Nuvellist,* a music magazine, to compose a series of twelve piano pieces, which became popularly known as "The Seasons" *["Vremena goda"].*

At the very end of 1875, the composer left Russia together with his brother Modest and the latter's deaf-mute pupil, Nikolay Konradi. The two brothers decided to go to Paris via Germany and Switzerland. Modest was planning to study the latest methods of teaching deaf-mutes in Lyons at a private school. While in Paris Tchaikovsky attended a performance of Bizet's *Carmen* at the Opéra Comique, which made a powerful impression on him. At the end of January he returned to Russia, but he met up with Modest in France the next June. After about a month there Tchaikovsky traveled to Germany, where he attended the first festival devoted entirely to Wagner's *Der Ring des Niebelungen.* During his stay he made the acquaintance of Liszt, but he failed to meet Wagner himself. Tired by his stay at Bayreuth, Tchaikovsky returned to Kamenka on 11 August.

On 14 October he completed the symphonic fantasia *Francesca da Rimini,* which he claimed to have worked on "with love, and that love, it seems, has come out quite well."[8] At the end of 1876 he was honored by a visit from Leo Tolstoy, whom he greatly admired. The premiere of *Swan Lake* took place on 20 February 1877. It was a dismal failure owing to terrible choreography and a poor orchestra, and after a few productions it was dropped from the repertoire.

Not many reminiscences survive about Tchaikovsky's period at the Moscow Conservatory. The most valuable are those of his students and friends at the time. One of them was Rostislav Genika (1859–1922), whom Tchaikovsky taught composition and orchestration. A well-known pianist and music critic, he studied piano with Nikolay Rubinstein from 1871 to 1879. In 1880 Genika himself began teaching piano at the Music School in Kharkov (Ukraine). His memoirs, first published in *Russkaia muzykal'naia gazeta* in 1916, vividly recreate the atmosphere of the Moscow Conservatory and the personality of its director, Nikolay Rubinstein.[9] We have included only those excerpts which are related directly to Tchaikovsky. The tone of his recollections of the composer, his teaching methods, and the students' response to him is clearly panegyrical, in sharp contrast to the recorded impressions of other, especially female students of the composer at about the same time. Since Genika mentions Tchaikovsky's 1872 textbook on harmony, the events he describes must have occurred around 1871.

Another student of the composer at the Conservatory, Mariya Gurye (1853–1938), took a very different view of the man: in her portrayal Tchaikovsky emerges as an extremely reserved, taciturn, and reluctant teacher, hostile to some of his students and implicitly a misogynist. One can only speculate on the extent to which this picture corresponds to real life and how much it owes to the author's antipathy to the man and frustration with her studies. Excerpts from Gurye's short recollections were published in 1940.[10] We have included all passages pertaining to Tchaikovsky.

Gurye's description of Tchaikovsky as a teacher finds confirmation in the reminiscences of the mezzo-soprano Alexandra Amfiteatrova-Levitskaya (1858–1947), who studied at the Moscow Conservatory in the mid-1870s. Her narrative is more lively than Genika's and provides many interesting details. Amfiteatrova-Levitskaya created the part of Olga in the premiere of *Eugene Onegin* in the Conservatory in 1879.[11]

Some further personal traits of Tchaikovsky have been preserved in the memoirs of the violinist Alexander (Samuil) Litvinov (1861–1933), the pupil of Ferdinand Laub.[12] The composer had been attracted to this young musician to the point that he supported him financially and paid his tuition. Not surprisingly, Litvinov's recollections are full of praise for his benefactor. Tchaikovsky's image at the Conservatory would be incomplete without a sketch by another of his students, the anonymous V. A., which was published in 1897 but never included in standard editions of memoirs about the composer.[13] On balance, it may be allowed that Tchaikovsky's response to his male and female students could have differed in terms of affection, concern, and sympathy owing to his own amorous predilections.

The most intimate memoirs regarding this period belong to Ivan Klimenko, who had became Tchaikovsky's close friend after meeting the composer several years previously. Their friendship was especially intense between 1869 and 1872, when Klimenko moved to Moscow.[14] Written in 1899–1900 at the request of Modest Tchaikovsky and addressed personally to him, Klimenko's memoirs were published in Riazan in 1908. Owing to their content, they were never reprinted in Soviet Russia.[15] Klimenko presents a Tchaikovsky quite different from the one familiar from the established Soviet canon, which portrayed the great man as a happy, playful person, full of energy despite the alleged atrocities of the Tsarist regime. The author strikes one as being extremely fond of his subject, and he obviously delights in sharing with his readers a number of amusing and often moving anecdotes. Here (as in chapters 2 and 9) Klimenko's memoirs are printed almost in their entirety. This is their first publication in English.

Rostislav Genika

As is well known, Tchaikovsky began his musical career while at the Moscow Conservatory. During the ten years he spent as a professor there he grew accustomed to the Conservatory, it became like a home to him, and he became attached to it with all his heart. The Moscow and Petersburg conservatories carried on a long-standing, though secret, rivalry with one another. To the end of his days Tchaikovsky championed the banner of the Moscow Conservatory. I recall a banquet during his visit to Kharkov in the spring of 1893, not long before his death, at which Tchaikovsky spoke passionately of the superiority of the Moscow Conservatory over the Petersburg Conservatory. In the heat of the moment, however, Pyotr Ilyich had put his foot in his mouth, for at this banquet were several graduates of the Petersburg Conservatory!

If Nikolay Rubinstein sacrificed his career as an artist to the business of the Conservatory, Tchaikovsky, on the contrary, broke with the Conservatory at the earliest opportunity for the sake of his freedom as a composer. The music trade, the drudgery, his professorial duties at the Conservatory all sickened him. This is quite natural, it could not have been otherwise. One must bear in mind the difference in the very nature of Rubinstein's position and Tchaikovsky's. Nikolay Rubinstein stood at the head of a large and complex artistic and pedagogical enterprise which he himself had created. Everything was under his direction and supervision. The organization of the Musical Society concerts and the associated conductor's duties satisfied his artistic needs and his self-esteem. And indeed, even his work with his piano class, as he taught it, held a strong artistic and ideological interest for him. In sum, how much luster, esteem, and beauty were connected with all this! Such work was utterly absorbing to an artist like Rubinstein. How dreary the duties of a teacher of music theory seem by comparison: what a truly dry, soulless, purely technical occupation it is! Student technique in this field, developed even to its highest perfection, may please the scholastic, but it often results in artistic nonsense. Nikolay Hubert loved to recall how at the Paris Conservatory, in a class in solfeggio, he happened to hear a chorus of students sol-fa a rapid fugue from the overture to Mozart's *Magic Flute*. The theorist has to analyze the forms, harmonic constructions, and polyphonic aspects of the great masterpieces; but this analysis is done from a purely technical point of view, and contains as little art as the research of an anatomist. The most prominent theorists, such as Dehn, Albrechtsberger, Fétis, and Gevaert, were devoid of artistic creative talent.[16] On the other hand, among great composers who were at the same time great theorists, Cherubini and Rimsky-Korsakov constitute exceptions.

For the genius, the lowly mechanical work is doubly difficult. What tragic irony there is in the fate of Sebastian Bach, who spent so many years drumming the musical ABCs into the pupils of a Leipzig parochial school! Tchaikovsky's hours of teaching theory passed for him in gloomy file. He was clearly bored, barely able to stifle his yawns. My youthful impressions of his first lessons in harmony are so vivid! How well I remember his appearance at that time: young, with fair, almost handsome features, a deep, soulful gaze in his handsome dark eyes, bushy, carelessly combed hair and a marvelous auburn beard, dressed rather poorly and carelessly, most often in a threadbare gray jacket, Tchaikovsky would enter his classroom in a rush, always somewhat embarrassed and irritable, as if annoyed at the tedium to come. He hated the mundane furnishings of the theory classroom with its school desks and ordinary old dilapidated yellow piano with jangling yellowing keys, and the blackboard with its red lines. Standing at this blackboard, Tchaikovsky would have to write for us problems and examples. I remember the squeamish gesture with which, after tossing away the chalk and gray dust cloth, he would wipe his fingers on his handkerchief. He bemoaned the slowness of most of the female students, the obtuse, superficial attitude toward the essence of art of all these future lady laureates who dreamed only of the stage and were convinced that the audiences applauding their playing would have no interest in their technical knowledge.

Reluctantly he would listen to students drearily banging out sequences and modulations on the dreadful-sounding piano, and patiently mark forbidden fifths and octaves with red pencil. When I entered Tchaikovsky's class his textbook on harmony had not yet been published; it appeared in Jurgenson's catalog the following year. Tchaikovsky, pacing about the classroom, would dictate to us slowly and very distinctly, and we would take notes. He spent the entire first semester acquainting us with the formation and relationship of different harmonies, explaining suspensions and anticipations, and making us solve problems in thoroughbass. Only in the second semester did he move on to melodic harmonization. Tchaikovsky's lectures, his comments, explanations, and corrections were remarkably clear, concise, and comprehensible. Later I took his class in orchestration and the theory of so-called free composition, creating orchestral arrangements for various piano pieces, and writing under his guidance a string quartet and, for the final examination, an overture for orchestra. Simplicity and clarity of exposition, fluidity of form, limpidity and lightness of orchestration were the ideals to which Tchaikovsky made his students aspire. He liked to illustrate various rules by citing Glinka and Mozart.

Pyotr Ilyich treated his students with amazing gentleness, tact, and patience. With some of the older students he was on intimate, purely friendly terms. His involuntary and sometimes sarcastic, but well deserved, remarks were never expressed at all rudely or offensively. The impossible musical absurdities that his students sometimes presented to him would cause the corner of his mouth to rise in a characteristic smile, at once good-natured and mocking. One of my fellow students in the composition class was Nikolay Klenovsky.[17] He was about three years my senior, and would work tirelessly and painstakingly. A music enthusiast who used to drop off to sleep in a bed heaped high with scores, he was fond of piling up complicated combinations and intricacies. Tchaikovsky, who disliked anything that was cluttered or ponderous, kept having to draw him away onto the path of classical clarity and simplicity.

From all this, it is clear that Tchaikovsky could not have regarded his professorial duties with much enthusiasm. As a teacher he was likable, efficient, conscientious—nothing more. But then, it was not for his teaching that everyone loved him, indeed worshipped him. His admirers were inspired by contact with his genius. How powerful and fresh were the impressions from each new work which flowed from his pen, to be performed immediately at one of the symphonic or chamber gatherings!

To understand the full intensity, the full unpredictability of these impressions, one must try to imagine what Russian music was like at that time, to make the mental transition to the early 1870s—for not a single composer who came after Tchaikovsky has escaped in one way or another his influence. Since then his methods have been so exhausted, so widely used! Many of them have become commonplace, even cliché. Nowadays Tchaikovsky is as popular, perhaps even as overplayed, oversung, as, for example, Chopin or Verdi. Musicians grow up with a knowledge of him. Today his music no longer has the charm of novelty, the fascination of the unfamiliar: everyone knows it too well. But one must imagine the sensitive listener who was encountering for the first time the beauties of his *Andante cantabile* for strings, *Romeo*, *The Tempest*, or the Piano Concerto! How vividly I recall the cloudy winter morning, the dark Hall of Columns in the Assembly of Nobles, and the rehearsal when I first heard, under Nikolay Rubinstein's direction, *Francesca da Rimini*. I happened just then to be reading Dante, his *Inferno*—in translation with commentary by Lamennais. I was utterly stunned by the power of the design, by the mastery of the colors with which Pyotr Ilyich painted his grandiose canvas. How meager the homogeneous works of Liszt or Berlioz seemed to me alongside this *Francesca!*

The knowledge that Tchaikovsky was still one of us, a Muscovite, a member of the Conservatory, that not only was he still unknown abroad but that even

Petersburg musicians had a rather negative attitude toward him, some envying him, others not comprehending him—all this made him all the more dear.

On the occasion of his *Snow Maiden,* the following verse directed at Tchaikovsky appeared in one of the popular Moscow newspapers:

> Save us, Lord, for pity's sake
> From this melancholy music!
>
> [Spasi nas, gospodi, pomilyi,
> Ot etoi muzyki unyloi!]

All the same, what charming simplicity and immediacy there is in this music of Tchaikovsky's, and what poetry and beauty there was in that first, memorable spring production of *The Snow Maiden* at the Bolshoy Theater! What a collection of first-rate artistic talent among the performers: Fedotova as the Snow Maiden, Nikulina as Kupava, Kadmina as Lel', Samarin as Berendey, Reshimov as Mizgir.[18] But the critics, instead of highlighting all the merits, the interest, the exceptional quality of such a production, dwelled on minor defects and cracked jokes about the fact that the extras portraying geese in the prologue appeared in blackened boots.

Of course, Pyotr Ilyich ignored both the acclaim and the minor jabs of the press. A consciousness of his own strength, his own genius, was the basis of his musical generosity, his shyness in everyday encounters, his surprising simplicity of manner, and his artistic nobility and dignity. I would sometimes see him at symphonic concerts, in the company of two or three students, in the gallery, sitting on the steps leading to the upper foyer; and meanwhile downstairs one of his masterpieces was being performed for the first time. When the rapturous audience loudly called for the composer, Pyotr Ilyich would appear on stage in his plain gray jacket looking bashful and embarrassed and, as if reluctantly, would give an awkward bow. But this unassuming manner of his only raised him in our eyes and made him even dearer to our heart.

For us, his students, the rising generation, Pyotr Ilyich represented as much of a musical ideal as Nikolay Rubinstein.

Mariya Gurye

Unfortunately my recollections of Pyotr Ilyich Tchaikovsky are quite sparse, firstly because it was so long ago—many decades, in fact—and secondly because Tchaikovsky was still a very young composer and was not yet surrounded by an aura of glory, since he himself had graduated from the Petersburg Conservatory not long before and had just entered the musical arena, and did not present for us any especial interest. Thirdly, for us Muscovites he was utterly foreign, a Petersburger, of whom we knew little and who was completely eclipsed by the spectacular array of foreign musician-professors invited by the Conservatory (that is, the Russian Musical Society), who were quite famous at that time.

As a teacher he did not leave a deep impression in my memory for the additional reason that the subject he taught, the theory of harmony, was not especially interesting for us (perhaps due to his teaching method) and was only of secondary importance in the Conservatory at that time. But then, Tchaikovsky himself did not exhibit any great interest in his subject and in our success at it (it is well known that he generally saw teaching as a burden and always dreamed of freeing himself from it). It was as if he tried to be unnoticeable. He isolated himself from his fellow professors, except of course Nikolay Rubinstein and Nikolay Kashkin, with whom he was friendly throughout. Tchaikovsky himself did not show much interest in his subject or in our progress. Extremely reserved, taciturn, sullen, as if dissatisfied with something, he excited neither attention nor liking. In his dealings with us he was very sharp and even rude, which probably stemmed from the fact that he found teaching a burden, which we sensed quite clearly, and he seemed to vent his dissatisfaction on his students, in particular the female students, whom he persecuted outright. With regard to our studies he was extremely demanding and became terribly annoyed at our evident inability to grasp harmonic theory in the way he understood it, demanding not only that we learn the rules by heart and fulfill the assignments, but also expecting a display of musical skill in our written exercises, interesting modulations at the piano, as well as rapid transcription from his dictation, and so forth. But we were truly not at all prepared for his course, since the course in elementary theory that we had with Nikolay Kashkin in our first year was quite episodic, with no system, textbook, or program, and therefore did not provide us with the necessary (solid) basis for the course in harmony. We were especially afraid of Tchaikovsky's caustic and at times rather harsh remarks when, sitting at the piano, we had, at his indication, to modulate boldly, swiftly, and without resorting to parallel fifths or octaves. Though himself very modest, diffident, even shy, Tchaikovsky had no patience for shyness and seemed even to despise it in his students and was particularly ruthless and sarcastic in his attacks on them. One example of Pyotr Ilyich's bashfulness is the embarrassment he showed by blushing to the roots of his hair every time he was asked a question, to which he would respond with irritation, obviously angry at himself for his embarrassment.

Today, when we know what a remarkably kind, considerate, and acutely sensitive man he was, his sharp outbursts of that time seem simply incredible, but nonetheless they occurred, and not infrequently, so that only two individuals at the Conservatory inspired fear and evoked timidity—Rubinstein and

Tchaikovsky. A feeling of timidity was also caused by his appearance, his expression, always sullen, even gloomy, so that I do not recall him ever smiling, even when making sarcastic comments. That is all I can recollect of my life at the Conservatory at that time and of my lessons with Pyotr Ilyich. I greatly regret that the impressions made on me at that time by the young Tchaikovsky were almost all negative, but these are, after all, recollections of the old Conservatory, of Pyotr Ilyich Tchaikovsky's first steps on the pedagogical stage, which was so burdensome for him. Such reminiscences must be first and foremost truthful and unembellished.

Alexandra Amfiteatrova-Levitskaya

When I entered the Moscow Conservatory, Pyotr Ilyich Tchaikovsky was professor of harmony and composition. Among his students, one found the most contradictory opinions about him as a teacher. Some considered him not only a brilliant composer but also an ideal teacher. According to them, Pyotr Ilyich always examined the work of his students with great interest and attention, patiently correcting errors, and gave remarkable instructions. Others maintained that Tchaikovsky treated them thoughtlessly, unfairly, that he devoted much of his time to a few students and paid no attention at all to the others. One of his female students recounted the following incident to me as an example of Pyotr Ilyich's uncaring attitude toward some of his students.

"Tchaikovsky is not only unfair, he's a terrible fault-finder. At the last lesson he picked on a trifle and crossed out my assignment without even looking at it."

"But why?" I asked.

"I attached the stems to the wrong side of some of the octaves. He grew angry and crossed out the entire page from top to bottom with a red pencil. Then, handing me back my exercise-book, he said irritably, 'First, you need to study stems, and only then can you solve problems in harmony!'"

In the view of most of Tchaikovsky's students, he was not fond of teaching in general and did not devote himself to it eagerly. He was only interested in those students in whom he saw some talent as a composer. Among these Pyotr Ilyich esteemed Sergey Taneyev, Nikolay Klenovsky, and Pyotr Danilchenko as outstanding, talented students who had a gift for composition.

I took harmony with Professor Nikolay Hubert and never had occasion to encounter Pyotr Ilyich as a teacher. Only once, at the finals in solfeggio, did I have to take an examination with him. Having heard contradictory stories about him, I became rather violently agitated when Pyotr Ilyich called me to the table. I remember that he chose from the music lying before him several bars with a difficult rhythmic division, where besides long notes there were also brief pauses and stops and syncopes. When I finished singing, Pyotr Ilyich said to me, "Correct," and asked: "Of what subdivisions does 5/4 time consist?" And I answered the question correctly as well. Tchaikovsky asked me to give an example. I named the chorus of maidens from the third act of Glinka's opera *A Life for the Tsar.*

"Can you sing a few bars from this chorus and conduct them?" suggested Pyotr Ilyich.

I sang, "The spring floods broke loose and flowed across the plains," conducting in 5/4 time.

"Fine, that's enough," said Pyotr Ilyich.

"Well, that wasn't as terrible as I expected," I thought as I proceeded on at the summons to Langer for dictation.

In his appearance Pyotr Ilyich was quite handsome, but the impression he gave was one of severity. His expression was such that he constantly seemed displeased with something. Gloomy eyes looked out from under a frowning brow. To the greetings of the students he responded with a barely perceptible nod of his head. He appeared stern and angry.

Such was Tchaikovsky within his official working environment at the Conservatory, and such he has remained in my memory of my Conservatory impressions.

Alexander Litvinov

I first saw Pyotr Ilyich Tchaikovsky in 1873 in the class in harmony that he taught at the Moscow Conservatory. He was a nervous and lively little man. He would enter the classroom at a brisk pace, with his hands behind his back, nodding slightly and staring ahead with a fixed and, as it seemed to us, sharp look in his gray eyes. Pyotr Ilyich would sit at the piano and pick up a pencil, passing it between his fingers so that his second and fourth fingers were on top of the pencil and the third beneath, or sometimes the reverse, and, without letting go of it, would play our exercises; stopping for a second, he would circle the parallel fifths and octaves with a rapid and abrupt movement, then continue on with the playing. It was clear that our mistakes irritated him. While explaining the rules of harmony, Pyotr Ilyich never stopped pacing to and fro about the classroom, typically clasping his hands behind his back and bending slightly forward. We were terribly afraid of him (I was then thirteen).

Once after a student concert at the Conservatory in which I had taken part (I was studying violin with Ferdinand Laub), Pyotr Ilyich, sitting in the first row next to Nikolay Rubinstein, called me over and showered warm words of praise on my playing. I was so encouraged by this that I experienced a redoubled burst of energy toward my violin lessons. After this I no longer felt any fear of Pyotr Ilyich as I had in harmony class where he was often sharp and impatient. Pyotr

Ilyich never missed an opportunity to praise me after one of my frequent appearances in student concerts, often adding his voice to the praises of Nikolay Rubinstein, our director.

With his gentle artistic nature, Pyotr Ilyich sensed how very important words of encouragement could be to nervous performers. And I did my very best.

Especially memorable for me is the following incident. It happened that my parents (I was born into a poor Jewish family), feeling that I had "learned to play the violin well enough" and, unable to afford for me to continue at the Conservatory, decided to remove me from there and prepare me for a different career. . . .

One morning, sitting at home in hopeless despair and holding my beloved violin in my hands (I never parted with it, even taking it to bed with me at night), I suddenly heard the sound of a carriage drive up and come to a stop near the entrance to our apartment. At once there came an impatient ringing at the bell and the tramp of hurried feet along the staircase, the door opened, and Tchaikovsky walked in. I rushed to greet him, and within a few minutes he and I were in the cab riding to the Conservatory. On the way, he told me that, having learned of my misfortune (I had stopped coming to classes) and the reason behind it, he had decided to make me his scholarship student, that is, to pay my Conservatory fees. . . .[19]

In 1879 I had the good fortune to play among the first violins in the lyric scenes from *Eugene Onegin*, which were produced for the first time at the Moscow Conservatory. In this same year, 1879, . . . I graduated from the Moscow Conservatory with the Great Silver Medal.

V. A.

In contrast to the other, "hardened" professors, [Tchaikovsky] treated his students with exceptional indulgence and tried to help them in every way possible. Among others who owed their graduation to his efforts was a Mr. Boits. In my time Boits was constantly roaming up and down the corridors, going from one professor to another for testing. He was a Jew, and so it was assumed he had a talent for music (it is well known that Nikolay [Rubinstein] belonged to this same race, though he was born in a small Bessarabian village to a merchant who was later the owner of a sealing-wax factory in Moscow). Boits's voice was actually not bad, but it tended to squeak, and sometimes one wondered where such sounds came from. At that, he would be sent from the Conservatory to the theater for an audition, and the small, dark, and slicked-down Mr. Boits would set off wandering anew. Studying the pages of elementary music theory without the help of a manual (I believe this was before the handbook of Nikolay Kashkin existed), he got bogged down in harmony. Pyotr Tchaikovsky not only enabled him to receive his diploma, he even arranged employment for him in the provinces. A few years later, having lost his position, Mr. Boits again turned to Tchaikovsky for help. This episode is described as here in one of the published reminiscences. (I apologize to the reader for this representative insertion, but I can attest to the truth of the episode, since I heard the story shortly afterward from one of those involved.)

Once, during Alexander Ostrovsky's tenure as director, the Bolshoy Theater was suffering a particularly acute shortage of tenors. Dmitry Usatov, who at the time was really the only one who sang the repertoire, demanded an increase in salary.[20] He was refused, but he stood his ground. The board of directors wanted to replace him, but there was no one available. Ostrovsky asked Tchaikovsky whether he could recommend anyone. Tchaikovsky promised to send a tenor to audition, describing his virtues in the most glowing terms. Ostrovsky, who was delighted, acted high-handed and haughty with Usatov, who re-mained steadfast in his demand. The auditioning tenor, having barely begun to sing, filled everyone with horror. "Wherever did this fellow come from?" Ostrovsky wondered aloud. It turned out to be Mr. Boits, who indeed had once had a fairly decent provincial tenor voice, but who for some years had not been able to find an appointment, owing to the loss of his vocal abilities, which eventually resulted in the collapse of the poor artist's nervous system and mental faculties. . . .

Ostrovsky made a bit of a scene with Tchaikovsky: "My dear fellow! Why are you making a fool of me? Who have you recommended to me?!"

"Oh, Alexander," replied the kindhearted Pyotr Ilyich, nearly in tears, "what was I supposed to do? Just look at what a pitiable fellow he is."

Ivan Klimenko

I recently recalled that, when I arrived in Moscow in 1868, Herman Laroche was sick with syphilis and it was necessary for him to take baths. It was very inconvenient to do this in the apartment of his mother, who worked as governess for the Katkov family and lived in the building of the editorial offices of *Moskovskie vedomosti*. Tchaikovsky, who was then living with Nikolay Rubinstein, dragged Laroche home and gave him his own room, while he fixed up a place for himself behind some screens in the back hall. That, at least, is what my recollection tells me. Not fully trusting my memory, I asked Jurgenson whether this was the case, and he replied that his memory seems also to depict something along these lines, though he would not be so bold as to swear on it.

Upon recuperating, Laroche chose a poor way of displaying his gratitude. He wrote a review for the *Moskovskie vedomosti* of a Musical Society concert that included a performance of dances from *The Voyevoda;* apropos of these dances he offered a general critique of Tchaikovsky's compositions, finding in them the imprint of the composer's "feminine" nature and clear traces of the influence of "imitators of Schumann and Mendelssohn." (Tchaikovsky despised these characterizations because they seemed to indicate that his muse was incapable of anything powerful, while by this time he had already written the *Scherzo à la russe,* the First Symphony, and the *Valse caprice*—all very masculine and powerful works; indeed, even in the *Voyevoda* dances there is nothing at all feminine about the cello theme, a fact that must have been clearer to Laroche than to anyone else.[21]) Pyotr Ilyich was especially offended by Laroche's second remark, since it showed the critic's clear intention to wound Tchaikovsky by implying that the composer was not mature enough to be influenced by Schumann and Mendelssohn themselves, but remained merely under the sway of their imitators. Tchaikovsky complained bitterly to me about how he, as a composer just beginning his artistic career, had naturally looked for support from Laroche, whose articles (such as, for example, his wonderful essay on "Glinka and His Significance in the History of Music") had already made a name for himself as an authoritative music critic; but, in the meantime, without any provocation on Tchaikovsky's part, Laroche had played a mean trick on him, sinning against both truth and friendship. Laroche, evidently wishing to soften the impression from his harsh and ridiculous stunt, charged someone (I don't remember who) to pass on a copy of his Glinka article to Tchaikovsky, and the next day Laroche, meeting the composer in the corridor of the Conservatory, asked, "Pyotr Ilyich, did you receive my article?" To this Tchaikovsky replied (without offering his hand): "Yes, I did, and I tore it up and threw it in the fire, as you deserve" (or, "as *a present from you* deserves"—I don't recall the precise words, but the scene I remember perfectly). I tell you this, of course, from Tchaikovsky's own words.

I also remember another incident where Tchaikovsky was hurt by Laroche. This time the latter was not so much to blame, since, in the first place, Pyotr Ilyich himself was in part the cause of the insult, and in the second place, it stemmed from somebody who was already on hostile terms with Tchaikovsky. What happened was this. Tchaikovsky's symphonic fantasy *Fatum* was scheduled to be performed at the Musical Society concert of 15 February 1869. Pyotr Ilyich brought me to the rehearsal. I was captivated by the work, being most affected by its second theme, in which I clearly heard heartrending weeping (Balakirev, meanwhile, according to Tchaikovsky, laughed at this same theme to his face, finding it comical [Tchaikovsky always explained Balakirev's comment about his works as envy on the latter's part]). Having been so strongly impressed by the work, I naturally wished to learn from the composer the true meaning of the work's title for a fuller understanding of it. Tchaikovsky flatly refused to offer any explanation, saying that the meaning of the title was a purely personal matter, concerning him and him alone.[22] After such a vigorous refusal, I sought just as vigorously to convince Pyotr Ilyich not to print the name *Fatum* in the playbill, since this title would inevitably pique the curiosity of any attentive listener and, in the absence of authorial explanations, might prove harmful (that is, might ultimately do harm to the interests of the composer himself). Were the composition to remain untitled it would be listened to as a work of pure music and, as such, produce a complete impression on the listener; but an intriguing title would make the listener search the contents of the work for the meaning of the title. The title would divide the listener's attention and would not only fail to clarify anything to him (as the composer evidently wished it), but, on the contrary, would completely obscure the meaning of the work.

On the Sunday following this rehearsal Pyotr Ilyich was visited by Sergey Rachinsky,[23] to whom I told the essence of my views expressed above, after which the following conversation took place among us: *Rachinsky:* "I quite agree with Ivan [Klimenko] and regret that I was not at the rehearsal, so as to second his opinion with greater confidence." *I* (to Tchaikovsky): "You must give the listener at least some clue for understanding such a vague title, and if, for some reason or other, you find it impossible to bare your soul to the listener and give a more or less detailed explanation of what you wanted to say in the work, then why not give him at least some hint in the form of an epigraph?" *Rachinsky* (to Tchaikovsky): "I fully respect the personal obstacles which prevent you, Pyotr Ilyich, from providing a detailed explanation, but I quite like Ivan's idea of placing some appropriate verse as an epigraph." *Tchaikovsky:* "Yes, but what poem?" *Rachinsky:* "What a pity that I haven't heard the work! But might not these lines by Batyushkov be suitable?[24] (I quote from the program.)

> Knowest thou what the gray-haired Melchisedek
> Said as he bid farewell to life? "Man is born a slave,
> A slave he goes to his grave,
> And even death will scarce reveal to him
> Why he walked this sorrowful vale of tears,
> Why he suffered, wept, endured, then vanished!"

> [Ty znaesh, chto izrek,
> Proshchaias' s zhizn'iu, sedoi Melkhisedek?
> "Rabom rodit'sia chelovek,
> Rabom v mogilu liazhet,
> I smert' emu edva li skazhet, zachem on shel dolinoi skorbnoi slez,
> Stradal, rydal, terpel, ischez!"]

Tchaikovsky: "Yes, perhaps that would be good." And Rachinsky at once wrote the poem down and it was printed. I was decidedly incapable of grasping the connection between the meaning of this poem and the music I had heard at the rehearsal, but Tchaikovsky's agreement confused me, and I, lending full authority to the composer's agreement, decided not to burden him for the time being with any explanations due to my fear of seeming annoying. I nurtured a strong hope of discovering the connection during the performance of the piece at the concert, but, alas, I did not find it, and the unfortunate epigraph gave Laroche occasion to reproach Tchaikovsky in a rather angry fashion, claiming that Melchisedek spoiled everything, casting obscurity into the listeners' minds. (I recall that Laroche responded to the piece, notwithstanding its name, in a quite flattering manner.) Tchaikovsky was saddened by the incident, and, I recall, *Fatum* was not performed any more in Moscow. You know, of course, that subsequently Tchaikovsky took the first theme for the romantic duet in *The Oprichnik,* but the second theme, as far as I know, was never repeated by him. I heard that Tchaikovsky, while living in Poltava somewhat later, destroyed the music to *Fatum,* thinking that the transcription for four hands by M. Ivanov, which Petya gave to me, was all that remained from the composition, which in my view was most superior. But it turns out (as Kashkin asserts in his *Memoirs*) that the orchestral parts survived and are held in the library of the Moscow Conservatory.

Necessary note. Keeping in mind that I am writing this exclusively for you, Modest Ilyich, as the beloved brother of my dear unforgettable friend, I consider it my sacred duty not to conceal from you anything that I know and remember. Therefore I beg you never for a second to think that in telling you of Laroche's behavior with respect to Tchaikovsky I had the intention of sowing in you hostility toward Laroche. I am no judge, only a truthful narrator. Besides, we both know that Laroche loved Tchaikovsky and was close to him in the final years. I am deeply convinced that Laroche always deeply loved Tchaikovsky, even when he caused him unpleasantness, and that he caused this unpleasantness with pain in his heart from some emotional factors, incomprehensible to me. In any case we should not judge Laroche for his old sins, which Tchaikovsky fully forgave him. We should not sin against Tchaikovsky's memory.

More on *Fatum:* soon after its performance in concert Tchaikovsky once thought out loud in my presence: "If only someone would give me a hundred good cigarettes." I immediately decided to play a harmless joke on Tchaikovsky, and the joke turned out wonderfully. On the very same day I asked Jurgenson[25] to print up three slips of paper—"FATUM" CIGARETTES, bought three boxes of cigarettes with glass lids, and glued these slips of paper onto the lids. The next Sunday morning I went as usual to see Tchaikovsky, gave the cigarettes to

Agafon (Nikolay Rubinstein's manservant), and asked him to place the boxes on their side on the desk, to make them more noticeable. Tchaikovsky sat down at the piano and played quite a long time for me. I impatiently awaited the moment when he would go to his study. Soon we were joined by Jurgenson, who knew about the merry scene that was to take place. Finally, thanks be to Allah, Tchaikovsky pulled himself from his chair and went to his study. We went after him. Entering his study and seeing the boxes, he joyfully exclaimed: "Ah, cigarettes! Where did they come from? Who brought them? Agafon!... Ah, my God! What is this? Look, kind sirs: 'Fatum' Cigarettes!" (At this for an instant his face showed an expression of real terror, quickly replaced by an expression of bewilderment.) I tried to continue the comedy and began to congratulate him on the success of his *Fatum,* which had apparently become an object of fashion, but I could not restrain myself, and Jurgenson and I cracked, and after us so did Tchaikovsky, who had understood the joke, of course. But he still hesitated for some time concerning the accuracy of his guess, having noticed that the labels were printed, so that cigarettes with that name must be available in the shops. When, however, he learned that only three labels had been printed, he laughed a lot, in the end approving of both the joke and the cigarettes.

I remember from this same period Tchaikovsky's concert in the Small Hall of the Assembly of Nobles, instigated by Nikolay Rubinstein, who convinced him to write a quartet for the performance. [Conservatory professors] Laub, Minkus, Kosman, and I don't recall who else (the second violin) offered their services for the concert. Rubinstein himself, of course, undertook to perform some of Tchaikovsky's piano pieces, besides which it was proposed that singers be found to perform his songs. Before the concert an unbelievably extravagant and amusing incident occurred. As the audience began arriving, I saw Apukhtin enter and take a seat, as usual, in the first row (naturally, wearing a frock coat and pale lilac gloves, and with an opera hat under his arm), after which Turgenev[26] entered with Kashperov[27] and, standing in the center aisle, talked among themselves. Suddenly I saw Apukhtin leave his seat, mount the steps to the stage, go over to the piano, slowly remove the glove from his right hand, lay it and the opera hat on the piano, raise the cover from the keyboard, and, with a perfectly serious expression, strike a single note with his finger and listen closely to the dying sound. He then drew up the bench, sat down, and played a major triad and listened to it for a long moment, cocking his head slightly to one side (his face toward the audience, his eyes toward the ceiling). Then, when the chord had died away, Apukhtin just as slowly closed the cover, took his hat and glove, pushed back the bench, and left the stage to return to his seat. Tchaikovsky, on hearing the first note, glanced curiously from the greenroom and, seeing Apukhtin, showed a momentary horror, which quickly changed to an expression of infectious merriment, whereupon he closed the door. The audience reacted variously to Apukhtin's prank: some were puzzled, others smiled broadly, and several clearly disapproved of Apukhtin's behavior, maintaining a severe expression. Turgenev was smiling goodnaturedly, while I and my friend Galliard for a long time were overcome with laughter, which Pyotr Ilyich seemed to be sharing in the greenroom. The concert, however, was not without some disappointment for Tchaikovsky, and the reason for this disappointment was Lavrovskaya.[28] The fact is that the concert was given by *Tchaikovsky the composer,* and such a concert only made any real sense if Pyotr Ilyich's works alone were performed at it. But the bitch Lavrovskaya, having accepted the invitation to participate in this concert of her former Petersburg Conservatory classmate whose career was only just beginning, nevertheless did not sing *a single one* of Tchaikovsky's songs, thereby imparting a note of insult to her participation.

Let me tell you about a misunderstanding between Tchaikovsky and Nikolay Rubinstein which, presumably, caused the two men much vexation, if not anguish, and which was resolved in a rather touching manner. When they were living on Znamenka (the apartment was laid out on two floors), I arrived in Moscow from Tsaritsin and stayed with them. Rubinstein, I remember, was then preparing three ambitious programs (for a concert in Vienna, for his annual concert in Moscow, and for a concert with his brother Anton in Petersburg). I tried to arrange my affairs so as to have the opportunity to spend as much time as possible with Nikolay Rubinstein while he was learning the aforementioned programs by heart. I was a diligent and attentive audience to him, and, of course, an ardent admirer. Such an attitude on my part evidently pleased him, and during those few days we became very close friends. One time I got back to the apartment from somewhere after midnight. Rubinstein was already asleep, but Tchaikovsky was in his room writing music (I don't remember what, exactly). I stopped in to chat with him a bit before bed and to listen to him lament about how difficult it was for him to make a name for himself in the face of the indifference Rubinstein showed toward his activities as a composer. "Why, Rubinstein obviously knows that here I am writing something close at hand in his own home, that this something cannot reach the public without his participation, and that in the end I shall be obliged to come to him and ask him to perform my composition at a Musical Society concert; and would you believe it, not once has he cared to find out what it is I am writing, while my own pride prevents me from forcing myself on his attention." The next morning at breakfast I told Rubinstein that I had got back rather late the night before and found him asleep, but that Tchaikovsky was still sitting at his work. With respect to this latter circumstance, Rubinstein, in his turn, complained to me about Pyotr Ilyich in approximately these words: "Well, here then, you be the judge! You know how fond I am of all of them. I love Modest and Anatoly like my own relatives, and Pyotr Ilyich more than a relative. So obviously it pains me to know that he's sitting there in his room writing something, and doesn't once call me in and show me his work, which of course I would be very interested in seeing and about which I might even be able to offer some friendly advice, as an experienced musician. And it hurts all the more since his work is sure to find its way into my hands in the end, but I would be curious to know something of it during its development."

When I told Rubinstein of Tchaikovsky's complaint against him and vice versa, you can easily imagine the sweet and touching conclusion to their mutual misunderstanding.

I remember going with Tchaikovsky to a rehearsal for the Musical Society concert at which his *Romeo and Juliet* overture was to be performed. The musicians took their places, and Nikolay Rubinstein mounted the stage, went over to his conductor's stand, and, rapping it with his baton, exclaimed: "Meine Herren! Bitte: Ouverture zu 'Romeo und Julietta' von Tschaikowsky." *I* (to Tchaikovsky): "How lucky you are to have your name uttered in such a noble connection!" *Tchaikovsky* (pressing my knee warmly): "Trust me, my dear fellow, I would be no less happy and proud if Rubinstein were to address this same orchestra with the words: 'Meine Herren! Bitte: Ouverture zu 'Macbeth' von Klimenko!'" And I firmly believe that, had I been a composer, there would never have been any jealous "rivalry" between us.

Just now I have recalled Kashkin's funny story, which might not be unknown to you, from the period of the late sixties or early seventies.

Tchaikovsky and Laroche met Professor Bugaev (then still a young mathematician) somewhere at an evening party.[29] Laroche asked him whether he would be able to explain to him, Laroche (who knew only arithmetic and some geometry), what a differential and an integral were. Bugaev agreed to explain. Tchaikovsky also took an interest in Bugaev's explanations. The listeners sat down with an expression of interest and full attention on their faces. Bugaev began to explain with enthusiasm what a differential was, and Laroche soon abandoned his place with the words, "No, I must be a complete idiot! I really cannot understand a word!" Tchaikovsky, however, due to his sincere kindness, remained to hear out the somewhat flustered professor, who continued his explanation with even more ardor, finishing it with a definition of the concept of the integral and displaying an expression of pleasure on his face that he had fulfilled his task in so brilliant a fashion. He was convinced, the poor thing, that his listener was naturally satisfied with the explanation, since he had attracted his full attention to the end. But, alas! He was in for a bitter disappointment. Tchaikovsky, sighing heavily, declared in an endlessly sad tone: "Lord! Are there really people on this earth who actually understand all that!"

And here is a story from Tchaikovsky about Kashkin. When Tchaikovsky became a professor at the Moscow Conservatory, he found Kashkin much more congenial than his other colleagues, and they began to meet frequently, discussing "important matters" and, at first, even playing four hands on the piano. Kashkin had long since acquired the curious habit of *constantly* rubbing the palm of his left hand with the middle finger of his right during conversations. The more interesting the topic of conversation, the more it excited Kashkin and the more intense became the rubbing of the palm (sometimes reaching almost a frenzy). (As an aside I shall note that Tchaikovsky assured me that Kashkin used the aforementioned method to wipe bits of grime from his palm, but this assumption is disproven by the fact that Kashkin sometimes made the very same motions, even with a passion, directly after bathing, when his hands were clean; thus it must be that the bits of grime that appeared during the rubbing were an accidental byproduct and not the intended target of the action.) During their playing four hands Kashkin (who played the bass part) became very excited and here the need to rub was felt in the form of an itch: Kashkin was able with wonderful virtuosity to use even pauses of an eighth note to this end. And if there were pauses of several beats, Kashkin would lessen the tempo of the rubbing, apparently experiencing indescribable bliss. Tchaikovsky told me that he experienced real torture as he had to force himself to refrain from bursting out laughing during the short pauses when Kashkin would quickly take his hands from the keyboard and pull at his palm with his finger, then pounce back onto the keyboard.

Given Tchaikovsky's penchant for laughter this must indeed have been unbearable. It was easy to make him laugh. We were members of the club called the Artistic Circle . . . and we attended it quite ardently. When we did not have dinner together we usually arranged to meet each other in the evening at the library of the Circle, which we called [using an archaic pronunciation of Russian "Biblioteka"] the "Vivliotheka." Once at a concert of the Musical Society I was silly enough to whisper in Pyotr's ear (during the performance of some piece) the word "vivliothekar [librarian]." My God, the results! He was immediately infected by laughter to such a degree that he gave a sort of groan with clenched teeth, and we barely managed to pull out our handkerchiefs and run out into the neighboring room with covered mouths. Thank God we were in the gallery so that no great impropriety came of our behavior.

The Artistic Circle was located, as you probably know, across from the side entrance of the Bolshoy. Once Tchaikovsky and I were at this theater to see some opera. After the performance, as we left the theater and were standing on the main steps, Pyotr Ilyich said to me: "Do you want me to ask the gendarme to summon General Tchaikovsky's carriage?" *I:* "Go ahead!" *He* (to the gendarme): "If you please, dear fellow, call for General Tchaikovsky's carriage." *Gendarme* (at the top of his voice): "General Tchaikovsky's carriage!" In a trice we retreated and ran to the porch of the Artistic Circle. *Gendarme* (still louder): "Gen-er-al Tchaikov-sky's carriage!!" On reaching the porch we dissolved into schoolboyish laughter. Finally the gendarme was shouting in a rage: "Gen-er-al Tchai-kov-skyyy's car-riaaage!!" And our laughter grew louder with every syllable of the gendarme's cry, much to the astonishment of the people going into the Circle.

But sometimes Tchaikovsky displayed amazing self-control in the most comic situations (even when he himself initiated them). One time he and I attended a quartet matinee. As we turned into Gazetny Lane, I said to him: "Let's bow to passing strangers" (which he and I would sometimes do for fun). No sooner had I spoken than Tchaikovsky all of a sudden leaped down from the cab and waved at some gentleman riding toward us. The gentleman stopped his carriage, gave Pyotr Ilyich a look of puzzled inquiry, and tipped his hat, whereupon Tchaikovsky said to him: "Oh, excuse me! My mistake! Please, forgive me!" He did all this with such an air of seriousness that it never occurred to me that this was Tchaikovsky's response to my suggestion that we exchange bows with strangers. Afterward, of course, we had a good laugh.

In another incident, our whole group (that is, Tchaikovsky, Nikolay Rubinstein, Jurgenson, Kashkin, Hubert, and I) made a trip to the Trinity–St. Sergius Monastery. We had a very jolly time and amused ourselves just as much on the way back, traveling in the saloon of the first-class carriage. The other half of the carriage consisted of individual (open) compartments, with which the saloon communicated by a narrow passageway. In the last compartment was a group of ladies. Tchaikovsky started playing about and imitating "ballet recitatives" (he did this marvelously), striking various ballet poses, and suddenly proposed to us: "Gentlemen, would you like me to dance the mazurka before the ladies?" And without waiting for a reply, he began a passionate rendition of the mazurka air from [Glinka's] *A Life for the Tsar* and dashed boldly and with an ardent expression into the last compartment, still dancing the mazurka, and then, addressing a humble "pardon" to the ladies, turned round before them and, with the same mazurka step, returned to us, maintaining a completely serious expression on his face. Then, of course, he joined in our friendly laughter.

At the monastery after a merry morning tea we all saw various points of interest. The Father-Treasurer showed us around them. When we approached St. Sergius' relics Tchaikovsky whispered an impromptu verse in my ear in order to make me laugh:

> When I saw the relics of Sergius,
> My earrings fell into my soup service.
>
> [Kogda videl moshchi Sergiia,
> Uronil vo shchi ser'gi ia.]

At the sacristy we were shown various icon medallions. Tchaikovsky again whispered in my ear a new impromptu verse:

> An icon shows a parson and deacon
> Dancing two *pas* with no clothes on.
>
> [Pop i d'iakon v panagii
> Dva tantsuiut *pas* nagie.]

We walked behind everyone and this was the only reason the Father-Treasurer did not see our laughing physiognomies. Desiring to have my revenge on Tchaikovsky and make him suffer in his turn in refraining from laughing, I whispered to him about the relics: "feather from the tail of the Holy Spirit" and "tooth from the Great Martyrs Boris and Gleb" (a shared tooth, you notice). Tchaikovsky controlled himself admirably and remained serious, and concerning the tooth he said that the monks would not acknowledge these relics, however they might want to.

Pyotr was a master of impromptu verse. I shall tell you everything that my memory has retained.

(1) Once before, Tchaikovsky, Jurgenson, and I went to the same monastery (that was Tchaikovsky's very first trip there). We were approaching Khotkovo Station, and Jurgenson said to Tchaikovsky: "Well, here's Khotkovo, and the monastery is next." Tchaikovsky, who had been in high spirits all the way, suddenly became lost in thought, and his face became so sad that we could not help noticing it and asking what was up. *Tchaikovsky:* "I can't find anything to rhyme with 'Khotkovo.' Maybe it could go like this?

> You've been invited for a cup of tea
> By your dear friend Tchaikovsky;
> Say: if you don't feel like "*tea*," [30]
> Perhaps you'd like some "*kovsky?*"
>
> [Na chashku chaia priglasil
> Tebia tvoi drug Chaikovskii;
> Skazhi: kol' "*chai*" tebe ne mil,
> Tak, mozhet mil khot "*kovskii?*"]

(2) When I lived at Tchaikovsky's house at Spiridonovka I used to travel for short periods to Poltava, where Kallivoda has a music shop. This same Kallivoda once asked me to convey a message to Jurgenson. The day after my return from Poltava Tchaikovsky met me at the Bolshoy Theater at the rehearsal of *The Voyevoda*. I asked him to come with me to Jurgenson's shop for a minute in order for me to communicate this message. After my conversation with Jurgenson Tchaikovsky asked me whether Kallivoda sold mineral water and, upon receiving an answer in the negative, said: "A pity! I just thought up this quatrain:

> Tell me, if the Kallivodas[31]
> In Poltava do drink water,
> Upon the fall of *Voyevoda*
> I shall drink, while weeping, water. . . ."

> [Ty skazhi mne, koli vody
> P'iut v Poltave Kallivody,
> Po paden'i *"Voevody"*
> Budu pit' ia, voia, vody. . . .]

(3) Laroche once told Tchaikovsky that it was difficult to find a rhyme for his surname, but Tchaikovsky, after a minute's thought, wrote:

> Already yellow are the crops
> And in the heat Laroche
> Bends over paper day and night:
> A symphony he does write,
> With a horrid pungency
> Poisoning the Muses and Charities.

> [Uzh pozheltela rozh'
> I v dukhote Larosh
> Den' i noch' nad bumagoi korpit:
> Pishet simfoniiu,
> Strashnuiu voniiu
> Nos otravliaia u muz i kharit.]

(4) Once in the evening at Jurgenson's house we had our usual game of *yeralash* with wild cards. Upon finishing the game we were sitting at the card table awaiting dinner and chattering away when Laroche suddenly looked at the clock and said with yearning in his voice: "God! How late! When will I manage to write my article?" Tchaikovsky improvised a note to Laroche in verse upon this occasion, but unfortunately I do not recall it, having retained in my memory only the final two lines, which really made us laugh quite a bit. They did not fit the meter of the poem due to the number of syllables, but Tchaikovsky, not hesitating for a second, squeezed them into the meter in the following way:

And he, instead'f writing h's article
Decided to play *yeralash* with us.[32]

[A on, vmesttvo, chtob stat'iu pisat',
Vzdumal s nami v *eralah* igrat'.]

After the first line he himself could not hold back his laughter. . . .

Once Cui, on the occasion of Tchaikovsky's visiting Petersburg, gathered the members of the Mighty Handful at his home and repeatedly asked Tchaikovsky to play the Romeo theme and the marvelous chords depicting the billing and cooing of the lovers from his *Romeo and Juliet*. Each time Cui expressed his delight, and toward the end of the evening Stasov,[33] taking Tchaikovsky by the arm and drawing him aside to a secluded corner, whispered to him that Cui used to say about the development of the Romeo theme, "It's beautiful! It's *even more passionate* than the duet in *Ratcliff*"[34] (such modesty!), and that he also had high praise for the love theme. Pyotr Ilyich, when he told me about all this, said: "How Cui and the whole of the Five would gloat and scoff at me should they ever guess that the melody of the love theme resembles a song of 'tip-cat.'. . . "[35]

I have just recalled Prov Sadovsky[36] and his tender love for Pyotr Ilyich. Sadovsky had hardly heard a note of Tchaikovsky's music and therefore Pyotr Ilyich must have captivated him exclusively by means of his attractive personal qualities. Sadovsky spent every evening at the Artistic Circle, usually in the company of Zhivokini.[37] At least I cannot remember an occasion when Tchaikovsky and I did not find them together. Whenever Tchaikovsky appeared Sadovsky bloomed into a blissful smile and then, greeting Tchaikovsky with a handshake, drew him to himself, kissed him, and sat him down for a few minutes next to himself on the sofa. Then, riveting his greedy gaze on Pyotr Ilych, Sadovsky would quickly grab him by the shoulders, draw him to himself, kiss him with a smacking sound in the nape of the neck, and, pushing him away, exclaim: "Who on earth are you?" Then he would repeat his drawing, kissing on the nape of the neck and pushing away. It was impossible to behold this funny scene without laughter, and Tchaikovsky laughed doubly, because the kisses on the nape of the neck were ticklish.

IV

The Socialite
(1866–1876)

In the spring of 1866 Tchaikovsky made the acquaintance of the actor and baritone Konstantin de Lazari, known to theatergoers by his stage name of Konstantinov. A companionable socialite, de Lazari knew everyone in Moscow theatrical circles and introduced his new friend to the actors and their milieu. It was de Lazari who brought Tchaikovsky to the club, the Artistic Circle, where Tchaikovsky enjoyed spending time, and it was he who brought Tchaikovsky to the home of Vladimir Begichev, the director of repertory for the Moscow theaters. Here the young composer was introduced to Begichev's wife, Mariya Shilovsky, and her two sons from her first marriage, Konstantin and Vladimir.

Mariya Shilovsky was a talented person: an amateur actress and singer, sociable and very active, she managed to unite all musical and literary Moscow around her home. Her elder son, Konstantin Shilovsky, wrote good verse and short stories, was a splendid singer, and composed gypsy songs famous all over Moscow. Later he joined the Maly Theater and became a good actor.

His brother Vladimir was of a very different mold: unsociable and ungenerous by nature, he led a secluded life. Nonetheless, according to Modest Tchaikovsky, "the chief interest for our composer in his acquaintance with the Begichevs lay in the personality of the younger of the Shilovsky brothers, Vladimir. He was then a fourteen-year-old boy, weak, sickly, with, as a result, a neglected education, but endowed, as it seemed then, with phenomenal capacity for music. In addition, his appearance was unusually lovely, his manners most originally charming, and his mind, despite his poor education, sharp and observant."[1] Vladimir Shilovsky apparently studied music for some time at the Moscow Conservatory and Tchaikovsky came to be his tutor in music theory after that. He was bound to his student not only by Shilovsky's talent, but also in great measure "by that love verging on adoration which he instilled in the boy."[2] Though Tchaikovsky's profound attachment to Shilovsky cannot be doubted, the emotional initiative almost always issued from the opposite direction, namely from pupil to teacher.

Initially Tchaikovsky appears to have been delighted with his new young friend, but in the following years their relations deteriorated, becoming stormy, unpleasant and uncomfortable, full of unpleasant scenes and ruptures, as a consequence of Shilovsky's intractable character.

During the 1866–67 season Vladimir Shilovsky's compositions were already being performed in public concerts and productions, while later he would be commissioned by Tchaikovsky to write the *entr'acte* to the second act of the latter's opera *The Oprichnik*. It was Shilovsky to whom Tchaikovsky dedicated his Third Symphony, as well as the two piano pieces, op. 10.

On 26 May 1868, Tchaikovsky departed on an extended European vacation in the company of Vladimir Shilovsky, his stepfather Vladimir Begichev, and their mutual friend Konstantin de Lazari. Shilovsky had not only invited Tchaikovsky to join them but also paid all his travel expenses. Returning to St. Petersburg in early August, Tchaikovsky went to visit his brothers in Estonia. According to Modest, it was around this time that the composer confided in him and Anatoly concerning his sexual preference.

It seems that Tchaikovsky enjoyed life in Vladimir Shilovsky's circle because of their mutual homosexuality. Recent archival studies have revealed the conventional perception of Tchaikovsky as a person tormented by his "difference" to be unfounded.[3] This perception was based on two largely unsupported assumptions: first, that nineteenth-century Russian society was characterized by sexual repression; and second, that as a consequence Tchaikovsky developed a particular fear of exposure and self-hatred. In fact, the Russia of that period happens to have been considerably more permissive than, say, Victorian England. Russia had no legal ban on homosexuality until the time of Peter the Great in the early eighteenth century. Even then the ban was only extended to the army. Homosexuality was criminalized in 1832 by Nicholas I, but the law was virtually never enforced. When homosexual incidents involved members of the upper classes, they were covered up by the authorities, the guilty parties, at worst, being transferred from one official position to another. Among Tchaikovsky's contemporaries, one may identify several homosexual members of the Imperial family, the most prominent of them being Grand Duke Sergey Alexandrovich, governor of Moscow. One of the most powerful statesmen under Alexander III and Nicholas II, Prince Vladimir Meshchersky (who was, incidentally, Tchaikovsky's schoolmate and friend) was repeatedly rescued by the two emperors from disgrace despite his flagrant homosexual activities. One may list many other individuals of similar status in Russian society.[4] Even after it was abolished in 1861, the tradition of serfdom continued to exert a powerful effect on social behavior of both upper and lower classes. According to established patterns of conduct, socially inferior people were expected to submit to the wishes of the socially superior in every respect, including the gratification of sexual desire. Russian peasants were traditionally tolerant of all varieties of sexual preferences among their masters and were often prepared to satisfy them on demand. This naturally resulted in boundless exploitation; at the same time, it explains the sexual affairs with servants and other lower-class persons so characteristic of Tchaikovsky and his milieu—a sort of hierarchical sex.[5]

As far as Tchaikovsky's own attitude is concerned, he could not, of course, fully neglect societal convention and, generally speaking, was rather conservative by temperament. In addition, in his youth he was repeatedly pressured to marry, and at some point he conceived the idea that he could change his sexual orientation and successfully live with a woman in order to ease his own life and mollify his relatives. Even at that stage, however, he considered his homosexual tendencies natural and nothing to be ashamed of.

The autumn of 1868 was marked for Tchaikovsky by an altogether new amorous development. This was an "affair" with the well-known Belgian mezzo-soprano Désirée Artôt, which, while ultimately and predictably doomed to failure, nevertheless proceeded to the point of betrothal. Artôt, having studied under the famous French singer Pauline Viardot, began singing with the Paris Opera in 1858. In 1868 she arrived in Moscow with a mediocre Italian opera company under the direction of Merelli. The fact that Artôt belonged wholly to the world of art and music formed the psychological basis of Tchaikovsky's infatuation. It seems that the composer fell in love not so much with her as with her voice and her performance, the more so as she was neither very young—being five years Tchaikovsky's senior—nor exceptionally beautiful, according to some contemporary memoirs.

Wishful thinking regarding his own capacity for a heterosexual lifestyle, and continuing pressure from his father, who passionately wished to see his son married, led Tchaikovsky to believe that he could marry Désirée Artôt. He met her for the first time in the spring of 1868, but her name does not begin to appear in his letters until her autumn performance in Moscow. He admits in his letter of 21 October to his brother Anatoly: "I am now on very friendly terms with Artôt and enjoy her very noticeable favor; rarely have I met a woman so lovely, intelligent, and kind."[6]

By the end of December Tchaikovsky's infatuation with Artôt was obvious to all. He wrote some music for her, and even began to discuss wedding plans with his father. On December 26, Tchaikovsky wrote him a lengthy letter describing his involvement with Artôt. The composer still maintained his personal and concealed preference for a homosexual lifestyle (of which there is abundant evidence), so it is not surprising that the account he provided his father displays little of the passion one would expect from such a sentimental man as Tchaikovsky. Below we cite the letter at length so that it might be compared to other, later sources on Tchaikovsky's relationship with Artôt:

Since the rumors have of course reached you concerning my intended marriage, and since you are perhaps annoyed that I myself have not written you anything about it, I shall now explain to you the situation. I became acquainted with Artôt last spring, but visited her only once, at a supper after her benefit performance. When she returned this autumn I did not visit her at all for a month. We met accidentally at a party; she expressed her surprise that I had not called on her; I promised to do so, but should not have fulfilled this promise (due to my characteristic reluctance to make acquaintances) had not Anton Rubinstein, who was passing through Moscow, dragged me to see her. From then on I began to receive invitations from her nearly every day, and little by little I grew accustomed to visiting her each evening. Soon we were inflamed with the most tender feelings for one another, and mutual declarations of them followed forthwith. It goes without saying that there immediately arose the question of lawful wedlock, which we both very much desire and which should take place in the summer, if nothing stands in the way. But therein lies the crux of the matter, for certain obstacles do exist. In the first place, her mother, who is constantly with her and has considerable influence over her daughter, opposes the marriage, finding me too young for her daughter and in all likelihood fearing that I shall force her to live in Russia. In the second place, my friends, and especially Rubinstein, have been taking most energetic measures in order that I not carry out my proposed plan to marry. They say that if I become the husband of a famous singer I shall play the highly pathetic role of my wife's husband, that is, that I shall travel with her to every corner of Europe, living on her earnings, growing unused to work and having no opportunity for it; in a word, when my love for her cools there will remain only broken pride, despair, and ruin. The possibility of such misfortune might be prevented by her decision to leave the stage and live with me in Russia, but she says that, despite all her love for me, she cannot resolve to abandon the stage, to which she is accustomed and which brings her fame and money. At present she has already departed to sing in Warsaw; we agreed that I would go to her estate (near Paris) in the summer, and there our fate is to be decided. Just as she cannot resolve to abandon the stage, I for my part hesitate to sacrifice my entire future for her, for there can be no doubt that I shall be deprived of the opportunity to proceed along my path if I follow her blindly. Thus, my dear father, you see that my situation is very complicated; on the one hand, I am bound to her by all the powers of my soul and it seems to me at the present moment impossible to live the rest of my life without her; on the other hand, sober reason forces me consider seriously the possibility of those misfortunes that my friends have drawn for me.[7]

Certainly in this letter, "sober reason" wins out over flaming passion. A few days later, Ilya Tchaikovsky, delighted by the news, wrote back, strongly disagreeing with the suggestion of Rubinstein and others that Tchaikovsky might lose his talent with the important change: "With such a person as your 'Desired One' [Désirée] you will rather perfect than lose your talent."[8]

It appears that Artôt's mother may have found out about Tchaikovsky's sexual orientation and taken control of the situation, for at the end of January, Tchaikovsky heard that his beloved had married a Spanish baritone, Don

Mariano Padilla y Ramos, in Warsaw. Although he was upset by the news, Tchaikovsky recovered from the disappointment quite quickly, as could be expected.

It may be surmised that some of Tchaikovsky's friends, knowing about his homosexuality, decided to help him to find a bride, and not only interfered but actually instigated the whole affair, exploiting Tchaikovsky's infatuation with Artôt's artistic personality. When it went unexpectedly well, some of them realized that, if the marriage did take place, Tchaikovsky would ultimately become a victim of his relationship to the famous singer and decided to undo their work. It is likely that gossip also contributed to the composer's relations with Artôt. For those who knew Tchaikovsky well, rumors of his possible marriage must have been incomprehensible. His brother Anatoly reported to him from St. Petersburg that "there's no need to mention what a stir the rumors of your marriage have caused here, for you yourself know to what extent those who know you might have expected such a trick from you."[9] Most likely he was driven to the brink of marriage by the situation itself, not by his feelings for Artôt.

In time, Tchaikovsky's relations with Artôt were exploited by sentimentally and romantically inclined memoirists and biographers so that they could satisfy their own psychological needs by mythologizing and idealizing the story to the point that it bore almost no resemblance to what must have happened in real life. Tchaikovsky's behavior following his separation from Artôt suggests that he suffered not so much from the pain of lost love as from a sense of humiliation and betrayal. Particularly interesting are his comments in a letter to Modest of February 1869: "The business with Artôt has resolved itself in the most amusing manner. In Warsaw she fell in love with the baritone Padilla, who here had been the object of her ridicule—and she married him! What sort of lady is that? One must know the details of her and my relations in order to have an idea of the ludicrousness of this denouement."[10]

Tchaikovsky continued his homosexual activities in Moscow and abroad. In the letter to his brother Modest written 23 June/5 July 1876 from Vienna he confessed that he had an encounter with a young man whom he called "she" (use of feminine pronouns was common among nineteenth-century homosexuals). In addition, Tchaikovsky could have resorted to this device in order to mislead the Russian censors, who could occasionally open letters of Russian subjects staying abroad:

> I do not like Vienna, and to spend several days here by myself seemed the height of tedium. Finally I decided that I would go to the Carre circus (which I found interesting because the program was full of old acquaintances, including the Nagels family, one member of which—August—was very close to my heart

ten days ago) with the thought that if I met *anyone* (the circus is in Prater) I would stay, and if not, that I would leave the next day for Geneva. . . . Just imagine: I met someone! Right here, even before buying a ticket! We quickly got to know each other (she's very young, fair and with hands worthy of the brush of a great artist), (oh! how sweet it was to kiss that wonderful hand!!!). We spent the evening together, namely at the circus and in Prater. Yesterday we spent the whole time together, namely we made an excursion far outside of the city. This morning she was with me, then I walked with her around the shops and *equipped* her from head to foot; we again spent the evening together and parted only this minute. . . . But I, unfortunately, am not [leaving] and therefore do not expect me before next week. The thing is that my beauty, a high-school student, is due to complete her exams on the 10th. It is impossible for me to leave before that day since she *wants* [I accept her will as law] to accompany me to Munich. For my part I am unable to refuse myself this bliss since up to this day I had had no *real thing* (namely, an entire night spent together in bed). So I'll leave here together *with her* Monday evening; on Tuesday morning we shall be in Munich, where we shall spend the day and stay the night, consequently only on Wednesday shall I leave Munich, directly for Lyons, where I hope to enclose you in my embrace.[11]

There are few accounts of the "Artôt episode." The most famous (although not entirely reliable) one is by Nikolay Kashkin in his memoirs, published in 1896. Less known, but perhaps more trustworthy, is the story told by Konstantin de Lazari (1838–1903), which has largely been neglected.[12] De Lazari was a gifted raconteur, and his narrative, which is here reproduced, is vivid, filled with anecdotes and telling details, even though some descriptions, and especially the dialogues, may have been fictionalized.

Another society acquaintance of Tchaikovsky, the journalist Alexandra Sokolova (1836–1914), who, like de Lazari, was close to the Shilovsky family, offers some additional information about less known facts of Tchaikovsky's special friendship with Vladimir Shilovsky and their entertaining habits.[13] Despite Sokolova's attempt to preserve a tone of objectivity, there are moments when one senses the author's personal dislike of the composer. As regards the masked ball in early March 1869, two versions of the episode have survived. One, by Nikolay Kashkin's daughter, claimed that Tchaikovsky made a bet with her father whereby each had to come up with a costume for the event so effective as to render him utterly unrecognizable: Tchaikovsky's solution was a domino, which he borrowed from a society lady he knew.[14] The second version belongs to Alexandra Sokolova and is printed below. In either event, the domino episode is consistent with Tchaikovsky's well-recorded fondness for mischief and practical jokes.[15]

The mastermind of the domino escapade was probably the young and notoriously reckless Vladimir Shilovsky. For Tchaikovsky, "the idea of appearing in female dress at a masked ball must have held. . . the allure of novel but safe adventure. Demanding a certain amount of daring, it was still within the bounds of convention, stretched as they were by the carnival-like nature of the event."[16]

The narrative of this chapter starts with the passage from Modest Tchaikovsky's *Autobiography,* in which he recalls the composer confiding to his younger brothers the truth about his homosexuality.

Modest Tchaikovsky

In the summer of 1867 in Haapsalu [Estonia] an important change occurred in our relationship: Anatoly and I ceased to be just children to Pyotr but rather became his comrades. It was then that he talked to us for the first time about his sexual anomaly, and I became a confidant in regards to all his amorous adventures. He always liked to recall things bygone in our presence, and now, when it became possible to speak not only about his childhood and the School [of Jurisprudence], but also about his experiences, I became closer to him than to Anatoly because of my greater affinity to him. . . . Nonetheless, it was Anatoly whom he loved. . . .

Konstantin de Lazari

In 1866, when I lived in Moscow, I was fortunate enough to belong to the innermost and most intimate circle of Nikolay Rubinstein's friends.

Apart from my salary at the theater I had no means of existence, but in spite of this fact I had the use of three apartments during the summer: the first was at Mariya Shilovsky-Begichev's summer home, the second at the estate of my close friend Setov[17] not far from Moscow, and the third at Nikolay Rubinstein's apartment, which was at my full disposal due to his having left Moscow [for the summer]. . . .

Once, in the closing days of August [1866], I went to the city and stayed at a friend's house until three o'clock in the morning. Since I did not want to return to the dacha that late, I set off to Nikolay Rubinstein's apartment to spend the night. I entered by the back entrance and asked [Rubinstein's new servant] Agafon: "Can I spend the night here?"

"Of course, of course, everything is ready for you. Just be quiet as you pass into the bedroom; there are two men sleeping in the study and drawing room."

I went straight into the bedroom and lay down.

"Bring me some tea, Agafon!" someone else's voice rang out a minute later.

"Agafon, will you bring us tea!" yet another minute later a third voice rang out, a voice that was mild and more similar to a contralto.

"Right away, right away! I'll get everyone some tea," Agafon answered, "Give me a chance to attend to it. Tea, rolls, you'll get everything!"

"Who else is here?" I asked when he served me tea.

"Kashkin's in the hall, and in that room. . . ."

However, I failed to catch who was there due to two voices making new demands that drowned out Agafon.

I put on a red dressing-gown and went into the room of the unknown man.

"Oh, oh! Who's there? My god, I'm not dressed! . . . What do you want?" asked a young man of charming appearance, as he covered his chest with his blanket.

"Why are you acting like a scared miss?" I asked. "What are you so scared of? Who are you?"

"I am a professor in the local conservatory, Tchaikovsky."

"You? A professor? Are you trying to make a fool of me? You're no professor! A student of some kind, more like it."

"As you wish," the lad answered, as if in anger. "And who are you?"

"Me? I'm a singer: in the theater I'm known as Konstantinov, but my real name is de Lazari."

"Ah, so that's who you are! Rubinstein has been talking about you for a long time."

"How did you end up here?"

"I arrived from Petersburg yesterday. I live here, only my lodgings are not ready yet, so I have been sleeping here."

"Oh, excuse me," I said haughtily. "Excuse me, Mr. Professor, *pardon,* that I disturbed you. With respect I take my leave."

"No, no, where are you going? Since you're here let's have some tea."

"All right," I said. "I'll go and bring my tea."

"My dear fellow, Konstantinov, tell them to give me fresh tea too."

"As you please. . . . But, you know, I must tell you, Mr. Professor, that you do not stand on ceremony: we have only just met and you want me to act as your servant."

"Well, you're a fine one too! You barge into my room without asking and then you tell me all these nasty things! It all seems rather curious and stupid!"

"Wha-a-at? Stupid?" I pretended that I was offended.

"No, no! I meant it seemed very intelligent. Do just hurry up and come back!"

This was the beginning of my acquaintance with Pyotr Ilyich Tchaikovsky. We were friends from that day on.

While we were sitting and drinking tea, he looked at me and said: "Do you know whom you remind me of? You look a lot like a friend of my father, the famous [actor] Samoilov."

I immediately entered like Samoilov and began to speak as if it were Samoilov speaking to Tchaikovsky's father. Goodness, what sweet, contagious laughter rang out at my performance! This finally won over Pyotr Ilyich to me. He kept asking me to imitate Samoilov. "I've never seen anything like it in my life!. . . It's simply amazing!" he muttered.

Then there was a voice behind the door.

"Pyotr Ilyich, what are you laughing about in there? What's so funny?"

"Come in and see for yourself," he said, still laughing.

Nikolay Kashkin came in. I was already acquainted with him.

"You know, Kashkin, I don't think I have ever laughed so hard in my life, thanks to this strange meeting. I thought that I would be horribly bored today, but instead I am laughing as never before!"

Kashkin left soon thereafter and we went to our rooms to get dressed. When we both entered the drawing room, Tchaikovsky sat down at the piano and, at my request, he played with great virtuosity some stirring piece, and then something melancholy and wonderful.

"What is that?" I asked.

"This is just my fantasy. . . ."

"Oh! You darling, that's really most talented! So you are really a professor? I didn't expect it!"

Then he asked me to sing something. I sang Dargomyzhsky's "I am sad" to his accompaniment.

"You sing with feeling and intelligent phrasing. I really didn't expect it."

"Why didn't you expect it? Do I have a stupid face?"

"No, on the contrary. I have now begun to like your face very much. . . ."

"Oh, like that, is it? Only now? But I did not like your face, I must honestly say, and right now I find it simply disgusting. But I'll kiss it anyway. . . ."

We embraced and kissed. It was already one o'clock in the afternoon.

"What are you going to do now?" I asked.

"Nothing. . . . I'll be at home."

"My dear man, my darling, let's go to the Hermitage [restaurant] for lunch."

"With pleasure," he answered joyfully. "But, actually, no, it would be better some other time."

"Why some other time? Have you no money?"

"I have some, but not enough."

That day I had two hundred rubles in my pocket that I had won the night before.

"And what is my money for, then? Look how much I won. If you want I'll give you half."

"Don't be silly! On what grounds?"

I started to beg him to go to the Hermitage and threatened that if he didn't go, I would throw fifty rubles out of the window right there in his presence, that I would break with him forever. . . .

He agreed and, taking the first coach we saw, we reached the Hermitage in a moment. The quick ride, which he always loved very much, gave him great pleasure, and we entered the restaurant in the best of moods.

I ordered a luxurious lunch and champagne with the self- importance and aplomb of a millionaire. The waiters simply hovered around us. Pyotr Ilyich looked around at the novel surroundings with surprise and gaiety. We drank to our friendship and began to converse as if we had known each other for a month without parting from one another.

In conversation he remarked that his only consolation when he had lived in Moscow during the winter was the Maly Theater, especially [the actor] Sadovsky. Upon hearing this I began to persuade him to go with me to the Begichevs' country estate. I explained to him that it was gay there, that it was a very musical household, that Rubinstein was like a member of the family, and that Begichev himself, as the repertory inspector, might one day be quite useful to him. I told him that there was one very talented boy in the family who would probably have need of music lessons, and that they would probably be ready to pay him large sums. Nothing had any effect. Pyotr Ilyich stubbornly refused to make this new acquaintance.

"But, my dear man," I tried to convince him. "Prov Sadovsky is there almost every day!"

This had a magical affect. His stubbornness gave way and in half an hour we were darting along in a coach toward the Begichevs'.

When we approached the estate, I left Pyotr alone and ran ahead to warn our hosts of the guest I had brought. I have a remarkable ability to fascinate others with what I am fascinated with, and I arranged it so that almost the entire household came out to meet Tchaikovsky, with Mrs. Begichev in front, and they didn't so much greet him as they almost carried him literally in their arms onto the terrace of the house.

Tchaikovsky's modesty, wonderful face, graceful laughter, and in general his special charm captivated everyone from the moment he appeared. Prov Sadovsky, who appeared as was his daily habit, was more delighted than anyone. He simply fell in love with him. If someone asked in his presence: "Just what is Tchaikovsky's talent?"

"What talent?" he would object. "Why talent? Just look at his face, Vladimir (Begichev's name), Mariya, look at this. It's pure wonder! Allow me to kiss you, my dear; God gave you a special mark. . . ."

No one ever saw Prov Sadovsky love anyone as tenderly and faithfully as he did Tchaikovsky.

That day was the beginning of Tchaikovsky's friendship with the Begichev-Shilovskys, in whose home he soon became like a member of the family.

I met him almost daily throughout the winter. We shared our last ruble.

Whenever we played cards, we bet the same way. And we mostly played in the singers' circle, our team consisting of us, Prov Sadovsky, and Alexander Ostrovsky. The latter, like Sadovsky, felt unusual tenderness for the young composer.

One had to see the faces of Sadovsky and Ostrovsky, who were bosom friends when apart but eternally argued whenever they were together, when playing cards with Tchaikovsky, in the minutes when the latter would lose and confusedly pull out, the poor thing, his last, crumpled three-ruble bill. How lovingly and sadly they would glance at their partner, how angrily they would glance at each other.

I never saw anyone so capable of experiencing joy in a sincere and contagious manner as Pyotr Tchaikovsky. There was an element of childlike sweetness and infinite pleasantness in his laughter.

I remember how once, in 1867 I think, I set off together with him at night to Ascension Cathedral on the day of Christ's Bright Resurrection. I won't describe the solemnity of the picture since I could not express the grandiose impression it made. During the service before matins, Tchaikovsky stood still, nervously looking around. Suddenly the cannon roared. The bells rang out, and he could not control himself. Crying out, he covered his face with his hands.

"What's wrong with you?" I asked in fright, thinking that he might have been crushed in the crowd.

"Leave me alone," he said, crying. "Let me enjoy it. . . ."

"Let the poet enjoy it, you Tatar," said Ostrovsky, who approached unexpectedly.

"Don't bother him!" suddenly and just as unexpectedly rang out the powerful voice of . . . Ivan Gorbunov.[18]

"Look at Pyotr Ilyich's face," Ostrovsky continued. "Even without the bells you could tell by his face that Christ is risen. Christ is risen, my dear! Christ is risen! How fine it is, eh? Gorbunov and I have meetings each year in this very place and on this very night. . . ."

With the following example I shall try to show how Tchaikovsky could be impulsively kind.

A certain tenor P——y once came to Moscow to take a few singing lessons from Setov and audition for the stage. He was of a large build, a complete brunette, with a wide chest and a wonderfully sonorous tenor, but he was deprived of any musical sense. He had no source of income whatsoever. Mrs. Shilovsky-Begichev rented him a room and invited him to dine with her. This gentleman had a feisty character. He ate enough for ten men and behaved so impolitely and rudely that he soon had to leave his lodgings. I don't remember why, but on the day immediately following his exile I hosted a lunch. Pyotr, of course, was one of my guests. At that time I lived at the house of the singer

Dmitriyev and had two rooms at my disposal. I must add that a week before this Tchaikovsky had received a magnificent watch worth about three hundred rubles as a present from Mrs. Begichev in return for the musical progress made by her son Vladimir Shilovsky, Pyotr Ilyich's pupil.

After lunch, the four of us sat down to play *yeralash*. Pyotr Jurgenson was the only moneyed person among us all.

At about six o'clock, when tea was served, suddenly and without warning, P——y ran in like a madman, clicking his teeth like a wolf and beating himself on the chest.

"Give me something to eat! I want to eat! Why am I perishing? I haven't eaten all day!"

"Why are you screaming?" I asked. "Are you crazy? Have a roll if you're so hungry, and stuff it down, and I'll arrange for you to be given something a bit more substantial."

He grabbed the roll like a hungry dog and began to tear it with his teeth, muttering: "They want to kill me! Why is Begichev persecuting me? I don't have a penny. I'm a pauper! I'm going to die of hunger!"

This scene made an unpleasant impression on everyone, but Tchaikovsky was most unhappy of all. He lowered his head and covered his face with his hands. Then he stood, quickly took his watch and chain, walked up to P——y and said quietly: "My dear man, what's wrong with you? Don't get upset. If you're in such straits, here, take this for now. You can pawn it or sell it."

"Thank you," P——y barked out. "You are the only decent man here!" With this he grabbed the watch and was ready to run off without waiting for the supper that had been promised him. But I ran after him, stopped him, took away the watch and asked Jurgenson to give him fifteen rubles. The furious tenor left and we were very happy to be rid of him, and because the watch that had so cheered Pyotr Ilyich had been saved.

Tchaikovsky's nervous impressionability is exhibited with particular clarity in the following episode.

In 1868, Begichev, Vladimir Shilovsky, Pyotr Ilyich, and myself spent the summer together abroad. Arriving in Berlin, we set off to look at the Tiergarten. We halted at the cage of an enormous boa constrictor. The monster was lying motionless, all curled up. We were invited to watch him eat and Begichev agreed. Right before our eyes a rabbit was let into the cage. The poor thing entered, stood up on its hind paws and began to stare at the frightening monster, unable to take his eyes off the serpent and, as it were, walking right into its mouth, which the serpent had opened on first sensing the presence of its victim. In an instant the rabbit disappeared in the repulsive maw.

At that instant a terrible cry rang out from Pyotr Ilyich. He broke down in tears and was overcome by violent hysterics, and we were obliged to take him home immediately. For a long time we were unable to make him take control of himself. He was racked by fever until evening, and was unable to consume any food.

Tchaikovsky's popularity grew before my very eyes not by the day, but by the hour. Anyone who entered into communication with him was immediately won over by his charm. By the start of the 1868–69 season he had become one of Moscow's biggest favorites, not only as a composer, but also as a man.

In Moscow, this season witnessed the blossoming of Italian opera. The Bolshoy Theater was filled every day from floor to ceiling. A great mob of people crowded every day at the ticket office from early morning on. People spared neither money nor their health in order to get a ticket to a performance featuring Désirée Artôt, who drove Muscovites mad in [Donizetti's] *The Daughter of the Regiment* and [Gounod's] *Faust*.

And indeed there was good reason for such fascination. This incomparable singer combined everything: her voice, both tender and passionate, stirred one's very soul; I know of no equals to her stage talent; her coloratura could be compared only to Patti; and then, finally, there was her musical sense. I have seen all the famous singers in my time: Pauline Lucca, Adelina Patti, and, finally, Bosio.[19] But in my opinion Artôt was better than all of them in her first Moscow season. Subsequently her voice deteriorated, and she became less impressive, but at this time she was the embodiment of operatic perfection. Whoever saw her then would remember all his life the highly artistic impression made by her inimitable performance.

While on stage she was the subject of universal adoration in Moscow; she was no less popular in private life. Her face was not beautiful: her nose was too broad, her lips a bit thick; but, despite this, there was such charm in the expression of her eyes, her exquisite and gracious manners, her conduct, her ability to utter a kind word to everyone and show her respect with warmth, etc., that her charm was communicated to literally everyone.

At the very height of her success in Moscow, Mariya Begichev invited Artôt to her house and gave a luncheon in her honor. The entire household was enamored of her. The delighted mistress of the house went so far as to kneel publicly before her esteemed guest and kiss her hand. But, of course, all of us together did not feel for her what Pyotr Ilyich was experiencing. Whether it is because I knew of his love, or whether it was so blatantly obvious, but I am left with such a vivid recollection of this luncheon that, although I have forgotten all the details, I see as if it was yesterday how Artôt and Tchaikovsky looked at each other. I remember their mutual embarrassment during their conversation, and their eyes shining with delight.

I remember that they sat rather at a distance from the others. I approached them.

"Pyotr," I addressed Tchaikovsky, "what luxury! She's the most beautiful woman in the world!"

"Que vient dire, monsieur?" Artôt asked.

"Il est fou de vous!"

She looked up at me with a smile that revealed wonderfully white teeth, and it was as if the room became warmer on account of her glance. Tchaikovsky's eyes were burning and he seemed entirely a different man.

When we all departed, Pyotr and I went to the Hermitage [restaurant]. Everyone knew him there already. Upon seeing us an entire regiment of waiters ran up to us, trying to entice us to sit in their area. The director of the restaurant came up himself.

"We don't need anything! Only some tea, please." He was not up to eating.

I began to speak of Artôt admiringly.

"Oh, Konstantin, what is your praise worth? Whom don't you admire, whom don't you praise?! I'm completely different: it's difficult to impress me, but that woman has really made me crazy. I swear, I never imagined that I could become so obsessed. When she sings I experience something I have never known before! Something new and wonderful! . . . What hands she has! . . . I haven't seen such hands for a long time! Those hands alone, with their grace in every movement, are capable of making me forget everything in the world. . . .

Whenever I hear "Romance without words," which Pyotr dedicated to Artôt, I once again hear his ecstatic words on that memorable evening.[20]

Soon all Moscow was talking about their love affair. People told each other as if it were a secret: "Have you heard that Artôt is to marry Tchaikovsky?"

Artôt lived with her mother at the Hotel Chevalier. As I already mentioned, she had tons of fans. At each performance she was literally covered in flowers and gifts, but no one gave her more valuable and attention-getting presents than a small, round, vivacious and energetic, dark Armenian [Ellarov], with narrow, sly eyes.[21] He invariably sat in the front row at every performance. He was crazy with love for Artôt and followed her every move. Whenever she drove up to the theater, [Ellarov] would be standing at the entrance, and would take the opportunity to help her from her carriage. She would come home and [Ellarov] would again help both her and her mother leave their carriage. In the theater hall, of course, no one shouted out the singer's name more loudly and clearly, no one stretched further over the barrier of the first row, no one brought her as many gifts. Above all he made it a rule to win the affections of her elderly mother by paying court to her. This was a sure strategy and he soon achieved the honor of being received by the diva. More visits followed the first, and soon he began to frequent the Hotel Chevalier. But he was not always received there, and what offended him most of all, sometimes he was forced to depart in disgrace, knowing for certain that the singer was not only at home, but was receiving other guests. This was more than enough for the passionate Armenian to flare up with an awesome hatred for the young composer.

Temporarily abandoning his siege of the daughter, he once again took to charming the elderly mother. As soon as he learned that Artôt was in rehearsal he would rush to her mother's hotel. He told her of his wealth in the Caucasus, of the magnificent palace he had there, of his really being a prince, and so on.

While praising himself, [Ellarov] did not neglect to slander his rival and set Artôt's mother against him. He would tell tall tales about Tchaikovsky really being Sadyk-Pasha's son, about him being a bankrupt gambler with huge debts, and other nonsense that the foreigner believed all the more readily as she was completely unacquainted with life in Russia. As a result, Artôt's mother became terribly hostile to Tchaikovsky. This led to conflict between mother and daughter, as the latter continued to put more faith in the young composer than in some roguish Armenian. But a drop of water can slice through stone, and so the mother's insinuations gradually began to disturb poor Désirée.

Meanwhile, Tchaikovsky, who had no clear concept of life and never considered what tomorrow would bring, who worried only about finishing today what he had begun to compose yesterday, was in the state of a fortunate man who can't believe in the possibility of evil due to his own surfeit of happiness. He noticed nothing and was completely absorbed with the upswelling of an ecstatic mood.

One day in December I went to his house and found him depressed and upset, whereas all the preceding time he had been quite buoyant.

"Pyotr, my dear man, what's wrong? Are you unwell?"

"Listen, Konstantin, I saw her yesterday. At first she was as nice to me as ever, but then I noticed that she was out of sorts, that she was worried about something. I asked what was up. Then her mother walked by and barely greeted me. Then I guessed that someone had told her some rumors about me. 'My mother is set against you,' Artôt told me, 'but whatever I am told, however others might try to divide us, remember that I will always be true to you and will never belong to anyone but you. But understand that it still pains me to see mother submitting to the slander that is raised against you.' No matter how I tried to find out who had said what about me, she refused to say and, while she continued to assure me that she loved me as before, she asked me to leave so that she might talk with her mother and try to calm her down. As you can see, I have nothing to be happy about!"

I tried to comfort him as best I could, but it was all in vain.

However, after some time Tchaikovsky's relationship with Artôt's mother was restored and, in the time before his bride's departure to Warsaw, Pyotr Ilyich began once again to frequent the Hotel Chevalier.

Their wedding was postponed until the summer and was to take place in France at the Artôts' estate. . . .

Nikolay Rubinstein was very much against the wedding and exerted all his efforts to preventing it from taking place. During the period when, due to [Ellarov]'s machinations, Tchaikovsky's relationship with Artôt was somewhat clouded, Rubinstein was extremely kind to his housemate, consoling him as much as he could, but in the depths of his soul he rejoiced at the possibility of a break. He was convinced that marriage to a singer, especially such a famous one, would have disastrous consequences for Tchaikovsky's musical career, that, trudging around various European cities in the role of the husband of a star, Pyotr Ilyich's pride would constantly suffer, that the petty concerns of his wife's success in one city or another would replace the pure and sublime concerns of art, that the intrigues of the theater stage would upset and burden husband and wife, and so on and so on. The main thing, however, was that Tchaikovsky's powerful talent would perish under such conditions.

In December Artôt left for Warsaw. Tchaikovsky was deeply saddened. He sat with head bowed, almost crying.

Why? Because he did not receive any letters from her.

"Well, what are you so depressed about? You're her fiancé, aren't you? She loves you, after all, doesn't she? She said she would write, and so she will. She has probably been unable to write."

You would bend down and kiss him.

"Konstantin, why are you smiling so stupidly?"

"It's not that; I was just thinking: how will you name your children? You can name a girl Artoshka, but a boy you should call Pyotr. He'll be a talented little rascal, but unbearable also. That's who I want to give a beating!"

"Why beat him? Our children will be so sweet, especially Artoshka. No, Konstantin, you shan't beat them!. . . "

And like a small child he would be consoled for a minute, but then he would become sad again.

Meanwhile there were still no letters from Artôt.

Once, at about seven o'clock on a January evening, Nikolay Rubinstein entered Tchaikovsky's room holding a letter and laughing loudly. "Pyotr, do you know what news I have just learned? Read it, or better yet I'll read it myself. Lord, how glad I am! Praise the Lord, praise the Lord!—Artôt has got married! And guess to whom. To Padilla! Well, wasn't I correct when I said that she didn't need you as a husband? He is a true match for her, but we need you, please understand, Russia needs you, and not as the partner of some famous foreigner. . . .

Tchaikovsky did not utter a single word. He simply turned pale and went out.

A few days later he had changed completely. Once again he was content, calm, and fully engrossed by his one care: composing. . . .

As I have already stated, at that time Tchaikovsky enjoyed universal favor and love in Moscow. But then it was impossible not to love him. From his youthful appearance and wonderful eyes with their profound expression, everything about him created an insuperable attraction, most of all his touching kindness and humility, which was surprising in one of such talent. No one was more capable of treating everyone sincerely and sweetly; no one's view of people had such childlike purity and radiance. Conversation with him made everyone feel a certain warmth, a certain caress in the sound of his voice and in his eyes. At the Conservatory he was the idol of the students, of both sexes, and among his colleagues he was a universal favorite, and he was the most desired guest in all circles of his acquaintance. He was inundated with invitations and, since he lacked the courage to refuse anyone, he accepted them all; this, however, was a great burden on him as it distracted him from his composing.

Whenever he dropped in anywhere, everyone's eyes would sparkle and everyone would be glad to see him. If he came to teach at the Conservatory, the young people would be delighted. If he looked in behind stage, everyone would gleefully extend their hands and greet him noisily. If he decided to drop in at the Artistic Circle, Prov Sadovsky, who was probably his most passionate admirer, would be waiting for him there impatiently. Although he was usually gloomy, taciturn, and unwilling to express his feelings for others, at the sight of Tchaikovsky he became friendly, tender, talkative, and cheerful.

You're my joy, my treasure!" Thus he would greet Tchaikovsky, who would walk with mincing step into the drawing room. "My dear little professor! Lord, just take a look at him! God has marked him for exclusively good things! Good gracious, my angel, that's all! What can I do with him? Oh, Lord!"

He would take a deep breath, take some snuff, and kiss his favorite.

And wasn't it just the same with Alexander Ostrovsky?

He would sit at his club, stroking his beard. Lost in concentration, he would look over the menu, choosing what he wanted to eat. As soon as he saw Tchaikovsky enter, however, the wrinkles of deep thought all disappeared. His face glowed with happiness.

"You made it, my dear, you made it, our loved one! Sit down here, my dear man, what can I offer you? Well, Pyotr Ilyich, I am trying, working away, writing a libretto for you. . . ."

In the last days of May 1868, Tchaikovsky, Begichev, Vladimir Shilovsky, and I went abroad. I have already told of the episode with the boa in Berlin. Leaving Berlin, as we sat down in our carriage, I took a book out of my pocket and began to read.

"Konstantin," said Pyotr Ilyich, "what book are you reading?"

"I never part with this book. It's a French textbook. We'll soon be on French territory and I want to speak to everyone and not depend on any of you!"

My fellow travelers all burst out laughing, but Pyotr laughed louder and more contagiously than anyone.

"We'll see how well you can get along in Paris without me!"

We reached Paris in the evening. Shocked by the noise and stunned by the brightness of the streetlights, by the luxury of the shops, which were still open, we got to Montmartre Boulevard and took a suite in the Hôtel Beau-Séjour. The luxurious suite on the mezzanine consisted of a drawing room and four bedrooms. We quickly got ready. Vladimir was sick and stayed at the hotel. Begichev immediately set off to a jeweler's to order a small medallion for his buttonhole. The two of us set off just to walk around and take a look at things. I held on to Pyotr since I was afraid to remain alone, knowing neither the city nor the language. The textbook had not yet begun to yield the results I had expected. . . .

Meanwhile my lessons with the textbook continued with regularity and zeal. While Pyotr Ilyich was working by himself, I would walk around the room and cram French words. I eventually got to the letter F. Once, without suspecting that Pyotr could hear me, I studied the words: étudier—to study, frapper—to knock, frire—to fry in oil, frotter—to polish. First I repeated them meaning-fully with full consciousness of what I was doing, but then I got lost in thought and began to repeat them automatically and even with a slight melody. Sud-denly I heard someone laughing. It turned out that Pyotr had long since been listening to me and had caught the melody that I had unconsciously developed. Approaching the piano, he began to play the melody, begging me to continue singing. Ever since, whenever Pyotr Ilyich was out of sorts, I only had to start singing "Etudier—to study, frapper—to knock, frire—to fry in oil, frotter—to polish," and he would start laughing and make me repeat my song endlessly.

At times we would begin to think up variations on it, and it would turn out very beautifully. He constantly promised me that he would introduce this little theme into some composition of his.

In general it would seem that no one was better at cheering him up than I was. He would listen endlessly to my stories. Twenty years later he would laugh at them just as much as the first time he had heard them. . . .

In Paris Tchaikovsky and I were almost never separated. Vladimir Shilovsky was ill the entire time. We always ate at the Diner de Paris (in the Passage Jofrois), and we took coffee at the Café-Riche. However, of an evening we would often go to the theater, and particularly frequently to the Opéra Comique. We attended the premiere of *Hamlet*, featuring Nilsson and Fauré.[22] Auber sat near us.[23] Pyotr Ilyich could not get enough of looking at him; staring with reverence at the features of this elder, he kept repeating to me: "How nice he is."

In November, on our return to Moscow, I became ill and Tchaikovsky visited me twice a day. . . .

In the spring of 1873 I was obliged to leave Moscow and settle in Petersburg. This did not affect my friendship with Pyotr Tchaikovsky and Nikolay Rubinstein, of which I repeatedly was convinced by each new meeting.

I made the acquaintance of Pyotr Ilyich's father and of his entire family, to which also belonged Herman Laroche, the most intimate friend of all three Tchaikovsky brothers, i.e., Pyotr, Anatoly, and Modest. At that time I was not yet acquainted with Nikolay and Ippolit.

Ilya Petrovich Tchaikovsky was a very elderly retired general. His relationships with his children were ideal; they all loved him to the point of adoration, but he returned their love with unusual tenderness. It was gratifying to witness the ecstatic gaze with which he looked at his sons, especially at the pride and adornment of the entire family, Pyotr Ilyich.

Often, coming to their house for dinner, you would find everyone gathered, even Laroche, but Pyotr Ilyich was absent.

"Ilya Petrovich," I asked, "Why is Pyotr so late! Why do you keep such a loose grip on him? I really think you should flog him, and then he would not be late!"

"Well, you see, as soon as he comes we really shall flog him, eh? It's gone five o'clock (the old man liked to dine early) and he's not here yet."

The doorbell rang, and Pyotr came in. In jest I threw myself at him in order to beat him up, but Ilya Petrovich immediately intervened on his behalf. "Forgive him this one time. He won't do it anymore, he will be a good boy. . . . Come here, my boy (Ilya Petrovich mostly addressed his sons in this way although the eldest were almost forty), come here and I'll defend you. . . ."

How tenderly he began to caress his Pyotr, as if a little child. . . .

We merrily sat down at the table, and there was no end to the laughter and jokes, especially with Laroche. Pyotr Ilyich had a very high opinion of the latter's abilities. "I can't compare with Laroche's huge stature, but laziness ruined him." At the same time he never laughed with anyone as he did with Laroche, and sometimes at him, for Laroche was unusually original, self-absorbed, and, at the same time, naive in the everyday matters of life.

Alexandra Sokolova

[Rubinstein] was decidedly upset by the failure of Tchaikovsky's first opera, *The Voyevoda.* . . . He upbraided Serov for refusing to find in this first effort by an emerging talent the same serious instincts that he himself saw, attributing this to a feeling of envy in the face of the vast composing career unfolding before the young musician, and it was with profound surprise that he met similar indifference in Prince Odoyevsky, whom no one, of course, could suspect of feelings of envy. . . .[24]

Prince Odoevsky, who attended the first performance of *The Voyevoda* in Mariya Begichev's box, took a thoroughly negative view of the young composer and did not see any future for him.

Serov also stopped by our box that evening and was somehow especially cool toward Tchaikovsky's first effort as a composer, remarking casually that the young representatives of the Russian conservatory had a gift for thinking that nothing was easier than writing an opera, and that all one needed was a knowledge of counterpoint, a suitable subject, a great deal of courage, and also a great deal of music paper. The arrogance of such a judgment was somewhat justified by the enormous success which greeted Serov's opera *Rogneda,* produced on the Imperial stage that same season. . . .

Dargomyzhsky, like Serov, showed not the slightest encouragement for Tchaikovsky's first opera . . . and never hinted by a single word that there was a great future musical talent lurking within it. . . .

I have a vivid memory of returning from the theater that evening to the Begichevs' home, where, as usual, Tchaikovsky also came, utterly dismayed by the result of his debut as a composer.

The Begichevs, who, as I have mentioned, were genuinely and warmly fond of Tchaikovsky, were no less dismayed and upset than he. Vladimir Begichev, well aware that, apart from the blow to his pride, the disappointment Tchaikovsky had suffered was also a material loss in terms of the vain hopes he had set on receiving royalties, hastened to console him, promising that no matter what it took, he would insist that the new opera be performed at least three or four more times.

In that comparatively recent time the famous composer dared not dream of anything more.

Rubinstein, who also came to the Begichevs', did everything he could to rouse Tchaikovsky from his doubts about his own abilities, insisting that those who failed to see the merits of his composing effort did not understand anything, or, worse still, "did not wish to understand" anything about opera. He chose even to ignore the fact that he was including both Serov and Odoevsky among those who "did not understand," but held his ground, declaring prophetically that Tchaikovsky had a serious musical future.

Meanwhile, Mrs. Begichev, who knew Russian folk songs better than anyone, sat down at the piano, and remembering the melodies from the opera we had just heard, she turned to Tchaikovsky in surprise:

"Oh, Pyotr! Why, you've stolen most of this!"

"What? From where?!" asked Tchaikovsky, horrified.

"Well, you've plucked bunches of it straight out of old Russian songs! Listen!"

And, recalling the melodies from the opera by turns and making the composer play each one, she herself then played several very old and little-known Russian folk songs, with which these melodies had so much in common that they did in fact seem to have been copied directly from them.

"That one's 'Little Gray Dove' [Sizyi golubochik]. . . . Listen!. . . That's 'In the Glade' [Vo luzyakh]. . . . And this one's 'In the wide meadow' [Na polyane na shirokoi]. . . . Well? Do you see?"

As Tchaikovsky listened, his head drooped lower and lower.

He saw indeed that the entire opera he had "composed" was a virtual repetition of the airs Mrs. Begichev played for him, but nevertheless he knew and was prepared to swear that he was utterly ignorant of these melodies and had never heard them anywhere before in his life.

"Oh, oh, oh! Whatever does this mean?" he exclaimed in horror, adding with his usual exaggeration: "Truly I must hide under the table, must I not?"

"You needn't hide anywhere!" interrupted Rubinstein with majestic certainty. "If you say you never heard anything like it, it means you didn't. No one will dare disbelieve you! You're not a liar! And this coincidence merely shows that, being a great talent, you have grasped completely the spirit of the Russian song and expressed it using the very same sounds in which it poured forth from the soul of the Russian people."

His words were prophetic.

Of course, Tchaikovsky was in that moment, as always, the original creator of everything he wrote and could never have "stolen" any melody in the world.

The composer did not begin to respond to Rubinstein's affection with the same warm feeling. Tchaikovsky was by nature cool and restrained, and he considered himself above everyone else. He was one of those egoists who do not care in the least about anyone else's heart or anyone else's fate. The feeling of gratitude was as alien to him as that of love or affection.

When [Mariya Begichev's first] husband Stepan Shilovsky died, he left her her own, quite independent fortune, which gave her an annual income of around twenty thousand, besides which she was a trustee over her sons' income, which amounted to seventeen thousand a year for each of the brothers. By carelessly managing both her own and her children's property and leading a royal lifestyle, Mariya Begichev contrived, with the help of her second husband, to run through absolutely everything that belonged to her and to her children, never mortgaging or selling anything only because she had no right to do so by law.

Everyone close to the Begichev family saw both the vast, unchecked expenses and the reckless losses, and at the same time knew their source.

Among those who were aware of all this was Pyotr Tchaikovsky, who was particularly friendly with Mariya Begichev's second son, Vladimir, at this time little more than a boy, being just barely sixteen. What lay behind this exceptional friendship, which amounted to schoolboy worship, was the topic of a great deal of quite unpleasant discussion at the time, but no one has the right to repeat any of these rumors. The only thing that is true is that when, in 1869, the elder [Konstantin] Shilovsky turned twenty-one and his mother asked him whether he wished to request of her a full account of the management of his property, he, taking such a question as a personal offense, signed without looking at it a statement of his complete satisfaction with the account, which he never laid eyes on, and according to which he personally was granted seventeen thousand rubles a year during his minority.

Vladimir Shilovsky was at this time only seventeen years old, and he had another year left until his first incomplete majority, which his friends exploited in the sense that, when he turned eighteen, giving him by law the right to choose his own trustee and demand from his guardians a full account of their trusteeship, the young Shilovsky refused his mother's continued management and not only demanded from her a full account of all his affairs for the entire time that had elapsed since the death of his father, but also expressed the desire that Pyotr Tchaikovsky be appointed his trustee. Such an election could not take place without the latter's consent; therefore, appended to the petition submitted by the younger Shilovsky was Tchaikovsky's formal agreement to undertake the aforesaid trusteeship.

Mariya Begichev was thunderstruck by such treatment from her beloved son, and she went after Tchaikovsky with her usual sharp words. Several extremely harsh letters were written. . . . Several less than rational threats were launched, and only through the energetic intervention of Konstantin Shilovsky was the matter settled in the sense that the account presented to the trusteeship was accepted, while the impromptu guardian voluntarily declined the flattering offer. . . .

[Tchaikovsky] was notable for the extraordinary likableness that colored his many distinctive traits. He was unquestionably kind, but it was a sort of lazy kindness, owing not so much to gentleheartedness as to a desire to avoid conflict at all cost.

He was always willing to let others have their way, though again not because of meekness or Christian humility, but simply because he either had no time or was just too lazy to argue.

In company, he was always reserved and very taciturn and only grew lively within his own circle, among people he knew well and liked. . . .

A masked ball had been announced and every hall in the Moscow Assembly of Nobles was taken, in expectation of a particularly large turnout. . . . People were talking about it everywhere, and a week before the ball it was the topic of passionate discussion during dinner in the Begichev home. At the table were all the habituees of that hospitable home, and everyone was taking part to some degree in the conversation.

Only those people who took no interest in the question of society pleasures were silent, among them Pyotr Ilyich Tchaikovsky, who almost never went anywhere.

The younger Shilovsky, who was especially friendly with Tchaikovsky, asked him whether he did not wish to take part in the masquerade as well, and the elder, Konstantin Shilovsky, offered to place at his disposal his entire theatrical wardrobe, which numbered several dozen costumes, from all countries and peoples. Tchaikovsky, always amenable to anything, readily consented this time as well and, rising from the table, went off to the young Shilovskys' wing to try on costumes.

They were at it a long time. Tchaikovsky ended up trying on everything in the closet, but not one of the costumes fit him quite right. Everything was either too short or too tight. The young men came back thoroughly disappointed. Mariya Begichev, who always had some unceremonious remark for every occasion, exclaimed indignantly: "What an ungainly fellow you are, Pyotr! You can't squeeze into anything!"

Tchaikovsky sadly lifted his hands to show that he personally had nothing to do with this costume mishap, but Mariya Begichev, for whom her husband's wish was law, seeing that Vladimir Begichev particularly wanted Tchaikovsky to be at the masquerade, suggested to Pyotr Ilyich that he wear her own costume which she had brought back from Paris, where it had been artfully executed from her design.

"What sort of costume is it?" inquired Tchaikovsky in his cool, indifferent voice.

"A witch costume!" replied Vladimir Begichev, instantly lighting up. "And what a costume, simply lovely! The gown is all made of smoke-colored barège and gauze, the outer tunic is held up on one side with green eyes, on the other with a black cat. Over the head goes a hood, also smoke-colored, with gray hair showing from under it—and the mask itself is the height of perfection! A hooked nose, bushy gray eyebrows, big crooked yellow teeth! This costume was an object of pride for the designer who created it and could definitely be included in any exhibition of theatrical costume!"

"But isn't it a woman's costume?" said Tchaikovsky, puzzled.

"So what?" Mariya Begichev shot back. "What the devil else are you going to wear, you ungainly man? Whose fault is it that nothing will fit you. . . ?"

A lady's maid appeared who did not understand a word of Russian, and at her mistress's order she brought the witch costume.

The costume turned out to be charming indeed and delighted everyone except Pyotr Ilyich himself, who showed not the slightest enthusiasm.

Mrs. Begichev explained in detail how to put on what; the Shilovskys headed with Tchaikovsky to the young men's wing, and several minutes later Tchaikovsky appeared among the guests and, to the loud laughter and applause of all those present, paraded the utterly original and striking witch costume.

It was decided that he would attend the Artistic Circle's masquerade in this costume, and everyone present, who were all enormously fond of Tchaikovsky, looked forward to seeing him, always so quiet and serious, in the new and unusual role for him of someone in disguise and having a jolly time.

The news spread quickly among his close friends, as well as within the theatrical community, which took an interest in everything that went on in the [Begichev-Shilovsky] household.

It was agreed that the following day Tchaikovsky would come for dinner as usual, rest for a bit after dinner, then put on his witch costume and head off to the Artistic Circle with Begichev and the two Shilovskys.

The following day I arrived for dinner, and everything that I shall now relate occurred in my presence.

We sat down at the table, as usual, around seven o'clock, the company including all the usual guests, with the exception of Tchaikovsky, for whom we waited in vain after dinner as well.

He never arrived.

At nine o'clock the Shilovskys and Begichev left, deciding that Pyotr Ilyich was simply too lazy to go to the masquerade, and had not come to dinner in order to avoid it.

When we had seen the men off, there were four of us left: Mrs. Begichev, the two Yazykov sisters, and myself, who because of illness did not go out at all except to a box at the theater or the most intimate gatherings. . . . It was after eleven when we heard a ring in the entrance hall, and into the room where we were sitting in front of the fire came Tchaikovsky.

It turned out that he had simply overslept and completely forgotten about the approaching masquerade, but as soon as he remembered, he had gotten dressed and come over.

The news that everyone else had left long ago did not upset him in the least. He admitted frankly that he would have had a boring time at the ball, and asked if he could sit and play lotto with us, insisting that this would be infinitely more fun that the Artistic Circle's costume ball.

But Mrs. Begichev would have none of it and demanded that Tchaikovsky at once put on the witch costume that had been made ready for him and go to the ball.

He tried to resist as best he could, but finally he gave in, Fanny [the maidservant] brought the costume, Vladimir Shilovsky's valet was summoned, and he and Tchaikovsky went off to the young men's wing.

A half hour passed, but Tchaikovsky still did not appear, and to Mrs. Begichev's repeated queries she was told that Pyotr Ilych was dressing.

"Why is he taking so long?' she wondered, but her surprise was even greater when, after such a long interval, Tchaikovsky appeared in his ordinary clothes, looking utterly perplexed and with a heap of skirts and tunics under his arm.

It appeared that neither he nor the valet could in any way penetrate the mysteries of the intricate female costume and that the experienced and skilled [valet] Alexey had proved quite inept as a lady's maid. . . .

"Good Lord! What a pair of blockheads!" exclaimed Mrs. Begichev with comic horror. . . . "Give the costume here!" she cried impatiently and, nearly tearing everything from the dumbfounded Tchaikovsky's hand, began, piece by piece, showing him what to put on after what. He watched this whole procedure apathetically, and when Mrs. Begichev, coming to the end of her manipulations, asked him whether he understood, he answered seriously and quite calmly that he had not understood a thing. . . .

"Now, listen, Pyotr, here's what I'm going to do! I'll go at once and put on this costume myself!". . . And, without waiting for his reply, she went out, trailed by Fanny carrying the various pieces of the costume.

A short time later she reappeared in full costume and wearing the characteristic mask of an old witch. . . .

"I'll remain in this costume, and you wear my domino. Any of my black skirts with a train will fit you, and the domino is so full and wide that it would fit anyone. I'll give you my black fan to hold, I'll put not a half-mask on you, but a real, full black mask, and you and I shall go to the ball!"

Tchaikovsky tried to make excuses, but alone against the rest of us he was powerless. . . .

Shortly after midnight Pyotr Ilyich came into the room, solemnly sweeping the long train of the rich black dress behind him and lazily flicking a sumptuous fan of black feathers encrusted with gold. He was so inimitably grand, and so unrecognizable in that costume, that we greeted him with a burst of unanimous applause.

Mrs. Begichev too was very pleased. Not only had her enterprise succeeded, but she seemed also to relish the prospect of unexpectedly attending the costume ball. . . .

And so, Mrs. Begichev set off with Tchaikovsky in the carriage and together the two entered the hall of the Assembly of Nobles. Everyone noticed the unique witch costume at once, and a murmur of approval ran through the hall.

Someone who had been privy to the intended plan mentioned that it was Tchaikovsky beneath the costume. This was repeated by someone else, and then by a third, and soon the entire hall "knew" who was dressed as the witch.

People came up to Mrs. Begichev and clapped her affably on the shoulder, saying again and again: "Pyotr! Great costume!"

Pyotr Ilyich, meanwhile, moved serenely and grandly through the various halls of the Assembly of Nobles, flicking his splendid fan with exceptional flair and swishing the enormous train of his costly gown.[25]

V

Marriage
(1877)

Bearing in mind his affair with Désirée Artôt, there is every reason to believe that until the middle of the 1870s Tchaikovsky did not take his homosexuality too seriously and, as is frequently the case, did not allow himself to think that his sexual preferences were irreversible or insurmountable. Most probably he thought that he could act on his inclinations for as long as possible, but that, when it became absolutely necessary, he could simply abandon these habits.

After traveling with his brother Modest and Nikolay Konradi in early 1876, Tchaikovsky clearly realized that the emotional atmosphere surrounding his brother's relationship with his charge was unhealthy and fraught with potential if not imminent danger. He became conscious of this on a very personal level, since he also felt an erotic attraction to the boy and had always been a role model for his younger brothers. And so the composer resolved to end the crisis in his own way by setting a good example.

On 19 August 1876 Tchaikovsky suddenly wrote to his brother: "*I have decided to marry.* It is inevitable. I must do this, and not only for myself, but also for you and for Anatoly, Alexandra [their sister], and all whom I love. For you in particular! But you also, Modest, need to think seriously about this. Homosexuality and pedagogy cannot abide in harmony with one another."[1] A month later, in a letter to Modest, he stressed the point further: "A man who, after parting with, so to speak, *his own* (he can be called your own) child [i.e., Nikolay Konradi] falls into the embraces of any passing trash [i.e. a male prostitute], cannot be the real educator that you want and ought to become."[2] Discussing with Modest the possibility of the three of them living together the following year, the composer touched upon another issue which no doubt had been weighing heavily on his mind: "I do not want evil tongues to wound an innocent child, about whom they would inevitably say that I am preparing him to be my own lover, moreover, *a mute one,* in order to elude idle talk and rumors."[3] Contemptuous though he was of public opinion, Tchaikovsky found that he could ignore it no longer. He was never a fighter by nature, and in the end he had no choice but to yield. His sudden and impulsive decision to marry was motivated primarily by an emotion more altruistic than selfish—a desire to ensure his relatives' peace of mind and to retain full and mutual understanding with them without the need for reticence or deception.

Until this time Tchaikovsky had treated his homosexuality as a morally indifferent phenomenon. Now it suddenly seemed imperative to suppress it and, what is more, to advise his brother to do the same. Indeed, his customary relationship with Modest dictated that Tchaikovsky set an example of behavior to be imitated, one that might save Modest from the danger of scandal without causing him to abandon a pupil who was so deeply loved by both brothers. That he himself would have to make certain sacrifices in this respect must no doubt have flattered the self-esteem of the composer, who may well have seen the decision as an almost heroic gesture. Nevertheless, however vigorous their intent, Tchaikovsky's preparations for marriage did not proceed without some severe setbacks. A few weeks after his somber letters to Modest about marriage, he went to the country estate of his friend Bek-Bulatov, where he discovered a veritable homosexual bordello and found himself infatuated with his coach-man.[4]

Tchaikovsky was torn by ambivalent feelings on the subject of sexuality and marriage. In a letter of 28 September 1876, after referring to three homosexual encounters since his last letter, he agreed with his brother that "it is not possible to restrain oneself, despite all one's vows, from one's weaknesses."[5] Moreover, at the end of the same letter he honestly confessed: "I shall not enter into any lawful or illicit union with a woman without having fully ensured my own peace and my own freedom."[6] He is obviously referring to the freedom to indulge in those "weaknesses" which could not be resisted, whatever vows one might make.

Some time later, at the end of 1876, he fell deeply in love with his Conservatory student, Iosif Kotek. This was a "passion" which, he admitted in a letter to Modest of 19 January 1877, assailed him "with unimaginable force":

> I am *in love,* as I haven't been in love for a long time. Can you guess with whom? He is of middle height, fair, with wonderful brown eyes (with a misty gleam characteristic of extremely nearsighted people). He wears pince-nez, and sometimes *glasses,* which I cannot stand. He dresses with great care and cleanliness, wears a thick gold chain and always pretty cuff links of the noble metal. He has small hands, but utterly ideal in form (I say "but" because I don't like small hands). They are so delightful that I readily forgive them certain distortions and ugly details stemming from frequent contact of the fingertips with the [violin] strings. He speaks with a heavily *nasal* voice, moreover tenderness and sincerity sound in the timbre of his voice. His accent is slightly southern-Russian and even Polish, for he was born and spent his childhood in Polish lands. But in the course of his six-year stay in Moscow this accent has been severely *moscovized.* On sum, i.e., adding this accent to the tenderness of his vocal timbre and his charming lips,

on which downy-fair whiskers are beginning to grow, the result is something delightful. He is quite smart, very talented in music and in general blessed with a fine nature, far from any kind of vulgarity and sleaziness. . . .

I have known him for six years already. I always liked him, and on several occasions I felt a little bit in love with him. That was like a trial run for my [present] love. Now I have momentum and have *run right into him* in the most decisive fashion. I cannot say that my love is completely pure. When he caresses me with his hand, when he lies with his head on my chest and I play with his hair and secretly kiss it, when for hours on end I hold his hand in my own and tire in the battle against the urge to fall at his feet and kiss those little feet (little and exquisite), passion rages within me with unimaginable force, my voice shakes like that of a youth, and I speak only nonsense. However, I am far from desiring physical consummation. I feel that if *that occurred* I would cool to him. I would feel disgusted if this *wonderful youth* stooped to sex with an aged and fat-bellied man. How horrible this would be and how disgusting I would become to myself! It is not called for.

I need only for him to know that I love him endlessly and for him to be a kind and indulgent despot and idol. It is impossible for me to hide my feelings for him, although I tried hard to do so at first. I saw that he noticed everything and understood me. But then can you imagine how artful I am in hiding my feelings? My habit of *eating alive* any beloved object always gives me away. Yesterday I totally gave myself away. . . .

I burst. I made a *full* confession of love, begging him not to be angry, not to feel constrained if I bore him, etc. All of these confessions were met with a thousand various small caresses, strokes on the shoulder, *cheeks,* and strokes across my head. I am incapable of expressing to you the full degree of bliss that I experienced by fully giving myself away.

I must tell you that yesterday was the eve of his departure for Kiev, where he is soon to give a concert. After my *confession* he suggested we travel out of town for supper. It was a delightful, moonlit night. I hired a carriage and we flew off. I cannot tell you the thousand details that caused me ineluctable bliss. I wrapped him up, hugged him, guarded him. He complained of the frost on the tip of his *nose.* I held the collar of his fur coat the whole time with my bare hand in order to warm this nosetip, so holy for me. The freezing of my *hand* caused me pain and, at the same time, the sweet thought of knowing that I was suffering for him. In *Strelna,* in the Winter Garden, I met the group of Lenin, Rivol [a group of homosexual friends from Moscow] and *tutti quanti.* Lord, how pitiful they all seemed to me in their cynical and ironic debauchery! From there we went to Yar and suppered in a private room. After dining he felt sleepy and lay down on the sofa, using my knees for a pillow. Lord, what utter bliss this was! He tenderly ridiculed my expressions of affection and kept repeating that my *love* is not the same as that of [his friend] Porubinovsky. Mine is supposedly selfish and impure. His love is selfless and pure. We spoke of the piece he *ordered* me to write for his Lenten concert. He repeated over and over that he would get angry if I didn't write this piece.[7] We left at three o'clock.

I awoke today with a feeling of having experienced happiness and with a complete absence of that emotional sobriety that used to make me repent in the morning for having gone too far the night before. I bore my classes today with extreme ease, was indulgent and tender with my pupils, and to their surprise made witticisms and jokes the whole time so that they were rolling with laughter. At eleven o'clock he summoned me out of the class to pay his farewell. We parted, but I ended class early and flew to the Kursk railway so as to see him once more. He was very tender, merry and dear. At half past one the train rushed him off. I am not upset that he left. First, he will soon return. Second, I need to gather my thoughts and calm down. I have done nothing recently and have seen absolutely nobody apart from those whom he visits. Shilovsky and Kondratyev are both angry at me. Third, I am glad that I shall have occasion to write to him and express all that I have not been able to say.[8]

On 4 May 1877 Tchaikovsky continued to share with Modest all details of his infatuation with Iosif Kotek:

> My love for a person known to you has ignited with new and unheard-of strength! The reason for this is *jealousy. He has tied himself to Eibozhenka,* and they have sex five and six times a day. At first they hid this from me, but my heart told the truth even earlier. I tried to distance myself from this thought, comforting myself with all sorts of inventions. But one fine day he confessed everything to me. I cannot *tell* you what torture it was for me to learn that my suspicions had basis in fact. I am not even in a state to hide my grief. I have spent several terrible nights. Not that I am angry at him or her, not at all. But suddenly I have felt with unusual force that he is *alien* to me, that this woman is millions and millions of times nearer to him. Then I became accustomed to this terrible thought, but love was ignited stronger than ever before. We still see each other every day, and he was never so tender with me as now. Do you know why I cooled to him this spring? Now I know for sure that it was due to that *disfigured* finger. Isn't that strange?. . . Shilovsky's wedding took place. Before that he was constantly drunk, howling all day and fainting. Now he is perfectly happy and content. He *has broken in* his wife (that's the utter truth) and spends all day making visits to aristocrats.[9]

It happened that about the same time, in spring of 1877, when Tchaikovsky's passion for Kotek suddenly declined, owing to the latter's infidelity and his disfigured finger, and when another close homosexual friend, Vladimir Shilovsky, was getting married, Tchaikovsky received several love letters from a former Conservatory student, Antonina Milyukova (1848–1917).[10] Tchaikovsky hardly remembered Antonina, since he had met her for the first time in Moscow in late May 1872, at the apartment of her brother, the staff-captain Alexander Milyukov (1840–85), whose wife, Anastasiya (neé Khvostova) was a close friend of the composer from his days at the School of Jurisprudence in Petersburg.[11]

Antonina later admitted, both in her letters to Tchaikovsky (1880s) and in her recollections (1893), that this first meeting made an indelible impression on her, resulting in a profound affection that lasted for many years. She lent

special meaning to the fact that her love arose from her attraction to Tchaikovsky's appearance and his purely human qualities, and that she was utterly
ignorant of his music and growing fame in cultural circles. On Tchaikovsky's
personal invitation Antonina attended the premiere of his cantata in honor of
the opening of the Polytechnic Exhibition in Moscow on 30 May 1872. Their
relationship, however, did not develop in the years after their first meeting, and
it was only during Antonina's studies at the Conservatory that they briefly saw
each other within the walls of this institution. As Antonina later wrote, she
loved Tchaikovsky "secretly" for over four years. In late 1876, Antonina
received a small inheritance due to the division of the family estate. This
potential "dowry" was apparently the immediate incentive for taking active
steps toward renewing her acquaintance with the composer.[12]

On 26 March 1877, Antonina sent Tchaikovsky a written confession of her
love for him.[13] Both Antonina and Tchaikovsky testify that they "began a
correspondence," as a result of which the composer received her offer "of hand
and heart" in early May 1877.[14]

On 20 May Tchaikovsky met with Antonina. An analysis of Antonina's
surviving letters suggests that in all likelihood their personal meeting was
initiated by Tchaikovsky himself. The threat of suicide, made in the last letter
Antonina wrote before their meeting, cannot be considered a serious factor in
Tchaikovsky's eventual decision; in the context of the entire letter, this "threat"
seems to be no more than a device in the tradition of sentimental models from
so-called "letter books," which were popular at the time and which contained
samples of fictional letters for all occasions.[15]

The meeting occurred in the house where Antonina was renting a room, on
the corner of Tverskaya Street and Maly Gnezdnikovsky Lane in Moscow. At the
next meeting, on 23 May, Tchaikovsky made an official proposal, promising his
bride only his "brotherly" love, to which she readily agreed.[16] But Tchaikovsky
chose not to mention this meeting in his letter to Modest, written on the same
day. Instead he tried to explain his cooling off toward Kotek and even began to
see the hand of Providence in various recent coincidences:

> You ask about my love? It has once again fallen off almost to the point of
> absolute calm. And do you know why? You alone can understand this. Because
> two or three times I saw his injured finger in all of its ugliness! Except for that,
> I would be in love to the point of madness, which returns anew each time I am
> able to forget somewhat about his crippled finger. I don't know whether this
> finger is for the better or worse. Sometimes it seems to me that Providence, so
> blind and unjust in the choice of its protégés, deigns to take care of me. Indeed,
> sometimes I begin to consider certain coincidences to be not mere accidents.
> . . . Who knows, maybe this is the beginning of a religiosity that, if it ever takes
> hold of me, will do so completely. . . . I send a photograph of myself and Kotek
> together. It was taken at the very peak of my recent passion.[17]

Alexandra and Ilya Tchaikovsky, Tchaikovsky's parents, 1850.
Photo credit: The State Theatre Museum (St. Petersburg).

Fanny Dürbach, Tchaikovsky's governess, in 1844-1848.
Photo credit: The Tchaikovsky State Archive and House Museum (Klin).

Tchaikovsky and his classmate Vladimir Gerard, 1859.
Photo credit: The Tchaikovsky State Archive and House Museum (Klin).

Sergey Kireyev, Tchaikovsky's close friend at
the School of Jurisprudence, 1858.
Photo credit: The Tchaikovsky State Archive and House Museum (Klin).

Rudolph Kündinger, pianist,
Tchaikovsky's teacher between 1850 and 1858.
Photo credit: The Tchaikovsky State Archive and House Museum (Klin).

Anton Rubinstein, pianist and founder of
the first Russian Conservatory, 1862.
Photo credit: The Tchaikovsky State Archive and House Museum (Klin).

Tchaikovsky, 1861.
Photo credit: The Glinka State Museum of Musical Culture (Moscow).

Ivan Klimenko, Tchaikovsky's close friend, 1872.
Photo credit: The Tchaikovsky State Archive and House Museum (Klin).

Mariya Gurye, Tchaikovsky's student, 1938.
Photo credit: The Tchaikovsky State Archive and House Museum (Klin).

Konstantin de Lazari, actor and socialite.
Photo credit: The Tchaikovsky State Archive and House Museum (Klin).

Tchaikovsky, 1868.

Photo credit: The Tchaikovsky State Archive and House Museum (Klin).

Vladimir Shilovsky, Tchaikovsky's society friend, 1868.
Photo credit: The Tchaikovsky State Archive and House Museum (Klin).

Désirée Artôt, Belgian soprano, 1868.
Photo credit: The Tchaikovsky State Archive and House Museum (Klin).

Tchaikovsky, 1874.
*Photo credit: The Russian Institute of the History
of the Arts (St. Petersburg).*

Tchaikovsky among his relatives;
left to right, sitting: Tchaikovsky, brother Nikolay, brother-in-law
Lev Davydov, sister Alexandra, brother Anatoly; standing: brothers
Modest and Ippolit, the latter's wife Vera, Nikolay's wife, Olga,
Lidiya Olkhovsky, Nikolay Litke and his wife Amaliya, 1874.

*Photo credit: The State Archive for Cinematographic, Photographic and
Phonographic Documents (St. Petersburg).*

Tchaikovsky and his wife, Antonina, 24 July 1877.
Photo credit: The Bakhrushin State Theatre Museum (Moscow)

The wedding took place at St. George's Church on 6 July 1877. The bridegroom's witnesses were his brother Anatoly and his friend Iosif Kotek, the bride's were her close friends Vladimir Vinogradov and Vladimir Malama. They were joined by the priest Dmitry Razumovsky, who was also professor of the history of church music at the Conservatory.[18]

The majority of biographical works on Tchaikovsky date the beginning of his relationship with Antonina Milyukova to early May 1877, the time of the genesis and first drafts of his opera *Eugene Onegin*. According to the composer's own testimony in his letters to Nadezhda von Meck, an important factor in the couple's rapid intimacy and marriage was Tchaikovsky's fascination with the plot of Pushkin's novel—his sympathy for the heroine and his desire to avoid "repeating" Onegin's cruelty toward a woman who loves him. Another significant factor was Antonina's own insistent requests for meetings, accompanied by suicide threats in case of refusal. The fact that there remained about two weeks before the idea of the opera *Eugene Onegin* took root in Tchaikovsky's mind, after being suggested by the singer Elizaveta Lavrovskaya on May 13, allows one to conclude that the choice of Pushkin's novel as the plot for an opera might possibly have been stimulated by Tchaikovsky's personal situation: a distant female acquaintance confessing her love in a letter.[19]

That evening, after the wedding, Tchaikovsky and his bride left for St. Petersburg to visit his family. He quickly realized that he had made a grave mistake. Moreover, he found himself unable to accept either the personality and character of his wife, or her family and circle of friends. After 20 days of cohabitation their marriage was still not consummated.[20] It is uncertain whether Tchaikovsky confided in his wife at the outset regarding his homosexuality. If so, she may simply have disregarded such a confession. On 27 July, Tchaikovsky left Antonina for six weeks, traveling to Kamenka to stay with his sister.[21]

After returning to Moscow the composer lived with his wife from September 12 to 24 at the apartment on Bolshaya Nikitskaya Street not far from the Conservatory, before leaving her for good. First, Tchaikovsky contrived to be summoned to St. Petersburg on a fictitious errand, and thereupon he departed abroad for a considerable period of time in order to recuperate from a nervous breakdown which, as it transpires from archival documents, was faked.[22]

Be that as it may, there hardly remains any doubt that his homosexuality, coupled with the psychological incompatibility on which he insisted in his correspondence, proved the ultimate cause of the breakup of his marriage. This recognition forced Tchaikovsky to admit that he had failed in his plan to enhance his social and personal stability. Most importantly, however, his impulsive marriage helped him to realize that his homosexuality could not be changed and had to be accepted as it was. There is not a single document from the rest of his life that can be construed as an expression of self-torment on account of his homosexuality. Some occasional expressions of nostalgia for family life are perfectly understandable in a bachelor and have nothing to do with sexual orientation. But even here the composer succeeded in creating an emotionally satisfying environment through his close relationship with his relatives and by surrounding himself with a group of admiring young men, headed by his beloved nephew Bob Davydov.

Tchaikovsky undertook several attempts at divorce in 1878–80 but without success; for a long time Antonina continued to believe in the possibility of future "reconciliation" and refused to agree to a divorce, invoking Tchaikovsky's wrath, accusations of stupidity, suspicions of "blackmail," etc. Only in 1881 did Tchaikovsky finally abandon the idea of divorce. At this time he ceased paying his wife the pension he had promised her (it had fluctuated from 50 to 100 rubles a month) due to her erratic and unpredictable behavior.

Antonina Milyukova's role in Tchaikovsky's life is no longer viewed in the one-dimensional terms that used to prevail. It is impossible to deny that she had a very negative effect on the composer's psychic and physical state, a fact that is confirmed by Tchaikovsky's own statements in his letters and diaries. Tchaikovsky called his wife a "terrible wound," he felt heavily burdened by his legal bind and sometimes even afraid of possible "disclosures" by her concerning his homosexual preferences.

Yet Tchaikovsky was also deeply concerned over the entire fiasco and felt sincere remorse for his seemingly cruel treatment of Antonina. Paradoxically, it is precisely the years 1877–80, the most difficult time in Tchaikovsky's marital drama, that stand out as one of his most productive periods in a creative sense. Subsequently Tchaikovsky was plagued with pangs of conscience, for instance in his letters to Pyotr Jurgenson (1883, 1888) where he asks his publisher to locate his abandoned spouse in order to help her materially. Tchaikovsky appreciated his wife's musical abilities, which is shown by a series of favorable judgments found in his letters. But Tchaikovsky often perceived Antonina's personal qualities unfairly, painting a distorted picture of her, based on his annoyance at this or that trait of her character (for instance, in his letters to his brothers, Nadezhda von Meck, and others). One of Tchaikovsky's more balanced statements in regard to his wife can be found in the letter to his sister Alexandra Davydova from Rome of 8/20 November 1877: "I give full justice to her sincere desire to be a good wife and friend to me, and . . . it is not her fault that I did not find what I was looking for."[23] The fact remains that, despite her ruined family life and perennial pain, not once did Antonina attempt to take revenge on her husband. On the contrary, she even slightly embellished the composer's human image in her following recollections: "No one, not a single person in the world, can accuse him of any base action."

Until recently, most of Tchaikovsky's biographers have recounted the details of Tchaikovsky's marriage in a superficial and tendentious manner, always with a bias in favor of the composer. Antonina Milyukova's own recollections, which present her side of the story, have been labeled the product of a rash and insane woman, and therefore ignored.[24] Recent archival studies have made it possible to clarify several key details relating to Antonina's origin, the history of the couple's acquaintance, their marriage, their later relationship, and Antonina's life after their separation.[25]

It is established that Antonina Milyukova was born into a family of the hereditary gentry that resided outside Moscow in the Klin region. The family traced its ancestry to the fourteenth century. Antonina's parents separated in 1851, and her childhood was spent in an unfavorable emotional environment. She was brought up in a private Moscow boarding school under the supervision of her mother (1851–55), and then at her father's Klin estate (1855–58). Together with her elder brothers Alexander and Mikhail, and her elder sister Elizaveta (or Adel), she received a standard home education, including the study of two foreign languages.

From early on, Antonina enjoyed music (her father Ivan Milyukov kept a peasant orchestra). She continued her education at the Moscow Institute of St. Elizabeth, completing the full course of study from 1858 to 1864. Here, apart from the required subjects, she took piano and voice lessons. In the 1873–74 school year she studied at the Moscow Conservatory, where her teacher in piano was Eduard Langer and her teacher in elementary theory was Karl Albrecht.[26] After leaving school, Antonina pursued a career in pedagogy, giving private lessons in Moscow in the 1870s, and then teaching at a school attached to the local House of Industry in Kronstadt in 1896. On several occasions Antonina attempted unsuccessfuly to become a teacher in various other educational institutions. From 1848 to 1893 she lived in and around Moscow, and from 1893 to her death she lived in Petersburg and its suburbs. In 1887 she made a trip to Italy. From 1880, Antonina Tchaikovsky lived in a free union with the lawyer Alexander Shlykov, and bore three children. Because of her financial vulnerability and "semi-legal" social situation, and the chronic ill health that afflicted both parents, Antonina surrendered all her illegitimate children to a Moscow foundling hospital, where they eventually died.[27]

In 1886, following a five-year silence, Antonina Milyukova asked the composer for monetary assistance, and suggested that he adopt and take in her youngest daughter, Antonina. Tchaikovsky readily agreed to the financial support, and once again assigned her a monthly pension of 50 rubles (later increased to 100, then to 150, finally lowered again to 100 rubles). He failed to respond to the idea of adopting her child, although it is known from Tchaikovsky's letters to his brother Modest and to Pyotr Jurgenson that he sharply condemned the fact that Antonina's children were at a foundling hospital.

In 1886–89, Antonina regularly wrote Tchaikovsky to thank him for his support, even sending him a shirt she had sewn as a sign of gratitude; she told him of her life and misfortunes (her civil husband died in 1888), asked him to increase the pension, and offered to join him again. Tchaikovsky reacted painfully not only to Antonina's letters, but also to information concerning her attempts to seek patronage from the Empress and Anton Rubinstein, in order to find a permanent teaching position. The composer considered the pension she was receiving fully adequate for a comfortable existence and viewed Antonina's "social legitimization" as a threat to his prestige. Throughout these years Pyotr Jurgenson served as the mediator between husband and wife, so that they could avoid personal contact. They met from time to time at concerts and operatic performances, seeing each other only from a distance. Antonina maintained that their last meeting took place in Moscow in the autumn of 1892 during a stroll in the Alexandrovsky Gardens. She recalled that Tchaikovsky walked behind her but "could not make himself speak" to her. This meeting was probably fictitious.[28]

After the composer's death, Antonina received a pension of 100 rubles a month which Tchaikovsky left her in his will. She moved to Petersburg and lived near St. Alexander Nevsky Monastery, where he was buried. Antonina's further fate was tragic: soon after Tchaikovsky's death she began to display signs of an emotional disorder (a persecution complex). By 1896 the disease worsened and Antonina moved to Kronstadt, where she sought spiritual support and a cure from the renowned miracle-worker Father John of Kronstadt. For some unknown reason the priest refused to help her. In October 1896 Antonina Milyukova ended up in the Petersburg Hospital of St. Nicholas the Wonderworker for the emotionally disturbed. After her relative recovery, in February 1900, she was released from the hospital, only to return there in June of 1901 with a diagnosis of *paranoia chronica*.[29] A month later, with the help of Tchaikovsky's brother Anatoly, she was transferred to a more comfortable psychiatric hospital outside the city, the Charitable Home for the Emotionally Disturbed at Udelnaya. The pension from her late husband covered her room and board. Antonina spent the last ten years of her life at this institution, more as a "resident" than a patient. The home provided her in her old age with medical supervision, attentive care by the personnel, and full living conveniences. She died of pneumonia on 16 February 1917, and was buried at Uspensky Cemetery in St. Petersburg. Her grave has not survived.[30]

In December 1893, the *Peterburgskaia gazeta* printed an interview with the composer's widow in which she warmly remembered her late husband.[31] Four month later, in April 1894, the same newspaper published Antonina's detailed recollections, written in late 1893, of her life with Tchaikovsky.[32] It was one of the first important published accounts relating to the biography of the composer. The first critical edition of her recollections appeared in Russia only a century later, in 1994, and they have never been anthologized or published in English.

Predictably, the version of their separation which she offers (that Tchaikovsky succumbed to his friends' threats that married life would deprive him of his talent) is, at the very least, naive and makes no mention of the real cause—his homosexuality. Despite her idealization of Tchaikovsky and occasional incoherence (perhaps a sign of her incipient mental disorder), there is no reason to question the reliability of her account as regards basic facts or revealing details. Based on recent studies of Antonina one can conclude that the recollections of Tchaikovsky's wife, in contrast to those of his brother Modest, are not only accurate with respect to the factual history of their failed marriage, but present—albeit from her peculiar and idealized perspective—a convincing image of the composer. Antonina's recollections are here published in full.

Another set of recollections covering about the same period belongs to Tchaikovsky's friend and fellow professor at the Moscow Conservatory Nikolay Kashkin (1839–1920). This particular narrative was written in 1918 and published in 1920.[33] According to Kashkin, Tchaikovsky confided to him the story of his marriage in a conversation that took place during one of his visits to Klin, probably in the summer of 1890. Predictably, Kashkin treats Antonina according to the "party line" taken by the composer's relatives and friends, emphasizing their psychological incompatibility, with strong hints of her potential mental disorder, and with no mention of any sexual problems.

The account of Tchaikovsky's marriage is here supplemented by a striking episode which Kashkin claims to have heard directly from the composer, that of his failed attempt to commit suicide sometime in the midst of his marital crisis in the autumn of 1877, before he had made up his mind to leave his wife for good and flee abroad. In this singular confession the composer is said to have described how one night, in a moment of dark despair, he purposely waded into the freezing waters of the Moskva River in the hope of contracting a fatal case of pneumonia. In this way, he reportedly told Kashkin, his death might appear to be the result of natural causes, thereby sparing his family any unnecessary additional pain. Fortunately, the adventure passed with no consequences.

It is not surprising, of course, that some biographers have seized upon this story as a major precedent for the composer's alleged suicide in 1893.[34] If Tchaikovsky had the heart to wade into an icy river in that moment of trial, runs their thesis, he would surely have had no compunction about poisoning himself in an hour of even greater stress, or if ordered to do so.

There are, however, more than a few problems with this argument, as well as a number of suspicious elements in the whole affair, beginning with Kashkin's memoir itself. Kashkin's account should be treated with extreme caution. He never belonged to the circle of Tchaikovsky's most intimate friends, and the composer was generally reticent with those who were not particularly close to him. Since Kashkin's story is not supported by any other evidence, direct or indirect, it must be doubted whether Tchaikovsky would have confided such a sensitive matter only to him.[35]

The device Kashkin chose for narrating events in the first person—that is, in Tchaikovsky's own voice—is surprisingly effective. But even if one concedes that Kashkin was a close enough friend of Tchaikovsky that the composer might have felt comfortable confiding in him so intimate an experience, it is nonetheless suspect that Kashkin chose to render this confession as a first-person narrative. As the student of memoir literature knows full well, the least reliable portions of any reminiscence are those that attempt to reproduce the direct speech of a famous individual.

Moreover, even if Tchaikovsky did in fact tell the story of his marriage to Kashkin just as the latter records it, he would have done so in retrospect, after an interval of thirteen years. It is not unreasonable to suspect that he may have indulged in a degree of fantasy or embellishment and tried to present himself in the best possible light for the sake of posterity. Kashkin's version of events creates the impression that Tchaikovsky, without ever having written a single line in response to Antonina's letters, simply went straight off to see her after receiving her threat of suicide; in fact, they had been corresponding for quite a while. It seems very likely that Tchaikovsky, Kashkin, or both sought to modify the course of events to better fit them into a Pushkinian literary framework. As I have pointed out elsewhere, "betraying the inherent romanticism of [Tchaikovsky's] mind, this wishful reversal reshaped events to accord more completely with artistic notions of coincidence and destiny. Fate, not his own folly, became for him the instrument of his undoing."[36]

Alternatively, Kashkin himself may well have elaborated upon the composer's brief mention of some momentary thoughts of suicide which he perhaps entertained during that very difficult time (and which indeed are reflected in some of his letters from the period), but without any clear notion of whether such thoughts were ever serious (which, again judging from his letters, they were not). It is important to realize that Kashkin could have learned much about Tchaikovsky's marriage (although, of course, not about the Moskva River episode) from Modest Tchaikovsky's biography, which was already published. It seems that Kashkin was not aware of some important facts, for example that the composer's embarrassing flight from his wife to St. Petersburg was not impulsive but arranged by him and his brothers in advance. It seems that Kashkin also did not know that Tchaikovsky's reported illness was actually fabricated in order to create an atmosphere of sympathy for him and avoid public condemnation for his hasty and ill-considered act.

A more realistic echo of the events, as well as Tchaikovsky's own feelings, can be sensed in Tchaikovsky's letter of 25 October 1877 to his colleague from the Conservatory Karl Albrecht, in which he explained his escape abroad by the need to resolve his matrimonial crisis. He wrote: "But what else could I do? In any event, it is better to be absent for a year than to disappear forever. Had I stayed but one more day in Moscow I should have lost my mind or drowned myself in the foul-smelling waves of the nonetheless dear Moskva River."[37]

This passage, however, displays a very different tone: Tchaikovsky speaks of drowning himself, not of catching his death of cold by wading into the freezing river; the treatment is ironic, which suggests that the whole idea of suicide remained firmly on the level of fantasy. It is possible that this very letter sparked Kashkin's imagination, since the composer mentions both "drowning" and "losing his mind." In Kashkin's account, that very expression ("losing his mind") took the form (not without Modest's help) of a "nervous breakdown" exaggerated to the point that it is portrayed as a major nervous crisis in Tchaikovsky's life. As for "drowning," since Tchaikovsky survived the crisis, it became a mere attempt to contract pneumonia by "wading" into the river. Whether consciously or not, there can be little doubt that Kashkin's memoirs contributed to the creation of yet another piece of mythology about the composer.[38]

Antonina Tchaikovskaya

I first met my husband at the home of my sister-in-law, the wife of my older brother Alexander. [Alexander] died about six years ago.[39] From childhood he, that is, my husband, used to go from the School of Jurisprudence to visit the home of my sister-in-law's mother, the widow of a consul general, Ekaterina Khvostova.[40] Her son—my sister-in-law's brother—was also a student at the School of Jurisprudence.[41] They got used to seeing my husband there from, I believe, the time he was twelve.

He grew up a very likable boy, and above all there was always a great deal of simplicity and kindness in his character. There was one time in school when for some reason he was particularly hungry, and on the spur of the moment he sent Ekaterina Khvostova, who was terribly fond of him, a note that said something like: "My dear Ekaterina, please send me something to eat! I'm dying of hunger!" This note had quite an effect, there was almost a furor in the house! Everyone laughed heartily and they all helped to pack up various things to eat—for Pyotr Tchaikovsky.

And he was always that way! Unaffected, sincere, ingenuous, and straightforward. He never, from childhood on, did any harm to anyone and never in his life did he speak ill of anyone. He never flattered people, never fawned or acted meanly—rather, his behavior toward everyone was always honest and noble.

And for this reason his eyes always regarded everyone so clearly. In them always shone the purity and nobility of his soul. No one, not a single person in the world, can accuse him of any base action. For this was not at all in his nature. I suppose he was foreordained by fate itself to live on this earth solely to help his neighbor. And who were his neighbors? All people. Here is a perfect example.

I was told that once some gentleman from the Caucasus came looking for a job. He was in a most critical situation. No money, no relatives, no connections! What was he to do now? Where could he go? To whom could he turn? Well, someone said to him, "Go see Tchaikovsky!" "But how can I do that?" he asked. "He doesn't know me, he'll send me away!" "Tchaikovsky? Go on with you! Do you really think Tchaikovsky could turn anyone away? He's incapable of it. Tchaikovsky's door is open to everyone: rich and poor, friend and stranger, even scoundrel or enemy. Everyone goes to him! Don't be afraid! You've no reason to be afraid of Tchaikovsky! It's impossible to be afraid of him! He's charity and kindness personified." After these words the man was no longer afraid and he went. The people who had advised him to go see Tchaikovsky stood at the entrance and waited. The visit lasted quite a long time. Everyone stood there impatiently, waiting and waiting. Why was he in there so long? They began to mutter with impatience. But then he came out, completely in tears. "Well, then?" "Ah!" he waved his hand and wept profusely. "You were right! He's the embodiment of charity and kindness." "Well, then? Didn't we tell you?" "Thank you," he bowed to everyone. "And again many, many thanks to you, gentlemen! And him? An enormous thanks to him. He gave me money and promised me a job and . . . everything . . . everything"—and he burst into sobs. Then he left.

Sometimes, indeed quite often, he, my husband, would be in a playful mood, and he would have a terrible urge to tease someone, most comically. Then he would think up some prank, something kind, never hurtful, and indeed so adorable that it made everyone laugh.

One time he picked on my *belle-soeur* [sister-in-law] in this way. It was when he had just graduated from the School of Jurisprudence.[42] He came rushing over, all decked out in spanking new clothes, to pay his first visit to Ekaterina Khvostova; but his galoshes were completely covered with mud. "What is this?" said my *belle-soeur,* "you should be ashamed, a dandy like you, going about in such filthy galoshes. Just look at yourself," she said, pointing to his feet, "how can you go walking along Nevsky in such boots? Why, it's a shame and a disgrace!" And he looked at his feet in embarrassment. "You're right! How could I have made such a spectacle of myself? I'm astonished. Still, I've long since noticed that I have this habit of invariably getting myself filthy somewhere. I won't think I've brushed up against anything, yet invariably I'll return home all covered in something, and almost always in chalk. I always inspect myself when I get home. And either it turns out that my sleeve is covered with chalk, or my back, or there's chalk somewhere else on my clothes." "Give me your galoshes right now! I'll give them to the maid at once. Otherwise you'll be ashamed to have them standing here. Everyone will know they're yours. Give them to me at once." "Here you are," he said, handing them over. "But I'll get back at you!" "How?" "I'll tell everyone that you cleaned my galoshes yourself." "You shameless man!" "Absolutely! But never fear! I'll only say it when you're around! But never ever when you're not there!"

She took away the galoshes. And afterward he always told everyone, in her presence, how she had cleaned his galoshes. He told me too, at our very first meeting, when she was there.[43] And all three of us had a good laugh. Then she said to him: "My *belle-soeur* here wants to enter the Conservatory!" "Really?" he said to me, looking at me with intelligent and infinitely kind eyes. "You'd do better to get married," and looked at me now with doleful eyes.

And for the rest of my life I never forgot them, those wonderful, marvelous eyes. They warmed me from afar, just as from close by. Those eyes conquered me for life, and always, always they hovered before me. I never forgot them as long as he lived. Yes, I remember them very well even now, and I shall not forget them to my dying day. . . .

After this I indeed entered the Conservatory and was extremely happy, running into him constantly: he was always terribly affectionate to me. . . .[44]

For more than four years I loved him secretly.

I knew perfectly well that he liked me, but he was shy and would never make a proposal. I made a pledge to myself to go every day for six weeks to the chapel at the Spassky Gates to pray for him, no matter the weather, always by six in the evening, when the lamp was lowered from above. I would offer a candle which they placed in the lamp in my presence, and while it was being raised I remained on my knees, sometimes in a puddle after the rain, and prayed fiercely. At the end of the six weeks I ordered a liturgy in the chapel and, having prayed some more at home, I mailed him a letter in which I poured out to him on paper all my love that had accumulated over so many years.[45]

He answered me at once, and we began a not uninteresting correspondence.

He always liked the way I wrote, and more than once he praised me to his friends. "How she writes!" he used to say almost in raptures. One day I received a short letter: "Tomorrow I shall visit you." And he came.[46] He could always charm the young ladies, and in those days, in particular, his gaze was enchanting. Among other things, he said: "But I am nearly an old man! Surely you will be bored living with me?"

"I love you so," I answered, "that merely to sit by you, to talk with you, to have you always near me will fill me with bliss."[47]

We sat together an hour.

"Let me think until tomorrow," he said as he left.

The next day he said: "I have thought everything through. Here is what I have to say. Never in my life have I loved a single woman and I feel that I am already too old for an ardent love. I shall never feel it for anyone. But you are the first woman whom I like very much. If you will be satisfied with a quiet, calm love, rather like the love of a brother, then I make you my proposal."[48]

Of course, I agreed to all his conditions. We continued to sit, however, very ceremoniously across from one another, talking a little bit about our future together. "Well then, it's time I went," he said, getting up and putting on his summer cloak (it was June),[49] then somehow especially charmingly and graciously turned to me, stretched his arms out wide, and said, "Well?" and I flung myself about his neck. I shall never forget that kiss.

Then he left at once.

I stood there like someone drunk; my knees were weak, but still I went immediately to share my joy with the lady who owned the house where I rented a room. She and I were quite friendly. When I came in she took a step back. "What's the matter?" she said in horror. "You look awful!" "I'm engaged," was all I could say, and then I began to cry. At first she did not believe me, but then she was happy for me with all her heart.

For a week he visited me every day after lunch.[50]

Once when he came to see me he said (we remained on formal terms until the very day of the wedding, and he would only kiss my hand, in greeting and as he took his leave): "Let us go for a walk tomorrow somewhere outside the city—to the Sparrow Hills, if you like."

But he sat with me a while, and by the time he left he had changed his mind. "No," he said, "I do not wish to compromise you; I want no one to have the right to say anything bad about you, and I don't want to give cause for any gossip from this walk." He never took tea when he came to see me, only seltzer water. I knew this. I used to pay in advance to have his water brought as soon as he arrived.

A week later, he asked my permission to go to his friend's estate near Moscow in order to write more quickly an opera he had already begun to compose in his head. This opera was *Eugene Onegin*, the best of all his operas.

It is good because it was written under the influence of love. It is based directly on us. He himself is Onegin and I am Tatyana. His operas written before and afterward are not warmed with love, they are cold and fragmentary. There is no wholeness in them. This is the only one that is good from beginning to end.

My husband left to write *Eugene Onegin* on 4 June, saying: "In exactly one month, on the fourth of July, I shall be here." It happened just as he said: between eleven and twelve in the morning of 4 July he approached the door of my house from the left just as I was returning home through another gate on the right, and we met at the door. . . .

When he returned on 4 July, Pyotr Ilyich informed me that he had invited only two people to the wedding: his brother Anatoly and a friend of his, though much younger than he, the violinist Kotek, who had then just graduated from the Conservatory. Kotek is dead now.[51]

Anatoly arrived on 5 July together with him, in the afternoon. Only my stepsister Mariya was with me. She was the only one of my relatives at the wedding. We introduced ourselves to one another and talked for a while about various trifles. After half an hour I took them both to see the couple who were going to be our sponsors at the wedding.

The day of the wedding arrived.

When I got to the church, we found that the rose satin cloth for under our feet had been forgotten (a bad omen). Someone was sent at once to fetch it, but it was brought only toward the end of the ceremony. My best man placed his white silk handkerchief under Pyotr Ilyich's feet, and I just stood as I was. After the ceremony Anatoly went alone with Pyotr Ilyich back to his bachelor apartment and I went back to the apartment of the director of girls' secondary schools, Gavriil Vinogradov. Gavriil himself, who was then living in Petrovskoe-Razumovskoe, had come expressly to be the first to greet me in his apartment after the ceremony. My sponsors were close relatives of his. My best men were his son Vladimir Vinogradov and an Ekaterinoslav landowner, the brother of a girlfriend of mine at the time, [Vladimir] Malama. Pyotr Ilyich and Anatoly liked my girlfriend [Elizaveta Malama] very much, and I had my photograph taken with her, in Russian costume.

Some time later, a carriage was sent for us and we went to the Hermitage Hotel. When we drove up, two footmen handed me down, as they say, from the carriage and led me in, one on each arm. At the foot of the staircase, Anatoly met me and took my arm. The room where everything was prepared was large and decorated with flowers. There were a great many dishes of every sort, but I barely touched a thing. Even then I had a presentiment of something bad. I simply felt cold from fear. Later, my cousin told me that it had been just like a funeral banquet, so cheerless was it.

After the dinner Pyotr Ilyich again went back to his bachelor apartment with his brother and I was again taken to the Vinogradovs'.

Toward seven o'clock in the evening we took a train on the Nikolaevsky railroad, and I departed for Petersburg with my husband.[52]

Our wedding was on 15 July 1877, and he left me in early November of the same year.[53] In the interim he went away for a couple of months, and instead of the Caucasus, where he had planned to go, he spent the whole time at his sister's estate. After returning from his sister's, he lived with me for exactly three weeks.[54]

I was incredibly funny then! For some reason I thought that the more trinkets I hung on myself, the more he would like me. This assumption later proved to be completely mistaken. He loved simplicity in women's clothes, and dark dresses. But it was summer, after all. And I always wore light-colored dresses.

Let me say a few words about something that happened a year before this time. One day I happened to be walking through the Solodovnikov arcade and, suddenly, in the window of Lebedev's store, I saw a coral set consisting of earrings with a brooch and necklace. They were a lovely color. The necklace was made so that the center bead was very large, and the other beads grew smaller and smaller, until they were quite tiny. I was terribly fond of the color. I went into the store and asked: "Are those real coral?" "Well, you see," the shop-assistant explained to me, "they're not completely artificial. They're made from leftover bits of coral. They've been crushed and made into a sort of coral mastic, and this set has been made from that." Maybe it was just a cock-and-bull story, but I believed it and bought the set, taking comfort in the fact that they were, after all, genuine, and I even wore them to parties at the Assembly of Nobles. They always made a big impression. And so, thinking only to please my dear husband, I appeared for morning tea fully dressed, wearing a light-colored dress (precisely the kind he could not stand) and my famous necklace. Indeed, I believe I had on the entire set.

There we sat, drinking our tea, he at his enormous writing desk, and I to one side near the window.

"Are those real coral you have there?"

"No!" I answered, very blithely.

He smiled faintly with just one corner of his mouth. "How nice!" he continued. "My wife wearing imitation coral."

"But what am I to do?" I replied, laughing. "I don't have any real ones, and I love them so!"

He said nothing in reply.

One Sunday he said to me: "Today we're going to have our picture taken! I'm going out for half an hour, and in the meantime you get dressed and ready and I'll come fetch you."

I put on my one formal black silk dress and sat down to wait for him. He was always punctual about everything. And indeed, he did not keep me waiting. From his face I could see that he was pleased with my costume. He suddenly became unusually cheerful, and kept hurrying me: "Come along then, be quick, let's go, let's go!" We went to Diyagovchenko's.[55] At that time Diyagovchenko himself was still alive. He received us very respectfully and the portraits were taken. As we came down the stairs, my husband said to me: "You know, they don't take my money at photographers' studios, but still many beg me to come, so long as I have my picture taken. For those where we're together, though, I have to pay half. But please don't think that this is because of you," he added. "It's because of me."

"Oh, but I know!" I replied, laughing. "Why should anyone take my photographs for free? I've done nothing to deserve it." And we both laughed merrily.

Never before or after this occasion did I see him as jolly as he was then. When we got to the street, he asked me: "Isn't there anything you'd like? Ask me for something. Why do you never ask me for anything? I'm terribly pleased when people ask me for things, especially you, my wife."

I said: "I'd love a cup of chocolate." We headed for Tremblé.

Tremblé was then located not far away, across from the photographer's studio. On the way he said to me: "But why don't you ask me for things more often?" When we entered the sweet shop, he was so jolly, and he looked round at everyone proudly as if to say: "Just see what a fine wife I have!" He ordered a chocolate for me, and cold water for himself. He could never stand sweets, and at this time he was already suffering from a bad gastric disorder and could not eat many foods. I never saw him touch apples or pears or grapes or anything that wasn't cooked. But his face at that time was so fresh that, surreptitiously and unnoticed by him, I was always admiring him, especially during morning tea. He just breathed freshness, always sitting there so handsome with his kind eyes that I was simply entranced by him. I would sit and think to myself while looking at him: "Thank God he is mine and no one else's! Nobody can take him away from me, because he is my husband!"[56]

In all, I remained in my husband's company no more than two and a half months. We were separated by the constant whispering to Pyotr Ilyich that family life would destroy his talent.[57] At first, he paid no attention to this talk; but then he began somewhat to listen to it more and more attentively. . . . There was nothing more dreadful to him than the thought of losing his talent. He began to believe their slanders and became listless and gloomy. Then one day, he told me he needed to go away on business for three days.[58] I accompanied him to the mail train; his eyes were wandering, he was nervous, but I didn't have the slightest inkling of the trouble hanging over my head.[59]

Before the first bell he had a spasm in his throat and went alone with jerky irregular steps to the station to get a drink of water. Then we entered the car; he looked at me plaintively, without lowering his eyes. When the second bell sounded, he suddenly threw his arms around me, clasped me long and hard to his breast, and kissed me, then, releasing me, he waved and said: "Go now, God be with you."[60] He never came back to me.[61]

Here are a few more memories about my dear husband.

Long before we were married, he was walking one day to the Conservatory. Suddenly, he met a group of children coming toward him carrying a little mongrel dog. "Where are you taking her?" he asked. "Oh, we want to drown her." At that, he began to shudder in horror. "Wait a moment!" he said, shaking—and he took out his wallet and gave it to them along with its contents. "Take it," he told them, "all of it, and give me the dog," and he went off with her in his arms. He later named her Bishka. She turned out to be a very smart dog and was terribly attached to him.

He very much disliked renting apartments and did not know how to go about it. He had a friend, an old man, who used to carry out all his errands, receiving from my husband twenty rubles a month. One time he needed an apartment. The old man—N[ikolay] B[ochechkarov][62]—went off to look; when it had been found, he said: "Now then, Pyotr, go away somewhere for the whole day, and at nine o'clock this evening go directly to the new apartment."

He did so. Everything was already put away, hung up and nailed in its place. No sooner had he finished his tea than he heard the sound of scales—a lady at her singing lesson. At first he listened patiently, then it began to irritate him and, finally, it simply drove him to the brink of despair. He had his own work to do, but it was impossible. These lessons did not let him think. Thus passed the first day. The second was the same. He listened and listened, then suddenly grabbed a poker lying nearby and started banging it against the ceiling, shouting: "Be quiet, for God's sake, be quiet!" But she just kept singing. Then he went straight to the old man and asked him to look for another apartment at once, even though he had already paid for the month, and he moved out.

There is a story that one time a lady said to him at a party: "Pyotr Ilyich, how lucky you are! Everyone so loves your music and worships you for your music!" And he replied thus: "Do you really suppose that music alone can bring me happiness? There are some moments when I hate it!" And tears came to his eyes. The lady was mortified. Afraid to embarrass him utterly for having seen his tears, she quickly moved away from him, saying: "A man, and he's crying? He must be very miserable indeed."

Pyotr Ilyich was extremely touchy. Alina Kh[vosto]va, the sister of my *belle-soeur*, graduated from the Conservatory at almost the same time as he, in the singing class. He very much liked her voice—a contralto. Once she was preparing to give a concert. My husband composed a song for her, which he dedicated to her, and on the morning of the day before the concert he hurried over almost at a run to deliver it. This song was "None but the lonely heart" ("*Net, tol'ko tot, kto znal*"). . . .[63]

He flew headlong into the house; there was only one copy finished and the sheets were still damp. She sat down at the piano, performed it, and for some reason did not like it. She thanked Pyotr Ilyich dryly but she did not sing the song at her concert.

He was terribly insulted and, I think, after that was always somewhat cool toward her. Later she sang the song at every one of her concerts and created quite a sensation with it. But all the same, his resentment remained.

Another time he composed a concerto, I do not know which one exactly, dedicated it to Nikolay Rubinstein, and brought the manuscript to the Conservatory, where he asked him to take a look at it.[64] Nikolay Rubinstein sat at the piano and played it all the way through, then said: "It's very good, but very long," and, saying that some things could be cut out, he began quickly striking out several passages with a pencil. Pyotr Ilyich was silent. Then he said, "Well, good-bye," left the room and with rapid steps headed home, where he went over to his writing desk, crossed out the dedication to Nikolay Rubinstein, wrote "Dedicated to Hans von Bülow," and immediately sent the manuscript to him by mail. Bülow gave a concert shortly thereafter and he played this piece. Everyone liked it enormously.[65]

Pyotr Ilyich was also friendly with Bülow, and for a long time I kept a letter from Bülow to my husband in which he wrote, shortly after our wedding, when we were still together: "Well, I've followed your example and have just gotten married too."

Let me conclude my reminiscences about my dear, unforgettable husband with his own definition of his character. "My character," he used to say constantly, "is a blend of an old man and a child." This was an extremely apt comparison. Everyone who knew the late Pyotr Ilyich closely will agree that his character cannot be better and more accurately defined.

Nikolay Kashkin

[In the summer of 1877] I heard from someone outside our circle, I don't remember who exactly, a report that Pyotr Tchaikovsky had recently married a former student of the Conservatory, and that the wedding had taken place in Moscow, at the Church of St. George, where the dean was a professor at the Conservatory, Dimitry Razumovsky, with whom our Conservatory circle was on friendly terms. The news was so unexpected and strange that at first I simply refused to believe it, for it was not unusual for the most ridiculous rumors to spread through Moscow (as I had experienced in my own regard). However, in this case one soon had no choice but to believe, and the news came to me like a blast of cold air when [Karl] Albrecht confirmed the report, he himself sadly wondering about its meaning and significance.[66]

It was not the actual fact of Pyotr Ilyich's marriage that struck me so unpleasantly, since he . . . himself had sometimes spoken to me of the possibility

and even desirability of such a step, though in a somewhat joking manner—
which, however, was his habit whenever he wished to find out someone's
opinion without asking the question directly. From Albrecht's account I learned
that Tchaikovsky had zealously hidden his intention, not even telling Albrecht,
with whom he was close friends, until after the wedding had already taken
place, and that before this he had even kept his arrival in Moscow a secret,
though it later turned out that he had not gone far, spending the entire period
before the wedding at Konstantin Shilovsky's country home near Novyi Yerusalim, where he and Shilovsky composed the libretto for *Eugene Onegin*.

In the secrecy with which Pyotr Ilyich had surrounded his marriage I
imagined that I saw something threatening, for given the close relations that
existed between Pyotr Ilyich and his nearest Conservatory friends, such secrecy
seemed utterly inexplicable. For the time being, however, everything was to
remain obscure and incomprehensible, since the newlyweds, as Albrecht told
me, had left Moscow.

Ordinarily I would stay on at my country home as long as possible, traveling into Moscow for the entrance examinations and even every day at the start
of classes. When I met Nikolay Rubinstein and Nikolay Hubert, we scarcely
spoke of Tchaikovsky and his marriage, as we were all quite at a loss, sensing
something bad about this event and fearing to speak of it. Being genuinely fond
of Tchaikovsky and valuing so highly his significance for art, our circle was
seriously worried about what consequences might result from the altered living
situation of our friend, recognizing, however, that everything depended on who
and what Pyotr Ilyich's chosen one, to us unknown, turned out to be.

Yet it turned out that this chosen one was known to at least a few people, for
several years before she had spent a year as a student at the Moscow Conservatory. At that time the number of students was less than two hundred, and we
knew almost all of them, at least by sight and in terms of their musical ability.
The student Milyukova, who was now Mrs. Tchaikovsky, was in this respect an
exception, and none of the individuals I have mentioned in our circle knew or
remembered her, with the exception of Albrecht, who had a fuzzy recollection
of a young woman from whom he, as inspector of the Conservatory, had
received documents when she entered the Conservatory and to whom he had
returned them when she left. That left only the instructor of the piano class in
which Miss Milyukova was enrolled, and whom she had also had for a class in
elementary theory. This instructor was Eduard Langer, a fine musician and a
good friend of ours, though he made relatively few appearances among our
group, as his cultural interests, apart from music, had little in common with
ours. When one of us asked him about Miss Milyukova, Langer mentioned that
in May Tchaikovsky had also asked about her and received in reply a sharply
laconic and coarsely negative characterization, which he now repeated, since

he had nothing more to add. We knew that Langer's judgments about his students were chiefly conditioned by the degree of attentiveness the latter showed to their studies in general and to his class requirements in particular, and therefore we could only conclude from his response that Miss Milyukova had proved an unsatisfactory student in his piano class.

From Albrecht we learned that Tchaikovsky had rented a new apartment on Nikitsky Boulevard. . . . At first Antonina moved into the apartment alone and set about putting it in order, with which Albrecht, at Tchaikovsky's request, helped her. He was the only one of us to meet her. Tchaikovsky himself was at this time staying with his sister in Kiev Province, having gone there alone upon returning with his wife from Petersburg, where he had presented her to his father and brothers.

When Tchaikovsky arrived in Moscow, having missed the beginning of classes, he came straight to the Conservatory. He displayed an exaggeratedly relaxed, cheerful air, but it smacked of artificiality. Pyotr Ilyich never knew how to dissemble, and the more he tried, the more obvious his pretense became. Noticing his nervous excitement, we all treated him most carefully, asking nothing, and waited for him to introduce us to his wife. But whenever Tchaikovsky came to the Conservatory for classes or on some other business, he was always in a hurry to leave, citing the fuss of putting the apartment in order.

We finally saw the young couple at the home of Pyotr Jurgenson, who arranged for this purpose a supper party, to which Tchaikovsky's closest Conservatory friends were invited. At that time I had a great many classes, often finishing quite late, and on this occasion I arrived at Jurgenson's to find everyone already gathered. There for the first time I met Antonina, who made a generally agreeable impression both by her appearance and by her modest manner. I struck up a conversation with her about something or other and could not help noticing that Tchaikovsky himself scarcely left us the whole time. Antonina seemed either shy or to be having difficulty in finding the right words, and occasionally Pyotr Ilyich during her involuntary pauses would speak for her or supplement what she had said. Our conversation was so trifling that I might never have been struck by his intervention, had it not been so overly persistent whenever his wife entered into a conversation with anyone. Such attention was not quite natural and seemed to be evidence of his fear that Antonina might have difficulty carrying on a normal conversation. On the whole, our new acquaintance made a favorable yet a rather colorless impression. A few days later, when some of us had gathered in the director's office at the Conservatory during a break between classes, Nikolay Rubinstein, recalling Jurgenson's party and speaking about Antonina, said: "She is pretty and has nice manners, but otherwise is not especially likable: as though she weren't real but just packaged goods." For all its vagueness, such a description was nevertheless fitting, since Antonina did in fact give an impression of someone who was "not real."

For most of those at Jurgenson's party this first meeting with Antonina was also the last, for the Tchaikovskys never again appeared in our midst as a couple. At Jurgenson's, Tchaikovsky, bidding us good-night, said that they had not yet got the apartment quite in order, and expressed the hope to have an opportunity to visit us soon, and later to welcome us in their home, and for our part we assured him of our willingness to comply with his wish.

The days went by, and Tchaikovsky showed up for his classes at the Conservatory with his usual undeviating punctuality, but he would leave as soon as they were over, obviously hoping to avoid conversation. His feigned calm and cheerfulness of the first few days after his arrival disappeared entirely, his appearance growing ever more anxious and gloomy, so that it became awkward even to try to talk to him, for, knowing him, one could expect a nervous attack at any moment.

In late September, he arrived at the Conservatory at the start of morning classes with such a painfully tortured look on his face that even now I remember it clearly. Somehow managing not even to look at me, he held out to me a telegram and said that he needed to leave. The telegram was signed by Nápravník and requested his immediate presence in Petersburg. He told Nikolay Rubinstein that he was leaving by the mail train and did not know when he would be able to return.

Two or three days passed, and we learned, I don't remember how, that no sooner had he arrived in Petersburg than Pyotr Ilyich suffered a violent nervous disorder, prompting very serious fears for his psychological state. A short time later Anatoly Tchaikovsky arrived in Moscow, staying with Nikolay Rubinstein and bearing not terribly comforting news. He told us that Pyotr Ilyich's disorder was of a most severe nature, and that the patient, on the advice of the then well-known psychiatrist [Ivan] Balinsky, was being sent abroad in the company of his brother Modest.[67] I do not know in what manner Balinsky acquainted himself with the general state and living conditions of his patient, but from the very outset he not only recognized the impossibility of his living together with his wife but emphatically insisted on the necessity of the couple's complete separation forever, and indeed even banning them from ever seeing each other in the future. No doubt the patient in his delirium said something that led him to such a conclusion, because neither the brothers nor the father could have told him anything, as they themselves knew nothing.[68]

The chief reason for Anatoly Tchaikovsky's visit was to inform Antonina of the psychiatrist's verdict and to work out the various property and other arrangements to result from the couple's permanent separation. On learning the purpose of his guest's visit, Nikolay Rubinstein, with his usual forcefulness, decided to intervene in the business, as he did not entirely trust Anatoly, fearing that his kind and gentlehearted nature might make him reticent, that he might not spell things out clearly enough and so leave room for misunderstanding. He therefore resolved to handle the more delicate part of the interview himself and went along with Anatoly to call on Antonina, having notified her of their visit beforehand.

I do not remember whether I ever heard anything from Rubinstein himself about his negotiations with Antonina, but Anatoly told me of the encounter immediately afterward, for the most part concentrating on Nikolay Rubinstein's role in it. According to Anatoly Tchaikovsky, they were met very warmly, and Antonina ordered tea prepared. Nikolay Rubinstein got straight down to the business at hand, describing Pyotr Ilyich's unhealthy condition and telling her, with unbending precision and determination, of Balinsky's conclusion that they must separate for good. Anatoly said that the cruel precision of the words made him go hot and cold all over, but his companion sternly and resolutely continued his harangue until he had said everything he had to say. Antonina heard him out with surprising calm, said that for the sake of "Pyotr" she agreed to everything, and offered her guests the tea that had been brought in the meantime. Having drunk a cup, Rubinstein rose and said that, adjudging the general situation to be clear, he would depart and leave the two of them to discuss, as he put it, "family" matters. Antonina saw him to the door and, returning with a radiant face, said to Anatoly: "Well, I never expected that Rubinstein would be drinking tea at my home today!" These words at such a moment astounded Anatoly, just as they astounded me when he told of them, and it was only many years later that I found what seems to me a likely explanation for them.

Tchaikovsky was taken to Italy. We at the Conservatory would receive news of his condition, which began to offer hope for his recovery. Nikolay Rubinstein expressed his firm belief in the patient's complete recovery and the restoration of his strength and abilities, but when speaking to me of this he would add sadly that, as far as the Conservatory was concerned, he believed Tchaikovsky was lost forever.

For a short time I became Antonina's piano instructor, thus forming a closer acquaintance with her. She always behaved equably and warmly with me, sometimes inviting me to have tea with her and conversing on various topics, and on occasion even referring quite indifferently to "Petya," which always jarred on me, for the intimacy of this diminutive form of his name [Pyotr] in the present situation seemed to me quite inappropriate, especially given her imperturbably calm tone. It seemed to me a remarkable anomaly that my short-term pupil combined such a fine musical ear with an utter lack of musical ability, something I have never encountered so vividly in my life since. Her hands were also nicely shaped, so that technically she played the piano rather well, but, at the same time, a faculty for artistic musical sensitivity and perception seemed to be completely absent, so that her playing was entirely devoid of life or meaning.

My lessons with Antonina soon ended, I don't remember why, and I never saw her again. When she left Moscow she sold all the furnishings in the apartment, which she had been allowed to keep, and through someone I managed to acquire an old writing desk of Tchaikovsky's which he had bought at Sukharevaya Bashnya and which had served him for a good many years. Recently I gave this desk to the Moscow Conservatory, where it is now housed in their museum. . . .

The Tchaikovskys' life together as husband and wife lasted a very brief time, only a few weeks, but it deeply affected my late friend, and, it seemed to me, the episode had a morbid effect upon his soul to the end of his life, like something painful and degrading that he could never shake off. Only after his marriage did that hopelessly melancholy furrow lay upon his face, which would later leave him only in moments of particularly cheerful animation or in those even rarer moments of a brief return to that sincere, half-childish merriment that had earlier been inherent in his nature.

On one of my extended visits to Tchaikovsky [in Frolovskoye, in the summer of 1890] we were sitting together one day after a walk. The day was drawing to a close, and though it was not yet late, the rooms were already growing dark. Some letters and newspapers had been brought from the post office, and I picked up the papers while Tchaikovsky began looking through his mail. We were both sitting near a round table, each engaged in his own reading. After glancing through the papers, I laid them aside and saw that Tchaikovsky was sitting with his gaze fixed somewhere off in the distance, lost in thought. We sat a long while without speaking; then Tchaikovsky, as if coming awake, turned to me, saying, "Read this letter, please," and handed me the folded sheets of writing paper he held in his hand. Taking the letter, I saw first the signature of Antonina Tchaikovsky, which quite surprised me, as I had heard from Jurgenson, who had been entrusted with paying Antonina the subsidy granted her, that no direct contact existed between the spouses. In my conversations with Tchaikovsky himself there had never been the slightest allusion to anything having to do with his marriage.

The letter turned out to be fairly long, for it took up two sheets of large-format letter paper, entirely covered with writing. The handwriting, to be sure, was large and spaced-out, but scrupulously traced and quite fine. The letter was well written and seemed to contain some passionate inquiries, since it was strewn with exclamation and question marks. When I read the letter through to the end and looked over at Tchaikovsky, he answered my silent question with another question: "Well, tell me, what is this letter saying?" Only then did I realize that the letter had no definite, actual content whatsoever, though it was not only perfectly grammatical, but even written in fine epistolary style. I had to tell him that I could not define the content of what I had read, in response to which I was told: "She always writes me such letters."

We sat for a time in silence. The shadows in the room deepened to the point where I could scarcely make out my friend's face. With no preliminaries, in a flat, seemingly cheerless voice, Tchaikovsky quite unexpectedly began to tell me his story, recounting it without ever changing his tone, as if discharging an obligation. As he spoke, he gave me a fairly detailed account of his initial acquaintance with Antonina and all the events which followed, up to his final separation from her.

I have thought so much about this account, comparing it with notes I made at the time, that I cannot set it down except as though spoken by Tchaikovsky himself, whom I see vividly before me even now, almost hearing the very intonation of his speech. My rendering will no doubt be somewhat shorter than the actual story, but to a large extent, indeed for the most part, it is a literal transcription of what I heard. Perhaps I have left something out, but in any event nothing has been added.

At first Tchaikovsky told me how, in the spring of 1877, Elizaveta Lavrovskaya suggested to him the idea of writing an opera based on *Eugene Onegin,* but since I have already spoken of this in my published *Reminiscences,* I shall not repeat it, but skip to the next stage of the story.[69]

"In April or early May of 1877," said Tchaikovsky, "I received a rather long letter containing a declaration of love for me. This letter was signed by Antonina Milyukova, who said that her love had been conceived several years before, when she was a student at the Conservatory. Even though, being at the Conservatory nearly every day, I knew most of the students there, I failed to recollect anything about Miss Milyukova. Her letter mentioned that she had been in Eduard Langer's piano class—and so, running into him at the Conservatory, I asked him about his former student Milyukova, whom he, it turned out, remembered, and whom he described (as he would later to me, as I mentioned above) using a single word of profanity, without offering any explanation. I never asked anyone else about Miss Milyukova.

"At this same time I was captivated utterly and exclusively by the thought of *Eugene Onegin,* and specifically of 'Tatyana,' whose letter had first drawn me to this composition.[70] Before I had a libretto or even any general plan for the opera, I began to write the music for this letter, yielding to an irresistible emotional need to set about this project, in the heat of which I not only forgot about Miss Milyukova, but even lost her letter or hid it away so well that I could not find it, and remembered about it only after receiving a second letter some time later.[71]

"Wholly engrossed in the composition, I had come to sympathize with the figure of Tatyana to such a degree that she began to seem alive to me, together with everything around her. I loved Tatyana and was terribly indignant with Onegin, who appeared to me a cold and heartless fop. On receiving a second letter from Miss Milyukova, I felt ashamed and was even angry at myself for my attitude toward her. In her second letter she complained bitterly about not receiving a reply, adding that if this second letter were to suffer the same fate as the first, there would be nothing left for her but to take her own life.

"In my mind, all this merged with the notion of Tatyana, while I myself, it seemed to me, had behaved incomparably worse than Onegin, and I was genuinely angry at myself for my heartless treatment of a girl who had fallen in love with me. Since included with the second letter was Miss Milyukova's address, I headed there at once, and thus began our acquaintance.

"In my new acquaintance I found a modest, pretty girl, who made on the whole an agreeable impression. At our very first meeting, I told her that I was unable to return her feelings of love, but that she inspired a genuine and kind affection in me. She replied that any sympathy on my part was precious to her and that she could be content with that, or something of the sort. I promised to see her often and kept my word.

"You probably remember my mentioning several times before all this my intention to marry someone who was not young, but who possessed certain qualities which might allow her to be a good friend and life-companion. Antonina did not fit this image in that she was relatively young, but she expressed such devotion to me, such a willingness to do anything to please me, that she set, as it were, an obligation upon me to respond in kind in some way, despite the deficiency of my feelings for her. Moreover, a sincere indignation at Onegin's negligent and thoughtless treatment of Tatyana was still strong in my heart. To act like Onegin struck me as heartless and simply inadmissible on my part.

"I was in a sort of delirium. With my thoughts constantly fixed on my opera, I responded to everything else almost unconsciously or half-consciously. I remember clearly, however, my firm conviction that I must tell none of you at the Conservatory of my dealings with Antonina or the intentions arising from those dealings. I was certain that if you were to know of this, everything would have to end and I would be unable to proceed as I wished. I quite failed to realize what such a certainty was based upon, but still it was there.

"All these vague hesitations did not so much worry or upset me as hinder my composition, and I decided it best to have done with this question so as to free myself from it. Having made my decision, I went to see Antonina in the evening after my day's work and told her again that I did not love her and would probably never love her, but that if, despite this, she wished to be my wife, I was prepared to marry her. She, for her part, expressed complete consent to this, and the wedding was set. She said only that she needed to make certain preparations, put her papers in order and in general arrange things, for which it was even necessary for her to leave Moscow for a time; but the wedding was to be held shortly after her return. I did not forget to tell Antonina that our decision must be kept a strict secret, otherwise the wedding could not take place. By this I meant, primarily, that it should be kept secret from Conservatory friends, who might, in some fashion—I did not quite know how—prevent me from carrying out my intention to marry Antonina.

"Having made my decision, I did not comprehend at all its importance or even realize its meaning and significance. It was essential for me to eliminate, for the immediate future at least, anything that prevented me from concentrating on this idea for an opera that had captivated my entire being, and it seemed to me most natural and simple to act as I did, and therefore, leaving all the care and preparation for the wedding to Antonina, and feeling as though a weight had been lifted from me, I immediately left for the country estate of Shilovsky, who was working on the libretto for *Eugene Onegin,* and spent nearly an entire month there, working constantly and feeling utterly content and happy, for there was no one to bother me, and Shilovsky was working so enthusiastically on the libretto that his good spirits infected me as well.

"The Shilovsky estate, Glebovo, near Novyi Yerusalim, is a wonderful spot, with amazingly beautiful environs through which it gave me great pleasure to stroll. The house and all aspects of life at Glebovo were fastidiously furnished with every comfort, but most precious of all to me was that I was granted as much seclusion as I liked, and enjoyed the company of my hosts only when I myself desired it. I scarcely ever remembered the new way of life awaiting me, and only somewhere deep inside of me did there stir an anxious anticipation of something, which I refused to think about, considering it completely unnecessary, and, mainly, worrisome and distracting.

"The Feast of St. Peter passed, and I received word from Antonina that she had completed all the preparations, and we could be married.

"Though I hated to leave Glebovo, where I had lived and worked so well, the possibility of postponing the wedding for any appreciable length of time never occurred to me. Still, I lingered for a while, wishing to finish some of my work. Of course, I never told Shilovsky what lay in store for me, and I believe I justified my departure by saying I needed to visit my father in Petersburg.

"On arriving in Moscow, I hastened to be done with the burdensome business as quickly as possible and wrote to my father, among others, about my plans to marry, fully certain that he would be quite pleased with my decision. I

invited only my brother Anatoly to come for the ceremony, which was scheduled for sometime in the next few days, and he arrived in Moscow at once.

"I carried on in a sort of daze. Turning to Dmitry Razumovsky, I asked him
to marry us in his church. With his usual infinite kindness, he had somehow a
good effect on me, boosting my spirits and freeing me from all the formalities,
and performing the sacrament of marriage with his characteristic artistic
beauty, which I could not help noticing, despite the importance of the moment.
But still I remained a kind of outside figure, uninvolved, until Dmitry Razumovsky, at the close of the ceremony, made Antonina and me kiss each other.
At this point, a pain struck my heart and such an anxiety gripped me that I think
I began to weep, but I made an effort to master myself quickly and assume an
air of calm. Anatoly, however, had noticed my state, for he started to say
something encouraging to me.

"That evening we left for Petersburg, where we spent, I believe, an entire
week, visiting relatives and a few friends. During those days I began to perceive
the whole terrible significance of my action and the desperateness of the
position in which I now found myself.

"I sincerely wished and tried to be a good husband, but this proved beyond
my strength. From the very first days of our life together I realized with dread
that we had no interests in common, and that everything I lived for was
absolutely alien to Antonina, though she evidently sought to comprehend me
and make herself agreeable to me. Her general development was quite peculiar,
indeed I had never suspected the possibility of anything like it. She had heard
and knew of a great many things, but she lacked utterly the ability to find in her
heart a response to anything but the most commonplace necessities of life. And
it was not that she refused to understand any of this—the most dreadful thing
was that she was absolutely incapable of assimilating anything, with the
exception of the most elementary conditions of existence. I cannot describe to
you my state when I realized that I would have to spend the entire remainder of
my life with this completely alien creature. The sympathy I was just beginning
to feel for her turned to revulsion, and, burdened by the intolerableness of my
situation, I shamefully fled under the pretext of needing to travel to the
Caucasus to take a water cure. I said I would stop on the way to see my sister,
in Kiev Province, and departed alone, leaving Antonina to put the apartment in
order.

"I did not go to the Caucasus, but instead spent about a month at my sister's
home, where I soon began to feel able even to work again. At Kamenka with my
sister I breathed freely again and tried to gather my strength for the battle with
myself, but, unfortunately, the rest ended all too soon, and I had to return to
Moscow for classes at the Conservatory.

"On my arrival in Moscow, I found my new apartment almost completely in order. Antonina had added some of the furnishings using her own money, and she had been helped in all this, as it turned out, by Albrecht, who had met my wife earlier. Everything in the apartment was comfortable and even quite nice, but this very comfort merely set off still more starkly what I already saw as the clear impossibility of existing under these conditions. Antonina, with her smooth, placid attitude toward everything around her, seemed to me even more narrow than before, and her mere presence oppressed me terribly. I was fully aware that I alone was to blame in all this, that nothing in the world could help me, and that therefore there was nothing for it but to endure it as long as I was able, and to hide my unhappiness from everyone. I don't know what exactly prompted this latter need to hide: was it only pride, or was it also the fear of causing pain to my family and casting upon them the shadow of what seemed to me my crime?

"In such a state it was quite natural to come to the conclusion that only death could free me, and this became my cherished wish, though I did not dare commit suicide obviously or openly, out of fear of dealing too cruel a blow to my elderly father, or to my brothers. I started thinking about ways of disappearing less noticeably, as though from natural causes. One such way I even attempted.

"Though no more than a week had passed since my return from my sister's, I had already lost all ability to struggle against the burden of my position, and at times my perception, as I myself could feel, began to grow dull. By day I would still try to work at home, but the evenings became unbearable to me. Not daring to visit any of my friends or even the theater, I went out to walk every evening, wandering aimlessly for hours through the remote and lonely streets of Moscow. The weather grew gloomy and cold, and the nights were freezing. On one such night I came to the deserted banks of the Moskva River, and the possibility occurred to me of catching a fatal chill. With this aim, seeing no one in the darkness, I waded into the water almost to my waist and remained there as long as I could endure the ache in my body from the cold. I left the water with the firm conviction that I could not escape death from pneumonia or some other respiratory illlness, when I got home I said that I had been taking part in some night fishing and accidentally fallen into the water. My constitution, however, proved so strong that I survived my icy bath with no ill effects.

"I did not have time to make any other attempt of this sort, for I had come to feel that I could not exist under these conditions and wrote to my brother Anatoly to telegraph me in Nápravník's name that I was urgently needed in Petersburg, which Anatoly did at once.

"Concerning my stay in Petersburg, I recall very little, and that by chance. I remember severe nervous fits, I remember [Doctor] Balinsky, my father and brothers, but nothing more.

"Modest and I went first, as you know, to Italy, probably at the doctor's instructions, but this was a most unfortunate choice, for the light and brilliance of the Italian sun and the splendor of Italy's autumn landscape suited too little my mood at the time and heightened my depression. Once I even tried, remembering stories about this, to drive away the melancholy with wine, but since Modest would not allow me to drink much wine openly, like a thief I secretly brought two bottles of cognac to my room and hid them. When we parted for bed that evening, I locked the door to my room and began drinking the cognac from a glass in large gulps. You know that in a normal state I probably couldn't finish a single glass before collapsing dead drunk, but this time I drank down both bottles without feeling intoxicated, whereas the depression gnawing at me grew to such an extent that I don't believe I have ever experienced before or since a state as dreadful as that in which I spent the rest of that night until morning. Of course, it never again occurred to me to get rid of my depression with drink.

"Finally I began begging my brother that we go somewhere else, somewhere more northerly—and we went to Vienna, where I felt far calmer and much better. It was in Vienna, I believe, that I received your letter, and you cannot imagine what a beneficial effect it had on me: it meant that there were people who did not despise me, but sympathized with me. Even though by this time I may have been somewhat recovered and more at ease, an active encouraging word was still precious to me.

"My material situation at this time, as you know, had changed, thanks to Mrs. von Meck,[72] but I still felt moral ties binding me to the Moscow Conservatory, and assumed that I would return to Moscow and my Conservatory duties the following year and so spend the remainder of my days. You know that it turned out otherwise, but when I tried in fact to resume my classes at the Conservatory, memories came flooding back which I could not endure, and so I quit both the Conservatory and Moscow, as it seemed to me, forever. With regard to Moscow, however, this feeling soon disappeared. It even disappeared with respect to the Conservatory, and before long I might easily have taken up my duties there again, but, in the first place, this would have interfered with my composing, and, in the second, [Sergey] Taneyev, who replaced me, was a far better teacher than I, of which I was perfectly aware. My attachment to Moscow even proved so strong that I am happier living near it than anywhere else. In addition, I have grown so fond of the environs of Moscow that there is no place more attractive to me among all the lands I have seen."

Tchaikovsky concluded his story as he began it, in a flat voice, his intonation barely rising, but at the same time, one could hear that he was extremely agitated and that the flatness of his voice was the result of a great effort to restrain himself and to keep his nerves in check. I myself, as his listener, was so agitated that later I could not for the life of me remember, even approximately, how long the tale had lasted. Apparently quite some time, for it grew completely dark, and by the end we could scarcely see one another. When the story was finished, we went to supper and spent the evening as usual—reading or playing piano duets—but neither that evening nor anytime later did we ever exchange any thoughts concerning the story. There was no way I could ever bring the topic up, for I saw that such memories cost Tchaikovsky dearly, nor did he ever again return to the subject with so much as an allusion. No doubt Tchaikovsky felt a need to unburden himself to someone close to him, and the arrival of the letter in my presence had provided the impetus for this—and I am probably the only person to whom Tchaikovsky ever spoke of this sad episode in his life.

VI

The Composer
(1878–1892)

At the end of 1876 a new woman entered Tchaikovsky's life. This was Nadezhda von Meck, the widow of a railway tycoon. She had heard and admired some of Tchaikovsky's music, and when she found out that he was encountering financial problems, she began to commission pieces from him. Both agreed on one condition, that they should never meet. Their strange relationship, carried on through over 1,200 letters, was to last for almost fourteen years. They only met twice, by accident, and hurried off without greeting each other. When Mrs. von Meck learned what had happened with Tchaikovsky during his abortive marriage, she agreed on his request to arrange for him to receive a regular allowance of 6,000 rubles. In this way the composer resolved his permanent financial crisis. Mrs. von Meck's money allowed him to dedicate himself to creative work.

At the end of 1877 and the beginning of 1878 Tchaikovsky and his brother Anatoly (later replaced by Modest) proceeded with their European tour through Switzerland, France, Italy, and Austria, hoping to put the disastrous business of Tchaikovsky's marriage firmly behind them. Iosif Kotek arrived at the end of November in Vienna and spent some time traveling with the brothers. By January 1878 Tchaikovsky had finished his Fourth Symphony, the first of his mature symphonic works, which he dedicated to Nadezhda von Meck. The other major work which occupied him during the period of his ill-fated marriage was the opera *Eugene Onegin*. At first the opera made little impression on audiences, and it took several years to achieve the public success it deserved. One other masterpiece also emerged from this period of self-exile: the Violin Concerto, written in Switzerland, which was inspired by Iosif Kotek, but which he dedicated for opportunistic reasons to the famous violinist Leopold Auer.[1] At first, however, the concerto suffered the same fate as the First Piano Concerto: Auer claimed it was far too difficult and refused to play it. In 1881 another violinist, Adolf Brodsky,[2] gave the first performance in Vienna, after which the famous critic Eduard Hanslick,[3] in his newspaper review of the concert, declared that the music "gave off a bad smell." Like the Piano Concerto, the

Violin Concerto is now established as one of the best-loved concertos by musicians and audiences alike.

In April 1878, Tchaikovsky returned to Russia depressed by the prospect of teaching and short of inspiration. Nevertheless, he finished some smaller piano pieces, including the popular "Children's Album" [Detskii al'bom]. Returning to Moscow after his usual summer visit to Kamenka, and also after a visit to Brailov, Mrs. von Meck's estate, he took a decisive step. He resigned his teaching job at the Conservatory, and shortly thereafter set off on his travels once again. He was to spend the next few years constantly on the move, avoiding Moscow and St. Petersburg as much as possible.

First he traveled to Florence, then to Paris, and then to Clarens in Switzerland, where he started to work on another opera, The Maid of Orleans [Orleanskaia deva], which was not one of his greatest successes. Back in Russia by autumn, he began a Second Piano Concerto. Later he traveled to Rome, where he composed the Italian Capriccio [Ital'ianskoe kaprichchio] for orchestra. Tchaikovsky then returned to his homeland, where he spent much of 1880 in the country. There he completed the Serenade for Strings and the piece most often associated with his name—the 1812 Overture, a commemoration of the historic Russian defeat of Napoleon's army. Early in 1881, still in Rome, Tchaikovsky learned that the seriously ill Nikolay Rubinstein had gone to Paris for treatment, where he soon died. Tchaikovsky rushed to Paris to pay his last respects to Rubinstein, and in December he began working on a musical memorial, the Piano trio dedicated "To the memory of a great artist," op. 50. This trio was first played on 11 March 1882 in Moscow with Sergey Taneyev (piano), Jan Hřimalý (violin), and Wilhelm Fitzenhagen (cello).[4] By now Tchaikovsky's music was being performed more often, thanks in large degree to the efforts of the late Nikolay Rubinstein, who had played and conducted a Tchaikovsky program at the Paris Exhibition of 1878 and premiered many of his new compositions in Moscow, though rarely with total success.

The main work of 1882–83 was the opera Mazepa, based upon Pushkin's epic poem Poltava. In the course of its composition Tchaikovsky's enthusiasm flagged considerably. Writing to Mrs. von Meck on 14 September 1882 he admitted: "Never has any important work given me so much trouble as this opera. Perhaps it is the decline of my powers, or have I become more severe in my self-judgment?"[5] Mazepa was performed in both Moscow and St. Petersburg in February 1884, but Tchaikovsky left for Europe without attending the St. Petersburg premiere, since the opera was not very cordially received in Moscow. He had hardly spent three weeks in the French capital before he was summoned back to Russia to appear before Alexander III, to receive an official decoration— the Order of St. Vladimir.

By the beginning of 1885 the composer was feeling the need to cease his restless wandering and settle down. He found a manor house in Maidanovo, near Klin, in the countryside outside Moscow. This residence also had the advantage of being on the direct line between Moscow and St. Petersburg. He moved there on 14 February. The view from the windows and the quiet and sense of being at home delighted him. Soon he settled down to a regular routine: reading, walking in the forest, working in the mornings and afternoons, and playing cards or duets with friends in the evenings. He wrote to his brother: "I am contented, cheerful and at peace."[6] He was occupied at this time with the revision of *Vakula the Smith*, with the new title *Cherevichki*, and also a new opera based on Ippolit Shpazhinsky's play *The Sorceress [Charodeika]*, a story about an innkeeper's daughter who is courted by two princes—father and son—with predictably disastrous consequences.[7] In May, Tchaikovsky began to fulfill a promise made to Balakirev to compose a symphonic work on the subject of Lord Byron's *Manfred*. This task cost Tchaikovsky an immense effort and was finished only in September 1885. All that autumn he continued to work on *The Sorceress* while traveling for a few days or weeks at a time to Moscow, St. Petersburg, and Kamenka.

On 11 March 1886, *Manfred* was successfully performed for the first time in Moscow, conducted by Max von Erdmannsdörfer.[8] Tchaikovsky was very pleased. At the end of this month he decided to visit his brothers—Ippolit in Taganrog near Rostov and Anatoly in Tiflis in the Caucasus. At Tiflis, where he spent the entire month of April, he met with a triumphant reception: a concert was organized on 19 April consisting entirely of his works, conducted by his great admirer Mikhail Ippolitov-Ivanov.[9] The concert was followed by a supper and the presentation of a silver wreath. From the Caucasus Tchaikovsky traveled by sea to France, where in Paris he met Léo Delibes, Ambroise Thomas, and Gabriel Fauré, and spent almost a month combining professional meetings with entertainment.[10] In the middle of June he returned to Russia to continue work on *The Sorceress*.

At the beginning of October the composer paid a visit to St. Petersburg in order to be present at the first performance of Eduard Nápravník's opera *Harold [Garol'd]* and to meet Rimsky-Korsakov, Glazunov, and Lyadov.[11]

The first performance of the new version of *Vakula the Smith*, *Cherevichki* took place at the Bolshoy Theater in Moscow on 19 January 1887. The experience had a far-reaching influence on Tchaikovsky's future, for it was then that he made his first successful attempt as a conductor. The opera was a great success, perhaps due to the composer's presence, but it lasted in repertory for only two seasons. Tchaikovsky appeared in the capacity of conductor again on 5 March at one of the concerts of the St. Petersburg Philharmonic Society, which was totally devoted to his works. Now he began to think of venturing on a concert tour abroad. He spent most of the spring at Maidanovo at work on the orchestration of *The Sorceress*. At the end of May, he set off on another Caucasian journey to visit his brother Anatoly, making a pleasant steamer trip down the Volga from Nizhny Novgorod to Astrakhan and through the Caspian Sea to Baku, then on to Tiflis and Borzhom. In Borzhom he received a telegram from his old friend Nikolay Kondratyev, who was near death in Aachen.[12] Tchaikovsky decided to visit him there, and on 15 July he was already in Aachen, where he spent over a month, pondering about God, life, and death, while watching Kondratyev's agonizing end.

On 20 October 1887 his new opera *The Sorceress* was produced at the Maryinsky Theater in St. Petersburg. Tchaikovsky conducted again but, in spite of a personal ovation, the opera left audiences cold. On the seventh night, the work was sung to a half-empty house and was soon withdrawn. On 14 November, Tchaikovsky conducted another successful concert in Moscow consisting of his own works, including the premiere of his fourth orchestral suite, *Mozartiana*. At the end of December he set out on his first European concert tour as a conductor, which included Leipzig, Berlin, Prague, Hamburg, Paris, and London. It was a very successful tour, especially in Prague, Paris, and London, where Tchaikovsky met several well-known composers (among them Brahms, Grieg, and Dvořák) and established good relationships with many famous musicians.

In the middle of March 1888, Tchaikovsky returned to Russia and visited his brother Ippolit in Taganrog and his brother Anatoly in Tiflis. He returned home only in the middle of April. This time he moved into a new house in Frolovskoye, a village which, like Maidanovo, was located near the small town of Klin. There he began a new symphony, the Fifth, inspired by the death of his friend Nikolay Kondratyev. The Fifth Symphony was first performed under Tchaikovsky's baton in St. Petersburg on 5 November 1888 and was well received, despite discouraging reviews. At the end of November Tchaikovsky traveled to Prague, where he conducted a successful performance of *Eugene Onegin*.

In December 1888 he retired to Frolovskoye for six weeks in order to compose a ballet, *The Sleeping Beauty [Spiashchaia krasavitsa]*, op. 66, based on the old French fairy tale and commissioned by the directors of the St. Petersburg Theaters. Tchaikovsky worked with genuine enthusiasm until he was forced to lay the work aside to go on another concert tour at the end of January 1889. He made his first appearance as composer on 31 January at a concert in Cologne, whence he traveled to Frankfurt am Main, Dresden, Berlin, Leipzig, Geneva, and finally back north to Hamburg. Here he found himself in the same hotel as Brahms and felt gratified to hear that the concert performance of his Fifth Symphony had pleased the latter, with the exception of the finale. Before going to London at the end of March 1889, as was scheduled, Tchaikovsky spent a few weeks in Paris. After the London concert he returned to Russia by way of the Mediterranean, stopping in Batum on the Black Sea and visiting his brother Anatoly in Tiflis. The local music society again celebrated his visit with concerts of his works. The summer of 1889 was spent as usual in his country home, and his time was occupied by the completion and orchestration of the ballet *Sleeping Beauty*.

Tchaikovsky spent the greater part of the autumn of 1889 traveling between St. Petersburg and Moscow, conducting concerts of his own works, those of Anton Rubinstein (on the occasion of the latter's Jubilee Festival), and rehearsing his new ballet at the Maryinsky Theater. The first performance of *Sleeping Beauty* took place on 3 January 1890 in a splendid production, choreographed by Marius Petipa.[13] The day before, Alexander III had expressed his approval of the ballet at a gala rehearsal attended by the Imperial Court.

On 14 January 1890 Tchaikovsky went to Florence where he began work on another opera, *The Queen of Spades,* op. 68, the libretto of which had been adapted from Pushkin's novella by his brother Modest. Tchaikovsky composed the opera with an enthusiasm almost without parallel in his career. The entire score was written in a fit of creative frenzy that lasted forty-four days. In the process, as we learn from Tchaikovsky's letters, the composer came to identify with its characters and its action. "I almost totally lost my appetite, my sleep, my cheerful disposition, in a word, all the attributes of health," he wrote to a friend soon after finishing, "but I really performed a heroic deed and wrote a great opera in seven weeks."[14] Elsewhere Tchaikovsky wrote: "I worked on [the opera] with unbelievable ardor and excitement, and actually experienced everything that happens in the story, at one time even fearing the appearance of the old dame's specter, and I hope that my authorial tumult and absorption will echo in the hearts of the audience."[15]

As was the case with almost every one of Tchaikovsky's major compositions, the immediate public and critical response to *The Queen of Spades* was mixed at the St. Petersburg production, first presented on 7 December 1890. While he never doubted the quality of his art, the composer was genuinely modest and sensitive to unfavorable feedback. Furthermore, he tended to deprecate his own work and lose interest in it upon completion. Not so with *The Queen of Spades*. Despite the skepticism of some, he adamantly held to the belief that the music of this opera belonged among the finest in the world. The judgment of posterity has proved him right.

All summer 1890 Tchaikovsky spent in Frolovskoye preoccupied with the finishing touches for this opera and composing the string sextet *Souvenir de Florence,* op. 70. On 19 December 1890 he was present at a very successful production of *The Queen of Spades* in Kiev. In September, however, he had received a letter from Mrs. von Meck informing him that she was on the brink of financial ruin and therefore unable to continue his allowance. This abrupt news wounded and depressed him for a long time.

His satisfaction with *The Queen of Spades* led Tchaikovsky to accept two more commissions from the Imperial Theaters, for the opera *Iolanta* and the ballet *The Nutcracker [Shchelkunchik]*. In the meantime, however, Tchaikovsky also accepted an invitation to conduct his own works in America on the occasion of the grand opening of Carnegie Hall in New York City. On 6 March 1891 he left Frolovskoye for Paris, where he was to conduct one of the Edouard Colonne concerts on 24 March. The success of this concert, which consisted entirely of his own works, was marred by the news of his sister Alexandra's death.

Nevertheless, he went ahead with the American tour. Tchaikovsky sailed from Le Havre on 6/18 April 1891 and landed in New York on the 14/26th. On the voyage, and throughout his American visit, he kept a diary of his experiences. Tchaikovsky conducted six concerts in which his own works were performed: four in New York, one in Baltimore, and one in Philadelphia. He also visited Niagara Falls. The composer was greatly impressed and heartened by the warmth and hospitality of his American hosts and by the enthusiastic reception given his music. On 9/21 May 1891 he sailed back from New York to Hamburg feeling fully gratified with his American tour.

Back home, Tchaikovsky returned to the composition of the ballet *The Nutcracker*, op. 71, based on E. T. A. Hoffman's fantasy story (but in the version by Alexandre Dumas *père*). This he finished at the end of June, whereupon he immediately commenced work on the one-act opera *Iolanta*, op. 69, the story of a blind princess, set in medieval Aix-en-Provence. In addition, Tchaikovsky composed a symphonic ballad, *Voivode*, op. 78, based on a poem by Pushkin and the Polish poet Adam Mickiewicz. On 4 November 1891, Tchaikovsky was in Moscow for the first performance of *The Queen of Spades* at the Bolshoy Theater and, two days later, to conduct *Voivode* at Alexander Siloti's concert.[16] This time, the opera enjoyed tremendous success. But after the performance of *Voivode* Tchaikovsky developed a strong dislike for the work and actually tore up the score, which was reconstructed only after his death.

At the end of 1891 we find Tchaikovsky traveling on a new concert tour. This time he visited Kiev and Warsaw before proceeding on to Germany. From Warsaw he went by way of Berlin to Hamburg in order to be present at a first performance of *Eugene Onegin*, conducted by Gustav Mahler. Toward the close of his life Tchaikovsky often felt overcome by the homesickness that attacked him whenever he left Russia. On this occasion he even abandoned a concert for which he had been engaged in Holland, going instead to Paris and then back home. At the end of February 1892 Tchaikovsky traveled to St. Petersburg where he conducted his *Romeo and Juliet* as well as the first performance of the *Nutcracker Suite*, which was received with immense enthusiasm.

On 5 April 1892 Tchaikovsky moved into another new home in the same area around Klin. This time it was a larger house on the outskirts of the town itself, right next to the Petersburg highway but surrounded by fields and woods. At the end of April he successfully conducted Gounod's *Faust*, Anton Rubinstein's *The Demon*, and *Eugene Onegin* in Moscow at Ippolit Prianishnikov's Private Opera. In May, Tchaikovsky began work on a symphony in E-flat, but the sketches he produced to this end—which were in some state of completion by October—did not satisfy him. Almost a year later they were used as the basis for the one-movement Third Piano Concerto, op. 75, and the Andante and Finale for Piano and Orchestra, op. 79, reworked by Taneyev after the composer's death. At the beginning of June Tchaikovsky went abroad with his nephew Bob Davydov to Vichy (France) for a short cure and spent some time in Paris. On 7 July he was back in St. Petersburg and four days later in Klin, where he dealt with the proofs of *The Nutcracker* and *Iolanta*.

Tchaikovsky and Alexander Glazunov (1865–1936) met for the first time in the autumn of 1884, at one of Balakirev's soirées, and they soon became close friends. Tchaikovsky met Glazunov on almost every visit to St. Petersburg, and they regularly exchanged letters and scores. At the Tchaikovsky Museum in Klin are many of Glazunov's scores with the composer's inscriptions to Tchaikovsky. Glazunov left few recollections about their friendship. Here are reproduced some little-known reminiscences of Glazunov, published in 1913 in the Russian newspaper *Birzhevye vedomosti*.[17] The short recollections of the conductor Eduard Nápravník (1839–1916) concerning *Eugene Onegin* have not been reprinted since 1913; they provide some additional facts about the history of the staging of Tchaikovsky's opera in St. Petersburg.[18]

The most important memoir of this period belongs to Vladimir Pogozhev (1851–1935), the manager of the Office of Imperial Theaters. It forms the centerpiece of this chapter. Pogozhev's reminiscences were written especially for the collection of letters and memoirs edited by Igor Glebov[19] and were first published in 1924.[20] Full of valuable and occasionally amusing details about the first performances of Tchaikovsky's operas and ballets, Pogozhev's memoirs show us a Tchaikovsky seen through the eyes of a Petersburg bureaucrat.

The French writer and musicologist Romain Rolland (1866–1944) observed Tchaikovsky during the composer's Paris concerts in 1888 and left a remarkable record of them in his diary.[21] The English music critic Herman Klein (1856–1934) also had the opportunity to see the composer during an 1888 concert, this time in London, which he described at great length in a London newspaper.[22] At the same time, at the end of 1888, Tchaikovsky met in Russia with Julius Block (1858–1934), an American businessman who specialized in importing to Russia the Edison phonograph and other technical equipment, and who owned a large typewriter and bicycle shop in Moscow. Block was a passionate music lover and something of a patron of the arts. In 1930, Block wrote his memoirs about his encounters with Edison, Nikisch, Tchaikovsky, and Tolstoy.[23] He appears to have shown Tchaikovsky the phonograph and, possibly, to have recorded the composer's voice on the cylinder, although no such recordings are known.

In December of 1890, Tchaikovsky traveled to Kiev to attend a production of *The Queen of Spades*. This event was recounted by Varvara Tsekhovskaya (1872–?), a reporter for the newspaper *Kievskoe slovo*. Her recollections were published only in 1913 and never appeared in standard editions of memoirs about the composer.[24]

Alexander Glazunov

I met Tchaikovsky quite often both at Balakirev's and at my own home. We usually met over music. He always appeared in our social circle as one of the most welcome guests; besides myself and Lyadov, Rimsky-Korsakov and Balakirev were also constant members of our circle. Tchaikovsky always conducted himself with great dignity and confidence.

I remember asking him a question once: "Have you right now a musical idea?"

"Not right now," he answered, "but if I were to spend a couple days in the country one would appear."

I think this was typical of Tchaikovsky, a composer who was able to surround himself with musical ideas in two or three days. In general he composed extremely quickly; thus, for example, he completed rough drafts of *The Sleeping Beauty* in two or three weeks. But, on the other hand, Tchaikovsky did not like working on the development of themes after he drafted them.

"I hate to write compositions that need development," he often complained to me. . . .

I recall several quite typical instances from Tchaikovsky's life. For some reason he disliked the waltz in *Eugene Onegin*.

"My God," he complained, "why on earth did I have to compose it! Now there isn't a single street musician or restaurant that doesn't persecute me with this vulgar music."

In general he wasn't an obsessive critic of his own works, but he often castigated himself for various slips. But he told me personally that he was satisfied with his Sixth Symphony (*Pathétique*) down to the smallest details.

Eduard Nápravník

Tchaikovsky was extremely sensitive to the success of his operas, and the cool reception given to his *Vakula the Smith* (1876) in Petersburg reduced him to sobs in the greenroom. For this reason he resisted all my efforts to persuade him to mount *[Eugene] Onegin* in Petersburg, especially as he himself considered this opera unsuited to a large stage. In order to gain Tchaikovsky's consent to a production of *Onegin,* I seized the following opportunity. Emperor Alexander III, who adored Tchaikovsky, had heard excerpts from *Onegin* when he was the heir apparent, at the musical evenings at the home of Count Adlerberg.[25] One day in a conversation with me His Majesty asked why *Onegin* had not appeared on our stage. I replied: "Tchaikovsky fears it will not do well and has refused his consent for a production of this opera. But if Your Majesty orders it staged, then the composer will certainly relent." "Tell Tchaikovsky, in my name," said the Emperor, "that I wish to see *Onegin* on our stage." I gladly conveyed His Majesty's words to Tchaikovsky, and the composer gave his consent. I rehearsed the opera, which the composer himself had considered inadequate for the large stage, and it was presented at the Bolshoy Theater [in Petersburg] on 19 October 1884. Since that time, *Onegin* has had the greatest success of any Russian opera. Of the (approximately) twenty thousand rubles that Tchaikovsky's compositions bring his heirs every year (in performance royalties), the majority comes from *Onegin.*

Vladimir Pogozhev

Before meeting Pyotr Ilyich personally, I knew him from his beautiful works, such as the opera *The Maid of Orleans,* numerous songs, and, finally, the portraits I had happened to see. I became personally acquainted with Pyotr Ilyich when I had already begun to work in the theater.

I cannot recall the precise year and circumstances of our first meeting. I know that by 1884 our friendship was already established, as I have preserved a photograph of Pyotr Ilyich with his autograph, dated 1884. I only recall the impression Tchaikovsky made at my first meeting with him in the office of Ivan Vsevolozhsky, director of the [Imperial] Theaters.[26]

The gray image of Pyotr Ilyich's pleasant face, with his extremely kind, tender eyes, seemed to me to be utterly unlike the portrait I knew of him as a young man. First of all I was struck by his extreme grace and courtesy, by his gentle manner and speech, and by the simplicity and, at the same time, elegance of his appearance and dress. This impression of elegance was strengthened and renewed in me whenever I met Tchaikovsky, regardless of the circumstances, whether he was wearing tails, a fur coat, or his customary blue suitcoat. At the same meeting in Vsevolozhsky's office I noted another of Tchaikovsky's peculiarities: when he praised anything, he frequently used the words "charming," "wonderful," "delightful"; moreover, he would pronounce the latter word with some particular stretching of the syllables, like "deel-i-ight-ful!" with a strong, drawn-out stress on the letter "i." I should note incidentally that Pyotr Ilyich's brothers, Modest and Anatoly, pronounced this very word with the same expressiveness. Apparently this was some familial peculiarity or habit of the Tchaikovskys. Subsequently, many years after the death of Pyotr Ilyich, whenever I talked to Modest or Anatoly, their use of the word "deelightful" vividly transported me to the past and my conversations with their brother.

At this first, memorable meeting with Tchaikovsky in Vsevolozhsky's office, I mostly listened to their conversation, which skipped from one topic to another. The main subject, however, was the opera: an evaluation of the repertory and singers. Before my entrance, apparently, they had already spoken of the staging of *Eugene Onegin,* which Pyotr Ilyich insistently avoided. When I entered, this conversation was already coming to a close. Vsevolozhsky seemed to be summing up their argument and his own conclusions in favor of producing *[Eugene] Onegin* on the main Petersburg stage. He gradually elaborated for Tchaikovsky his thoughts concerning the details of the staging: on the balls, the costumes of the dancing choristers and ballet, the need for accuracy in the officers' dress; on the set for the first scene, with the country house of Larina; on the duel scene with its setting at a windmill in winter, and, finally, on the final scene, in which the director was especially eager to show the view from the windows of Tatyana Gremina's room onto the Neva and the Peter and Paul Fortress.

One could tell by the animation in Pyotr Ilyich's face that he was tempted by seeing the convergence of an entire series of external factors necessary for the success of his opera on the main stage, which indeed led, as is known, to *[Eugene] Onegin's* appearance at the Bolshoy Theater in Petersburg. This circumstance, Vsevolozhsky's increased pressure on the composer to agree to a staging of *[Eugene] Onegin,* was vividly recalled to me later on when I heard the clearly slanderous rumor that had been persistently circulating in society that the opera had made it into the repertory of the Petersburg theaters against the director's wishes, owing to the composer's lobbying, which in turn had elicited pressure from above.

I am not always able to sort out the dates of my many memories of Tchaikovsky. I remember only that I became closer to him after the staging of *[Eugene] Onegin.*

Memories about such a great artist as Tchaikovsky are inseparable from recollections of his works, and thus I consider it relevant to share with my readers the materials I have preserved concerning the stagings and performance of his works. The appearance on the Petersburg stage, one after the other, of *Eugene Onegin, The Sorceress, Sleeping Beauty, The Queen of Spades, Iolanta,* and *The Nutcracker* will comprise the stages of my recollections of Pyotr Ilyich.

I have preserved vague memories of the staging of *Mazepa,* Tchaikovsky's first opera, which was performed in Petersburg under the auspices of my theatrical agency. My archive contains information indicating Vsevolozhsky's interest in this opera, an interest he showed, it is true, in all of Tchaikovsky's works. Not long after the celebration of the coronation [of Alexander III] reached its culmination in 1883, on 7 June of that year to be precise, Vsevolozhsky wrote to me: "Before leaving Moscow I learned that Tchaikovsky has completed his opera *Mazepa.* It is essential that it be acquired immediately for production on the Petersburg stage. I have likewise accepted it for Moscow. Domershchikov should read the libretto and consider how and when it might be staged."[27]

Eduard Nápravník or Gennady Kondratyev[28] probably raised some objections concerning *Mazepa's* sudden inclusion in the repertory for the 1883–84 season, because in his letter of 21 June Vsevolozhsky writes: "It is essential to stage *Mazepa,* if only in January or February. I do not insist on an early date; but I am instructing the management of direction to stage the opera in any case in *this season.*" Several days later Vsevolozhsky, having evidently seen the libretto of *Mazepa* and become concerned about the historical accuracy of its setting, wrote me: "I am sending you a telegram about [Serov's] *Rogneda.* It is probably possible to postpone this opera by an announcement, although the newspapers have already put it abroad that a most grandiose setting is being prepared for it. But it is necessary to give *Mazepa* a luxurious staging. All of Petersburg will probably come to see it."

My hypothesis concerning the existence of objections to the sudden inclusion of *Mazepa* in the 1883–84 repertoire might find some support in the following lines of Nápravník's letter to me of 2 July 1883: "I am glad that we are going to have an interesting new work, that is, Tchaikovsky's opera *Mazepa,* but I am afraid that his hurried 'composition' and ignorance of the stage will introduce into it all the previous faults that so harm his doubtlessly talented dramatic compositions." The staging of *Mazepa* occurred almost simultaneously in both capitals: first on 3 February [1884] in Moscow; then on 6 February in Petersburg. Many, including myself, expected more from this work. As far as I remember, only individual sections enjoyed success: for instance, the Gopak scene, the scene with Kochubey and Orlik, the funeral march during Kochubey's walk to his execution, Mariya's lullaby, and the symphonic picture of the Battle of Poltava. In general the opera seemed tedious, and the performers were also unsatisfactory; even the talented Pavlovskaya[29] failed to save it. Incidentally, I noted that, at the first performance of *Mazepa,* when Tchaikovsky emerged in response to the curtain calls—probably owing to his characteristic extreme shyness—what I would call starched awkwardness replaced his usual elegance. As he bowed, Pyotr Ilyich made several steps forward, and then he threw an impulsive, quick bow into the audience, indeed he not so much bowed as bent his body without lowering his head, moreover with something between a smile and a pitiful, mournful grimace.

In 1885, there was talk of Pyotr Ilyich creating an opera based on Pushkin's *The Captain's Daughter [Kapitanskaia dochka]*. I suppose Vsevolozhsky gave Tchaikovsky the idea. Apparently there were considerable limitations for creativity in this work, since it was impossible to avoid a musical development of the Pugachev rebellion, a sensitive topic at that time. This problem led the composer to continued doubt and hesitation. Vsevolozhsky, notwithstanding his customary modesty and shyness when dealing directly with requests for the Emperor, was so carried away with the idea of staging *The Captain's Daughter* that he decided to discuss with the Emperor the creative difficulties presented by the Pugachev rebellion.

On Wednesday, 16 January 1885, the sixteenth performance of *Eugene Onegin* was given. Alexander III was in the audience for the second time, and Vsevolozhsky used the occasion to seek permission to stage *The Captain's Daughter*. The permission was granted. But Pyotr Ilyich was fully absorbed at this time in his ideas for reworking his opera *Vakula the Smith* as *The Slippers [Cherevichki]* and, primarily, in composing *The Sorceress*. The plot of *The Captain's Daughter* apparently did not inspire him, and Pushkin's wonderful work was not fated to see the light of day in the musical interpretation of this composer. However, this question was fully resolved only much later; on 13 May 1888, Vsevolozhsky wrote to me: "I received a letter from Tchaikovsky in Klin. He writes that he has fallen out of love with the plot of *The Captain's Daughter* and wants to abandon it."

Pyotr Ilyich's work on *Eugene Onegin* did not end with its staging at Petersburg's Bolshoy Theater. Director of Theaters Vsevolozhsky always took a deep interest in Tchaikovsky's works and constantly attempted to perfect their staging. Having noticed that *[Eugene] Onegin's* sixth scene (the second ball) suffered from an absence of stage movement and from the insufficiently full development of its finale, he decided to enliven it by strengthening its choreography. Ivan Vsevolozhsky wrote me on 12 August 1885, "I have received a telegram from Pchelnikov: [Anton] Barzal should have arranged with Tchaikovsky for the addition of a song to *Eugene Onegin*, so it is necessary to do the sets for this opera."[30] In the end, Vsevolozhsky persuaded Pyotr Ilyich to add to this scene some dances, in particular the écossaise. Tchaikovsky carried out the director's request quickly, by the beginning of the 1885–86 season. . . .

After the staging of *Eugene Onegin* there is a kind of gap in my memories of

Tchaikovsky. He and I met every time he came to Petersburg, either in the theater or in Vsevolozhsky's office during his visiting hours. Sometimes Pyotr Ilyich came to my office at the theatrical agency to discuss musical notations or to receive his honorarium (10% of all box-office receipts from the performance of his works). These meetings were always friendly. I can't remember even a shade of disagreement between us. But then there was no occasion for such, considering Pyotr Ilyich's politeness and sensitivity and my unwavering readiness to meet the desires and interests of our respected artist. On the other hand, I can't remember any details from our conversations at these short business meetings. Our close and, alas, extremely brief friendship formed, as far as I recall, only after the staging of *The Sorceress*.

The schedule in the coming season was usually compiled in the spring, during Great Lent, by the Directorate of Theaters, consisting of all of the managing personnel of the administration, the head directors of the troupes, the orchestra and ballet masters. All gathered at the director's office. Stagings were decided upon for all the months of the season. The resulting schedule determined the assignment of both repertory and set-design work, that is, the preparation of costumes, set decorations, and props. Of course, the pieces to be staged had been chosen before such general repertory meetings.

Two productions were penciled in for the first half of the 1887–88 opera season: Tchaikovsky's *The Sorceress* and Verdi's *Otello*. The most favorable time for new productions was always considered to be the height of the season, when Petersburg was overflowing with the most worthy theatergoers—that is, from mid-November to mid-December. As far as I remember, Vsevolozhsky, for Tchaikovsky's own benefit, marked the end of November 1887 for the staging of *The Sorceress,* making it the second new work of the season, after *Otello*. Ivan Shpazhinsky, the author of the drama *The Sorceress* and of the libretto to the eponymous opera, who sometimes visited from Moscow, learned of the director's intention and informed me that Pyotr Ilyich's wishes did not coincide with this intention, and that for Tchaikovsky it would be more agreeable to stage his new opera at the beginning of the season. Having learned from experience to exercise caution in accepting such declarations through intermediaries instead of directly from the interested parties, I advised Tchaikovsky to make a corresponding written declaration. [Tchaikovsky wrote to Pogozhev with the request that his opera be staged first in the new season.]

Naturally, Pyotr Ilyich's wishes were carried out and, at the regular spring repertory meeting at Vsevolozhsky's office, the production of the opera *The Sorceress* was set for the latter part of October 1887. Its first performance took place in Petersburg at the Maryinsky Theater on 20 October 1887.

My frequent conversations concerning *The Sorceress* with the singer Emiliya Pavlovskaya, and, in part, my impressions from talks with Tchaikovsky himself, led me to expect great success for this opera. The tragic romance of this Russian Carmen, the conflict between father and son over their passionate love for the debauched Kuma, the intrigue of the vengeful civil servant Mamyrov and, finally, the haughty princess' cruel retribution after she had been doubly insulted in her pride and in her maternal and wifely feelings, all of this seemed to provide the talented composer with sufficient scope to develop fully musical illustrations of the heroes and dramatic situations, as well as of scenes from everyday life. But, to universal regret and to the deep disappointment of the composer, fate decided otherwise.

Aside from miscalculations in the musical composition, of which much has been said and written and about which I cannot judge, the reasons for the lack of success of the opera *The Sorceress,* its short life in the Petersburg repertory, and the transfer of its set to the Moscow Bolshoy Theater must be attributed to a significant degree to the thankless nature of the title role's vocal part. Moreover, by the time of the production of *The Sorceress,* Pavlovskaya's voice had become considerably fatigued, and the role of Kuma, as conversations with the singer herself gave me some reason to believe, was unsuited both to her taste and to her abilities.

My friendship with Pyotr Ilyich was facilitated by our mutual friendship with Pavlovskaya. It is with great affection that I recall this talented woman, who, incidentally, was endowed with neither a particularly beautiful face nor outstanding natural vocal qualities. Her husband, Sergey Pavlovsky, was also an opera singer—a baritone—and an extremely well educated person. We met at their house from time to time, and those evenings were sweet, cozy, and unpretentious, with a small number of invited guests, always interesting people.

Conversations at the Pavlovskys' dealt primarily with the opera, the lives of the artists, and art in general. Sometimes, when we asked her, the hostess would sit at the piano and perform romances or arias from her repertory. (She had completed the piano course at the Conservatory and was an outstanding pianist.) As if it were yesterday I can remember our delight in her stunning, remarkably pure rendition of a famous waltz by Venzano, which she usually inserted into her performance as Rosina in [Rossini's] *Il Barbiere di Siviglia.* Time flew, thanks to the level of conversation, the guests' stories, and especially the hostess herself. A German by birth, Pavlovskaya's spoken Russian was artistic and vivid, and she could make her listeners vicariously experience the multifarious adventures and successes of a singer's life, particularly those from earlier years on the island of Malta, where her artistic career had blossomed.

A simple supper and a little wine at the end of the evening usually loosened the guests' tongues. Pavlovskaya knew how to animate her guests, and the usually taciturn Pyotr Ilyich unhesitatingly contributed anecdotes about his travels and artistic performances, meetings with celebrities, adventures, successes, and failures. Pyotr Ilyich was rarely so gregarious as at Pavlovskaya's parties. His speech could be extremely tender, quite smooth and rounded; at times he uttered energetic or laconic judgments: "delightful! disgusting! charming!" The story might be humorous or vitriolic. If his subject was an unpleasant one, his tone would betray rancor and aloofness, and even his facial expression would become angry. The two things that most irritated Tchaikovsky were unfair and biased music criticism and praise of musical works he didn't care for. He especially hated, as I recall, two of Verdi's operas: *La Traviata* and *Rigoletto*. In his judgments on artists, the theater administration, orchestra directors and musicians, and composers, Tchaikovsky was diplomatic and even, I would say, insufficiently sincere, often exaggerating his praise. But when conversation turned to the so-called Mighty Handful, led by César Cui, his affability and tranquility would be displaced by rancor. He also exhibited malice and irritation toward the composers Galler and especially Lishin, Tchaikovsky's *bête noire*.[31]

Once I told Tchaikovsky about an especially nasty cartoon that had appeared in one of the satirical magazines, perhaps *Strekoza*. It depicted a Roman circus. César Cui was seated in the Imperial loge. A group of gladiators passing through the arena were bowing to César. Interspersed with them were characters from Cui's unsuccessful operas, *Angelo, William Ratcliff,* and *The Captive of the Caucasus [Kavkazskii plennik]*. The caption contained the traditional gladiatorial greeting before setting off to fatal battle: "Ave Caesar! Morituri te salutant! [Hail, Caesar! Those who are about to die salute you!]." Pyotr Ilyich, who evidently already knew of the cartoon, laughed long and infectiously. I hope I am mistaken, but I fear that in his laughter was a note of malicious exultation.

This asperity somehow conflicts with the established view of Tchaikovsky's unique affability and tenderheartedness. But it must be noted that Tchaikovsky's ill will was free of any tinge of envy. As far as I could tell, it was always directed toward people standing considerably lower than Tchaikovsky on the ladder of artistic reputation.

On the other hand, there were also conversations with Tchaikovsky in which he exhibited his characteristic warmth and even, I would say, sentimentality. Such were conversations about children, whom Pyotr Ilyich especially loved, and about human—especially female—self-sacrifice. A tale about someone in dire economic straits would have a powerful effect: his eyes became moist, a pitying, even mournful smile appeared on his lips, his face expressed compassion, and his arm involuntarily moved toward his pocket in order to free from captivity an unneeded, or perhaps often quite needed bill. . . . His friends learned to exercise caution in opening up to a man who suffered to such an extent from the atrophy of centers of restraint in his charitable instinct.

Tchaikovsky loved to speak of his dislike for society and of the discomfort caused him by acquaintanceships and especially by social visits. Nonetheless, at a propitious moment during one of our meetings, I got up the nerve to invite him to my apartment. To my delight, Pyotr Ilyich immediately agreed to come on the appointed evening. As a necessary precondition, I directed that he avoid any ceremonial visits, which visibly pleased him. And in fact, we initiated a friendship that was quite animated for busy people, especially people of the theater whose evenings are occupied by performances. We then began a correspondence that further enhanced our friendship.

My friendly relations with Pyotr Ilyich continued for more than five years, and it is remarkable that, despite Tchaikovsky's frequent evening visits, never— not once—was I at his home, nor did he ever invite me. . . .

Pyotr Ilyich began to visit my home and became acquainted with my family in 1887, if I am not mistaken. I didn't hold regular parties. Once in a while —three or four times a season—I invited my friends and others whom the former might find it pleasant and interesting to meet. . . . The program for passing the time was most unremarkable: conversations, primarily in small groups, a couple of tables for card players, a bit of music, Leonid Yakovlev's singing,[32] and, over dinner, and especially over dessert and coffee, a general discussion. . . .

Tchaikovsky loved to play a game of *vint;* he played without any apparent skill, but excitedly, with enthusiasm, avoiding arguments and experiencing sincere disappointment with his mistakes.[33] He did not mind female society and was quite ready to converse with the ladies.

At one of his first visits to one of my parties, Pyotr Ilyich met and befriended General Dragomirov. A widely educated and talented man and an interesting interlocutor, Mikhail Dragomirov immediately won Pyotr Ilyich over with his unique mindset and witty speech; the general, in turn, was very interested in the talented composer and became most fond of him. Once, at a dinner I hosted, Tchaikovsky extended his wine to clink glasses with Dragomirov and said to him: "To your health, Your High Excellency!"

"It is mutual, Your Excellency," Dragomirov answered, clinking his glass.

"I'm not excellent!" Pyotr Ilyich objected in embarrassment. Then, as if it had just occurred to him, he laughed and added: "It's really quite remarkable! At the Klin train station, where I often have occasion to be during trips in the country, all the lackeys always call me 'Your Excellency'!"

This rather inept emendation was greeted with a friendly chuckle from the others at the table. Dragomirov, taking no offense at being compared to lackeys, laughed more than the others, so that Tchaikovsky's understandable discomfort in such a situation passed unnoticed without leaving a bad impression. After this conversation Dragomirov gave Pyotr Ilyich the nickname "the Klin lackey."

In the period after 1887, following the staging of *The Sorceress* but without the least connection to this work, Tchaikovsky enjoyed the particular, outstanding sympathy and concern of the Directorate of Theaters in the persons of all its influential representatives. Pyotr Ilyich's economic situation at that time was far from good. News of his circumstances reached the sympathetic Vsevolozhsky and motivated him to campaign for the assignment of a regular Imperial stipend for the needy composer. On New Year's Day 1887, the Directorate of Theaters received notice that the Tsar was awarding the composer Tchaikovsky a yearly pension of 3,000 rubles. This was an unheard-of benefaction for an artist in those times, and its magnitude can be explained by Alexander III's particular appreciation for Pyotr Ilyich. Tchaikovsky was then on what I believe was his first artistic tour abroad. Vsevolozhsky telegraphed him in Lübeck with notification of the Tsar's material support. I sent Tchaikovsky my own heartfelt congratulations on this same occasion to the same place. . . .

As I have mentioned above, my recollections of Tchaikovsky are grouped in periods associated with the musical works he created for the stage. Thus, all of 1889 is connected with the production of [the ballet] *Sleeping Beauty*. Pyotr Ilyich had spent the spring of 1889 on a trip abroad. Arriving in the Caucasus from outside the country, he felt fatigued and was not particularly inclined to compose music for a ballet.[34] Having happened to read an article in *Novoe vremia* about the alleged postponement of the production of *Sleeping Beauty*, he seems to have been happy to grasp the opportunity to delay work on the commission he had accepted. However, this postponement rumor was baseless. The ballet was set for the 1889–90 season, for early January 1890, as I hastily informed the composer. Pyotr Ilyich finally got to work, and in autumn, after the Directorate received the music, we began our fevered preparations for the production. My meetings with Tchaikovsky also intensified beginning in that autumn, at Vsevolozhsky's office and the Theater Agency, at the theater, and at my apartment. Wherever we met, the primary topic of conversation was *Sleeping Beauty*.

Much time was devoted to a review of the costumes and stage sets, and subsequently also to individual and orchestral rehearsals. Periodic business meetings and conversations with Vsevolozhsky, Petipa, and the orchestra director [Riccardo] Drigo became part of Pyotr Ilyich's routine life.[35]

The end of 1889, especially December, brought many worries to both Tchaikovsky and the Directorate of Theaters. The staging of *Sleeping Beauty* was the outstanding event of Petersburg theatrical life, thanks to the artistic efforts of the ballet's three creators, Tchaikovsky, Petipa, and Vsevolozhsky, to the luxury and complexity of the sets, and to the financial expenditures associated with it. As far as I remember, the wardrobe, sets, machinery, and props for

Sleeping Beauty came to about 42,000 rubles, that is, slightly more than a quarter of the yearly budget of the production (that is, set design) department of the Petersburg theaters. Despite the generous amount of time allotted to the production, a certain degree of haste was, as usual, unavoidable. There was always something: changes in costumes, additions to the sets and props, the organization of mechanical tricks and the movement of the panorama, insertions and changes in the choreographic composition, and finally, necessary corrections in the score and orchestral parts. A particular abundance of trouble ensued from the setting up of the marvelous depiction of the sleeping kingdom. All of this unnerved Vsevolozhsky, Petipa, the artists, the administration, and, of course, it all affected Tchaikovsky.

The dress rehearsal took place on 2 January 1890, and on 3 January was the first public performance. It had enormous success. It is no exaggeration to say that the poetic music of the moving panorama, the marvelous waltz, and numerous other interesting portions of the score all charmed the ear. Petipa outdid himself with the choreography. The dancers also excelled, and Sleeping Beauty herself—Aurora, Miss Carlotta Brianza—and the other personages elicited delight.[36] I remember that the dancer Anderson was especially sweet as a small cat; she later paid for her carelessness with fire when, at a rehearsal of the ballet *Cinderella [Zolyshka]* on 3 December 1893, she received serious burns when her tutu caught on fire, forcing her to leave the stage.[37] A considerable share of the success should be attributed to the staging itself, to the set design, and especially the costumes, created according to Vsevolozhsky's own designs. The success of *Sleeping Beauty,* as is known, grew with each performance. This was one of those special musical-choreographic works, the details of whose beauty are revealed as one's acquaintance with it deepens. The ballet music quickly became popular: the waltz and many other numbers were soon to be heard both on concert stages, in home piano recital, and, finally, on mechanical instruments.

The idea of writing an opera based on Pushkin's *The Queen of Spades* had long before occurred to the Moscow musician and composer Nikolay Klenovsky,[38] who as early as 1886 had asked Modest Tchaikovsky to write the libretto for it. With the passage of time Klenovsky lost enthusiasm and abandoned the idea. I cannot be sure whether it was a coincidence that Vsevolozhsky thought of creating an opera of *The Queen of Spades,* or whether he learned of Modest Tchaikovsky's work on its libretto, but I remember that in December of 1889 there was already talk of an opera on this subject.

Vsevolozhsky reacted very enthusiastically and insistently to this plan, and he immediately related it to Pyotr Ilyich. Tchaikovsky willingly agreed to write the music. During that same month of December, Modest Tchaikovsky acquainted the Directorate with his libretto, and Vsevolozhsky, taken with the subject, applied his artistic imagination and unique talent to the development of many details of the staging and even to the planning of the opera itself. Moreover, he drafted the scene of Herman's meeting with the Countess in her bedroom. He also recommended to Pyotr Ilyich the old collection of eighteenth-century French arias, songs, and romances which would inspire the melody for the dozing countess, which Tchaikovsky then wrote in such a touching fashion to the words: "Je sens mon coeur qui bat, qui bat, je ne sais pas pourqois [I feel my heart beating, beating, I do not know why]."[39] At the same time, Vsevolozhsky drafted the staging of the intermezzo at the ball with its singing and dances, in which he decided to make all the characters into a group of antique Sevres porcelain figurines; for this he commissioned the talented sculptor Pavel Kamensky, who then managed the prop workshop of the Directorate, to construct porcelain-like pedestals of white with blue and gold.[40] Vsevolozhsky also thought through most of the details of the *mise-en-scène* and many parts of the composition. There is no doubt that Vsevolozhsky's contributions earned him a portion of the laurels which crowned the opera The Queen of Spades.

Soon after launching *Sleeping Beauty,* Pyotr Ilyich set off abroad and settled in Italy, in search of creative solitude. He took an apartment on the poetic Lungarno,[41] and it was the lot of charming Florence, world capital of art, to become the place where Tchaikovsky created the musical work that strengthened his reputation as a highly gifted artist. Composition proceeded at an unusually rapid pace. All seven scenes of the opera were ready at the very beginning of March 1890, and by May the score of *The Queen of Spades* was already at the music printing shop of the publisher, Mr. Jurgenson. In May 1890, Vsevolozhsky mentioned to me in a letter from the country that Tchaikovsky had asked him to arrange for the appearance of Catherine the Great at the ball in the third scene, but this proved impossible owing to the censorship of that era.

In November of 1890 Tchaikovsky temporarily moved to Petersburg, where he, the Directorate, and all involved in the staging of the opera experienced the typical nervous anticipation of first performances, the worries that comprise the inevitable fate of people poisoned by the stage, drawing such people together like a magnet. There were a multitude of changes, insertions, omissions, and reworkings in all the elements of the staging, especially in the set design. There were also quite a few conflicts, arguments, altercations, and reconciliations, even verbal abuse, but still the work went forward in a friendly and purposeful manner. As always during Vsevolozhsky's tenure at the helm of the Imperial Theaters, everyone put his heart and soul into it in the fashion of Peter the Great: everything was done "without tedium."

In the theatrical world, especially in the provinces, there is a superstitious belief that "a rough dress rehearsal bodes a successful show, and, vice versa, a smooth rehearsal bodes failure!" This superstition was brilliantly justified by the staging of *The Queen of Spades*. There was plenty of roughness at this dress rehearsal!

Indeed, there was a lot of nervousness at that truly "rough" rehearsal on 5 December. The singer Nikolay Figner,[42] who usually was nervous before his first appearance in a new role, won leave of the head director to put on his costume at his own apartment, which was quite a distance from Maryinsky Theater, on the condition that he show up at the theater at the proper time ready to go on stage. One of the component parts of Figner's costume was a pair of tights, which split when he was putting them on. The tailor and dresser who had been assigned to Figner had to travel back to the theatrical wardrobe to choose another pair of tights or to repair the split ones. I don't recall which of these solutions was resorted to, but in the end it turned out that Figner was not only late for the agreed time of arrival, but also came much later to the theater and made Alexander III wait a good twenty minutes for him.

Now, from a distance of more than thirty years, this event seems not even an event, but rather a curious theatrical- workplace anecdote. But at the time it was an occurrence of great significance. More than an hour of alarm and unrewarded expectation, of the fear that the angered Tsar would leave the theater, the terror of the theatrical administration for the consequences of what had happened, all of this together could knock anyone off his emotional balance. Everyone was wandering about as if under water and in an eerie silence; all faces displayed the expectation of some catastrophe. I was not in the audience; instead I roved back and forth across the stage in nervous expectation. I remember that Pyotr Ilyich was performing the same exercise, but on the other side of the curtain, pacing around pale-faced and with plaintive eyes, sighing from time to time. According to those who were present in the audience, the Tsar and his family settled in the sixth row of seats and observed with curiosity the entrance of various civil servants with their monotonous reports to Vsevolozhsky concerning Figner's continued absence. Eduard Nápravník stood at his podium, his back to the stage, periodically glaring behind stage in case the director Alexander Morozov might appear bearing good tidings.

"What's causing the hold-up?" asked the Tsar.

Vsevolozhsky, seated in the seventh row behind the Tsar, bowed and said quite loudly: "Figner's pants split, Your Majesty!"

The Tsar burst out laughing. As one could have expected, he regarded the entire event with tolerance, patiently awaiting Figner's arrival without expressing displeasure.

Once Figner finally arrived at the theater, the administration naturally refrained from reproach in order not to worry him before the performance of his part. But when the rehearsal ended and Alexander III left, the reprisals began. First of all, as is proper, everyone searched for the guilty party, and, of course, this was primarily Figner. Vsevolozhsky was truly enraged, insisting on meting out the most severe measure of punishment, up to the cancellation of Figner's contract. Kondratyev tried to put all the blame on the assembly crew, whose representative, Platon Domershchikov, in his turn blamed the costume master and Kondratyev, who had allowed Figner to dress at home at a great distance from the theater and the wardrobe. The latter opinion, in my view, was the most correct. But the storm nonetheless gathered over Figner, and quite a storm at that. Foreseeing the unpleasant consequences of punishing Figner severely— the possibility of the theater losing a talented singer, the public's darling, who had gathered large receipts, a loss whose consequences could have a negative effect on the interests of the Directorate itself and on the representatives of the administration—I decided to intercede for Figner. Pyotr Ilyich supported me in this initiative after I explained my reasons. I well remember my conversation with Vsevolozhsky. It was quite enthusiastic; I pointed to the lack of ill will in Figner's errant act, to the fact that he had on the contrary striven to do his best, and to the Tsar's own magnanimous and understanding attitude; finally, I referred to the success of The Queen of Spades and Figner's artistic performance. My advocacy was convincing. A man of the kindest heart, Vsevolozhsky was not spiteful; he managed to calm down and agreed with my reasoning, turning his anger into benevolence. In the end, Figner's punishment was a mere reprimand.[43]

The "roughness" of the dress rehearsal of The Queen of Spades was not limited to Figner's unfortunate tardiness. Figner's nervousness and somewhat fidgety manner on stage gave the entire audience a worrisome minute. In the scene at the guardhouse, despite the choir's wonderful recital of the funeral motif "I pour out my prayers to the Lord," at the moment when the countess' ghost appears, Figner, illustrating Herman's horror, accidentally knocked a candlestick with a burning candle from the table behind which he was moving. It rolled across the floor and, as if on purpose, stopped with its flame under the edge of the curtain at the backdrop of the set. The candle continued to burn and, of course, the public's attention, attracted by the sound of the falling candlestick, was riveted to the candle's flame and to the curtain, which had already begun to smoke. The prompter, Josef Paleček, standing in the first curtain entrance, immediately ran behind the curtain, from which a hand soon appeared to remove the candlestick from the stage. Everyone breathed a sigh of relief.

With the exception of these two disagreeable occurrences, the rehearsal was a triumph for the composer, the singers, and the production. Of the play's decor the costumes and accessories of the "pastoral" were particularly popular. The set for the countess' bedroom, the work of the artist Konstantin Ivanov, made a particularly strong impression.[44] Many refused to believe that it was all painted on a single surface. The set depicted the countess' room with an alcove illuminated by a hanging lantern; behind a screen in the alcove was the countess' bed. People went backstage with the sole purpose of convincing themselves that there was nothing on the stage, apart from the countess' chair, that everything, including the alcove, the bed, the screen, and the other furniture, was all painted on a single curtain, with a painted lantern and light falling from it onto the bed and other objects.

The first performance of *The Queen of Spades* took place on 7 December 1890. It went brilliantly, without a hitch.

As I already noted, Pyotr Ilyich was not in the habit of asking others for their opinions on his works. Despite his remarkable humility and, on the other hand, despite his great pride, he was afraid to seek either compliments or the elusive comments that hide negative opinions. Pyotr Ilyich was very sensitive and even excessively suspicious with regard to the way his works were treated, for example, the postponement of a production, cuts, works being excluded from the repertory, etc. . . .

But at the same time Tchaikovsky was distinguished by a rare magnanimity with regard to verbal and even written (but not journalistic) criticism of his works and did not take offense at disapproving reactions to some part or number in his works. I will adduce the following example to characterize his magnanimity: in 1885 I think (I don't remember precisely), the Mikhailovsky Theater staged a small German ballet *Der Gestiefelte Kater,* that is, the fairytale "Puss in Boots." For some reason this merry piece ended with an apotheosis including a humorous procession of German opera composers and the antagonists of their works. Thus, for example, Faust walked together with a caricature of Margarita, the composer Wagner walked together with Lohengelb instead of Lohengrin, and the procession was accompanied by the performance of parodies of the corresponding melodies. The head director of the German troupe, Philip Bock, told me that he regretted that there would not be any parody of Russian opera in the closing procession of the opera on the Petersburg stage. I expressed the thought that there was no point in parodying an unsuccessful opera, and that in any case this would be disingenuous on the part of the Directorate; I mentioned the possibility of parodying an opera with an established reputation, such as *Eugene Onegin.* I also alluded to a certain similarity between the famous song "Little Archer" and the melody of Onegin in his scene with Tatyana in the garden, when he sings: "I love you with a brother's love, a brother's love." This might make occasion to present a caricature of Onegin in the musical procession, with Onegin crossing the stage singing: "I want to tell you, to tell you." Bock liked this idea very much, and I, meeting Pyotr Ilyich, risked asking his permission to stage the parody I had thought up; of course I was ready to abandon my intention at the smallest hesitation or hint of displeasure. But my fears were groundless. Tchaikovsky burst out laughing and immediately agreed to my project. However, as far as I remember, this project was left unfulfilled out of caution.

Pyotr Ilyich had a custom of disappearing quickly from the theater after the first performances of his operas. At subsequent meetings one could see in his eyes a silent, yet worried question: "Well, what do you think?" After the dress rehearsal of *The Queen of Spades* there was no time to exchange impressions of the opera and its performance. Everyone was shaken by the fright occasioned by Figner's tardiness. But when I met Tchaikovsky several days after the premiere on 7 December, Pyotr Ilyich for some reason, contrary to his custom, asked me my impression of *The Queen of Spades*. In all sincerity I expressed my delight with the opera, but immediately declined to give my detailed impressions, promising to find a free hour to write them down and send them to Pyotr Ilyich in the country. At the first opportunity, which came only during the Christmas holidays, I fulfilled my promise.

Romain Rolland

4 March [1888]

At the concert conducted by Tchaikovsky at Châtelet.

His head is that of a diplomat, or a Russian officer. Sideburns and square beard. An open forehead, bony, divided in the middle by a deep wrinkle; strongly vaulted brows; a gaze very focused, immobile, staring directly ahead and, at the same time, it seems, directed within. He is tall and thin, with an irreproachable demeanor, white gloves, and a white necktie. When he is conducting, his tall figure does not bend, while his right arm, firmly, dryly, sharply marks the beat in the air, occasionally (at the end of the Third Suite) emphasizing the rhythm with heavy force and violent energy, which makes his right shoulder shake, even though the rest of the body remains unmoved. He bows like a true automaton, dryly, rapidly, with his entire body, three times in a row.

I enjoyed the concert. I don't like Tchaikovsky much as a melodist. There is too much convention or inflexibility in this aspect of his work. The Concert Fantasia for piano, played by Diémer, is an accumulation of acrobatic difficulties, with a vague Schumann-like sentiment. But I was struck by the Serenade for Strings. The first part throughout, with its modest title (*pezzo in forma di sonatina*), is simplicity itself, full of grandeur, even though it is a little rigid. The finale is a fugue on a Russian theme. The same style in the fragments of the

Third Suite (theme and variations), of which the end makes a powerful rhythm. One would like to hear from him an oratorio, or a grand prelude and fugue. This is a vigorous modern orchestration, Handelian in form.

I am pleased to say that there still is a man of classical, almost scholastic, age—a man who experiences powerful pleasure in listening to the vibrancy of a grand perfect chord, and who makes you listen to it, just simply, without trying to uplift it by some harmonic zest.

(N.B.—At performances of Tchaikovsky's music, above all remember to observe the rhythm of implacable rigor).

11 March [1888]

A new concert of Tchaikovsky. The theme and variations of the Third Suite was performed again, and a symphonic poem, *Francesca da Rimini*; its orchestration is more modern, with the same grave and galloping rhythm; also a beautiful concerto for violin, well played by Marsick.[45]

Herman Klein

M. Tchaikovsky made his first bow—or, rather, the first of several very profound and rapid bows—before an English audience at the Philarmonic Concert on Thursday [22 March 1888]. A hearty reception awaited him as was fitting in the case of one of the most distinguished of Russian composers. . . .

M. Tchaikovsky is not quite forty-eight, but he looks older, his hair and close-cut beard being perfectly gray. By his intelligent and animated beat, I should judge him to be a good conductor. It was a pity, though, that he should not have been represented in Thursday's scheme by a work of first-class importance, instead of a Serenade for Strings and a movement of a suite, neither of them worthy of his genius in its highest phase. The predominant impression left behind is tinged with a certain coarseness, not to say vulgarity of treatment. M. Tchaikovsky had to respond to two recalls after the Serenade, which brought out the tone of the Philharmonic strings with wonderful sonorousness and purity of quality.

Julius H. Block

One cold winter's night in 1888 I stepped out of the Moscow–St. Petersburg express at the station of Klin. While hastily swallowing down a glass of hot tea, among a crowd of fellow travelers, I recognized Tchaikovsky sitting next to me. I had long wanted to meet Tchaikovsky. Ever since 1876 I had been burning to tell him of his great popularity among music lovers in America; for I felt sure that, if he would make the voyage, a great triumph awaited him across the water.

The opportunity had come at last. But my heart beat so violently, I was in such a state of excitement, that I had not the courage to address my neighbor. And a year was to pass before another chance came.

One autumn morning, lifting my head to glance through my office window, I recognized Tchaikovsky walking in. This time I did not hesitate. Rushing out, I boldly engaged him in conversation and asked him for his autograph then and there. He kindly promised to send it; and, on afterwards opening his letter, I found not only his autograph, but the motif of the second part of the *andante cantabile* movement of his First Quartet, written out in his own hand as a souvenir. Deeply touched, I wrote a letter of thanks; in which, to reciprocate his courtesy, I offered to demonstrate Edison's latest invention, the phonograph. I asked him to keep the letter a secret; for I had only just brought the instrument into Russia, and wished to give my first demonstration in the Czar's presence before making the new marvel public.

Tchaikovsky called the following day to thank me. "I quite understand," he said, "you wish to keep the matter a secret." He paused a moment. "I suppose— I suppose you could not make just one exception?" With some embarrassment he went on to explain that he wanted to bring his great friend Sergey Taneyev with him. "I was unable to conceal the contents of your letter from him," he explained, "and now he is as anxious to hear the phonograph as myself."

The great composer arrived with his friend at the appointed hour. Once again, as he shook hands, his manner seemed a little embarrassed. I had not to wait long for an explanation. "We have just been dining with Rukavishnikov, the mayor of Moscow," he began. "Safonov was there too.[46] But we were in such a hurry to leave that they would not let us go until they had learned why we were going. And—and, somehow or other, I burst out with the secret! Naturally, they both authorized me to ask if they might join us and," he added with a smile, "they are waiting for you to pass judgment on them now." The cat was out of the bag; I could not help smiling in my turn, and Taneyev went to the telephone to tell his friends that they were welcome.

Later, I had the pleasure of meeting the great Russian Maestro at Taneyev's house; when I told him of his great popularity in America and suggested a tour of the States, I discovered that the scheme had already been mooted. . . .

Lovers of this great artist's music are already familiar with the main facts of his life. They know something of the tragic dualities of his nature which so often find a voice in his great compositions. Yet, as it was my good fortune to number Peter Ilyich and his brother Modest among my best friends, it may not be uninteresting to mention some further episodes in the life of a genius, in whose sensitive nature joy and gloom were closely intertwined. . . .

It is in this very matter of friendship that the dualism . . . stands most clearly revealed. For whenever Tchaikovsky felt the need to seek out his friends, his melancholy changed as if by magic into optimism and cheerfulness. In that mood, a nimbus of charm, endearment, of enchantment even, seemed to emanate from him; the very atmosphere of any room he entered seemed to glow, and it would be hard to imagine a more sympathetic and delightful companion.

Many are the stories illustrating his unselfish devotion to his friends. Tchaikovsky repeatedly journeyed for days and nights to stand by some sickbed, although he suffered profoundly when sharing the sorrows or suffering of those he loved. And seldom have servants been so appreciated and so lovingly and generously treated by any man.

His modesty and simplicity revealed a truly great spirit. When the first performance of his ballet *The Nutcracker* and the opera *Iolanta* were to be given at St. Petersburg Opera House, I had traveled from Moscow to be present and ran into Tchaikovsky as I entered the house. He expressed surprise and said: "I'm afraid you'll be sorry you came! It really wasn't worth the trouble and expense of such a long journey." His tone was so sincere that it was impossible to mistake his words for a mere conventional phrase of politeness.

Here is a story showing he was sometimes the victim of his own kindheartedness. When Tchaikovsky gave up his flat in Moscow he used to stop at the Great Moskovskaya Hotel during his visits to the ancient capital. This hotel contained a number of grand halls and apartments for festivals and banquets. Some students had arranged a meeting at the hotel. It was late; supper was over, and having given Bacchus his due, they felt the desire to prolong the night with dancing. But a "tapeur" was wanting. Then one of the students informed the company that Tchaikovsky was staying at the hotel; why not send a deputation up to ask him to play for them? Poor Pyotr Ilyich was just going to bed. Tired, he did his best to persuade them to abandon their idea. But they insisted on his dressing, and down he went to play dance music.

To illustrate his modesty: when Tchaikovsky was teaching at the Moscow Conservatoire, Sergey Taneyev was one of his pupils. They later became intimate friends. Taneyev, a bachelor and nonsmoker, had a very small apartment, in which he received his friends and pupils on certain days. During one such evening, a very animated conversation, led by Tchaikovsky, was in full swing, when the speaker pulled out one of his cigarettes and his matchbox. The host, *sans gêne,* prevented his lighting up, stopped his most interesting debate, and directed him into the narrow corridor, where several men were standing, smoking into the chimney pipe of the stove. Like an obedient schoolboy Tchaikovsky went to join the smokers, there he lit his cigarette and, smoking into the stovepipe, continued his conversation in a louder tone. But evidently he felt not very pleased. In a good-humored way he made the remark to his host: "Well, Sergey, after all you might have made an exception, and let me smoke there. You know, I am gradually becoming quite well known. And I can prove it to you— the orchestrion (mechanical musical instrument) at the Hermitage (the famous Moscow restaurant) is playing a potpourri from my *Eugene Onegin*." But his friend remained unmerciful, and made the composer first finish his cigarette near the stovepipe. . . .

Another incident, showing how depressed he could be at times, happened when I was present. Pyotr Ilyich had just conducted his new symphonic poem *Voivode*. It was on 6 November 1891, at Moscow. The concert had been arranged by Siloti, who asked his friend the composer to conduct his new work in person. Although the public received their favorite with great ovations, the applause at the end seemed to the author but meager, and on returning to the greenroom he destroyed the manuscript of the score and told the attendant to collect all the orchestral parts and bring them to him. Luckily Siloti's energetic revoke saved the composition. "Excuse me, Pyotr Ilyich, but I am master here, and I alone can give orders." Thereupon he had the orchestral parts carried to his own house. All this was done in such a downright manner that poor Pyotr Ilyich was stunned and said, *sotto voce:* "How dare you talk to me in such a way!" to which Siloti answered: "Well, we'll talk about it some other time." At that moment I entered the greenroom with several other friends to greet the composer and to congratulate him. Pyotr Ilyich walked up to me rather quickly and I noticed he was excited. He stretched out both hands and leaned forward. Assuming that he intended to whisper into my ear, I turned my head and he pressed his lips to my cheek. It is the custom in Russia for good friends to kiss each other, but as I had never been embraced by the great maestro before, I felt much embarrassed. Still more so when I heard Peter Ilyich ask if he could come and see me. Very ungraciously, I am afraid, I proposed *any* evening, for I was really too flustered to know what I was saying. The upshot was that a meeting was arranged at my house for the following night. A few of our mutual friends—his brother Modest, Taneyev, the cellist Brandukov[47]—were asked to help in dispelling the gloom that would surely fasten upon Tchaikovsky after an unsuccessful concert.

I had looked forward to his visit and had prepared a few phonograph records of his famous trio, played by Taneyev, Hřimaly, and Brandukov, as a surprise. The composer's friends were the first to arrive, and Modest Ilyich told me his brother had been very despondent and quite poorly all day; indeed, it had been hard to persuade him to join us that night, for he had shut himself up in his hotel room ever since the concert of the night before.

As he came into my house, his first words were: "Well, what do you think of my *Voivode*? Rotten, isn't it?" Just before his arrival, his friends had been talking of the work in lukewarm phrases so that silence followed his question. Tchaikovsky then turned to Taneyev and asked for his opinion. "Well," said his outspoken friend, "it *is* rather poor. You see, your love scenes—Romeo, for instance, and Francesca, are so fine, but *here*—!" To which poor Pyotr Ilyich replied: "Yes, you are quite right, it's a rotten piece."

Seeing how depressed he was, we did our best to cheer him up during supper, but his gloom did not disappear until well on in the phonograph seance. Our maestro was so taken by some of the musical recordings that he continued to listen until the clock struck half-past two.

When he took his leave he seemed a different man. "Julius, I have to thank you heartily for this delightful evening. I came here feeling quite sick and tired out, but I leave you completely cured and happy. Allow me to repeat the cure whenever I feel depressed." That evening, I may add, was one of the happiest I ever had.

Varvara Tsekhovskaya

I remember Pyotr Ilyich Tchaikovsky's visit to Kiev and the production at the City Opera Theater (the old one that later burned down) of *The Queen of Spades*, which first saw the glow of the footlights in Kiev. The Kiev music world was buzzing about Tchaikovsky's visit well beforehand, and everyone was looking forward to it as a major event. When Tchaikovsky arrived, he plunged into rehearsals at once, endeavoring to make the production of the opera as perfect as possible. They said that at the very first orchestra rehearsal he declared himself satisfied. Later he praised both the performers and the set decoration, and he especially liked the view of the Winter Canal from the Winter Palace.

On 17 December 1890 the dress rehearsal of *The Queen of Spades* took place with full set and costumes. The management of the Opera Theater was at that time in the hands of the famous singer Ippolit Pryanishnikov, who distributed invitations to this rehearsal all over Kiev.[48] By seven o'clock that evening, the theater was surrounded by carriages and people on foot. Everyone entered the theater building from the stage side, and it was so strange to pass across the raked stage, where the singers and performers, already dressed and made up, were all gathered and milling about. The theater was brightly lit, the musicians were in position, everything looked as it would for a regular performance. There was only one difference: at the left side of the proscenium, near the lettered boxes, a little bridge had been thrown across the orchestra pit connecting the stage with the parterre. The invited guests crossed over this little bridge and down some little steps into the hall. We all sat where we wanted in the parterre, but the tiers of boxes and gallery remained empty. The parterre was full when, from behind the curtain, appeared the small, thin, and elegant figure of Pyotr Ilyich Tchaikovsky. Following him were Ippolit Pryanishnikov, Lev Kupernik,[49] and two or three other prominent citizens of Kiev. Loud and enthusiastic applause greeted the composer, everyone rose as one, and the orchestra struck up a flourish. Pyotr Ilyich descended to the parterre to listen to the flourish, after which he acknowledged the applause with several bows. Then, leaving his companions, he proceeded to a side box above the orchestra. A hush fell, the conductor, Josef Přibyk,[50] solemnly raised his arms, and the first notes of the overture rang out. Pyotr Ilyich leaned his elbow on the rail of the box, as if intending to hide his face from the public's gaze with his hand. He sat alone in the box, concentration personified. The overture ended, the curtain rose. The scene was the Summer Garden, children playing with their nannies and wet nurses. Standing in splendor on the stage was the singer Mikhail Medvedev—the darling, even idol, of the ladies of Kiev—more impressive than ever, in the costume and role of Herman. Both the music and the singers' voices soared ever more surely and harmoniously, and Pyotr Ilyich Tchaikovsky continued to listen with his brows knit and his face reflecting anxiety and something like self-constraint. He seemed to be trying to forget that he was the composer and to hear *his* work calmly and critically, as if it were *someone else's*, but in that he could not quite succeed. . . .

He was nervous, and it showed. His fine-featured, seemingly chiseled face was far paler than usual and his anxious gaze never left the stage. . . .

The audience was carried away by the opera. The tumultuous ovations and applause during the entr'actes were unabating. People in the crowd were humming the melodies they had just heard, praising and admiring them. . . . The opera's motif of "Three cards! Three cards! Three cards!" rang out through the hall, and it was impossible to tell who was taking up the cry. The longer it went on, the more fired up the audience became. They called for Pryanishnikov, the performers, the conductor Přibyk. The anxiety faded from Tchaikovsky's pale, refined face. He turned nearly pink, his eyes glistening as he looked about and bowed with a slight smile, and in front of the entire audience he embraced and kissed Mikhail Medvedev, who had played Herman so well.[51]

The first performance of *The Queen of Spades* on 19 December turned out to be a sheer triumph for Pyotr Ilyich. The elegant and by now eagerly impatient audience filled the theater to overflowing. Frock coats, epaulets, ball gowns, and a crowd of heated and wildly exuberant young people formed a continuous dark semicircular swath in the gallery beneath the roof. The composer sat at the side of the stage in the "director's" box and this time did not seem nervous. Whether this was due to greater self-control than at the dress rehearsal, or because the dress rehearsal had quieted the composer's doubts and anxiety, who can say? But Pyotr Ilyich appeared quite calm, and this time he did not hide behind his hand. When the curtain fell at the end of the first scene amid claps of thunder and flashes of lightning, the hall burst forth with its own storm of vigorous cries. "Tchaikovsky! Tchaikovsky!" came the shouts from every corner of the theater, without subsiding. Tchaikovsky came out to take a bow, and again—like two days earlier—the entire audience rose to its feet and greeted the composer with a spirited ovation. The orchestra played a flourish, but no one could hear it, and the conductor Přibyk also rose and warmly applauded Tchaikovsky. The ovations were repeated many times, after every scene. At the conclusion of the second act, the curtain rose and the composer was surrounded on stage by the entire opera company: the singers, the whole chorus, and the musicians from the orchestra. The evening's hero was presented with a beautiful large silver wreath with the simple inscription: "To our dear guest Pyotr Ilyich Tchaikovsky—the Kiev Opera Association."

VII

The Man
(1878–1892)

Considering the emotional tension of Tchaikovsky's works, one might legitimately ask whether its creator ever enjoyed happiness in the course of his life. The answer, as for the rest of us, is yes and no. Happiness is by no means a permanent condition; rather, it constitutes a momentary experience. Browsing through Tchaikovsky's extensive correspondence, one often encounters a reflection of poignant bliss, as, for instance, in an exclamation written in 1879: "O God, how happy I am now, did I ever dream that I should enjoy life so much?" And ten years later, when he had already become a European celebrity, he recorded a moment of "*absolute happiness*" during his visit to Prague where he attended the production of his own *Swan Lake*. As he is careful to emphasize, however, this was "only a moment."

More lasting was the sense of joy that accompanied his work-in-progress. Tchaikovsky was more than merely a hard worker. He eventually learned to organize his everyday routine in a manner that allowed him a maximum of concentration. His strict exercise of discipline enabled Tchaikovsky, in addition to his regular work, to write up to twenty letters every day, and to compose the entire *Queen of Spades* within forty-four days. Besides his musical oeuvre, which alone comprises seventy-six titles, he left over sixty articles on a great variety of topics and a dozen volumes of correspondence.

All this does not mean that he was devoid of the need for pleasures, some of them addictive, like playing cards, a habit that became almost a necessity which he resented; or enjoying a good drink, although he rarely drank to excess; or occasional smoking. Exceptionally generous, he was always willing to provide help to his friends and even casual acquaintances; and he could spend vast sums of money without account. In a playful mood, he enjoyed children and pets, and was not above participating in practical jokes. On a loftier plane, Tchaikovsky possessed a passionate love of nature. When finally settled on his Klin estate near Moscow, he would take a daily six-mile constitutional, regardless of the weather. Music was naturally his chief artistic preoccupation, but he was very well read, particularly in Russian and French, and a devotee of theater. In sum, his public persona was an embodiment of the cultivated Russian-European, and many contemporaries describe the composer as a person of extraordinary charisma.

Conventional wisdom also holds that, along with joy, creativity entails suffering. This wholly applies to Tchaikovsky: a hypersensitive artist, he often could not help appearing neurotic. In his habits and attitudes he seemed a living paradox. He loved traveling and spent almost half of his life abroad, but he invariably fell prey to homesickness as soon as he left his beloved Russia. A popular socialite, he was subject to fits of misanthropy when he felt that people interfered with his work or mood. He suffered from multiple fears, most of them irrational, and more than once, while exaggerating his immediate concerns, such as his health, he drove himself into states of extreme anxiety. At the same time, he never reached the "verge of insanity," as some of his later biographers would have us believe. In fact, Tchaikovsky strikes us as a highly self-conscious individual capable of laughing at his own foibles.

The extant portraits and photographs of him show us a man of distinguished appearance. The composer's hair and beard turned gray quite early, and at the time of his death he looked much older than he was. He cut a fine figure of a late nineteenth century gentleman artist, with a high proud forehead, "as if chiseled by thought," in the words of one contemporary. Tchaikovsky's eyebrows finely outlined the rather deep arches under which his wide-open dreamy blue eyes stood out. He had a well-formed nose and a mouth with sensual lips, which his moustache leaves visible, and the chin and lower part of the face was completely covered by a white, neatly trimmed beard. His voice was a pleasant low bass. Tchaikovsky liked to talk and his speech was gentle and fluent. When praising something he loved to use words like "enchanting, ravishing, charming." Of moderate height and well groomed, he knew how to dress well and was often taken for something of a dandy.

The composer's love life was complex owing to his homosexuality, although he eventually succeeded in adjusting those tastes to the conventions of contemporary Russian society. That Tchaikovsky at some point came to think of his homosexuality as a natural inclination follows from his use of that very word in a letter to his brother Anatoly on 13/25 February 1878 from Florence: "Only now, especially after the tale of my marriage, have I finally begun to understand that there is nothing more fruitless than not wanting to be that which I am by nature."[1] Tchaikovsky's correspondence with Modest in following years, after his matrimonial fiasco, particularly from abroad, is full of graphic and unhibited descriptions of erotic encounters with homosexual prostitutes which were hitherto censored in all publications of Tchaikovsky's correspondence. In order to understand Tchaikovsky's state of mind in the 1870s and 1880s, it is very important to take note of this revealing letter by the composer, written in Paris to his brother Modest on 26 February/10 March 1879:

> Yesterday was a day of very strong agitation. In the morning there was a concert at the Châtelet and the performance of [my] *Tempest*. The torments I experienced were the strongest proof that I should only live in a village. Even that which was formerly my deepest pleasure, namely listening to my own compositions, has became a source of torture and nothing else. The conditions in which I listened to *The Tempest* would seem to have guaranteed my utter calm. But it was not to be. On the evening before the concert I began to suffer from diarrhea and nausea. My agitation crescendoed right up to the initial chords, and while they played, I thought that I would die that very instant, such was the pain in my heart. And this agitation was not at all from a fear of failure, but because for some time each new listen to any of my compositions has been accompanied by severe disappointment in myself. As if by design, right before *The Tempest* they played Mendelssohn's "Reformation" Symphony, and despite my terrible emotion I was constantly surprised by his wonderful mastery. I lack *mastery*. To this day I still write like a talented *youth* from whom one might expect much but who gives quite little. More than anything I am surprised how badly my orchestra sounds! Of course, my reason tells me that I somewhat exaggerate my faults, but this is a poor comfort for me. They performed *The Tempest* quite well, although not in a first-class manner. The tempos were absolutely correct. It seemed as if the musicians were playing diligently but without delight and love. One of them, on whom my eyes were riveted for some reason, smiled and made as if to exchange glances with someone, as if to say: "Excuse us for presenting you with such a strange dish, but we are not guilty: we are told to play and we play!" When the last chords were done, there rang out quite feeble applause, then it seemed as if a new salvo was gathering force, but here three or four loud whistles were heard, and then the hall was filled with cries, "Oh! Oh!" that signified a favorable protest against the whistling, and then all fell quiet. I bore this without particular grief, but the thought was killing me that *The Tempest,* which I am accustomed to consider a brilliant work of mine, is essentially so insignificant! I immediately left. The weather was marvelous and I walked continuously for a couple of hours, after which I came home and wrote [Edouard] Colonne a note in which I lied and said that I had only been in Paris for a day and therefore could not attend personally. The note expressed sincere gratitude, and he really did perform *The Tempest* very well. Here I was considerably calmer, but I decided that I had to spend some time in pleasure. Therefore I dined quickly and went to search for *Luisa.* For some time my search was unsuccessful until suddenly: there she was! I was unimaginably glad for she really was quite attractive to me. We immediately turned into a deserted street and had an explanation. It turned out that she had not come to the *rendezvous* that other time because she had had a very unpleasant accident. A carriage had struck her on the leg and hurt it considerably. She was in bed for two or three days and still walks with a slight limp. She suggested we go to her place. She lives immeasurably far away. We walked for a long time, then took an omnibus, then walked some more, moreover I spent the whole time engrossed in her chatter, as if it were the most wonderful music, and in general felt quite in love. Finally we reached rue de Maine. That is an area of petty

tradesmen. On this and the following street, de la Goite, there was a mass of revellers, bar after bar, dancing halls with open windows from which music thundered. In order to get to her *mansarde* it was necessary to enter an *Assomoir,* drink *une mante avec de l'eau frappe,* slip through a small door, then climb up a narrow and dark staircase leading to a tiny room with slanted ceiling and a window not in the wall, but in the ceiling!!! All that the room contained was a bed, a sorry trunk, a dirty table with candle- stub, several pairs of holey trousers and shirts hanging on nails, an enormous crystal glass won in the lottery. And nonetheless at that moment I felt that this miserable room was the focus of all human happiness. He (I can't use the feminine pronoun talking about that dear person) immediately showed me passport and diplomas, which fully proved the truth of all that he had told me about himself. Then there were various *calinerie* [tender words], as he put it, and then I became possessed with amorous happiness and the most improbable pleasure was experienced. With no exaggeration I can say that it has not only been a long time, but that I have almost never been as happy in that sense as yesterday. Then we went to some kind of entertainment: something between a *café chantants* and a theater, then we were in some café and drank a lot of beer, then walked for terribly long on foot, again drank beer, and parted at one in the morning. I was so exhausted by the mass of impressions that I was not able to make it home and engaged a cab. Reaching home I fell onto the bed and fell dead asleep, leaving Alyosha a note in giant letters asking him not to wake me up before ten o'clock.

However I awoke at seven o'clock, with a terrible weight in my head, with tedium, with pangs of conscience, with a full consciousness of the falsity and exaggerated nature of the happiness I felt yesterday and which, in essence, is nothing but a strong physical attraction founded on the fact that Luisa corresponds to the capricious demands of my taste and on his prettiness in general. However that might be, the youth has *much that is fine* in the root of his soul. But my God, how pitiful, how profoundly debauched he is! And instead of encouraging his improvement, I only help him to descend further downwards. I shall tell you at our meeting many charming details bearing witness to his naiveté combined with debauchery. Honestly speaking, he really should return to Lyons, where his father and mother have a hat shop. But he can't return other than as *a decent young man,* and for this he needs at least five hundred francs. I read his parents' letters, which show that they are decent people. As if on purpose I shall have to leave without being in a condition to give him real help, namely to send him to Lyons. I shall tell you about how radically mistaken I was in some of my calculations, or how Nadezhda Filaretovna [von Meck] was mistaken in hers, but God grant only that I have enough money to get to *Berlin.* I have already written to Jurgenson asking him to wire me a transfer to a Berlin bank for five hundred marks, in order to get to Petersburg.

I must leave quickly, and without delay I am departing the day after tomorrow, on *Wednesday.* As far as *the failure of The Tempest* is concerned, this has faded into the background and depresses me little today. *That is,* I mean the failure it evoked *in me.* I have reconciled myself to this circumstance based on the fact that, after the opera and suite, I shall finally write a model symphonic composition. So, up to my last breath, it seems, I shall only strive for mastery and never achieve it. I lack something, that much I feel, but there's nothing I can do.

My head no longer aches. The weather is marvelous, and I have been walking like crazy. I breakfasted in a stylish restaurant. I send you a newspaper clipping on yesterday's concert. The newspaper is *Paris-Journal*. Kisses. Show Anatoly this letter. I ask his forgiveness that he will have to read of my amorous adventures. [2]

The remorse which Tchaikovsky experienced the following morning after meeting with a prostitute and the sentiment it reveals is clearly that of social, rather than sexual, guilt; it resembles the sensibilities of some of Tolstoy's or Dostoyevsky's characters. Recent studies of the composer's archives in Klin strongly suggest that "it would be a profound mistake to believe that Tchaikovsky all his life suffered from his 'anomaly.' As can be seen in his letters, in the last decades of his life he achieved a happy psychological balance—after fruitless attempts to struggle against his nature."[3]

In the course of many years, Tchaikovsky demonstrated a particular devotion to his extended family, which included not only his father and his siblings but nephews and even more distant relatives as well. Toward the end of his life Tchaikovsky found himself surrounded by an adoring group of young male relatives and their friends. Their presence must have contributed to his sense of contentedness when he achieved the peak of world fame with his triumphant tour to the United States, where he presided over the inauguration of New York's Carnegie Hall, and later to England to receive the degree Doctor of Music *honoris causa*.

In the memoirs of Konstantin de Lazari we find glimpses of Tchaikovsky's life immediately after his flight abroad in 1877 and the records of their occasional meetings during the following years, all incorporated into his habitually chatty narrative.[4]

Of particular interest are diary entries of the poet and amateur composer Grand Duke Konstantin Konstantinovich (1858–1915), nephew of Tsar Alexander II. These entries begin on 19 March 1880, when the Grand Duke met Tchaikovsky for the first time. The Grand Duke was twenty-two years old and created a most favorable impression on the composer. Tchaikovsky wrote about this meeting to Mrs. von Meck: "The young man proved to be extremely pleasant and very gifted in music. We sat from nine o'clock until two in the morning talking about music. He composes quite nicely, but unfortunately does not have the time to work at it persistently."[5] They forged a strong friendship and were in correspondence right up to the composer's death. Konstantin Konstantinovich dedicated a poem to Tchaikovsky, and Tchaikovsky wrote the Six Songs, op. 63, and the chorus "Blessed is he who smiles" [*"Blazhen kto ulybaetsia"*], to verses by the Grand Duke.[6] The excerpts below are taken from the Grand Duke's unpublished diary, preserved in the Russian archives.[7]

It seems that at about the same time, Tchaikovsky also met Konstantin Konstantinovich's father, the brother of Alexander II, Grand Duke Konstantin Nikolayevich, who had personal interests in art and literature. During this meeting Tchaikovsky made the acquaintance of another composer, who wrote music mostly for ballets, Baron Boris Vietinghoff-Schell (1829–1901).[8] The latter published reminiscences of this event in the Moscow newspaper *Moskovskie vedomosti* in 1899.[9] The Baron's recollections emphasize one moving feature of Tchaikovsky's character—his remarkable capacity for gratitude.

In the spring of 1888, while visiting his brother Anatoly in Tiflis, Tchaikovsky met a young officer, Vasily Korganov (1865–1934), who would later become a pianist and musicologist. In 1902–1904, Korganov studied the theory and history of music in Berlin, but the rest of his life he spent in Tiflis and Erevan, teaching music. Korganov wrote several popular books on Mozart, Beethoven, and Verdi. In his recollections he described his meeting with Tchaikovsky in great detail. The narrative betrays, sometimes amusingly, the personality of its author in a mixture of dilettantism, ambition, arrogance, and naiveté. Published in 1940, Korganov's memoirs have never been included in standard editions of memoirs about the composer.[10]

In 1912, Tchaikovsky's physician, Vasily Bertenson (1853–1933), published memoirs in which he wrote about the composer and many other Russian celebrities whom he met during his life.[11] Bertenson's attempts to analyze Tchaikovsky's personality in psychological terms are not completely satisfactory, but, since he often had the opportunity to observe the composer at close quarters and under strain, he offers a few valuable insights. Still, his conclusions are not only confused, but they also betray the influence of the "canonical" portrait of Tchaikovsky created by Modest, which Bertenson knew both from the latter's biography of Tchaikovsky and through his personal correspondence with the composer's brother.

The next reminiscences are from the pen of the famous Russian actor Konstantin Varlamov (1849–1915).[12] The anecdotal story from Tchaikovsky's life that we find there is obviously told for reasons of entertainment and is based on fact. It is known that Tchaikovsky greatly feared death and anything associated with it.

When, in 1890, Tchaikovsky traveled to Florence with the express purpose of composing the opera *The Queen of Spades*, he took with him Modest's manservant Nazar Litrov (?–1900), leaving his own servant Alexey Sofronov behind in Klin with the latter's dying wife. During his stay abroad, Nazar Litrov kept a diary in which he recorded his conversations and observations with Tchaikovsky, as well as his impressions of Florence.[13] This diary, written by a minimally literate but intelligent and imaginative individual, is a unique document of daily life that records many valuable particulars about Tchaikovsky himself and the composition of the opera. In it one finds Tchaikovsky perceived through the eyes of a servant fully devoted to his master and touchingly concerned with his well-being. The diary has never been published in its entirety. Below we have included both published and hitherto unpublished excerpts from Nazar Litrov's diary.

Konstantin de Lazari

In the fall of 1877, I met Modest Tchaikovsky on the platform of the Nikolayevsky Train Station, and here I learned that Pyotr Ilyich had fled Moscow, married, and fallen ill. At that time there was concern for his mental health. But the decisiveness with which he underwent treatment, and his trip abroad for this purpose in the company of his brother Anatoly, completely eliminated the early stages of illness. In early 1878, when his brother Modest traveled abroad to replace Anatoly at Tchaikovsky's side, everything reached a happy conclusion, and the patient needed only complete rest and a warm climate in the company of a loved one. He spent the greater part of the winter in San Remo, the spring he spent in Clarens, and the summer at the estate of his sister [Alexandra] Davydova, in the village of Kamenka in Kiev province.

In the fall of 1878 he made an attempt to return to his professorial duties at the Moscow Conservatory, but he withstood this for no more than a month and abandoned teaching forever.

During this time I was able to see him only after he had decided to abandon the Moscow Conservatory, i.e., in October or November of 1878. He was staying with his brother Anatoly in Pushkin Street. Seeing him for the first time after such a long separation, I found him greatly changed. As if by magic, the youth had turned into an old man. Such was my first impression. I went to see him on a day when he was particularly upset, so that at first I was even denied entry to see him. But, hearing my voice, he insisted that I enter. The first minute I could hardly overcome my shock at seeing the change in him, but immediately I began to joke and tease him, recalling how he had conducted in 1872 in Moscow. That was always the first thing I used to cheer him up. I mimicked all the awkward movements he made while he was making his way to the conductor's podium, the way he said something to the first violins, less because he had something to tell them than to conceal his confusion, the way he took up the baton, "found the vein" (he had a strange, nervous movement of the upper lip), and began to wave it confusedly.

In less than half an hour Pyotr Ilyich was as animated and cheerful as his former self, and he succumbed to his charming, childlike laughter.

He spent only a few weeks in Petersburg at this time, and, of course, I saw him almost every day.

Soon all trace disappeared of the nervous disorder that had almost killed him, and, since he was free of all obligatory duties incidental to his creative work, he began to compose more than before, and he won increasing fame with his trips abroad.

In this period of his life, i.e., from the late 1870s to the end of his life, I saw him much less frequently than before, but all the more sincere and friendly were our meetings whenever he was in Petersburg. Until 1885, he resided in the small town of Kamenka, where his sister's family lived. After 1885 he arranged himself an independent lodging outside Moscow, at first near Klin, and then, in the final year of his life, in Klin itself.

Of our numerous meetings in this period of his life, best of all I recall how he came to my house directly from the palace after his second performance for the Emperor. It is necessary to add that Pyotr Ilyich had long felt a particular adoration for the person of Alexander III, from the time the latter was Crown Prince. When this memorable monarch ascended the throne, His Majesty's graces flowed onto Tchaikovsky one after the other. In 1883, he was commissioned to compose a cantata for performance in the Granovitaya Hall during the coronation banquet, and for this he was given a marvelous gift from His Majesty's office. Soon after he was awarded the Order of Vladimir. . . . This was the occasion for Pyotr Ilyich's first performance for the Emperor in Gatchina. The second time he was deemed worthy of similar honor was in 1891, when he was awarded a lifetime pension of 3,000 rubles.

After this second performance he came to my house. I will never forget how nervous he was! The main cause of his torment was that the official circumstances of His Majesty's reception, and also his natural confusion, had not permitted him to express the full degree of his gratitude and adoration for the Emperor.

On this visit he gave his photographs to all my family with affectionate inscriptions. When I upbraided him for not dedicating a single song to me, he threw himself on my neck and begged me to forgive him, swearing that he would dedicate pieces to all of my family, and that to me he would dedicate the polka which I myself had composed, and which I had always played in jest on a toy pipe.

"I'll not only dedicate this polka to you, Konstantin, but I'll work it into a ballet. Play it for me, please."

Sometimes he would come to my house to play cards. What an idiosyncratic gambler he was! He was terribly fond of playing; he would get angry when he was losing, but he seemed even more distressed when luck was on his side. He immediately began to feel sorry for the loser, and when it came time to settle accounts, he would not accept money for anything, even from his most intimate friends. He only took money when it would be insulting to his partner to refuse.

His attention span sufficed only for the first rubbers (except for *yeralash* and *vint* he didn't enjoy playing any games), but the further things went, the worse they became. Woe if he happened to get a stubborn partner; on such occasions Tchaikovsky would become utterly confused and play even worse than he was capable of playing. There was no end to his apologies to his partner for each mistake; however, he not only did not get angry over his partner's own mistakes, he would even try to defend the partner if others criticized him.

Grand Duke Konstantin Konstantinovich

19 March 1880

I spent a delightful evening at the house of Vera Butakova.[14] She had promised to introduce me to Tchaikovsky, our finest composer, whom she also invited. His brother Anatoly, Apukhtin, and Shcherbatov were also there.[15]

Pyotr Ilyich Tchaikovsky is about thirty-five years old, although his face and graying hair make him look much older.[16] He is of small height, quite thin, with a short beard and meek, intelligent eyes. His movements, manner of speaking and entire appearance reveal an extremely well-bred, educated, and dear man. He was educated at the School of Jurisprudence, was very unlucky in his family life, and now only works at music.

Apukhtin is famous for his immoderate obesity and wonderful poetic works, which he will never agree to publish. He remembers them and recites them by heart. Butakova persuaded him to read us something. He recited "Venice," not a well-known poem. It is so good that, as he recites it, one becomes afraid that it might end soon; one wants to keep on listening for longer.

I was forced to play; I wanted to play a song by Tchaikovsky, but was afraid to. His brother sings; I accompanied him on "A tear trembles" [*"Sleza drozhit"*]; then I played "None but the lonely heart," and then [my] romance in B-flat.

Tchaikovsky was asked to play something from his still unfinished opera *Joan of Arc*.[17] He sat down at the piano and played the chorus-prayer. We were all enraptured by the marvelous music. This is the moment when the nation recognizes Joan's prophetic gift, and she utters a prayer to the Lord God. The form of the composition is reminiscent of the prayer in the first act of *Lohengrin:* the voices gradually rise, constantly increasing in intensity, until finally they reach the fortissimo and highest note together with the orchestra. This *morceau d'ensemble* must be especially good and effective on stage.

After supper Apukhtin recited several more poems of his own composition. We parted at two o'clock. Tchaikovsky made the most pleasant impression on me.

30 March 1880

I am writing late at night under the impression of a delightfully spent evening. My guests were Pyotr Ilyich Tchaikovsky, Shcherbatov, and Nilov,[18] and the conversation mainly touched on music, especially opera. We decided to ask Tchaikovsky to go with us around the world on [the Imperial ship] *Duke*. He is very tempted by our invitation. But there is a steep obstacle: whether the authorities in command will agree to it. It would be good if fate arranged this.[19]

My comrades found at my piano the romance I once wrote to the words of Tolstoy: "When the sleepy forest is silent all around."[20] They made me play it. Since it is written in rough copy and without the words I could hardly make it out; Pyotr Ilyich wouldn't stand a chance. They liked the final high phrase "and I want to *press* your dear hand," which had made me work like a horse with a painted-on feedbag. And they sang it for long afterwards.

Although there were only four of us we sat until two o'clock without noticing the time, engrossed in unceasing conversation. We, that is I, bade farewell to Tchaikovsky with visible mutual joy, as if we had already known each other for a long time and were already close friends. His nearsighted eyes shone with a kind, tender light; his intelligence shows through them.

Boris Vietinghoff-Schell

[Tchaikovsky's] name, so dear to Russian art, immediately brings tears to one's eyes. Some kind of evil destiny follows our outstanding artists and unmercifully plucks the best of them from our midst at the very zenith of their artistic careers! How many wonderful creations were still to come when this bright ray of our national glory was extinguished.

Tchaikovsky himself told me how difficult was the beginning of his musical career. Due to circumstances beyond his control, he decided to devote himself to his musical vocation comparatively late, thus losing quite a bit of time. Financial straits forced him to resort to giving lessons and translating the texts of various songs from foreign tongues into Russian, for which he was paid by the line. All of this took time, distracting him from his work.

I knew Tchaikovsky when he was still working at the Conservatory. People were already saying that he was very promising; some were quick to say that promises are not always kept, but no one could guess at that time that his name would become one of the most popular in the musical world.

In 1880, I met Tchaikovsky at the house of Grand Duke Konstantin Nikolayevich, who was hosting a performance of my oratorio *John Damascene,* with organ, piano, and a string quartet. The Grand Duke himself played the cello.

During the intermission a conversation arose concerning the difficulties connected with an artistic career; turning to Tchaikovsky, the Grand Duke said: "A composer's career is also not without its thorns."

To this Tchaikovsky answered: "Yes, Your Highness, there are many such thorns and they prick one most painfully. But after all, the world is not without kind people." Here he named Nikolay Rubinstein, and then, pointing to me, he said: "The Baron is also a good man. I recall his favor with gratitude."

I was very surprised as I had absolutely no idea what he was talking about. The Grand Duke started to ask what this favor consisted of. Tchaikovsky said that, many years ago, when he was still at the Conservatory, he experienced great hardship due to his poverty. He decided to give lessons and came to me to ask me to recommend him as a teacher of music to my rich friends the B[egichev]s. My recommendation had the desired effect, the lessons were frequent and generously paid, and this helped him considerably.

"And I remember this favor," he added, "because I felt terrible, and 'a beautiful egg is always best at Easter.'"

I didn't remember any of this, and if Tchaikovsky had not named my friends I would have thought him mistaken. I didn't even remember the name of the man I recommended; and who could think that fifteen years later the fame of this poverty-stricken worker would shine brightly in the musical firmament. Few are able to make it on the composer's path of thorns. It is difficult to climb up. The slope is very steep. Few have enough talent and strength to overcome the various obstacles, both material and moral, and also the "indifference of society, the bias of epigones and the judgments of dandies," as Dargomyzhsky once wrote in my album. I myself would also add: it's difficult to overcome one's envious detractors.

Tchaikovsky was able to overcome all of this in a comparatively short time thanks to the fact that, in addition to his extraordinary talent, he enjoyed the friendship of Nikolay Rubinstein, who immediately raised the price and significance of this musical pearl and did much to ease Tchaikovsky's way to fame and to make his works well known. Nikolay Rubinstein was fully rewarded by the touching sense of gratitude he encountered in Pyotr Ilyich, and which Tchaikovsky clearly expressed in this case.

This trait is rare among those who have risen high above the general level, and it works to increase Tchaikovsky's honor. He was very kind, polite, sensitive, and was always ready to help however he could. In general he was a most pleasant man.

As an artist he was a rare phenomenon. All of his music is filled with poetry. His *Francesca da Rimini, Italian Capriccio, The Tempest,* all of *Eugene Onegin,* his symphonies, [the overture] *1812,* all of these works captivate one's soul. When one listens to them one experiences them, so to speak, together with him. And all the gracious charms sprinkled in his *The Sleeping Beauty,* and his songs, his romances! And so many more precious contributions would he have made to Russian art had he not gone so early to his grave.

Once, at a performance of the ballet *The Harlem Tulip [Garlemskii tiul'pan],* for which I wrote the music, Tchaikovsky said to me: "You know, Baron, that I have been commissioned to write a ballet. So I have come to listen closely and learn how ballets are written, since I have never had the opportunity to do one before."

"Why are you pulling my leg, Pyotr Ilyich?" I answered him.

"You are wrong to think that," he objected. "I especially chose your ballet for this because I love your music. The tulips' waltz is charming, and so is the entr'acte. Afterwards I shall come to visit you, to ask you to tell me how you undertook this, how you came to terms with the ballet director and coordinated the length of the musical numbers with the dance requirements. I was told that ballet masters are very free with the music when they stage a ballet, demanding many changes and revisions. It is impossible to write under such conditions. We can also speak about how to avoid this."

I took all of this as a polite joke on his part, but in several days he came to visit me and we discussed it in detail.

I keep in my album Tchaikovsky's note, where he asks me to come to the general rehearsal of *The Sleeping Beauty* and promises to get me a seat in the theater for the first performance.

And for his autograph he chose a page in my album that already bore the autograph of Nikolay Rubinstein, and asked me to allow him to write on the same page, saying, "so as not to part with this dear friend, to whom I owe so much." What a charming and touching character trait!

His precious autograph consists of three measures of music, under which is written, "To Baron Boris Alexandrovich Vietinghoff-Schell, in memory of his sincere friend, P[yotr] Tchaikovsky. 3 November 1887. St. Petersburg."

Both this autograph and the sincere content of the note written under it are extremely valuable to me.

Vasily Korganov

[At the end of March 1888] a rumor spread that Tchaikovsky was expected to come [to the rehearsal of our concert in Tiflis], but this did not bother me because for some reason I was sure that he would not attend an amateur concert.

One feast-day morning we began to rehearse the Polonaise; then we took up the *Souvenir de Hapsal.* The concert hall was empty, not a single person in the audience. Suddenly the door opened at the opposite end of the hall and [our concert's sponsor] Goncharova[21] came in accompanied by five or six people, among whom I recognized Tchaikovsky, whose appearance I knew from photographs! . . . It is difficult to describe my reaction! I lost my confidence, became shy, my hand began to shake, everything went dark. Leaving the group of visitors at the end of the hall, Tchaikovsky set off right toward the stage with soft, inaudible steps.

I continued to wave my hand, but only in a mechanical, unconscious way, cursing the day when I had agreed to take up something I knew so little about. But Tchaikovsky continued to move toward me, toward the steps that lead from the audience to the stage. His straight, well-built figure was coming on me like a ghost; he rose up, walked around the piano and approached from behind. The piece is short, about five minutes in length, and this was just long enough for him to cross the hall and turn up behind my back at the last sound of the piece's dwindling finale.

"Allow me to introduce myself: Tchaikovsky," he said to me, extending his hand.

I froze and waited: what next?

"Why do you wave your baton beneath the music stand? The ladies can't see the baton."

Gathering my strength I answered, "It's a good thing that I myself didn't crawl under the stand and spread out on the floor."

"Well, well, you must be bolder. What else are you playing? The Polonaise? *Egmont?* . . . Bring your notes and come to see me tomorrow at nine in the morning. I am staying with my brother on Consul Street. We can study all three pieces together. Good- bye."

Then, turning to the girls at the pianos, he said, "The ladies have learned their parts well. Everything will be great. It's only necessary to fine-tune a couple of things."

Then, apparently having noticed the startling impression he had made on me, which had also been communicated to the girls, Tchaikovsky gave us all a bow and walked off toward the exit, and the entire group of visitors disappeared, leaving us with the most "disheveled feelings." We quickly finished up the rehearsal and parted, so as to gather again at the following rehearsal the next Sunday, when I would appear as "Tchaikovsky's protégé. . . ."

At the appointed hour I was at Tchaikovsky's place, where there was hardly enough room for a bed, table, and piano. He asked me about my past musical activity and then, opening up the two-handed transcriptions of the three pieces I had brought and which I was to conduct, he, I remember, made several hasty comments regarding the Polonaise and "Souvenir," noting with a pencil several nuances right on the score. The score with his handwritten notations is probably at the Tiflis Conservatory, to which I gave my entire music library in

1921. We spent about half an hour on the third piece, *Egmont*, and Tchaikovsky made more pencil marks on the score and, learning that I did not know the program of this overture, began to tell about the heavy steps of the Spanish soldiers sent to pacify the rebellious Dutch, which are depicted in the chords of the Andante, 3/2, about the pleas of the repressed nation, about the latter's final victory, etc. He advised me to conduct the Andante with six thrusts: two down, two to the left, two to the right, and the finale with one thrust on the beat. After this "lesson" we talked for about half an hour, moreover he noted that I often glanced at his unusually red hands.

"That's from my nerves; the French call this disease 'rougeur.' Because of it I sometimes conduct in gloves."

I had already known of the composer's extreme nervousness, but I had heard that this nervousness was mostly manifested in frequent tears, crying and even sobbing, which almost always occurred in solitude, after reading something touching, sometimes from sad thoughts, sometimes after abundant libations to Bacchus, in which he did not refrain from indulging even in company, even at invited dinners. Throughout our conversation I could not take my eyes off his straight, large and beautiful hands; I kept wanting to touch them; it seemed that they would seem hot, flaming. However upon parting I was even more surprised to feel their normal warmth.

Hearing out my request for a page of manuscript score, Tchaikovsky at first fell into deep contemplation, then dug around for a long time among his papers and got out three sheets of score paper filled with pencil marks and a multitude of corrections.

"I don't understand, how did this get here?" he said, extending to me the three sheets, with which I acquainted myself at home. These twelve pages contained the waltz (scherzo) from his Fifth Symphony. I effused in expressions of gratitude as much as I was able, and I preserved this manuscript, covering each sheet with transparent (calque) paper, until the spring of 1923, when I was forced to sell it to the Berlin antique dealer Joseph Altmann (Lützow Ufer, 13), who placed it on auction on May 5 and 6, together with my entire manuscript collection. In his printed catalogue no. 25 this manuscript is no. 254: "Pracht-stück: Skizze zum Walzer aus V Symphonie"; the same collection held a note by Tchaikovsky with an envelope (no. 255 in the same catalogue) regarding the piano of Diderichs' factory and the orchestral ballad *The Voivode*, about which see below.

Learning that I was a native of Tiflis, Tchaikovsky began to praise to the skies our natural surroundings, climate, and society.

"For us northerners everything is marvelous here. We aren't spoilt by frequent sun. There is still snow in Petersburg right now, fog. . . . Unfortunately all of my family is occupied with work during the day, while I, after working until noon, set off to walk on foot, most often to Mushtaid Gardens, from which I have simply become inseparable. Everything is so good there, delightful! Despite my tendency toward solitude, sometimes at home or on walks it would be nice to share one's impressions with someone, but I always have to walk alone. Don't you work at the same place as the unfortunate Verinovsky?[22] He also had to stay at work until dinnertime. Did you know him? Poor man!"

"No," I answered. "He wasn't at engineering school when I was there, and I returned to Tiflis when he had already passed away. Sometimes," I dared to add, "I am free during the day, and if you would permit me, I could accompany you to Mushtaid."

"Good. Your work is near the Cadet Corps. You see, I even know where the sapper barracks are located. We can meet above the upper entrance to Alexand-rovsky Park; I pass by there at about half-past twelve."

"No," I objected. "My work is near the train station, and I would prefer to wait for you in Mikhailov Street, near the German church."

"Well, all right, we can meet that way. Are you often free?"

"Once or twice a week, from twelve to two," I lied, and, taking up the score, I began to take my leave and thank him for the "lesson."

"Good-bye, then. I pass by the German church when its clock shows one o'clock sharp. Well, keep in mind that I sometimes go to the Botanical Gardens, and don't blame me if you don't meet me."

Returning home, I noted in my diary my impressions from this visit and considered both it and the future strolls at some length. Tchaikovsky's tone of voice seemed to me to be simultaneously polite and sincere, but at times cold and condescendingly proud, which did not make me feel much sympathy for the great composer. "And what kind of artist is he, what kind of genius?" I thought. "He is so dapper; his bearing is that of director in the civil service, of a real jurist! He takes delight in nature, but sounds like the straight-laced ladies and cavaliers of the beau monde in their salons." At the same time I was strongly attracted to him, the author of thousands of wonderful harmonies. I wanted to learn a lot from the first famous composer whom I had chanced to meet, who was the first to invite me to his home, and who had given me the honor of an interesting music lecture. Before, I only knew César Cui, but more as a general and professor of fortifications who would give me tickets to the exams of the Petersburg Conservatory and who printed my correspondence in his journal, *Muzykal'noe obozrenie*.

I had worked for periodicals, and had already (in late 1887) published my first book, a thin little brochure about Beethoven. But I was attracted and fascinated by something else, I was obsessed by the "cursed questions" of the philosophy of art. I greedily attacked books by Hegel and Proudhon, Taine and

Cherbuliez, but I found answers, although ones that did not fully satisfy me, in Hanslick and Helmholz.[23] I was surprised and scandalized to find that, not only in society, among acquaintances, but even among performers, musicians, teachers at the Tiflis Musical School, I could not find anyone with any knowledge of these writers, let alone any interest in the fundamental principles of art, which seemed to me to be correctly expounded only by Hanslick and Helmholz. This mood evoked in me the need to teach the public, and in 1889 I read two public lectures in the "Tiflis Circle," where I expounded the ideas of Hanslick and Helmholz in a popular and concise manner. At the time I was delirious with them, I sought someone to talk to about them, but I could not find anyone. Moreover I craved to hear from an outstanding musician quite a few clarifications and developments of fundamental principles of musical art, quite a few answers to questions that remained unresolved for me, but I could not find such a mentor.

And lo and behold fate was sending me one of the best imaginable mentors! I dreamed of hearing from Tchaikovsky confirmation of the correctness of the ideas I had arrived at, or else their well-grounded rebuttal and critique. Being unsociable by nature, reticent, loving solitude (later on I had on the doors of my office a printed poster with a quotation from Cicero: "Only in solitude do I not feel lonely") and avoiding contact with "society," I nonetheless decided to skip out of work twice a week under various pretexts in order to accompany Tchaikovsky to Mushtaid, or to hear from him words of revelation.

Two days later, not without agitation and a shudder, I awaited him on the corner of Kirochnaya and Mikhailov streets, searching the distance for the well-built figure and gray beard of the composer. He appeared at the appointed hour and we set off at a quick and steady pace toward Mushtaid. I wanted to start interviewing him immediately, but at the same time it seemed awkward to do so. Tchaikovsky, probably taking my silence for shyness, began to speak of the features of street life near the bathhouses in the old part of the city, which he liked for their original and exotic nature.

"Have you never had the occasion," I asked, "to hear a zurna or sazandar, the music of those Asiatics who flood the bath district?"

"Oh, no! I avoid it, I can't stand Asiatic music. It is often quite original, but in general I find it unpleasant; I get convulsions from it, nervous twitching, especially in the face muscles. . . . And how are your symphonic concerts going? I recall that I was at one which was held with an empty hall. But the public here, it seems, likes serious music."

"Yes, symphonic concerts are not catching on here; the hall is rarely full; it seems that the public is not mature enough yet."

"You have to train it, attract it, at least by inviting famous pianists or singers to take part. . . . Gradually you will be able to attract the public and elicit interest in these concerts. After all, the same thing has happened everywhere, and even now quite a few concerts are held everywhere to a half-empty auditorium."

I began to examine Tchaikovsky regarding his concerts in Europe, but he answered somehow reluctantly, recalling his appearances with some agitation in his voice.

"It seems," he said, "I shall never get accustomed to appearing on stage. What tortures I endure before every show! How horrible I feel throughout the concert and what a loss of strength, what exhaustion appears afterwards! . . . Where did you read about these concerts?"

"In *Muzykal'noe obozrenie*."

My maneuver seemed close to its goal. Having already mentioned the concerts, it would be easy to shift the conversation onto the critics' reviews, and then to the "cursed questions" of musical aesthetics that interested me, although certain circumstances presented dangerous underwater reefs on my chosen path. The very mention of the journal had apparently annoyed the composer, since it was run by César Cui, who often wrote in a malicious manner about Tchaikovsky. In addition, I was aware that foreign critics, especially the Viennese, led by Eduard Hanslick, also had an almost hostile attitude toward him. However, I quickly conceived of a way to avoid the reefs. By this time we were already in the park. Tchaikovsky set off in the direction of the Kura [River] and, settling on a bench, began to express delight at the view of the opposite high bank with steep cliffs. Only after we began our return path did I renew our interrupted conversation about the composer's trip abroad.

"I read that the public received you wonderfully everywhere, but that the press expressed contradictory views. I am particularly interested by one question: are there any general principles of aesthetics in European music criticism? For example, does it recognize Hanslick's ideas? . . . "

"Oh, that Czech . . . only writes nonsense!" Tchaikovsky interrupted me and fell silent somewhat gloomily.

It was as if I had been struck on the head. I was stunned.

The conversation was not working out. We parted near the German church without saying a word about a future meeting.

Tchaikovsky's attitude failed to lower my esteem for Hanslick, but it dug such a chasm between myself and the composer that I could not find any way to reach Tchaikovsky.

But still I was attracted to him. I did not yet feel any vainglorious self-satisfaction from meeting famous people, as I did subsequently, when I would seek an opportunity to meet and speak with certain famous composers and writers, from whom I would request signed portraits. It was difficult for me to part with my illusion, and I still hoped to find in Tchaikovsky even a vague affirmation of the correctness of my thoughts. After all, it would not be polite for me to avoid showing up at another rendezvous and cut off our relations so rudely and stupidly.

Of our second stroll I remember only that I found it necessary to spend about half an hour with the famous composer, that I prepared myself for this stroll and thought through a series of questions about the composer's opinion of Wagner, of the Mighty Handful (Balakirev and Co.), about the organization and charter of our conservatories, etc. I did not get up the courage to mention the forthcoming concert which I was to conduct: I felt ashamed and awkward, and he did not ask me about it either. I also did not mention my recently printed brochure about Beethoven, although these two subjects were the most "topical" for me at that time.

Once again I escaped from work, again I met with Tchaikovsky, but the composer's cold and dry tone paralyzed all my prepared questions; noticing his taciturnity, I began to tell all sorts of stories from the history of Tiflis: something from the history of Mushtaid Gardens, about the past of Mikhailov Street or the "German colony," etc. Tchaikovsky seemed to listen readily to my chatter, but as soon as I tried to shift to a musical theme the expression of his face became gloomy and he answered with fitful phrases, as if he wanted to get rid of his insistent companion.

I did not seek a third meeting with Tchaikovsky. He left Tiflis five days before the Goncharova concert.

Vasily Bertenson

It is certainly true that Tchaikovsky was a surprisingly complicated character. It seems to me that two distinct personalities were blended in him. One manifested itself when he was calm, rested and creative, and completely happy in his solitude. The other was sickly, restless, and misanthropic, and it provided little inspiration for his creativity.

The predomination of the minor tone in many of his works and, more importantly, the tragic mood that ends his swan song, the Sixth Symphony, have established the opinion that he was a pessimist. However, the pessimism of his works is only a reflection of his own profound optimism.

Indeed, it is difficult to imagine a purer optimist. His bright vivacity, his love of life and of every living thing, his faith in the triumph of good and in people, and his capacity to be moved by the beauty of every blade of grass: these qualities never left him from the first moment of his conscious existence until the day before his fatal illness.

Pyotr Ilyich never used the expression, "I love," but always, "I adore." He applied the phrase to everything—Mozart's compositions, Tolstoy's works, flowers, dogs, pancakes with jam. This constant panegyric to life, together with his capacity for enthusing ecstatically over everything he encountered on the road of life, especially people, made him appear quite charming to all who met him.

In his presence everyone felt himself set on a pedestal created by Pyotr Ilyich's fiery imagination.

Always carried away by the impression of the present moment, always governed by his emotions rather than by his mind, he could not help being changeable—especially when his enchantment turned unmercifully to disappointment.

This is the source of his constant mourning for "what had been": not just because it had "passed," but also because it was no longer the "same" as it had seemed at that time.

This explains the minor mood in Pyotr Ilyich's creations and the fact that, entering the valley of old age, so to speak, he was able to write such a profound piece, such a deeply felt work, as his Sixth Symphony—under the influence of all that he had loved, that he had hoped for, that he had considered unfadingly beautiful, and that now appeared to him corrupt and decrepit, like his gray hair.

Many people called Tchaikovsky a misanthrope. Is this so?

True, he used to avoid people and he felt best in solitude, and this to such a degree that even people as close to his heart as his sister and brothers could be a burden to him, and sometimes he could be happy only when there was no one except the servants about him. Anyone who broke his measured routine of life was his personal enemy. During an artistic triumph his most intimate and gnawing desire was to flee from his admirers and hide from his friends.

Yet all this in no way stemmed from a dislike for people, but, on the contrary, from an excess of love for them. Anyone who is acquainted with his biography knows that his entire life was one of boundless love for everything: from the tiniest bug to a man, and from the smallest violet to the bright and fragrant talent of a young artist. He wished everything and everyone well and was only truly happy when he had succeeded in making someone else happy, or helping someone, or supporting something beautiful.

Tchaikovsky avoided medical treatment and was afraid of doctors; but, paradoxically, he was in constant need of them. In the well-known biography of Tchaikovsky by his brother Modest . . . it is stated that the only physician in the world of whom Pyotr Ilyich had no fear was myself.

Pyotr Ilyich was sick often from a young age. His brothers claimed that his main sickness, extreme oversensitivity, manifested itself not only in early childhood, but also in adolescence.

As a young boy, Tchaikovsky would wake up often during the night in hysterical fits. As he grew older, and in more mature years, this oversensitivity took the form of insomnia and fits he himself described as "slight strokes of paralysis." He would wake up suddenly, trembling with unconquerable fear, as though he had been struck by someone. These "slight strokes," at times recurring nearly every night, drove him to a hatred of going to bed that sometimes lasted for months, and during this time he would fall asleep only in his robe, sitting in his armchair, or curled up on the sofa.

But the main source of suffering, which afflicted him constantly from the age of thirty, was acid indigestion, which caused continual heartburn. In the 1870s he learned to avoid heartburn by taking sodium bicarbonate. When one of his friends recommended it to him for the first time, he told him to use a spoonful of soda in a glass of water. Pyotr Ilyich got it mixed up and put a spoonful of water in half a glass of soda. Despite the deplorable results of this first test of the remedy, from that day no one ever could visualize Tchaikovsky without a little jar of soda and Vichy lozenges in his pocket.

Despite all of this, Tchaikovsky's appetite was excellent, and he never had to watch what he ate. He always praised whatever was served to him, and, in later years, when he had his own household, he frequently called his cooks into the dining room to compliment them; his guests, who did not always agree that compliments were in order, had to avert their gaze so as not to contradict and displease their host.

Pyotr Ilyich drank a great deal, both vodka and wine. In the evening, especially during the periods of "slight strokes of paralysis," he abused cognac; there was even a time, according to his brothers, when he was close to actual alcoholism. Whenever he came from the country to the city, especially to Moscow, he took great pleasure in visiting restaurants, and then his favorite beverage was champagne, always sweet, with sparkling water.

He smoked from the age of fourteen without respite, especially during periods of work. He inhaled not only cigarette smoke, but also cigar smoke.

In general Tchaikovsky was absent-minded. This absent-mindedness, when combined with his organized nature, was at times the cause of various incidents. In this connection I recall the following occasion.

Arriving in Petersburg one summer, Tchaikovsky sent for me, but not as a doctor. Knowing my love for music, he wanted to give me the pleasure of going with him and his young nephews Vladimir Davydov and Count Alexander Litke[24] to the restaurant Aquarium. At that time the Aquarium was not a gathering of *étoiles* [stars] as it is today, but a modest garden where Engel's quite tolerable symphonic orchestra performed.[25]

That evening, incidentally, was the first performance of Tchaikovsky's famous Third Suite, with which several months previously the famous conductor Hans von Bülow had fascinated the overcrowded hall of the Assembly of the Nobility.[26] Pyotr Ilyich had been present behind the columns at this wonderful performance. The public, recognizing its favorite, began wildly to call the famous composer out, and the ovations for Tchaikovsky and Bülow reached such Homeric proportions that I remember them to this day.

Unfortunately the same Suite, performed on the evening I am describing at the Aquarium, failed to make any impression whatsoever either on Tchaikovsky or on us simple music-lovers. The orchestra of the Aquarium played without nuances, without inspiration, lifelessly. We left the concert in a state of disappointment.

Then Pyotr Ilyich invited us all to supper in order to erase what he saw as the unpleasant impression left by the evening. A good supper, he said, could cheer up anyone.

We went to Leiner's restaurant. The menu was very elaborate. Pyotr Ilyich ordered, among other things, a yard-long sterlet, etc. In a word, it was a grand repast. Then the bill was presented and Tchaikovsky discovered that he had left his wallet at home and had with him only a small purse with some change. Embarrassed, Tchaikovsky asked his nephews to help him out, but the young men, who had not counted on such a large expenditure, had not brought enough money with them either. Fortunately I turned out to be the "capitalist" of the evening.

The next morning Pyotr Ilyich sent me a note that read, "I return herewith my debt and thank the healer not only of my body but also of my pocket."

Pyotr Ilyich was unusually ignorant and naive regarding the simplest necessities of life, and age did not improve him. As a young man, having already graduated from the School of Jurisprudence, Tchaikovsky, according to his brother Modest, could not tell shot from gunpowder. Once he was found lighting shot and running to the opposite corner of the room in expectation of an explosion. As an old man, he would perplexedly ask questions he considered insoluble, such as: where does one buy nails? How might one, for example, get ahold of window putty? Pyotr Ilyich was not fully sure of how to pour the water or coal into a samovar! He would show off his ignorance before equals without a whit of embarrassment, but when he really had to display his helplessness he felt truly ashamed and would spare nothing to conceal it.

This was the basis of the following story, which one of Tchaikovsky's brothers related to me. . . . It occurred in the 1880s, when the composer was staying with his brother in St. Petersburg. Being fond of solitary walks, he avoided populous locales and chose the most secluded places.

Once, in bad weather (it was windy), he decided to walk to the Church of the Savior by crossing the frozen Neva River by the foot planks laid across the ice. After walking a good distance he realized that he had no cotton-wool in his ears—a precaution he was usually careful to take. With the sharp wind he might end up with the hated dental abscess he was susceptible to. At once the impossible question arose as to where he could get some cotton-wool. It was too far to go home, and by that time he would already be ill. No, he had to buy some cotton-wool, but where? Since the Petersburg Embankment was closer, he should obviously go there. But in which shop? Since he could not answer this question himself, he had to find out from someone else. But whom should he ask? Any passerby would think he was crazy.

Therefore, to disguise his ignorance, Tchaikovsky decided that the best thing to do would be to hasten to the first corner store, which was on the other side of the embankment, purchase something, and then casually ask where he could buy some cotton-wool, that is, to address a purely local question instead of a general one concerning the location of the cotton-wool.

He had not thought through what he was going to buy at the shop, so when the clerk asked him what he wanted Tchaikovsky was at a loss. Instead of cigarettes, matches, or any small article he could carry in his pocket, he impulsively asked for some apples. For the help the clerk was supposed to render him, Tchaikovsky was ready to give him his entire purse; therefore, when he was asked how many apples, he answered, "A dozen."

"What kind?" asked the salesman.

"The very best," said Tchaikovsky.

Then, while the biggest and best apples were being put into a bag, he casually asked the clerk where he could buy some cotton.

To which the answer was, "In the store next door."

With a bag full of apples, and overjoyed that the problem had been solved so easily, Tchaikovsky entered the next shop.

"What would you like?" asked the clerk.

"Some cotton-wool," replied Tchaikovsky.

"And how much?"

This question was quite unexpected. He realized that he could not ask for just enough cotton-wool to put in his ears. But, how is cotton-wool sold? By the yard? By the pound? Tchaikovsky was perplexed. When he heard the clerk's voice suggesting a pound, in a rush of thankfulness he cried, "Certainly, a pound!" The clerk told a boy to bring a pound of cotton-wool. An instant later from the depths of the store emerged a whole cloud of cotton, behind which the boy was lost. Tchaikovsky was horrified, but it was too late to confess that he only needed enough cotton-wool for his ears without seeming an idiot. The horror of contemplating an endless quantity of cotton- wool soon passed, as the experienced hands of the clerk turned the cloud into a reasonably sized packet.

With apples in one hand and a pound of cotton-wool in the other, Pyotr Ilyich left the shop and, stopping in an empty lane, decided to utilize his purchase. Without ceremony he made a hole in the packet and pulled out the necessary quantity for his ears, planning to take his purchases home. But then there occurred something utterly unforeseen. The cotton-wool had been so tightly packed by the clerk that it began to stretch, expand, and stick out of the hole Tchaikovsky had made, slowly turning back into a cloud. What could he do? Take a cab? But there were none around. He had to walk back over the foot planks. His hands, one holding the apples and the other holding the cloud that kept growing and bursting out of the packet, began to freeze in the wind. He began to think of ways to get rid of his unbearable load. He could throw both things under the planks. But passersby would take him for a madman or, more likely, for a criminal concealing the traces of some theft. He had to drink the cup to the bitter end and cross all the planks, and he was able to find a cab only on Gagarin Square.

Needless to say, this ill-starred cotton-wool was used for many months in the house of Tchaikovsky's brother.

Konstantin Varlamov

Pyotr Ilyich and I were friends, and my memories of this surprisingly modest, dear, and kind man have remained the brightest, best, and most unforgettable of recollections.

His modesty was such that when people would ask him about music he always made some excuse or other and tried to change the subject. But if pressed, he used to say: "I like all kinds of music. I like the music of a street-organ. I like hearing the sounds the metal combs produce. I even like the music that the musical clowns at the circus make with their bells, bottles, and the other instruments they've invented, because in every kind of sound, in every kind of music, I feel music."

He was the kindest of men. I never had occasion to observe in him the slightest arrogance, or to see him point out his own superiority or strength in anything. Of course, there can be no question that he was strong. A man of remarkable spiritual beauty, modest in the extreme, he charmed everyone around him with this quality.

He and I met often. He was a frequent guest at my home, and I never saw him other than calm, tranquil, and thinking only about his brilliant work.

His only peculiarity was his dread of ghosts. "You know, Konstantin, if someone wants to rob you, well so what, let them rob you; if they want to kill you, you can take a revolver and defend yourself, and the killer will head for the door or the window; but you can never escape from a ghost: through a crack, through a keyhole, it will find a way in." Now one day, he happened to receive an invitation to visit a certain estate. Pyotr Ilyich accepted. The family who had invited him had no idea what to do to prepare for his reception. He arrived at the estate, it should be noted, toward evening. He was welcomed, of course, with outstretched arms. They had tea, then the host said to him: "Dear Pyotr Ilyich, if it pleases you, we've prepared a separate pavilion for you, far from the main house, with a piano, where it's peaceful and quiet and no one will disturb you. Come, I'll show you." Off they went. Everything, indeed, was beautifully furnished and pleasant, and he thanked his host. "And there's a park," said his host, as he raised the window-blind. "Isn't it a wonderful view?"

"And what's that? What is that cross?" asked Pyotr Ilyich.

"Oh, that's nothing, just a grave, the late X is buried there."

"He left," Pyotr Ilyich told me, "and I lowered the blind and went to bed. I don't remember when, I believe around midnight, I woke up, my face and my entire body drenched in a cold sweat. I saw something white fluttering. I screamed—and fell to the floor. How long I lay there I don't remember. When at last I carefully opened my eyes, I saw it was already light—it was after four. After this I decided to leave there at once. Painful though it was for me to leave in this way, and thus disappoint the people who had been so delighted to have me stay with them and who had gone to so much trouble—still I left.

"I invented the excuse of having accidentally forgotten to take care of some pressing business."

After a while the whole story came out. Pyotr Ilyich himself said that the "white something" had been a towel hanging across from him, and his hosts, when they learned what had happened, said: "If only he'd told us, if he had told us he was afraid of ghosts, we would have given him the whole main house!"

Nazar Litrov

18/30 January 1890. Florence
Hotel. Settled in well, a separate apartment. We drank some tea. . . . We changed clothes. Pyotr Ilyich took us to show us the city, some rain, yet light air. . . . I began to figure things out. But Pyotr Ilyich left in order not to see the unpacking. The servant called to lunch, but I didn't understand anything.

Pyotr Ilyich has a drawing room, second is a bedroom, third a darkish room in which I put the suitcases and trunks. Half-past three Pyotr Ilyich came, began to read, and at four called for a bath—ordered tea, we admired the embankment, a piano was brought. Pyotr Ilyich played some chords. Went to the bath. I am very interested in the statues and paintings in the shops and on the buildings. Their baths are not like ours, only bathtubs. To the Hotel Washington. The Lungarno Embankment, what surprises me is boys' whistling, quite a lot and grown-up, they walk along the pavement and whistle some tunes. And also that at almost every building one can urinate on the street without any ceremony, ladies and girls don't pay any attention. . . . Pyotr Ilyich is writing a letter. Seven o'clock Pyotr Ilyich had dinner. . . . I went to buy tea and an ashtray. We went to bed at ten-thirty.— All is well.

19/31 January

Morning. . . . I got up at seven o'clock, a bit cold. Perhaps even nice for me. Got dressed, went to wake up Pyotr Ilyich, lit the fire, opened the shutters. Pyotr Ilyich was smoking a cigarette. He got up and was a bit upset that the maid had not cleaned the room, but that's because he didn't know yet that it is cleaned only when no one is in the room. Lord bless. Pyotr Ilyich breakfasted, questions about how my stroll was, the servant came, called me to breakfast. . . . Pyotr Ilyich returned from his walk and noted: "Smoke, which is why they called me." Pyotr Ilyich also began to drink tea. I went for a walk. What I admire is the statues and paintings in almost every window. Very nice. Came home. Pyotr Ilyich is working. . . . The day of the 19th went well, soon ten o'clock. Pyotr Ilyich was at the theater, returned about eleven o'clock. I slept in the other room, very big, seven paces across, eleven long, a very wide bed . . . and very comfortable, I slept like never at home.

20 January/1 February

Morning, Saturday, got up at seven o'clock. Lit the fire in Pyotr Ilyich's fireplace. I won't recall everything because now it's everyday monotony. At eight o'clock Pyotr Ilyich drinks tea, and I go to the general cafeteria and drink coffee, as much bread as I want and butter, because I like it very much. . . . Pyotr Ilyich is at work. . . . Pyotr Ilyich is concerned that I am cold and begs me to light the fire, but I refuse. First, firewood is very expensive, and we have to pay extra for it, and second, I don't find it necessary, because I love [to sleep] and sleep deeply in a chill. Pyotr Ilyich went for a walk and apparently will go to the theater. . . .

21 January/2 February

Pyotr Ilyich is working. I am in the bedroom and watch strolling people, who have been strolling in a mass. Pyotr Ilyich came in and tried to get me to go for a walk. Twelve o'clock, all is well. At lunch we drank madeira. On the occasion of Sunday. . . .

Pyotr Ilyich returned from his walk. Tea. We look out the window and curse everyone who looks intently at us, in Russian of course, and really very fun, he looks at us, and we make impudent remarks at him, of course with a smiling face. . . .

25 January/5 February

Now I only feel sorry for myself, that I am so ignorant and can't communicate what I feel and that it is too late for me now. But still I am very happy and don't know how to thank [Pyotr Ilyich] for such benevolence and how I can merit [it], no merit of mine can be higher than this virtue which I have been feeling all this time for Pyotr Ilyich. I don't know if I help any with my presence and such small service, which is my obligation: the service consists of him not being alone, and that's it. But then I am such a bad companion that I doubt that I give him a drop of pleasure, except for large expenses. Maybe that is why he took me since he said when we were leaving that he's scared of being alone, in case he gets sick.

29 January/10 February

Pyotr Ilyich is in a good mood today. Yesterday he began a new scene, and I observe it is going well. He praises Modest Ilyich's libretto. Each time before the end of his work I enter the room and say that it is time to eat lunch or dinner. I don't know, perhaps this disturbs him, but he doesn't seem to express dissatisfaction. If I noticed, of course, I wouldn't enter. This is the problem. Perhaps Pyotr Ilych thinks that I enter just out of boredom, that he is unoccupied at that time, and he just puts a tender and good-natured face on it. But no, I'm not bored at all yet. And I enter only in order to take his own mind off of things, and if I didn't do that, perhaps he himself would think that I am unhappy with him over something, but it's all the same while everything's all right, and thank God. I entered at seven o'clock. Pyotr Ilyich wasn't finished yet. I said: "Time to finish." He replied right away but continued to draw little hooks. "Yes," I said, "it'll soon be seven o'clock." "Coming," he said, and did one more little hook, and struck the lid of the piano with his hand. I stood still. He took out his watch and opened it. "It's only twenty of, I can work another ten minutes." I said something. And he: "Let me work just another ten minutes." I left. In ten minutes he came out to me. "Well, I'm finished," and began to ask me what I had been doing (I had been writing; as soon as he walked in, I closed my notebook), and we went to his room. Pyotr Ilyich took to walking back and forth around his room while I stood by the table. We spoke about Feklusha, Alexey, etc.[27] For the first time I heard Pyotr Ilyich talk about his future composition with praise. "It'll be an opera, God grant, it'll work out so well that you'll burst out crying, Nazar." I said: "God grant that it goes well," while to myself I said: "and God grant you good health."

1/13 February

Good weather. Pyotr Ilyich is healthy and as I see his work is going well. At least he himself says so.

3/15 February

At twelve o'clock I came to Pyotr Ilyich. For the first time he complained that his work went badly.

11/23 February

I am not bored at all, but I fear that Pyotr Ilych is displeased: the doctor and masseur attend to him and bother him, and Pyotr Ilyich hates this terribly, although he tries not to show it. But I know for sure that he is terribly displeased.

13/25 February

Pyotr Ilyich went for a walk and bought some flowers and three vases, in which I placed the flowers, but I couldn't put them on the table. That's how good a servant I am for Pyotr Ilyich at the present time. I feel that he now regrets taking me. Of course, that's my supposition, but still one might think that. For ten days already I have been hobbling on four legs. Pyotr Ilych is constantly teasing me for having one leg shorter than the other, especially when I try to serve him something: "Well, where are you scrambling to, stubfoot?" And, of course, he himself fetches what I was supposed to serve him. That's my situation.

20 February/4 March

Pyotr Ilyich began to write a letter to Modest Ilyich, and he promised to pay my respects. Pyotr Ilyich said that he will have to do a good bit of work on this scene, despite the fact that it's small. He says that the fifth scene is quite hard— the ghost appearing to Herman, the way the Queen of Spades appears to him, and the funeral singing. Pyotr Ilych proposed that I might do it quicker. I answered that, without a doubt, I'd do it quicker.

27 February/11 March

Modest Ilyich sent the seventh scene. When I came after coffee, Pyotr Ilyich read me the scene he'd received and said: "Now this scene is bigger than all the previous ones," and he showed me that he'd already composed the first page. I also took a look at the half-sheet: there were lines and hooks drawn on it. I asked whether he'd finish it this week, but Pyotr Ilyich said: "I think not.". . . At six-thirty Pyotr Ilyich finished work. Today it was pretty good, did some good work. When I entered I could guess by Pyotr Ilyich's cheerful face that everything had gone all right. "If," he said, "it continues this way, I'll finish by Sunday." Pyotr Ilyich told me that in the morning he had absentmindedly lit the candles on the piano and some time later noticed that in his head he'd lost all connection to his hands. Probably at this moment in his head there swarmed a swarm of musical notes, and they wove around and opened up and combined several together, and at this time his hands also needed something to do, and they unconsciously lit those candles during broad daylight.

2/14 March

Pyotr Ilyich finished his work at seven o'clock. While he was washing, Pyotr Ilyich said that he had finished the opera; Pyotr Ilyich has recently begun to tell me everything, I suppose because apart from me there's no one else to tell. "Well, Nazar," he addressed me and began to tell how he finished Herman's last words and how Herman committed suicide. Pyotr Ilyich said that he had cried all that evening, and his eyes were still red then, and he himself suffering terribly. He was tired, and, despite this fatigue, he still wanted to cry, it seems . . . . I love these tears, and think that everyone who has experienced it [must love such tears]. Pyotr Ilyich is the same way. He feels sorry for poor Herman, and therefore he was quite grieved. When Pyotr Ilyich played the death of Herman as he composed it, he then also shed the tears that filled his soul while he was composing. . . . It is important for me to note Pyotr Ilyich's tears. If, God grant, Pyotr Ilyich finishes just as well, and if I get to see and hear this opera on stage, then probably many will shed tears just like Pyotr Ilyich. After his walk Pyotr Ilyich returned early. Tired, he put on his dressing gown and sat by the open window. Clear sky. The stars seemed especially bright to him. All the time he looked at this stillness and into the heavens' depths and said: "Look at this little star, I love it very much." Spent this evening quietly, as if he had really buried that poor Herman.

VIII

The Celebrity
(1891–1892)

When Tchaikovsky arrived in America in April 1891 for the opening of Carnegie Hall, he was amazed by how much attention the American media paid not only to this event but to his participation in it. On 15/27 April the *New York Daily Tribune,* describing the arrival of the famous composer, mentioned that he came to New York "accompanied by his wife," mistaking the president of the Music Hall Company Morris Reno's daughter Alice for Tchaikovsky's spouse.[1] In the *New York Herald* a few days later Tchaikovsky saw himself described as "a tall, gray, well built, interesting man, well on the sixty. He seems a trifle embarrassed, and responds to the applause by a succession of brusque and jerky bows. But as soon as he grasps the baton his self-confidence returns."[2] It so happens that Tchaikovsky was one day short of fifty-one, and the idea that the reporter described not only his performance but also how he looked seemed to him quite bewildering. He even quoted this passage with three exclamation marks in his diary entry. "It angers me," Tchaikovsky put in his diary, "that, not satisfied with writing about my music, they must also write about my person too. I cannot bear to think that my shyness is noticeable or that my 'brusque and jerky bows' fill them with surprise."[3]

On 25 April/7 May, after the splendid performance of his Third Suite, Tchaikovsky had the chance to meet with the reporters ("oh, these reporters, among them the very famous Jackson" he wrote in his diary)[4] and forcefully destroyed the myth about his age: "No, I am not old. I am celebrating my fifty-first birthday today. My hair is gray, and the work of conducting makes great demands upon my vitality, but I hope that in the future I still may be permitted to enjoy the honors that American audiences are so willing to give me."[5]

After this initial encounter with journalists Tchaikovsky granted several interviews. A reporter from the *New York Times* remembered the composer during these occasions as "one of the most modest and unassuming of men" with "charmingly unaffected manners."[6]

Here I choose to include several of the interviews Tchaikovsky gave to American and Russian reporters. As documents, interviews provide more reliable information than reminiscences, even though there is always a risk of errors or confusion on the reporter's part if the text was not authorized by the person interviewed. On the other hand, the reporter and the interviewee engage in active conversation and this conversation is recorded by the reporter almost immediately, often with many valuable details about the personality, which are usually given between questions and answers and at the beginning of an interview. Of course, much depends on the skill and the experience of the interviewer.

In the case of Tchaikovsky, whom we know quite well from his own writings, letters, and diaries, it is interesting to learn how he was perceived by his contemporaries, whose perceptions were recorded not many years later, when memoirs are penned, but under the fresh impression of a first encounter. In some interviews one can actually feel the living presence of the composer—talking, smoking one cigarette after another, sitting across from the reporter. Some interviewers no doubt even picked up his intonation, which helps to imagine his normal manner of conversation with others. Moreover, in such free exchange of ideas with the interviewer, Tchaikovsky would often say new and unexpected things about himself, his own music, or the music of others, since his mind worked differently while talking than while writing. The interviews also give indirect evidence regarding contemporary attitudes toward Tchaikovsky and his music, reflected in the selection of questions and the actual description of the man.

On 2/14 May Tchaikovsky was interviewed by a reporter from the *New York Herald*—"a very appealing man."[7] This interview was published on 17 May 1891. Many other American reporters were watching his every step and produced various descriptions of the Russian composer for their newspapers. In order to provide a glimpse of how American journalists imagined Tchaikovsky, I have included here two pieces by staff reporters: the first is an article from the weekly magazine *The Musical Courier*, the second, an interview from the *New York Herald*. The first piece was apparently produced by a brash and eccentric journalist, Marc A. Blumenberg, in characteristic American style—a mixture of appreciation and irreverence (such as applying diminutive names to the famous personages he mentions).[8] The article is somewhat disjointed and occasionally pretentious. It seems curious that at one point the writer compares Tchaikovsky with Walt Whitman. The interview is written in a much more traditional mode and contains, rather unexpectedly, a discussion of church music for which Tchaikovsky otherwise showed little interest. This interview contains a number of errors which probably originated from the lack of clear communication, perhaps since Tchaikovsky's French was translated into English.

The second interview, from the *New York Herald*, conducted by a very sensitive and sympathetic correspondent whose name is lost to oblivion, is much better. Even Tchaikovsky's brother Modest acknowledged later that this interview "is reproduced with astonishing fidelity. As we read it, we can almost imagine we hear the voice of Tchaikovsky himself."

The Russian interviews presented here can be found in the Moscow newspaper *Novosti dnia,* the weekly *Peterburgskaia zhizn',* and the *Peterburgskaia gazeta.*

The *Novosti dnia* reporter, most likely Semyon Kugulsky (the interview was signed with the initials "S.K."), met with Tchaikovsky in early April of 1892, when the composer started rehearsals in Moscow, while conducting a few operas for the private Pryanishnikov Opera Company at Shelaputin's Theater. The reporter mentions that he had at least two sessions with Tchaikovsky, which enhances the value of the final interview. In its text, one may feel particularly surprised by Tchaikovsky's ruminations regarding his intent to abandon composition in order to leave room for younger talents. This piece appeared on 13 April 1892.

Another interview was published on 12 November 1892 in the weekly supplement to St. Petersburg's major newspaper *Novoe vremia.* It appeared under the title "Conversation with P[yotr] I[lyich] Tchaikovsky" and was signed with the initials "G.B." Judging from the interview's rich professional contents, it was most likely conducted not by an ordinary journalist, but by the music critic Grigory Bloch, who often contributed to various Petersburg papers at this time. In it the composer offers elaborate insights on such topics as Russian music criticism, the damage brought about by conflicting music ideologies, and the prospects for music teachers in Russia. Bloch probably met Tchaikovsky during rehearsals of *Iolanta* and *The Nutcracker* at the Maryinsky Theater at the beginning of November 1892.

The final interview, by an unknown reporter, was published in *Peterburgskaia gazeta* under the title, "With the composer of 'Iolanta'" on 6 December 1892, the day of the first performance of Tchaikovsky's new opera and the above-mentioned ballet. It provides a vivid cameo of the composer, caught at a moment of respite amidst continuous pressures, talking about his work habits and future prospects.

Musical Courier

Walter Damrosch appeared to be very little more than a figurehead last week at the May Music Festival.[9] But a modest, amiable figurehead, I admit. Tchaikovsky—what a delightful surprise he was to all of us!

The personality of conductors is not always a pleasant one, but in Peter

Tchaikovsky one finds a cultured man of the world, excessively modest and retiring.

We have entertained a musical god during the past week and I fear me greatly that many of us were not aware of the fact.

I bethought me, as I looked on his earnest face, heavy brow, with its condensed look about the eyes, that there stood a man who might be called the greatest in the country.

Do you notice I don't say the greatest musician but the greatest man?

Let me see; of individualities living among us we still have dear old Walt Whitman, who represents a primal force, but in the best of whose work, despite its rugged sincerity, there is always an unfinished quality. . . .

We have a few strong painters, fewer sculptors, our poets are mainly imitative or echoes; in a word, where in art, music, literature, politics, religion, is just such a forceful, fiery, magnetic man as Peter Tchaikovsky?

You can't name him.

This man epitomizes young Russia in his music, he preaches more treason in his music than Alexander Pushkin ever uttered. He is not as profound as Brahms, but he is more poetic.

Above all he paints better than the Hamburg composer.

His brush is dipped into more glowing colors, his palette contains more hues and the barbaric swing of his work is tempered by European culture and restraint.

Take the piano concertos in B-flat minor and G-minor. They are about as unorthodox as we can well imagine.

I like the second better, but in neither of them do I find real writing for the instrument. Tchaikovsky thinks orchestral, and if the idea does not suit the keyboard—well, all the worse for the keyboard. There was a story afloat that Nicholas Rubinstein helped him to fix up the piano part of the two concertos.

From Tchaikovsky I indirectly got the true story.

When Peter (Pete, to be a little familiar—I don't like his middle name at all, do you?) had finished the first work he showed it to Nick Rubinstein, whom he pronounced to have been a better pianist than his brother Tony. They all lived in the same house in Moscow, Rafael Joseffy occupying the top floor, and he says that whenever he wanted to practice Tchaikovsky always wanted to sleep, so that trouble ensued daily.[10]

Well, Rubinstein looked through the concerto and dismissed it disdainfully. "Unklaviermassig [unpianolike], mein lieber Tschike." He called him Tschike for short, and that reminds me that all rumors current about his inability to pronounce his own name were set to rest last week by the publication in the Novgorod "Bi-daily" of an article on the "use and abuse of the letter 'j' in Russian proper names." Mr. Tchaikovsky is a member of the Moscow Philological Society, admission to which august body depends on the applicant's ability to pronounce his own name. It goes without saying that these learned men can carelessly remark "Prejavolowski" at any hour of the day.[11]

Tchaikovsky bided his time and gave the work to von Bülow, after erasing Rubinstein's name on the dedication and substituting that of von Bülow. Rubinstein suddenly discovered the merits of the work and to him Tchaikovsky dedicated the second concerto in G.[12]

The brilliancy and daring of the great Russian are particularly well illustrated in his Third suite, with its national coloring and complex rhythms. I like the fifth symphony better, and I am sorry he didn't conduct it while he was here.

Tchaikovsky sometimes says great things in a great manner, and that is why I think he is the greatest man in the country at present, for we have many men saying things which are not great, nor are they said greatly.

The figure of Tchaikovsky looms grandly over these petty personalities as a poetic, intense thinker, who in an age of self gain and grasping greed looks afar, as from a peak, and sees beautiful things, which he repeats to us afterward in his music. I like, I admire, I even reverence, his kindly love of his fellow men which throbs through his scores.

He has suffered much. No man could pen that wonderful "Nur wer die Sehnsucht kennt," which interprets Goethe's idea better than Goethe himself, without having tasted at the acid spring of sorrow.[13] He had loved, else his "Romeo and Juliet" overture is a farce and make believe, and the passionate heartbeats it causes in you lie, too.

That were hard to believe.

He knows his Hamlet, he knows his counterpoint, and, above all, he knows himself.

He is a strong man.

He says great things in a great manner, and that is why I call him the greatest man at present in this broad and fair land.

For the rest, he is a pleasant appearing gentlemen who perspires audibly and puts his pocket handkerchief in his left hand trousers pocket (Moscow etiquette I am told) and always looks for it during a fermata.

I was amused at John Rietzel in the orchestra after the suite was finished. He stood up and in the most significant manner touched his forehead and pointed out to Pete, who was bowing his acknowledgments, as one should say "a great head". . . . A great head indeed! . . . .

So it is. Tchaikovsky is with us, a noble thinker in tone, who will be honored when these United States have had another centennial celebration. . . .

And forsooth if I express my keen admiration for beautiful music I am paid for it! Yes, I am paid for it and a thousand times repaid for it, for can I not listen to Tchaikovsky's music, and is that not magnificent pay for my petty praise?

Let us salute Peter Ilyich Tchaikovsky. He does not compose like Bach, Beethoven, nor yet Wagner, but he has given us new thoughts, a broader vision, a new gleam of beauty from that wonderful ocean called music; so Salutamus te, Petrum Tchaikovskiensem, and a short shrift for your detractors.

New York Herald

Tchaikovsky seems to be as fond of American audiences as they are of him.

"They are so warm—so sympathetic," he said to me the other day, "so like the Russian public, so quick to catch a point and so eager to show their appreciation of the good things offered them."

We were sitting in his little room at the Normandie, and between his nervous puffs at his cigarette the Russian composer waxed eloquent over the great American public.

"When I say they are enthusiastic," he added, "I do not mean they applaud anything and everything. Far from it. They are delicately discriminating and slight the weak musical points quite as decidedly as they applaud the strong. Their perceptions are fine and their appreciation honestly and frankly expressed." Another cigarette.

"Of course I can speak only of the New York audiences, as I know no others. But after my return from Baltimore and the South I can tell better about the public gatherings of your other cities. Not even in the music centers of Europe have I found such musical sympathy as in New York.

"London audiences, you know, are proverbially cold, and people will tell you to seek for all that is responsive in listeners found in France, Germany and Italy. But St. Petersburg and New York are good enough for me."

Not so bad a compliment!

"And then your musicians," he continued. "They are thoroughly capable and conscientious performers and would quite put to blush some of our players across the water in the matter of sight reading.

"Here again I can only speak of one body—your New York Symphony Society—but I sincerely trust that I may find equally good players in your other bands."

"And you were satisfied with the people to whose bands your orchestral works were intrusted at the festival?" I inquired, as still another cigarette was lighted. "Quite," came the answer between the puffs. "Quite. I must confess to a genuine surprise to find at my first rehearsal that the men had so little trouble with some of my music.

"Now, my scherzo was by no means easy and I expected a good deal of hard work at its first trial. Judge of my astonishment then to hear it played as correctly as at the public concert.

"'Gentlemen,' I said, 'you have rehearsed this with Mr. Damrosch.' But they all denied having seen the music before.

"As for the composition of the band, I admire the flutes and strings particularly. The flutes are beautiful and sweet and your string orchestra is sonorous and rich in quality."

"M. Tchaikovsky," I asked, suddenly changing the subject, "how much truth is there in the rumor that you are to return in the fall with a choir of Greek Church singers?" for I knew that he was an enthusiast upon this branch of music, and had shown his partiality to sacred choral writing by the selection made of his own works sung by the Oratorio Society last week.

"There is a possibility that such an engagement may be made," he answered, "and the idea was first started in this way:

"When Mr. [Andrew] Carnegie was in Moscow he was particularly pleased with the harmonies produced by the singers in the Cathedral, and wished his friends in New York might hear them. Now that I am coming back in the autumn, it may be that such a company may be brought back with me. I shall certainly bring the best if I bring any, and have them sing some of their own folk songs as well as their church music.[14]

"But our church music! How beautiful it is! And did you know that until very recently no one in Russia was permitted to write anything new for the church, and that nothing but the olden time music was allowed to be sung?"

I did not know it but kept my ignorance to myself and allowed my host to continue.

"Dimitry Bortnyansky, the Russian Palestrina, was the last of the old school, and long after his death, in 1825,[15] his influence remained—a stumbling block to progress in the music of the Greek Church, and it was a long fight that finally opened the doors to the new school of music, and to Davidoff, Degteroff, Beresovsky, Tourtchonihof and Wedel belongs much of the credit of the work.[16]

"To-day these writers do nothing but compose for the Church.[17]

"I had a little experience myself that will illustrate the high feeling about the admittance of anything new within the sacred precincts of the church.

"I had written a mass and given it to my publisher, who was almost immediately served with an order from court that the work must be destroyed, and, this order was speedily followed by fire before my publisher's very eyes.[18]

"The music of the Greek Church of to-day, however, is beautiful beyond expression, and I trust you may have pleasure of hearing it in all of its grandeur and beauty in my home (Russia) some day," smiled my host.

His cigarette was reduced to ashes.

"Some day," I answered, as I picked up my hat and bowed myself out.

Novosti dnia

Today our renowned composer is conducting at the Pryanishnikov Opera.[19] This provides me with an occasion to reproduce my conversation with Pyotr Ilyich at our two last meetings.

Three days ago I saw Tchaikovsky at a rehearsal at the Shelaputin Theater. Everything in Mr. Pryanishnikov's office bears the stamp of particular respect for our famed composer: Tchaikovsky's portrait hangs in a conspicuous spot, crowned with the laurel wreath that was presented to Mr. Pryanishnikov on opening night.

"This is to whom the laurels belong, not to me," the head of the opera seems to be saying with modesty.

"Well, now we too have a fashion for interviews," the renowned composer told me when he heard of my intentions. "In America, interviewers besieged me by the dozen; you can imagine how difficult it is to find a common language with people who have little competence in music and have utterly savage ideas about Russian music in particular, not to speak of how difficult and unpleasant it is to speak of oneself, especially abroad, where people have the most improbable ideas about Russia and Russians.

"A crowd of American reporters awaited me at the New York harbor on the day of my arrival," Pyotr Ilyich added with humor. "They even tried to marry me off: I got into a carriage with my friend's daughter, and the next day I read that I had arrived with my beautiful, young wife."

The next day, the composer of *Eugene Onegin* received me in his room at the Grand Moscow Hotel. Of course, anyone with any interest in Russian music, anyone who has been in the foyer of the Bolshoy Theater, knows Pyotr Ilyich's portrait. This relieves me from the need to describe his appearance. Since he is a European down to the tips of his fingers, Tchaikovsky is charmingly polite and kind, and he readily speaks on his favorite topic—music. At the present moment the most interesting question concerns Tchaikovsky's relations with the Pryanishnikov Opera.

"Pryanishnikov's company was deeply offended in Kiev," my gracious host explained to me. "The city took away their theater after they had been conducting business in good faith for three years. They asked whether I would advise them to move to Moscow; I didn't try very hard to persuade them, but promised to help them however I was able. In general, I have great sympathy for opera companies. In this particular company I like the way they do things, the lack of intrigues; they have a pleasant spirit. And if they continue in the same way, without promoting individuals, caring about the ensemble and the overall level, then they will do well."

"So you are even indifferent to the fact that things in Moscow began with an advertising campaign for [Borodin's] *Prince Igor,* which is a work by the Mighty Handful, a camp to which you don't belong?"

The renowned composer became animated.

"I am always outraged when people speak of camps in music. Well, what party do I belong to? They don't exist for me. What can I have against the music of the late Borodin, who was my good friend? I don't belong to the Mighty Handful because I don't live in Petersburg, but I am friendly with Balakirev, Rimsky-Korsakov, Cui, and other representatives of this group. Any talented and pleasant man in the sphere of music is my friend and brother. And if I ever needed to join a camp, I would of course join the group of these honest people rather than any other.

"If I don't in fact belong to this circle," said Pyotr Ilyich with renewed animation, "then this is partly explained by the inflexible nature of its founder, Balakirev, with whom I am nevertheless quite friendly. Having founded this circle thirty years ago, Balakirev sticks hard to the views and principles he marked out from the first, and all of his followers feel solidarity with him. I always wanted to preserve a certain amount of freedom for myself. As far as Borodin in particular is concerned, he was not a furious revolutionary [in art]. And in his *[Prince] Igor* he holds to the old traditions and stands firmly on the soil of traditional techniques, avoiding musical anarchy. He introduced new techniques in *Igor* only in the part of the pipers and in a few other places."

From this general question we inevitably moved on to a more specific one, the question of how Tchaikovsky composes and what he has planned for the future.

"I just finished the opera *Iolanta* and the ballet *Nutcracker,*" Pyotr Ilyich said, "and now I am working on a new symphony.[20] I will be in Moscow all April in order to conduct the operas I have promised Pryanishnikov. Then I will travel to Vichy to take the waters, and, upon returning to Russia, I plan to settle in Moscow Province, specifically at my friends' estate, where I shall compose my symphony."

"And tell me, by the way," I asked, "is it true that you are composing an opera based on Lermontov's 'Bela,' and that Vasily Nemirovich-Danchenko is writing a libretto for you?"[21]

"Yes, Nemirovich-Danchenko, whom I met recently in Moscow, urged me to write an opera on this theme. . . . In view of Nemirovich's insistence, I proposed that he do the libretto. When I return from abroad I shall meet with him."

"And are you planning to go back to America, where you created such a sensation?"

"It is quite likely that I shall go there, as a gentleman named Wilson is traveling to Europe with the aim of inviting me and some other European musicians to an exposition in Chicago. I have already been informed of this by our ambassador, and if I am offered advantageous conditions, I shall go; they are planning some stupendous concerts there.[22] But in general," Pyotr Ilyich noted after a moment's pause, "I must tell you that I am planning to give up both composing and traveling."

Noticing my astonishment at this unexpected declaration, the renowned composer added in a contemplative tone:

"One has to stop at some point. I don't want to write myself out. Of course, out of mercy for my egoism, no one is going to tell me that I have written myself out, but I will sense it myself. I assure you, as soon as I sense it, I shall quit. Moreover, when we are young, no one pays serious attention to our operas, people are unwilling to accept them. When we achieve fame, we in turn close the way for the young. I know that the artistic director will always accept an opera of mine, but, if he didn't accept mine, the way would be open for a young talent."

While I was there, a man came by from the theater, and Tchaikovsky gave him instructions for adapting the conductor's podium for the day's performance.

"I can't conduct sitting down; I feel as if I am sinking," the composer said to me. "And so I am asking them to remove the support, since I shall conduct standing up. Incidentally, I am not the only one who does this: Colonne also always conducts in a standing position."[23]

Pyotr Ilyich spoke a great deal about music, about plots, about the fact that Italian music is taking up real subjects, something that was especially prominent in *Cavalleria rusticana* and facilitated its success.[24] Tchaikovsky regretted that this opera had not been performed on the imperial stage, although he added that its success and significance were transitory.

"In Russia, Italian opera is sometimes necessary: it is beneficial for the singers and satisfies the needs of the public," Pyotr Ilyich noted in this regard. "But, of course, filling the Russian stage with Italians wouldn't be healthy. I remember a time when the only Russian operas performed were *A Life for the Tsar* and *Ruslan [and Lyudmila]*—and how terribly pitiful it all was! Now we are witnessing a golden age in Russian music! . . ."

In parting, Pyotr Ilyich told me a curious story. There was a coachman at the restaurant Moscow, a twenty-year-old boy from the Kolomna region. The doorman brought him to Pyotr Ilyich, who found that the driver had a wonderful, velvet baritone. Although he had never set foot in a theater, the driver had learned "They sense truth" and "In olden days forefathers lived" by hearing them from other drivers, and he sang them wonderfully. Pyotr Ilyich furnished the driver with a letter to Vasily Safonov, the director of the Conservatory, and expressed his willingness to sponsor his training.

"Perhaps in five years he'll be a singer," said Pyotr Ilyich, who always patronizes singers and composers, indeed everything that bears the stamp of giftedness, talent, and ability.

Peterburgskaia zhizn'

At the present time our renowned composer Pyotr Ilyich Tchaikovsky is staying in Petersburg, where in the near future the Maryinsky Theater will present productions of his new works: the one-act opera Iolanta and the two-act ballet Nutcracker.[25] We had the opportunity to speak to Tchaikovsky, and he expressed so many things of interest and value for passionate devotees of art that we consider it most appropriate to give a printed exposition of the contents of this discussion, with Pyotr Ilyich's gracious permission.

First of all we must note one detail: Pyotr Ilyich is distinguished by a rare modesty and he speaks of himself with unusual taciturnity and restraint. He is always calm and gentle, but he becomes extremely animated when he speaks of music, and his words convey a sense of genuine fascination with, and boundless devotion to, his dear art.

The first question we presented Pyotr Ilyich concerned, of course, himself.

"Where do you usually live?"

"I live at a small estate near the city of Klin, but the life I lead should more likely be termed nomadic, especially in the last ten years."

"When do you work?"

"In order to work I retire to my Klin refuge or to some quiet corner abroad, and there I lead the life of a hermit. I work from ten in the morning to one in the afternoon, and then from five to eight in the evening. I never work late in the evening or at night."

"It would be interesting to learn how you conceive your musical ideas."

"My system of work is purely craftsmanlike, that is, absolutely regular, always at the same hours of the day, without any leniency with respect to myself. I conceive musical ideas as soon as I take up my work, as I turn my attention from thoughts and concerns that are foreign to my labor. The majority of ideas, incidentally, arise in me during my daily walks; moreover, in view of my unusually poor musical memory, I carry a notebook with me."

"Some people believe that it is difficult for a composer in our day to provide anything that is truly new, without repeating to a certain extent what has already been said by the great masters of the musical art."

"No, that's not true. Musical material, i.e., melody, harmony, and rhythm, is absolutely inexhaustible. Millions of years will pass, and if music in our sense still exists, the source of musical ideas will be the same seven main tones of our scale, in their melodic and harmonic combinations, animated by rhythm."

"What kind of music do you prefer, operatic or symphonic?"

"Tous les genres sont bons, hors le genre ennuyeux [All genres are good, except the boring]. Both kinds of music have given equally great exemplars."

"Everyone is awaiting the debut of *Iolanta* on the local stage. Why did you pick this particular plot?"

"Eight years ago I came across an issue of *Russkii vestnik,* in which there was the one-act drama of the Danish writer Henrik Hertz, translated by Fyodor Miller, with the title *King Réné's Daughter.*[26] This plot captivated me with its poetic and original nature and its abundance of lyric moments. I immediately promised myself that one day I would put it to music. Owing to various obstacles it was only last year that I was able to fulfill my resolution."

"In operatic compositions music serves to illustrate, complement, and clarify the text; but if the musical idea is to merge with the word, how is this merging actually achieved?"

"It is difficult to say. There can be a greater or lesser degree of inner identity between the word and the music that illustrates it, and this is the result of a mysterious process in creation that doesn't depend on one's own will and is not subject to description and expression."

"How satisfied are you with the performance of your operas on the Maryinsky stage at the present time, as compared to former times?"

"The general performance, the ensemble, is just as good as it was formerly, and for this there is a very simple explanation: the very same, incomparable Eduard Nápravník graces the conductor's podium. As far as the scenic decorations go, it is simply ridiculous to compare the present sparkle, luxury, and wonderful taste with the comparative poverty of former times. The role of the director has also risen to great heights and it might well be that no other capital-city stage in Europe can boast such painstaking attention, such vitality and intelligent acting in the choral ensembles."

"You must of course have your own favorite composers, whom you prefer to others?"

"I was sixteen when I first heard Mozart's *Don Giovanni.* This was a revelation for me: I am incapable of describing the vast force of the impression I experienced. It is likely as a result of this circumstance that, out of all great composers, I nurture the most tender love for Mozart. I think that the artistic delights one experiences in the years of one's youth leave a mark on one's entire life and have enormous significance for one's comparative evaluation of works of art even in old age. It is by just such an accident that I explain why, after *Don*

Giovanni, I most of all love *A Life for the Tsar,* precisely *A Life for the Tsar* and not *Ruslan and Liudmila!* And also Serov's *Judith.* The latter opera was first performed in May 1863, on a wonderful spring evening. And the delight I experienced from the music of *Judith* always merges with some indefinite springtime sensation of warmth, light, and rebirth!"

"What do you think of the contemporary state of music in the West and of its future?"

"I think that music in Western Europe is experiencing a transitional phase. Wagner was for a long time the only significant figure of the German school. That genius stood in a certain magnificent solitude, and not a single one of the European composers of the second half of our century escaped his powerful influence. Both during his life and now, there was and is no one capable of replacing him. In Germany there is, to be sure, the widely respected and highly valued composer Brahms, but the cult of Brahms bears more a character of protest against the excesses and extremes of Wagnerism. Despite all his mastery, despite all the purity and seriousness of his aspirations, Brahms has hardly made an eternal and valuable contribution to the treasure-trove of German music. One can, of course, name a couple more outstanding German composers: Goldmark, Bruckner, young Richard Strauss; one might also mention Moritz Moszkowski, who, despite his Slavic name, works in Germany.[27] But, in general, one notices a certain poverty of talent in the classic home of music, a certain lifelessness and stagnation. Only in Bayreuth, at the center of Wagner's cult, is there something really happening, and, however we might feel about Wagner's music, it is impossible to deny its strength, its capital significance, and its influence on all contemporary musical art."

"And in other countries?"

"Until very recently Italian art suffered from an even more serious decline. But we seem to be witnessing the dawn of its rebirth. An entire pleiad of young talents has appeared, and of them Mascagni attracts the most attention, it is only fair to say. It is wrong to think that this young man's colossal, fairytale success is just a consequence of able publicity. No matter how much you publicize a giftless work or one that has merely fleeting significance, you won't do anything and you will never make the entire European public simply choke from fanatical delight. Mascagni is obviously not only a very talented man, but also very intelligent. He realizes that at present the spirit of Realism is everywhere, the spirit of merging art with the truth of life, that Wotans, Brunhilds, and Fafnirs are essentially incapable of evoking vital participation in the listener's soul, that man with his passions and sorrows is more understandable and closer to us than the gods and demigods of Valhalla. Judging from his choice of plots, Mascagni is not ruled by instinct, but by a profound understanding of the needs of contemporary listeners. Moreover, he avoids doing what some Italian composers do, trying to look as much as possible like Germans and feeling almost shame at being children of their fatherland; Mascagni illustrates the vital dramas he chooses with purely Italian plasticity and beauty, and as a result he achieves works that are almost incomparably pleasant and attractive for the public. One notes a lot of life and forward movement in France, which is right to be proud of such artists as Bizet, Saint-Saëns, Delibes, Massenet. . . . Scandinavia has given us much of value: it is the homeland of Grieg, who is full of originality and freshness, and also of Svendsen, who is witty and rich in mastery.[28] Of Slavic nationalities the Czech lands are giving much promise: Dvořák is in the full bloom of his talent; but, apart from him, there are several young people who are catching attention: Fibich, Bendl, Kovařovic, Foerster."[29]

"Wonderful; but what is your opinion of the state of music in Russia today? Many claim that it is extremely pitiful."

"I think that it is generally quite difficult to agree with the absolutely pessimistic views on the state of modern music and its future which Anton Rubinstein expressed in his renowned book, which caused such a sensation last year.[30] There is still less reason for despair at the progress of music in Russia. If I recall what Russian music was at the time of my youth, and compare that situation with what obtains today, then I cannot help but celebrate and place the best hopes on the future. At that time there was nothing, apart from the cornerstone of Russian music, Glinka, who was, however, mistreated and who was completely strangled by the Italomania that ruled then. No matter how modest and strict we are with respect to our own art, we have reason to be proud of the successes we have achieved. Both the aging figures of today and the brilliant talents of the numerous young musicians who have appeared over the last decade are a guarantee of the best hopes for the future. These latter are luckier than people of our generation. They were able to receive a comprehensive and correct musical education at the correct time in their lives, to devote themselves to the work to which they are called in early youth, and immediately occupy a suitable position without struggle or hesitation."

"What significance do you attribute to Russian music criticism?"

"For certain reasons, music and theater criticism have acquired a greater significance and weight than in Western Europe. There, the major interest of a newspaper is politics; there is a music and theater section, but this is a secondary section, which people look at only incidentally. There are special press organs for art. But a newspaper needs *current events*. Yet here, our newspapers very often shift their gravitational center onto the theater and art, and it is in the section devoted to them that the reader finds the portion of *current events* that he needs to consume. This is why a satirical article on literature, theater, or music is sometimes an entire event for us. All the more caution, care, objectivity, and sincere aspiration for truth should our respected art critics have with respect to their work. Meanwhile—at least as far as music is concerned—we find the absolute opposite to be the case. At every step we meet such curious violations of the most elementary ideas of justice, that it is either annoying or sad, or else simply ridiculous. One of the reasons for this unfortunate situation is that music criticism is in the hands of people who often do not limit themselves to this branch of musical activity, as is true for the most part in Western Europe. At the same time these people compose and attribute more significance to their composing than to their reviewing! . . . A lot of unfortunate things stem from their one-sided and inevitably biased attitude toward their critical work. I can boldly point to this all the more as I myself was once a reviewer on a Moscow weekly and, judging from the way that I quickly created many enemies for myself, I must have succumbed quite often to the mistakes of a composer taking out his own authorial grudges in the space granted to him in a newspaper."[31]

"What can be done to eliminate this unfortunate phenomenon?"

"Reviewers and critics should be people who have devoted themselves especially to this work, who love it boundlessly and follow what is happening in this sphere only as an impartial witness. By such a voluntary renunciation of the role of judge, a composer who writes reviews would prevent much harm that is inevitably done to his work, and would win back for himself a tranquility and emotional calm that would be unthinkable for him if he were to try to combine both kinds of activity."

"Both in society and in the press there are constant discussions concerning the so-called Mighty Handful; are the goals it pursues anything unique?"

"At the end of the sixties and in the seventies the word 'Handful' was taken to denote a circle of musicians who were joined by personal friendship and identical musical tastes and opinions; the soul and mind of this circle was Mily Balakirev. The musicians of this circle found joy and moral support in intense contact with each other. It would seem that such a union of talented people would not be capable of arousing anything but warm sympathy. As a matter of fact, however, the 'Handful' gradually created an enormous number of enemies for itself. The reason for this should be sought in the fact that the 'Handful' had its own representatives in print, who, in their admirable, if you will, effort to glorify their warmly beloved friends, often went too far and succumbed to exaggerations, committing themselves to an excessively sharp ridicule of any figure or phenomenon that was alien and disagreeable to the circle. If we were to look in their compositions for a fundamental principle that the members of the circle applied to their work, it would be difficult to find it. Quite often the composers of the 'Handful' were called radicals, revolutionaries, and innovators; although such a characterization often seemed to be true, these were more likely exceptional cases. The circle never broke all ties with the past, as Wagner and the Wagnerites did. The more outstanding participants in the circle never avoided old, traditional forms. Some considered the works of the 'Handfulites' to be filled primarily with the 'Russian spirit'; but this is also only partly true, as some of them did not write a single line in the 'Russian spirit' in their entire lives. We will not find a single particular unifying principle in the activity of the circle. Meanwhile, the antagonistic attitude that they inadvertently adopted with respect to the rest of the Russian music world gave rise to the impression of a struggle between two parties of some kind, of which one was the 'Handful,' or, as I think Mr. Cui named it, 'the New Russian School,' and the other was everyone outside of the 'Handful.' The latter party was for some reason called 'conservative.' This division into parties is a strange confusion of ideas, a colossal mixup, whose time has come to step aside into the realm of the past. As an example of the impracticality of such a division into parties, I would point to the following fact, which I find most unfortunate. According to the view that is widespread among the Russian music public, I am associated with the party that is antagonistic to the one living Russian composer I love and value above all others—Nikolay Rimsky-Korsakov. He is the finest decoration of the 'New Russian School'; I, on the other hand, am associated with the old, retrograde school. But why? Rimsky-Korsakov felt the influence of contemporary art, to a greater or lesser degree, and so did I. He composed programmatic symphonies, and so did I. This did not prevent him from composing symphonies in the traditional form, from willingly writing fugues, and, in general, from working in the polyphonic genres; and so it was with myself. In his operas he succumbed to the style of Wagnerism or some other, in any case innovative, attitude toward the operatic texture; and I, perhaps to a lesser degree, also succumbed to it. This did not prevent him from inserting into his operas cavatinas, arias, ensembles in old forms; and I, to a greater degree, was likewise not prevented from doing this. For many years I was a professor at a conservatory that is supposedly antagonistic to the 'New Russian School,' and so was Rimsky-Korsakov! In a word, despite our different musical identities, it would seem we are following a single path; and I, for my part, am proud to have such a fellow traveler. And meanwhile, quite recently, in Mr. Gnedich's serious work on the history of Russian art, I have been associated with the party antagonistic to Mr. Korsakov. There is some strange misunderstanding here, which has caused and continues to cause unfortunate consequences. It upsets the public's correct understanding of phenomena occurring in the realm of Russian music, giving rise to an utterly pointless antagonism in a sphere which should, one would think, be ruled only by a harmony that cannot be upset by anything; it sharpens the extremes in both directions and, in the end, it compromises us, the musicians, in the eyes of future generations. A future historian of Russian music will laugh at us, just as we now laugh at the Zoiluses who upset Sumarokov and Tredyakovsky's peace and quiet!"[32]

"To be honest, I didn't expect to hear this from you."

"You see! But why? For example, Lyadov and Glazunov are also numbered among my opponents, yet I sincerely love and value their talent."

"What then, in your opinion, is necessary for the development of musical life in Russia?"

"Much has already been done, but more must be done. The merits of our two conservatories are very great. They have given many talents the opportunity to receive a comprehensive musical education at the right time in their lives, and they have raised the level of musical comprehension to a comparative height among the intelligentsia; but one must admit that these are, to a degree, greenhouse plants, artificially cultivated on a soil that is still unworked. They are like universities that exist in a country without secondary and elementary educational institutions. One might ask how to put an end to such an unhealthy situation? I think this might be attained in the following way. It is necessary to build, both in the capitals and in all provincial and large local cities, schools that would correspond to gymnasia; the goal of these schools would be to prepare young people for admittance into an institution of higher education, a conservatory. But, so that the level of students in the conservatories not be random, in order that only those who actually have a musical calling be admitted, it is also necessary to execute the strictest discretion in accepting students into these secondary schools: only a man with special talent can serve art. It is also necessary for the required study of choral singing to be developed and strengthened in all elementary educational institutions of our Fatherland."

"Do you propose that all this can occur on private initiative?"

"That is equal to asking whether Russian music would thrive if each of these initiators solved the question of musical education in his own way? Hardly. I think it would be the greatest boon for Russian art if the government took concern for all of its branches into its own hands; only the government has resources, strength and power, that are required for this great task. Only the institution of a ministry of fine arts can allow one to hope for the quick and brilliant growth of all branches of art, only then will there be a unity of actions, a normal correlation and organic connection between all institutions devoted to art.

Peterburgskaia gazeta

In the corridor of the Grand Hotel, on a coat rack in front of the door to Room 67, several laurel wreaths with many-colored ribbons are displayed.

This is where Tchaikovsky is staying.

"May I come in?"

The room is quiet and dark. At my appearance, Pyotr Ilyich rises from the divan, on which, apparently, he has just been lying, and says kindly: "Please, by all means—I'll just light a lamp." He performs this operation himself, and we sit down near the writing table. . . .

"It seems I've disturbed your rest? . . . "

"I wouldn't say you disturbed me, but—I admit you find me extremely tired. These daily rehearsals are unbelievably exhausting. However, now I can relegate them to the past and in a week and half or so leave Petersburg."

"Do you really intend to leave?"

"Absolutely. I go first abroad to Hamburg, Schwerin, and Brussels, where they are putting on my *Iolanta,* then to Odessa to conduct two concerts, and then from there, through Moscow, I shall return to Petersburg around 23 January. After this trip, I mean to settle in Petersburg permanently, because I can't stay in the country any longer. At present I have such trouble with my eyes that I must give up entirely my customary evening pastime in the country—reading. In the past, I used to work during the day, then relax with a book in the evening. Now, once I have settled in Petersburg, I shall continue to work, as before, from ten to one o'clock and from five to eight, and then spend the evenings with friends."

"You work six hours a day!"

"Without fail, every day."

"But what if you don't feel the desire or ability to work?"

"Then I force myself to feel that ability. Nowadays young people wait for inspiration before setting to work, but I consider this quite mistaken. Could Mozart, who died at such a young age, have written so many marvelous works if he had constantly been waiting around for inspiration?"

A pause. Pyotr Ilyich gazes pensively at the lamp's flame and suddenly says: "I'm afraid of only one thing—not sensing the moment when I begin to be played out. Still, I'd like to continue for another five years or so, then stop. I'm fifty-two now, so I can keep writing until I'm fifty-seven."

"I should think that you need never fear that danger."

"Who knows? No one will ever say it to our face. Would anyone dare tell Anton [Rubinstein] that it's high time for him to give up writing? Of course not, and so he just keeps on writing. No, one must make way for the younger forces."

"Who do you have in mind?"

"We have a great many talented young composers in Russia at the present time. Here in Petersburg there's Glazunov, in Moscow there are Arensky, Davydov (the nephew of our celebrated cellist), Rakhmaninov, who has written a splendid opera based on Pushkin's *The Gypsies [Tsygane].*"[33]

"And when will we hear something about your new composition?"

"If you mean an opera, then not for a couple of years at least. During this time

I don't wish to write anything more for the stage, since I've quite neglected everything I used to work on. Symphonies, quartets, songs. I've recently started a symphony."

There is a faint knock at the door, and Mr. Dalsky, an actor . . . enters the room.[34] I take my leave of Pyotr Ilyich, and as I go out I hear, from the corridor, his words, apparently addressed to his new visitor: "Not only do I have no box for tomorrow, I don't even have the slightest glimmer of one. They gave me only three boxes in the dress circle, and some forty people have come wanting them."

IX

The National Treasure
(1892–1893)

At the beginning of September 1892 Tchaikovsky planned to conduct a concert in Vienna. However, after he arrived and learned that it was to be played by a scratch orchestra in a mediocre restaurant, he took offense and left. His old friend from the Moscow Conservatory, the Austrian pianist Anton Door, who had not seen him since the late 1860s, not surprisingly found him looking older than his years. From Vienna the composer traveled to be a guest of the pianist Sophie Menter[1] at the Castle of Itter, in Tyrol, and thence to Prague in order to attend the first performance of *The Queen of Spades*. Early in November Tchaikovsky had to return to St. Petersburg to take part in the rehearsals for *Iolanta* and *The Nutcracker*, originally intended as a double bill.

On 6 December both the opera and the ballet were performed in splendid productions at the Maryinsky Theater in the presence of the Tsar and the court. The opera was conducted by Eduard Nápravník, and the ballet by Riccardo Drigo. Alexander III was cordial with respect to both pieces, but it seems that the music of *Iolanta* did not appeal to the public. *The Nutcracker* was more fortunate: most critics approved of its music and choreography. Tchaikovsky left the capital on 12 December, disappointed by the lukewarm reception of his new creations.

This time he traveled to Switzerland, visiting his old governess, Fanny Dürbach. He wrote to his brother Nikolay: "The past rose up so vividly before me that I seemed to breathe the air of Votkinsk and hear Mother's voice."[2] The last days of 1892 Tchaikovsky spent in Paris and in Brussels. In the Belgian capital he successfully conducted on 2 January an all-Tchaikovsky concert, then traveled home by way of Odessa.

The composer was fêted in Odessa for almost two weeks. He conducted five all-Tchaikovsky concerts, supervised the production of *The Queen of Spades*, and attended several banquets held in his honor. Returning to Klin in early February with renewed confidence and inspiration, Tchaikovsky started work on the Symphony No. 6 in B minor. He worked so vigorously that in the week after his arrival, the first part of the symphony was already complete and the rest was clearly outlined in his head.

On 11 March, Tchaikovsky arrived in Kharkov for a scheduled concert appearance. A great crowd gathered at the train station to greet the famous composer. The response to the concert itself three days later, at which Tchaikovsky conducted his Second Symphony, *The Tempest,* and the *1812 Overture,* surpassed all expectations: the hurrahs and bravos seemed to continue on without end, and as soon as the famous man appeared in the doorway he was lifted up and carried to his coach.

Tchaikovsky returned from Kharkov on 18 March and resumed work on his new symphony. He finished the finale first and only then took up the second movement. Within five days he completed the full sketch of the entire work. After finishing the score by mid-August, he wrote to his publisher, Pyotr Jurgenson, "On my word of honor, I have never been so satisfied with myself, so proud, so happy to know that I have done something so good!"

In April, Tchaikovsky began to compose the Eighteen Pieces for Piano, op. 72, commissioned by Jurgenson, and Six Songs, op. 73, to the text of the poet Daniil Rathaus. In May, he traveled to St. Petersburg, Moscow, and Nizhny Novgorod, where he visited his brother Anatoly, now the deputy governor of that city. During his visits to Petersburg Tchaikovsky's meetings with Nikolay Rimsky-Korsakov and with the younger generation of composers, such as Alexander Glazunov and Anatoly Lyadov, grew more frequent and productive.

On 13 May the composer set off for England to accept the honorary degree Doctor of Music *honoris causa* from Cambridge University, which had been conferred upon him earlier. The London Philharmonic Society intended to give two concerts at which all the foreign composers who had recently received honorary degrees at Cambridge would conduct their own compositions. At the first of these concerts, on 20 May/1 June Tchaikovsky was represented by his Fourth Symphony, which appears to have been an enormous success. The festivities at Cambridge, in honor of the Jubilee of the University Musical Society, began on 31 May/12 June with a concert whose program included one work by each of the five doctors of music: Boito, Saint-Saëns, Bruch, Tchaikovsky, and Grieg; the latter was not present at the ceremony for reasons of ill health. Tchaikovsky conducted the first English performance of *Francesca da Rimini* and then attended a "gala dinner and still more gala reception." The next day saw the ceremony awarding him the honorary doctorate. The composer left London on 2/14 June for Paris where he could finally relax after three weeks of tension and exertion. A few days later he traveled to the Tyrol to spend a week with Sophie Menter and the prominent Russian pianist Vasily Sapelnikov (1868–1941), whose interesting reminiscences about Tchaikovsky's visit are presented in this chapter.[3] By 18 June 1893 Tchaikovsky was back in Russia.

While Tchaikovsky was abroad he received a continuing flood of bad news from Moscow and St. Petersburg: his old Conservatory and society friends Karl Albrecht and Konstantin Shilovsky both passed away, in late June Vladimir Shilovsky also died, and he was led to expect similar news concerning Alexey Apukhtin and Professor Nikolay Zverev.

In late August, Tchaikovsky visited Hamburg briefly to attend a production of *Iolanta* conducted by Gustav Mahler. Upon his return he visited his brother Anatoly and family in Nizhny Novgorod. In September, he worked on his Third Piano Concerto. Furthermore, he started to consider the possibility of writing a new opera. A few ideas had already occurred to him. One was Shakespeare's *Merchant of Venice,* another *Nal and Damaianti* (adapted from Vasily Zhukovsky's *Mahabharata*), but he was especially enthralled by the plot of George Eliot's tale *Mr. Gilfil's Love Story.*

His engagement calendar for the forthcoming concert season was extremely full. On 16 October, at a concert in St. Petersburg, he planned to conduct for the first time his new symphony, which he decided to call the *Pathétique.* On 27 November Tchaikovsky expected to return to St. Petersburg for a concert. On 4 December he was to appear at a concert in Moscow, although on 15 and 29 January 1894 he had two more engagements in St. Petersburg. In March he was to go on tour to Amsterdam, in April to Helsinki, and in May to London. In addition he had invitations from Odessa, Kharkov, Warsaw, Frankfurt am Main, and other places.

In the beginning of October the composer finished scoring his Third piano concerto. He enjoyed the visits to Klin by two young cellists: his old friend and former pupil Anatoly Brandukov, and a new, promising young musician, Yulian Poplavsky (1871–1958). A year later, Poplavsky wrote an excellent recollection about his visit to the composer.[4] On 8 October he went with his guests to Moscow, and from there he proceeded to St. Petersburg on 9 October.

We have included in the present selection reminiscences of Tchaikovsky's relatives, friends, colleagues, protégés, and admirers who happened to witness the composer's incredible popularity at the end of his life. Indeed, by this time Tchaikovsky had reached the pinnacle of his fame, enjoying a kind of "superstar" status in Russia and America. The memoirs of that period amply document the genuine love and admiration many felt for him at the end of the century.

The recollections of the émigré writer on music and composer Leonid Sabaneyev (1881–1968) present Tchaikovsky through the eyes of a seven-year-old and, later on, a twelve-year-old boy, and they are especially interesting due to Sabaneyev's observations on the relationship of Tchaikovsky and Sergey Taneyev.[5] In other factual respects, Sabaneyev is not trustworthy as a memoirist.

He compromised himself when he wrote a devastating review of Prokofiev's *Scythian Suite* at a concert that never took place.

Some of Tchaikovsky's lesser-known character traits may be seen in the short recollections of the cellist Mikhail Bukinik (1872–1947), which discuss the author's encounters with the composer in Moscow,[6] and in the account of the Austrian pianist Anton Door (1833–1919) regarding Tchaikovsky's visit to Vienna in 1892.[7]

Mikhail Bukinik's brother, the student Isaak Bukinik (1867–1942), left vivid reminiscences about Tchaikovsky's stay in Kharkov early in 1893.[8] His memoir demonstrates the extraordinarily enthusiastic response to him by the provincial populace. The journalist Abram Kaufman (1855–1904) left his anecdotal impressions of the composer's Odessa concerts.[9] The violinist Konstantin Dumchev (1879–1948) wrote about meeting Tchaikovsky in Odessa when he was only 13.[10] A unique blend of emotional involvement with the famous composer is reflected in the recollections of two of Tchaikovsky's intimate friends, Ivan Klimenko, whose memoir is written in a chatty style,[11] and the cellist Yulian Poplavsky, whose reminiscences have never been published before.[12] Poplavsky later abandoned the study of music and went on to enjoy a successful career at the Moscow Stock Exchange. After the Revolution he emigrated to France and died there. He was the father of the Russian émigré poet Boris Poplavsky, much admired by Vladimir Nabokov.

Leonid Sabaneyev

I made my first acquaintance with Tchaikovsky in about 1888, when my brother (later a professor of organ at the Moscow Conservatory from 1915 to 1917) and I began studying the theory of music, harmony, and counterpoint with Sergey Taneyev. I remember well our first lesson with Taneyev in his small apartment in Sivtsev Vrazhek (in Moscow), where he lived together with his old nanny Pelageya, who had been with him from the days of serfdom. She refused to abandon her "little sire," and she remained with him almost as a mother right up to his death. . . .

I remember how my brother and I came to him together with our tutor (we were not allowed out alone, such was our parents' rule). We rang (with the sound of a little bell) at the door of his small house, and the nanny let us in, sat us down, and said: "Sergey is out. He asked you to wait for him."

Our tutor left us, in order to come back later and take us home, and we remained alone. Then the little bell sounded again. Pelageya opened the door and informed us: "That wasn't Sergey."

Then everything went silent once more. Another ring at the door. This time Pelageya opened the door wide and informed us: "And this is Pyotr Ilyich."

Then Tchaikovsky entered. I knew him not only from portraits, but also from concerts, which he always attended when in Moscow. As boys of a proper upbringing we continued to sit quietly. Tchaikovsky was himself apparently quite shy, and he did not seem to take much interest in such musical children as ourselves. He took to examining some sheet music lying on the piano. I looked at him reverently.

This continued at some length. At last the heavy silence was interrupted by a new ring at the door. This time it was Taneyev himself. To our great surprise he immediately "sent" his beloved Tchaikovsky out of the room, telling him: "I have a lesson right now, go along to the kitchen."

"That's an excellent idea," said Tchaikovsky. "I can have a cigarette while I wait."

Taneyev had a rule in his house: smoking was allowed only in the kitchen, and then only by the window. All visitors, including renowned people of the time—Tchaikovsky, Anton Rubinstein, Borodin, Balakirev, Rimsky-Korsakov— were obliged to smoke by the window. Only Lev Tolstoy was not forced to go there, but he no longer smoked by that time.

Thus began my "acquaintance" with Tchaikovsky, whom we thenceforth no longer called Tchaikovsky but Pyotr Ilyich. . . .

Pyotr Ilyich was extremely shy and modest, extremely nervous and absent-minded. He spoke in a somewhat raspy voice, and was not especially talkative. . . .

I noticed that Tchaikovsky was "afraid" of Taneyev in some ways. I think that he was unnerved by the overt frankness with which Taneyev reacted to Tchaikovsky's works: Taneyev believed that one must indicate precisely what one finds to be "faults," while strong points would make themselves evident. He was hardly fully justified in this conviction: composers are a nervous lot and they are often particularly dissatisfied with themselves. Tchaikovsky was just such a person: he worried himself almost sick over each work and often tried even to destroy them. . . .

I recall that I was not very impressed by Tchaikovsky in those years. His entire external appearance seemed too "average" and cozy, and his conversations on music did not last long, veering off onto everyday concerns. I think that this was part of his "Petersburg finish." This occurred because such conversations were conducted at tea with my parents, who were not musicians, and Tchaikovsky with his sensitivity was probably concerned not to overburden them with "professional" talk. He himself did not like to speak about his works.

I also "didn't like" the fact that Tchaikovsky was basically a bad pianist and was utterly incapable of playing the violin. Almost the entire piano part of his famous concerto was redone by his friend Nikolay Rubinstein.[13] The violin part of his violin concerto was essentially "rewritten" by Ferdinand Laub.[14] As a conductor he was excessively shy and modest, and too sensitive: this profession demands a commanding temperament, of which Tchaikovsky had not the slightest. Nonetheless his concert appearances were a success both in Russia and abroad, but this was the success of his works, not of his conducting.

I recall individual incidents from the past. I remember once Tchaikovsky brought Taneyev seven romances which he had only just composed. Taneyev, who never missed an occasion to crack a joke or make a pun, took him aback by saying: "My word, Pyotr Ilyich! You always wrote works by the ordinary dozen, and now you bring music in extraordinary amounts."

Before Tchaikovsky had always brought in romances by the six or twelve.

I also recall an incident concerning his Fifth Symphony, which was unsuccessful at the first performance, sending Tchaikovsky into utter despair.[15] He brought it to Taneyev, with whom he always conferred, in order to ask his opinion. With characteristic pedantry Taneyev began showing Tchaikovsky what he considered to be faults, thereby sending Tchaikovsky into even greater despair. Tchaikovsky grabbed the music and wrote across the page with a red pencil: "Awful muck." Still not satisfied with this punishment, he tore the sheet of music in half and threw it on the floor. Then he ran out of the room. Despondently Taneyev picked up the music and told me: "Pyotr Ilyich takes everything to heart. After all, he himself asked me to give my opinion. . . ."[16]

Among other events of that time connected to Pyotr Ilyich I recall his attending Erarsky's children's orchestra. . . . Of course, Taneyev brought him here, too. The tiny orchestra players (the eldest was under 12 years of age, and some were as young as 5) welcomed him with a flourish and played his works. Tchaikovsky was moved and expressed a desire to conduct one of his works that Erarsky had orchestrated for the orchestra. This was accepted with fear and with joy. Upon leaving Tchaikovsky promised to write a special work for the children's orchestra. Alas, he did not manage to do this.

Another recollection concerns Tchaikovsky's visit to the apartment of [Julius] Block (not the poet, but the owner of a large typewriter and bicycle shop in Moscow who was a passionate music lover and something of a patron of the arts). Block had a phonograph, which he had received from America immediately after its invention. It was the first and only one of its kind in Moscow. . . .

Block treated us to the "phonograph," which was then a primitive system with a wax cylinder. Various things were recorded on the cylinders: Pabst (a professor at the Moscow Conservatory) playing his paraphrase of Tchaikovsky's *Sleeping Beauty*, the voice of Lev Tolstoy, and something else. It was far from perfection; after all, Edison had only just invented it. Block asked Pyotr Ilyich to play something or, at the least, to say something. Tchaikovsky frowned and tried to disappear before refusing decisively.

"I am a bad pianist and my voice is raspy. Why should one eternalize it?"[17]

This is one of my last recollections.

Mikhail Bukinik

In the 1891–92 season I had the good fortune to play twice under [Tchaikovsky's] baton. At that time I had stopped feeling like a modest and shy newcomer at the Conservatory. I played in the orchestral and chamber classes under the direction of Vasily Safonov, I was a member of the symphonic orchestra of the Music Society, and I already knew Tchaikovsky's Fourth Symphony, his *Romeo and Juliet,* and many other major compositions. The prospect of playing with Tchaikovsky filled my youthful heart with pride.

Symphonic rehearsals, like the concerts of the Imperial Russian Music Society, took place at the main hall of the Assembly of the Nobility. The rehearsals usually began at nine o'clock in the morning and ended at twelve. The large columned hall of the Assembly was dark; it was illumined only by the chandeliers that framed the stage. In the semi-darkness the hall's columns seemed to be the masts of ships, and the high ceiling—the dark sky. The figures of those who gathered at the rehearsals seemed small, and Tchaikovsky did not stand out among them in any way.

But suddenly the orchestra inspector summoned the musicians onto the stage, all took their places, and Pyotr Ilyich appeared at the conductor's podium. Everyone stood and greeted him by tapping their bows against their instruments. Tchaikovsky, apparently touched by this ovation, bowed with embarrassment and showed his gratitude. Then he tapped his baton, and everything became still. We began to rehearse the overture to *Hamlet.* The music of the piece seemed uneven, patched together and diffuse. And it went badly. Tchaikovsky started to show impatience. He treated the musicians with such delicacy and benevolence that everyone tried to please him. But the composer/conductor was following the directions printed on the music less than the performing musicians. The composition remained vague and incomprehensible for the musicians. Tchaikovsky apparently sensed this himself. All my life I remained indifferent to this composition.

I would like to describe Tchaikovsky's appearance. Despite his comparatively young years (he died at the age of 53), Tchaikovsky already looked almost like an old man at that time. He was of medium height, completely gray, thin hair, a multitude of wrinkles on his face and yellowed teeth. He spoke with a quite husky voice; Tchaikovsky won one over with his pure, clear and trusting eyes, his warm smile, and such sincere laughter. He was quite active and well-built. His figure gave the impression of an aristocrat. He always came to rehearsals neatly dressed, buttoned all the way up, and made the impression of a European.

I remember a rehearsal when the musicians had gathered in the smoking room during the intermission. Tchaikovsky came in to smoke a cigarette. We, the musicians, surrounded him and began to ask what he was writing at that moment. Tchaikovsky said that he was writing a ballet on commission from the Imperial Theater on a fantastic theme, and that it would be called *The Nutcracker.* He added: "It's awfully fun to write a march for tin soldiers, a waltz of the flowers, etc."

Apart from the overture to *Hamlet*, we worked on another of his new pieces, *Voivode*, based on Mickiewicz's ballad in Pushkin's translation. The piece begins with the agitated sounds of stringed instruments, which grow and lead to a grand love duet. Tchaikovsky was very nervous while rehearsing this piece. His anxiety was communicated to the musicians, and the piece sounded weak and uncertain. . . .

The concert went well in a technical sense. Tchaikovsky's appearance on stage elicited such a furor that the applause lasted as long as ten minutes, preventing him from beginning. Moreover, flowers began to pour down, enormous bouquets from the balcony, so that the musicians had to protect their instruments from harm. Finally, Tchaikovsky gave the sign and the audience began to calm down. We, the musicians, were crowded on stage due to the mountain of flowers that had formed.

I observed Tchaikovsky during this rapturous ovation. To my surprise, I noticed on his face a kind of sadness, as if he felt sorry for himself. For a long time I was unable to explain to myself this sadness in the fervor of triumph.

Anton Door

On the occasion of the Theater and Music Exhibitions of 1892, the most outstanding composers, among them Tchaikovsky, were invited to Vienna to conduct their own compositions. This wonderful idea evoked very little interest among the public, who strolled along the alleys of the exhibition, visited the exhibition halls, but who seemed very reluctant to look in on the concert hall.

How glad I was after so many years of separation to have an occasion to see my old friend Tchaikovsky!

One day I was informed that a gentleman wanted to see me, and then the long-awaited guest entered the room and embraced me in a friendly and joyful way. But how frightened I was at his appearance! He had aged so much that I recognized him only by his wonderful eyes. An old man of fifty years stood before me instead of the near youth I had left in the early seventies! I did my best to conceal my surprise. His delicate constitution had broken under the weight of colossal labors.

The next day, when I arrived at the rehearsal, I found there Tchaikovsky, Sophie Menter, and Sapelnikov.

After rehearsing the first orchestral suite, Tchaikovsky took up the second number of the program. After the very first beats, he tapped with his baton and asked where the first trumpet was. He was told that the musician was very tired from the rehearsals, but that he was such a good musician that he would be able to play his part at the concert without rehearsals. The surprised Tchaikovsky then countered, "But, my God, it is impossible, I have here a trumpet solo and the part includes such difficult passages that the most experienced artists are unable to perform it from sight!" Despite this, he rehearsed the entire work to the end. The three-hour-long rehearsal exhausted him, and, sweating heavily, he got down from the stage with difficulty and asked for his fur coat, although it was a summer day. He sat down at a table, rested for a quarter of an hour, drank a glass of beer, and left with Menter and Sapelnikov. I accompanied him to his carriage; he shook my hand firmly and, looking at me affectionately, said farewell. I did not completely understand his behavior then, but at nine o'clock in the evening I came home to find the solution to the mystery on my desk. Not long before my return home I had been brought a note, in which Tchaikovsky informed me that he was going to Itter, to Sophie Menter's, in order to rest up from the unpleasantries and exhaustion. Two days later I received a letter, in which he explained that at the rehearsal he had decided to leave Vienna and not conduct the concert.

Abram Kaufman

I saw Tchaikovsky for the first time at the Odessa Municipal Theater in 1893. He had been invited to Odessa to conduct two symphonic concerts and direct the staging of his opera [*The Queen of Spades*].

When the public learned that Tchaikovsky was sitting in one of the boxes, the theater was filled with loud applause which took a long time to quiet down. Hiding behind the backs of his neighbors, the composer was forced to lean out of the box and take a bow. Ivan Grekov, the impresario of the theater, asked Pyotr Ilyich in vain to show himself to the public from the stage.

On one of the first days of Tchaikovsky's stay in Odessa I paid him a visit at his hotel in order to thank him for his response to a written request I had made of him. While compiling a literary collection in aid of the famine victims of 1891, I asked Pyotr Ilyich to send me a sheet of music manuscript for reproduction in the appendix to the collection. In his letter, Tchaikovsky, with the modesty that always distinguished him, declared that he was somewhat reluctant to have his manuscript appear among those of the outstanding Russian writers and public figures who would doubtless respond to my request, but, in sympathy with the noble cause of the collection, he was sending me his manuscript, a line of notes with a small text, which I subsequently reproduced.

[The collection contains a fragment of the arioso of Nastasiya ("To look from Nizhny Novgorod") from Tchaikovsky's opera *The Sorceress.*]

In Tchaikovsky's hotel room I found several "Wunderkinder"—violinists and pianists—to whom Pyotr Ilyich was listening patiently. Some parents of the adolescent musicians were in attendance, and they were not satisfied with the composer's verbal expressions of approval and demanded written attestations. Against his will Tchaikovsky sat down at the desk, although he did not like the little virtuosi.

"Often nothing comes of Wunderkinder," Pyotr Ilyich declared. "Spoiled by expressions of praise and ovations during their performances, they stop working and soon leave the stage. . . ."

On the initiative of Lev Kupernik and the author of these lines a banquet was organized in Odessa (on 22 January) in honor of Tchaikovsky, who was visiting there. The banquet was a lively affair; participants included the artists of the opera troupe, prominent figures of musical society, music lovers, and admirers of Tchaikovsky. Kupernik in his brilliant speech gave an appreciative evaluation of the unforgettable composer's musical works; the author of these lines, pointing to the interest which Pyotr Ilyich had inspired among Odessans in opera in such a short period of time, expressed the hope that every average household should certainly own at least one musical instrument, along with the chicken for dinner of which King Henri IV [of France] dreamed.

Tchaikovsky found Kupernik's praise to be fulsome, but he agreed with the hope I expressed.

One can verify the popularity Tchaikovsky enjoyed in Odessa then by looking in old Odessa newspapers, whose columns were filled with the composer's name. Interviewers raced after Tchaikovsky and besieged him with questions, to which he gave written answers, in order to be more precise. . . . Indeed, he did not surrender immediately to the interviewers and tried to avoid conversations, noting good-humoredly that his opinions were of no interest to anyone.

But Tchaikovsky was unable to refuse anything, to cause anyone displeasure, or to offend anyone. I recall that at one rehearsal of Pyotr Ilyich's opera, the orchestra conductor [Nathan] Emmanuel noted: "Do you know, Pyotr Ilyich, in *Mazepa* one finds nuances from *Eugene Onegin, Oprichnik,* and other operas?"

"And do you know, maestro," Tchaikovsky answered him in the same tone, "that *Mazepa* is also my opera, just like *Eugene Onegin* and *Oprichnik?*"

Emmanuel realized the impropriety of his remark.

Before his departure from Odessa, Tchaikovsky promised the impresario Grekov that he would attend the staging of his opera *Iolanta.* Subsequently he confirmed his promise in writing, but two days after the letter was received, on 25 October 1893, Pyotr Ilyich Tchaikovsky passed away.

At Anton Rubinstein's fiftieth jubilee [on 20 November 1889], Tchaikovsky conducted Rubinstein's oratorio "The Tower of Babel" at the Assembly of the Nobility.[18] Unexpectedly Pyotr Ilyich, all red, flew into the musicians' room with a yell: "I'm dying! . . . "

The composer Nikolay Solovyov, who was present there, as he told me later, hurried to tear off Tchaikovsky's tie, unbuttoned his shirt, and, laying him down on the sofa by a window which he opened, ran for seltzer water and brought the half-dead Pyotr Ilyich back to his senses, perhaps even saving him after a stroke.[19]

It was said that the seizure was caused by anxiety and some unpleasant conversation. It must be said that Tchaikovsky, despite all of his talent, was not a first-class conductor and orchestra leader, and at Rubinstein's jubilee he was making his first appearance as a conductor.[20]

The day after his seizure, Tchaikovsky met Laroche, a famous music critic in his day, and told him that Solovyov had displayed such magnanimity and sincerity, and that perhaps he had even saved his life.

Konstantin Dumchev

In January 1893, I was performing in Odessa when our famous composer Pyotr Ilyich Tchaikovsky, who had been invited to direct the staging and performance of his most recent opera *The Queen of Spades,* arrived there. A local piano teacher, Rudolph Feldau, who accompanied me at my concerts, invited me to a luncheon one day where my first meeting with Pyotr Ilyich took place.

I must mention Pyotr Ilyich's wonderful delicacy. After lunch at Feldau's, before I had to start my concert appearance, a young girl pianist appeared, the daughter of a friend of the composer's brother, Ippolit. The girl played one of Liszt's fantasies (on *La muette de Portici*) with great sincerity, but with little musical talent. After her performance Pyotr Ilyich approached the piano and picked several notes in order to test the pianist's musical ear, but she could not name a single one of the notes. Since she played by the music, Pyotr Ilyich proposed that she play something by heart, but she couldn't do that either. Then Pyotr Ilyich told her father, in very polite tones but with apparent annoyance: "It is to the great merit of your daughter's piano teacher that he was able to achieve such results with her." The father of the pianist immediately went home in embarrassment.

After lunch I played several pieces from my repertory at Pyotr Ilyich's request. Pyotr Ilyich treated me with charming warmth and sincerity, taking my word that I would visit him daily and join him for morning tea. And thus every morning, just before nine o'clock, I would be at his room at the Hôtel du Nord, and revel in conversation with him.

After breakfast we went together to the rehearsals of the symphonic orchestra or his opera (*The Queen of Spades*).

Pyotr Ilyich, Sophie Menter, and Vasily Sapelnikov unexpectedly came to my third concert in Odessa [on 17 January 1893]. Although none of Pyotr Ilyich's compositions were on the program of that concert, I still greeted him with the performance of one of his pieces, the op. 5, transcribed for the violin. After performing this work the audience gave an extended standing ovation in honor of its famous guest.

Upon parting, Pyotr Ilyich gave me his portrait with a warm inscription: "To Konstantin Dumchev in memory of his sincerely sympathetic old friend P[yotr] Tchaikovsky."

Almost forty-seven years have passed since the moment of our last meeting, but I remember Pyotr Ilyich as if it were yesterday. I have never in my life met such a charming man, neither before nor after him.

Isaak Bukinik

Tchaikovsky arrived in Kharkov at nine in the morning on 11 March 1893, on the express train from Moscow. A great crowd had gathered at the station to welcome him. I have never seen such a splendid welcome. There were members of the Music Society, led by its conductor, Ilya Slatin; there were teachers and students from the Music School; among the welcomers were also students who were music-lovers, as well as other admirers of the great composer's talent. When the train approached, Slatin and the [violin] teacher Konstantin Gorsky entered the carriage and soon returned together with Pyotr Ilyich, descending onto the platform. Those who had gathered greeted the important guest with loud applause. He was presented with many fresh flowers. Everyone tried to squeeze forward the better to see him and shake his hand. But he seemed embarrassed and worried; he shook the hands of those who stood at the front and slowly made his way toward the exit, surrounded by the public. There were phaetons waiting by the station, and Pyotr Ilyich, accompanied by Slatin and Gorsky, got into one. The crowd surrounded the phaeton, began to applaud once again, and for a long time prevented it from setting off. Slatin told me that they were going to the Hôtel de l'Europe, that two hours later they would arrive at the rehearsal together with Pyotr Ilyich, and that he wanted me to tell the orchestra to be in their places at that time.

The composition of the orchestra that was to take part in the planned concert was unusual. Never before in Kharkov had there been an orchestra of more than forty or forty-five people. This time, the orchestra had been expanded to seventy people. It was composed of the orchestra musicians of the Opera Theater, teachers and graduates from the Music School, and even musicians invited from other cities, along with the best students in the Music School. All members of this orchestra were anxiously awaiting the arrival of the genial composer, exchanging impressions of his welcome at the train station, discussing the works that were to be played, guessing about his manner of conducting. In the hall, apart from the orchestra, was also a chorus composed of students of the Music School. At about one o'clock in the afternoon someone ran into the hall and shouted: "They're coming, they're coming, they have arrived." We all took our places immediately, everyone took up his instrument, and the entire orchestra froze in expectation.

Soon the teacher, Konstantin Gorsky, who was concertmaster and soloist in the orchestra, entered the hall. He informed us that Pyotr Ilyich and Slatin were already here, that they were taking off their coats and would be in directly. Gorsky sat next to me, took up his violin, and at that moment Pyotr Ilyich Tchaikovsky and Ilya Slatin appeared in the doorway. Tchaikovsky was of medium height, all gray, very elegant, and dressed in a brown suit of French cut. He bowed to us from the doorway and quickly headed toward the orchestra. Everyone stood up. The orchestra and chorus welcomed their dear guest with a musical salute. We performed the "Glory" from his opera *Mazepa*. When the salute stopped, Pyotr Ilyich ascended to the conductor's podium and addressed the orchestra: "Allow me to introduce myself. I'm Pyotr Ilyich Tchaikovsky." The orchestra and chorus once again broke out in loud applause. When quiet fell, Pyotr Ilyich shook my hand and asked how many first violins there were. I answered that there were sixteen. How many second violins? Twelve. How many violas? Eight. How many cellos? Eight. How many double basses? Six. Having acquainted himself with the entire composition of the orchestra, Pyotr Ilyich seemed satisfied; he took the baton and said: "Well, let's rehearse." All of the orchestra's attention was riveted on the conductor. I recall how surprised everyone was by Pyotr Ilyich's manner of conducting. He held the baton not in his fingers, but firmly gripped in his fist. He raised it above his head, on the first beat he brought it down sharply, on the second, he raised it to his left shoulder, on the third, he drew it over to his right shoulder, and on the fourth, he once again raised it up. The players were not accustomed to such a manner of conducting. Everyone exchanged glances, but the knowledge that we were to be conducted by the composer himself of the work that we were to play made us soon forget this immediate awkwardness, and we tried to play as well as we were able; by the end of the rehearsal we had become used to Pyotr Ilyich's idiosyncratic conducting style.

We rehearsed Tchaikovsky's Second Symphony. The orchestra players, carried away by their performance, were unaware that Pyotr Ilyich was constantly listening to and watching each performer; a smile never left his face during the entire rehearsal. I remember that during the performance of the main theme by the principal French horn, Pyotr Ilyich paid special attention to the hornist. The latter sang out his part with such inspiration that Pyotr Ilyich seemed all illumined and nodded his head at him gratefully. During the break, Pyotr Ilyich approached the principal hornist, offered him his hand, and expressed delight at his playing. A friendly conversation was struck up between them. Pyotr Ilyich was interested in his biography; it turned out that this hornist was the peasant musician of some Kursk landowner. The hornist's surname was Volkov, and his son, a trombonist, was professor of trombone at the Petersburg Conservatory. Pyotr Ilyich embraced him and said: "You are a very musical person and understood me well. When I wrote this symphony I thought that the hornist should perform his part in precisely the way that you did. Not a single hornist up to now has satisfied me as you have. I am sincerely grateful to you."

After the break we rehearsed Tchaikovsky's fantasy for orchestra, *The Tempest,* based on Shakespeare. The rehearsal lasted more than three hours. When we finished rehearsal, Pyotr Ilyich thanked the orchestra; everyone was charmed by the great composer. The orchestra players followed their unusual conductor out with loud applause as he left together with Slatin and Gorsky.

After the rehearsal, I was invited to dine at Slatin's. I had been to Slatin's before, informally. To my embarrassment, I found Pyotr Ilyich there. I asked him to excuse my informal attire, but he was so forthright and gracious, and seemed so glad to see me, that I immediately forgot my embarrassment. Pyotr Ilyich took me by the arm, sat me down on the sofa, sat himself down across from me in an armchair, and said: "You know, during the rehearsal I constantly watched you and kept meaning to ask whether you are related to Edvard Grieg. . . . You look so much like him that I thought I was looking at him." I became flustered and didn't know what to say. Afterwards, I took a good look in the mirror and found that I did indeed bear some resemblance to Grieg. At that time I had a great head of hair, I wore a mustache, and the yellowish color of my hair was like Grieg's; my flat nose and my characteristic facial and eye structure could really lead anyone to make that mistake. . . . I recall that I answered Pyotr Ilyich that I had been born in Kharkov, that my parents were from Volhynia Province, and that neither they nor I had even been abroad, neither were we related to Grieg. Pyotr Ilyich waved his arms: "Well, you know, a striking resemblance, striking." Slatin's entire family, Gorsky, and another guest whose surname I do not remember all congratulated me on my newly invented relative, Edvard Grieg.

After dinner, Konstantin Gorsky addressed Pyotr Ilyich with a proposal: "I have prepared all of your new, recently published pieces for violin and piano: 'Melody' and 'Waltz Caprice.'" Pyotr Ilyich expressed joy and said: "Well, come on, come on, let's play them." He was in a very good mood. Gorsky took up his violin, tuned it, and Pyotr Ilyich sat down at the piano. They played "Melody" and began to play the waltz, but Pyotr Ilyich was having some trouble with the accompaniment. Several times they broke off and began again. Something was wrong, it was not working out. So they stopped the concert. Pyotr Ilyich closed the piano, stood up, and said with annoyance: "Well, what a pianist I am; what a no-good accompanist." After dinner, I went home to change for the opera (*Rigoletto*) later in the evening; I did not want to miss it, since Ilya Slatin had told me that they all, including Pyotr Ilyich, would be there.

I arrived at the theater long before the performance began. When the theater was filled to overflowing, a rumor that Tchaikovsky would be coming began to spread, and all awaited his arrival with impatience. When Pyotr Ilyich appeared in a box, in the blink of an eye the audience rose and gave him an unprecedented ovation: for about ten minutes everyone stood and applauded. The orchestra joined the audience and three times played a fanfare, but one could hardly hear it.

Pyotr Ilyich bowed to all sides and several times tried to take his seat, hoping that the ovation might stop; it did not cease but continued with equal force. Finally the curtain was raised and all was quiet. When the performance ended, the curtain was immediately raised again and the entire opera troupe, together with the conductor, [Nathan] Emmanuel, saluted Tchaikovsky, and the crowd followed the composer out in a friendly manner.

The next day, 12 March, at eleven in the morning, the second rehearsal took place. A military band, led by V. O. Katansky (a graduate of the Kharkov Music School), took part in this rehearsal for the finale of the *1812 Overture*, and bells were also featured. The opera singer Tamarova also rehearsed (Liza's aria by the canal from *The Queen of Spades*), as did Gorsky (the Concerto for Violin and Orchestra in three movements by Tchaikovsky). It was a very long rehearsal, about four hours. Pyotr Ilyich kept working with the sound of the military band and the bells, changing their seating and location, until at last he decided to put the band in the next room and place the bells several rooms away from the hall. After rehearsing the military band, we moved on to Tamarova's singing. She sang very well. Pyotr Ilyich liked her voice, and he was quite satisfied with her performance, thanking her and kissing her hand. Less successful was Gorsky's rehearsal of Tchaikovsky's Violin Concerto. They rehearsed all three movements, but Gorsky apparently did not want to play all the movements on the day of the concert. Pyotr Ilyich agreed to this.

The rehearsal on 12 March showed that all of the performers were ready for the concert. Pyotr Ilyich announced that it was unnecessary to rehearse any longer, and that next day there would be a dress rehearsal, after which on the 14th at two o'clock would be the concert.

Following the second rehearsal [on 12 March] it was learned that all of the tickets for the concert on 14 March had been sold out in one day, that demand for tickets was still great, and that the public at large had asked that the largest possible number of music lovers and students be given the opportunity to attend. Pyotr Ilyich then suggested that the public be allowed to come to the dress rehearsal at the most accessible price of one ruble per ticket. This was agreed. The dress rehearsal was set for 13 March at eleven in the morning, with tickets at a ruble a seat, and the hall of the Assembly of the Nobility was packed. Never had that hall seen so many people within its walls. Tchaikovsky was given such a warm reception that the program could not begin for a long time. Pyotr Ilyich was noticeably tired after all these salutes. . . .

The long-awaited concert took place on 14 March 1893, at two o'clock in the afternoon, in the hall of the Assembly of the Nobility. This was a real celebration. The hall and stage were decorated with fresh flowers and tropical plants. There was scarcely room to cross the stage, as it had been difficult to fit in the orchestra, enlarged to twice its normal size, along with the chorus of the opera theater. We were so excited that it took us a long time to take our seats, prepare ourselves, and get in the right mood. I awaited the beginning of the concert with a shiver of emotion. It began in an unusual, uniquely triumphal manner. Pyotr Ilyich, in a tuxedo with a white tie, entered the stage unobtrusively and modestly, and began to make his way through to his place. The public noticed him before the orchestra did. They applauded, shouted "Hoorah! Bravo! Welcome to the great composer, welcome to our guest," and everyone applauded and applauded. The orchestra stood up and with the chorus performed the "Glory" from the first act of *Mazepa*. The applause did not cease after the "Glory," and everyone in the entire hall and on stage was focused on Pyotr Ilyich, who stood near the conductor's podium, a bit pale, leaning with his hand on a chair and looking straight down in front of him. Several times he bowed, and this evoked even more applause. Finally he stepped up to the podium and the hall fell silent. We were prepared to play, but there was a long delay before the beginning of the concert. Suddenly [Ivan] Velitchenko, a member of the Music Society, ascended the stage and read an address to Pyotr Ilyich on behalf of the Directorate of the Music Society. . . .

While Pyotr Ilyich listened to the address, the public once again applauded furiously. And when Velitchenko left the stage his place was taken by another representative of the Music Society who presented Pyotr Ilyich with a wreath on behalf of the members. Then he was presented with a silver wreath from his admirers, a silver wreath from the opera troupe, a wreath from the newspaper *Iuzhnyi krai,* and a wreath from the Music School teachers. From the students of the Music School there were wonderful flowers. The public continued to applaud loudly. It seemed that there would be no end to this stream of salutes and ovations. They continued throughout the concert and reached their peak upon the completion of Tchaikovsky's *1812 Overture.* The overture was performed well during the dress rehearsal, but it was performed better yet at the concert proper. The performers joined with the conductor into one whole, united creative impulse.

I recall that this universal impulse led to an incident. The concert had long since ended. Pyotr Ilyich had descended from the podium and bowed to the audience, yet somewhere in the distance the bells continued to peal. The public had come up close to the stage. Everyone was in a joyful and excited mood. But the bells continued to ring at full strength. Pyotr Ilyich several times frowned and said: "Well, why don't the bells stop ringing? Are they planning to bury me?" Since I sat nearest the podium, Pyotr Ilyich turned to me: "Can't you get those bells to stop ringing, it's upsetting me." I ran to the room where the bells were set up. It turned out that Slatin had assigned the bells to a Music School student from the singing class, a tall and healthy lad who was a great music lover. He was located several rooms away from the orchestra. Because of the loud ovations he had not been able to hear when the orchestra had stopped playing and the concert had ended. He was still ringing the bells when I came in.

The bell-ringing ceased, but the ovations continued. Pyotr Ilyich regained his composure and joined in the festive mood, bowing to all sides and raising the orchestra players' hands so that they also stood up in acknowledgment of the public's gratitude. The younger audience members and the Music School students ran onto the stage, sat Pyotr Ilyich down in a chair, and lifted it up, carrying him seated in the chair throughout the entire hall, accompanied by salutes and applause. The members of the Music Society, led by Slatin, then deposited Pyotr Ilyich in a phaeton and carried him off in his tuxedo and white tie to the photographer, [Alfred] Fedetsky.

After the concert the Music Society organized a ceremonial dinner at the Hôtel de l'Europe in honor of Pyotr Ilyich. It is difficult to list everyone who participated. All those active in Kharkov's music scene and all the cultural forces of the city gathered at the dinner to salute the great Russian national composer, expressing delight at his genius. There were so many toasts, so many speeches, that it is impossible to describe their content, even in general terms.

Pyotr Ilyich expressed gratitude for the reception, saying that he was very touched by such attention, that he was enjoying his stay in Kharkov, and finally that he would keep the very best memories of Kharkov musicians. Most clearly imprinted in my memory was not so much the dinner as the conversation that spontaneously arose afterwards. A small group gathered around Pyotr Ilyich and he began to tell of his trips abroad, of his impression of concerts abroad, about his meetings with local composers there. Pyotr Ilyich spoke with special sympathy of Bizet and Edvard Grieg, whom he loved both as a person and as a great composer. He also spoke of his Violin Concerto as played by Gorsky.

Incidentally, Gorsky had played only the first movement, and those present expressed regret that he had not played all three, as at the dress rehearsal. Pyotr Ilyich, laughing, told how the concerto had been criticized abroad, that it had been called "stinking music," and that regarding its finale foreign critics had written that "it whiffs of vodka." Pyotr Ilyich was in an excellent mood. He joked, laughed, made witticisms, and paid compliments to one beautiful lady who could not take her eyes off of him. He kept filling her wine glass and said that there were many beautiful women in Vienna, but that he had not seen any like her. The lady melted before him and asked him to tell something "from his private life."

Pyotr Ilyich told of an unusual romance he had had with a student at the Moscow Conservatory. It turned out that he himself had not known of her love for him. And he was horribly shocked when she showed up at his apartment, kneeled down and declared that she could not live without him, and that she had come to die at his feet. And indeed she took out a revolver, intending to shoot herself. Pyotr Ilyich said that he had been horribly afraid, had promised to marry her, and that he had a lot of trouble getting rid of this unbalanced woman. . . .[21]

All were enchanted with Pyotr Ilyich. He was so forthright, so humanly open, and he was very good at telling stories. Somehow everything he did turned out well. About both serious and trifling matters, he spoke and listened in such a way that he was constantly the center of attention.

We, the musicians, were naturally most of all interested in his creative work—how he wrote, how he created, and what plans he had for the future. Pyotr Ilyich said that he had been approached to write an opera about the Pugachev uprising, based on Pushkin's The Captain's Daughter. This subject attracted him greatly, but he had been obliged to abandon it for censorship reasons. The censor would never have allowed the figure of Pugachev to appear in an opera. For similar considerations he had abandoned the subject of Turgenev's On the Eve [Nakanune], since it was an event very close to our time.[22]

Pyotr Ilyich related much about his work on Eugene Onegin, the idea for which had been given to him by a famous opera singer, professor of the Moscow Conservatory Elizaveta Lavrovskaya. He told of his work on the opera The Sorceress, in which the opera singer Pavlovskaya had refused to sing the leading role, and then had relented and sang and acted marvelously. It is a pity that I neglected to record immediately all of the ideas Pyotr Ilyich expressed. After forty-seven years quite a lot has unfortunately slipped from my memory. . . .

That dinner lasted a little more than two hours. For myself and for all those present it was really less a dinner than several unforgettable hours of interesting contact with a great composer and great man.

[On 15 March 1893] at nine o'clock in the evening, Tchaikovsky left

Kharkov. His leavetaking was even more ceremonious than his welcome, and the crowds were even larger. There were all of the members of the Music Society, all of the performers at the concert, all of the pupils, many admirers, and very many members of the public. Pyotr Ilyich was again presented with flowers. At first he accepted the bouquets himself, then he passed them over to the [train] conductor, who carried them into the carriage by the armful. So many people crowded the platform that there was nowhere to go for the public who came to see him off. Before the train's departure, Pyotr Ilyich ascended the boarding steps, bowed to his well-wishers, and entered the carriage. The public ran after Pyotr Ilyich's carriage as the train set off, throwing flowers after it. Suddenly the window opened, and Pyotr Ilyich blew a kiss, but the carriage was already receding into the distance.

Ivan Klimenko

My final meeting with Pyotr . . . was in Kharkov at the beginning of March 1893. . . . Learning from the papers that he would be conducting his works at the Kharkov Music Society, I wrote him a letter in Kharkov asking him to inform me when the dress rehearsal would be. I received a telegram from him on 11 March: "Last rehearsal Saturday morning; will be terribly glad to see you!"

I arrived in Kharkov on Friday evening. I took a room at the Hôtel de l'Europe, where he was also staying. In the hotel office I was told that Slatin had come for Pyotr that morning and that Pyotr had not returned since. I went to search for him around town. I was given the wrong address for the Music Society. I arrived and found some kind of club there. I went to the correct address, but there I was told that there had been a minor rehearsal that morning, that the next day there would be a major one, but that no one knew where Mr. Tchaikovsky was now. Craving to see my friend as soon as possible (you understand!), I had wasted a lot of time with no result, and meanwhile it was nine o'clock (?!) already. Just in case, I went to Slatin's. I knocked, and the maid said that the master was out, that he was having dinner with Tchaikovsky at the governor's (eh?!!). I was in despair, since I naturally could not go to the governor's and pull my friend away. I stood for a while before Slatin's closed door, then turned with an empty feeling to find a cab, when suddenly someone jumped from a cab and ran up to the very door from which I had just walked away. This someone looked at me questioningly and asked: "You're not looking for me by chance? I'm Slatin." *I:* "Of course, for you! Allow me to introduce myself: I'm Klimenko." *He:* "Oh my God! Pyotr Ilyich has been waiting for you for a long time. He thought you'd come yesterday." *I:* "For God's sake tell me where I can find him!" *He:* "Pyotr Ilyich just set off for the opera, box number four. Go right there. He will be very glad to receive you. I myself shall be coming to the theater directly." (They were performing *Aida*).[23] Naturally, I flew right there *poco à poco accelerando*. I arrived, released my cab, took off my coat and, without waiting for the intermission, ran straight to the box, quietly opened the door, and saw *him* in the company of a *lady* (!!), which I did not at all expect. The creak of the door made Pyotr turn to me. Seeing me he smiled joyfully, showed me to a chair next to himself, firmly shook my hand and kissed me on the lips. Then he addressed the lady with a whisper: "Anna Nikolaevna! Allow me to introduce you to the friend I was telling you about." This lady was the wife of a professor of pharmacology (or something like that), Zalessky. During the intermission the lady, after a few words of conversation with me, told me that Pyotr Ilyich had promised to have lunch at her house the day after the rehearsal, and that, knowing how eagerly Pyotr Ilyich had been waiting to see me, she would not want to deprive him of my company and would therefore be much obliged if I also came to lunch. Naturally, I accepted with delight. Pyotr thanked her sincerely for granting this favor to his friend.

While conducting a conversation with this delightful lady (she really was quite nice), I unintentionally looked at the neighboring box, number five, where the quite unattractive woman who sat there had fixed an intent gaze on Pyotr. Seated with this woman was a man of middle age, looking at the audience through his binoculars. Pyotr decided to go for a smoke, and when we got up from our places, the woman walked out of her box with the man. I stopped Pyotr for a moment and told him about the woman looking at him intently. Leaving the box, we saw this woman standing with the man at her door and looking in our direction (we had to walk by her). Pyotr stopped, shuffled his feet, and bowed to the lady, who did not take her severe (even somewhat angry) eyes from him, inquiring of her shyly: "Madam Shidlovskaya, if I am not mistaken?" *The lady* (preserving her regal and self-important visage and nodding her head slightly): "Yes! You are not mistaken. Is your concert tomorrow?" *Pyotr* (shyly and unsure as before): "Yes, tomorrow." The man stared at us throughout the entire exchange with unusual condescension.

When we had moved off to a polite distance, Pyotr addressed me: "Did you see how self-important that lady was? If only you could have seen how she hung onto me in Tiflis and followed me around! At that time, she was separated from her husband; now they must have got back together and she's become all-important. Well, can one really greet a person like that, when before she visited me dozens of times in the role of petitioner? What is wrong with her? She utterly embarrassed me!"

After the performance, Pyotr treated me to a marvelous dinner; moreover, we drank some of our favorite "Sivoucha litowska." That evening at our hotel there was a gathering of some sort of agricultural society, and a lot of people were dining, snacking, drinking, smoking, arguing, shouting, and walking around the halls. We sat by ourselves in a cozy corner and talked quietly. Suddenly Pyotr whispered to me with horror: "My God! What a gathering! Whatever brought them here?" I saw two men approach with a loud exclamation of delight at glimpsing Pyotr. Both kissed him, moved chairs up to our table, and sat down. Pyotr introduced me to the younger, calling him Kondratyev, and then added: "This is the very Sergey Kondratyev you met once in Gurinsky Tavern and, you remember, you almost got into an argument with him."[24] Naturally we treated each other in the friendliest way and told each other that we really could not remember what had happened between us before. (I do not know how sincere Kondratyev was, but I really had forgotten; I only remember his face then, a very young, clean-shaven face, and its unusually eager expression during conversation at our first meeting.) The other, a bit older, was, I believe, Kondratyev's brother-in-law. Of course, this intrusion utterly spoiled our intimate conversation, and, in order to lessen Pyotr's grief over this unpleasant encounter, I took energetically to telling jokes, which, thank God, Pyotr had not heard, so that in the end our supper was not boring or burdensome after all.

The rehearsal was on the next day. It made an indelible impression for several reasons. First, I heard a superb orchestra and, having been starved for this pleasure, was simply enchanted by it. Second, I heard major compositions by Pyotr that were hitherto utterly unknown to me (*The Tempest,* the Second Symphony, and *1812*). The main thing, however, was that I was overcome by delight in seeing my close friend being shown respect that bordered on veneration, and the small audience at the rehearsal expressed warm and, of course, sincere pleasure.

After the rehearsal, Tchaikovsky and I had lunch at Madame Zalesskaya's, where we made the acquaintance of her husband, a kind, modest, and very shy man, who to our great surprise turned out to be a lover of rare and expensive drinks. He pulled from his cellar (which might very well have been in his study) some wonderful old vodka and some rare wine, which we drank with great enjoyment. Soon after lunch, Pyotr, the poor thing, was supposed to go to dinner at the governor's (it was Slatin who had arranged for him such despicable entertainments), but for the life of me, I cannot recall how and where I spent the remaining part of the day. But then I remember the following day (Sunday, the day of the concert) down to the smallest details.

The concert took place during the day (it began at one o'clock). The public's enjoyment was indescribable. Pyotr's triumph was so grand that I hardly dared to admit to myself that he was my close friend, such was the chasm that divided me—a modest, mere mortal—from him, the hero of the day! The significance of the triumph I witnessed was augmented by the fact that it was a tribute not only to a great artist, but also to a man who was charmingly kind, cultured, and sincere to everyone. At the concert, apart from the wreaths and baskets of flowers (which were largely plucked away right then and there by the ladies), Pyotr was presented a silver lyre. This latter was presented, I believe, by the local branch of the Music Society. (As an aside I shall note that I thought that all of the enormous proceeds from the concert would go wholly for Pyotr's benefit, but, with a feeling of pride in my noble friend, I learned from him personally that when he received the Music Society's invitation to give a concert of his own works, he considered it an honor shown to him by the Society, and that the concert would not only bring him nothing, but that it would also cost him about four hundred rubles of his own money. I recall that he made a considerable financial contribution in his own name in aid of music classes.)

The day before, we had agreed to dine together after the concert. . . . This dinner, however, could not take place, because during the concert, Pyotr received an invitation to an official dinner as the guest of honor. While waiting for this ceremonial dinner, Pyotr came to sit at dinner together with me and my wife for half an hour. . . . Pyotr in his sincere kindness expressed regret that the official dinner had deprived him of the opportunity for us to dine together merrily, and that, more importantly, the official dinner would doubtless tire him out, and that it might even drag on to a late hour, thus preventing him from spending the evening with his friend, whom he had not seen for a long time and with whom he must discuss certain things. Therefore he proposed that we have supper together. Naturally, we gladly accepted his proposal and it was agreed thus: after dinner he would lie down for a rest and regain his strength for supper, while we would set off to hear *Faust*. Moreover, I proposed to the group and to Pyotr that we sup not at the Hôtel de l'Europe but at Ruf's restaurant, where they made a wonderful Salade Olivier (for which Muscovites have a soft spot), and where there is a large mechanical organ which plays, among other pieces, a potpourri from *Eugene Onegin,* which I did not yet know very well. Pyotr also did not have anything against the organ, which might remind us of our dear Moscow.

In the end it turned out so ridiculous, unfortunate, and sad that I still cannot remember it without a feeling of pain. The thing is that I made the arrangements and therefore could not help but remember them. They were that we would return from the theater to our (both mine and Pyotr's) Hôtel de l'Europe, whence we would get Pyotr (and if we were to find him asleep we were to awaken him), and set off together for Ruf's. Returning from the theater, I went straight to Pyotr's room and, to my surprise, found him pacing the corridor, hat in hand. Upon seeing me, Pyotr asked in a sad voice: "Tell me please how this happened? *I:* "Lord! You're frightening me! What happened?" *He:* "Well, we agreed to meet at Ruf's. After resting up I went there and began to wait. After sitting quite a long time I finally saw some men walk in, who approached the buffet, and I overheard them discussing *Faust.* Ah! I thought to myself, that means that you and the rest will soon be here! But after waiting quite a bit longer and eating some horrid food, I returned here and have been waiting for quite a long time without knowing what was going on, quite naturally. Where on earth have you all been? *I:* "We only just got back from the theater. Those men who were discussing *Faust* apparently did not stay to the end of the performance. But why did you go to Ruf's without us when we had all agreed to meet here and set off together? *He:* "I must have misunderstood you."

My wife thought the same as Pyotr, but the rest had understood my arrangements in accordance with my own interpretation. Later Pyotr told us that at Ruf's, both the customers and the staff had looked at him strangely. It is highly probable that the customers recognized him and were baffled as to why he should be there alone. (This is my idea, not Pyotr's.) In order to dispel the staff's confusion at seeing a person unoccupied for so long a time, he had ordered himself something, which had finally killed any desire for supper. The boredom of a long wait by himself was exacerbated by the fact that Ruf's restaurant (the dining hall, I believe) was being remodeled at the time, according to Pyotr, so that it was filthy, crowded, and uncomfortable.

Although Pyotr was, as always, charming and gracious at supper, my supper was spoiled by the knowledge of my unintentional affront to him. I could not free myself from the torturous thought that he, today's idol of a crowd of thousands, whom many would consider it a great stroke of luck and honor to have as their guest, whom many probably asked to do them this honor, had refused these requests in favor of his unworthy friend and had ended up in a situation far from fitting for the hero of the day. I believe, *I know,* that he forgave me, with such sincerity did he, so to speak, cover my mouth, as it were, at the very beginning of my apologies, but this does not prevent me from experiencing an extremely bitter feeling upon recalling this sad occasion. It is unfortunate that it all occurred on my account, although through no fault of my own. It is unfortunate that fate chose me of all people as an instrument for causing unpleasantness to my deeply loved, unforgettable friend.

The day after the concert I was to return to Poltava on the morning train and could therefore spend only a few minutes with Pyotr, and then we embraced like brothers and bade each other farewell. How could I imagine that I was bidding him an eternal farewell? . . .

Vasily Sapelnikov

We met in the Tirol, at the castle of the famous pianist Sophie Menter, where Pyotr Ilyich had come to spend a few days [in June 1893] en route from London back to his estate Kamenka, in Podolsk Province. He had traveled to London on the invitation of the London Academy, which had recognized Pyotr Ilyich as one of the great men of his time and honored him with the title of "doctor," which for the English was the highest degree of honor for famous foreigners.[25]

Despite his fifty-two years, Pyotr Ilyich felt wonderful. His spiritual and physical powers were in full blossom. He hoped to create many more new musical works and was burning with a thirst for work. In his imagination swarmed the sounds and melodies that were to find expression in new symphonies and an opera that he was planning to compose. Despite the fact that the entire world considered him to be a great composer, Pyotr Ilyich absolutely refused to acknowledge his past merits. He said that he wanted terribly to compose a really good opera.

Pyotr Ilyich, this highly educated and cultured man, was not and could not, of course, be superstitious. . . . All the more mysterious, of course, is the presentiment of approaching death that he had several months before his demise. This presentiment seemed immediately to grasp Pyotr Ilyich's entire being and made him unrecognizable. . . . He turned from a merry and buoyant man into one oppressed by the thought of approaching death. . . .

The evening before his departure for Kamenka, Pyotr Ilyich was unusually animated and in a good mood. But then, at tea, he suddenly became serious and taciturn. He cut the conversation short and became lost in thought. I looked up at him and took fright. His eyes were set fast on a single point. The expression of his face became sad and concentrated. He continued looking in this way for a few minutes.

His departure was set for the next day. Pyotr Ilyich was pensive the entire way. In the buffet at the train station, Pyotr Ilyich asked for a bottle of seltzer water. Pouring out two glasses, for himself and for me, Pyotr Ilyich drew the glass up to his lips, but then suddenly lowered the glass in his hand, without having even touched it. Again, his face adopted its sad expression of the previous day, and he became lost in thought. The second bell rang. It was time for him to take his place in the carriage. We stood up. Pyotr Ilyich took my hand and held it in his for a long time. "Farewell," he said finally. "This is perhaps the last time we shall see each other."

It was as if I felt in the sound of his voice the final salutation of a man dear to me. Tears appeared in his kind eyes.[26]

Yulian Poplavsky

The house at Klin where Tchaikovsky lived and created his wonderful works stands at the end of Zaretskaya Street, at the very edge of the city. At the time, Zaretskaya Street did not even exist in reality, for this became the name of a part

Nikolay Kashkin, professor of Moscow Conservatory.
Photo credit: The Russian Institute of the History of the Arts (St. Petersburg).

Eduard Nápravník, conductor and composer, 1897.
Photo credit: The Russian Institute of the History of the Arts (St. Petersburg).

Vladimir Pogozhev, the Director of St. Petersburg branch of
Russian Imperial Theaters, 1885.
Photo credit: The Bakhrushin State Theatre Museum (Moscow).

Grand Duke Konstantin Konstantinovich, 1892.
*Photo credit: The State Archive for Cinematographic,
Photographic and Phonographic Documents (St. Petersburg).*

Tchaikovsky, 1884.
Photo credit: The Russian Institute of the History of the Arts (St. Petersburg).

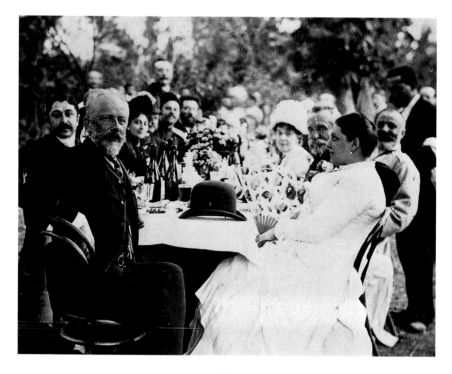

Tchaikovsky in Tiflis, 30 April 1889.
Photo credit: The Russian Institute of the History of the Arts (St. Petersburg).

Tchaikovsky in Tiflis, 2 May 1889.
Photo credit: The Glinka State Museum of Musical Culture (Moscow).

Nazar Litrov, Tchaikovsky's manservant, 1890.
Photo credit: The Tchaikovsky State Archive and House Museum (Klin).

Tchaikovsky, 1891.
Photo credit: The State Theatre Museum (St. Petersburg).

Pianist Vasily Sapelnikov and Tchaikovsky, 1892.
Photo credit: The Tchaikovsky State Archive and House Museum (Klin).

Konstantin Dumchev, violinist, 1893.
Photo credit: The Bakhrushin State Theatre Museum (Moscow).

Yulian Poplavsky, 1892.
Photo credit: The Tchaikovsky State Archive and House Museum (Klin).

Modest Tchaikovsky, 1895.
Photo credit: The Russian Institute of the History of the Arts (St. Petersburg).

Nikolay Mamonov, Tchaikovsky's physician, 1904.
Photo credit: The Tchaikovsky State Archive and House Museum (Klin).

Lev Bertenson, physician, 1904.
Photo credit: The Tchaikovsky State Archive and House Museum (Klin).

Tchaikovsky in London, 1893.
Photo credit: The Royal College of Music (London).

of the Petersburg Highway in Klin, bordered on both sides by fields and gardens.

The composer's house stood by the very gate at the entrance to the city, on the side opposite the Klin railway station. The house was wooden and with two stories. Around it were a small garden and outbuildings. Tchaikovsky himself occupied the upper part of the house. Downstairs was a small dining room with a terrace, as well as the living quarters of his servant and his family. Almost half of the upstairs was occupied by a spacious room with a small windowed balcony in the shape of a lantern. Tchaikovsky was especially fond of resting with a book in this "lantern." Next door were the bedroom and two guestrooms. The large room was Tchaikovsky's salon, study, and library. He went downstairs only for meals. Along the walls of the salon stood bookcases filled with music and books. In the middle of the room stood a piano. By the fireplace were an old-fashioned sofa and a desk. Above the desk hung portraits of Pyotr Ilyich's most dearly loved composers: Bach, Mozart, Beethoven, Glinka, and Rubinstein. In general there were a large number of portraits in the salon, arranged every-where. Here was also a little collection of gifts presented to the composer by admirers in various cities and countries. The composer's workroom was actu-ally his bedroom, where a simple, unvarnished table stood in the corner next to the window. Tchaikovsky worked at this table every day. He had a stunning capacity for work. He wrote systematically at the same hour every day, hardly managing to note down the compositions which he composed and developed in all their smallest details in his head. Moreover, Tchaikovsky could abandon for years at a time any melody or sketch which he had begun and, as soon as he returned to it, all that he had conceived was resurrected in his head in its original form. Tchaikovsky often said that if only our Russian composers worked regularly, like Beethoven, Schumann, or Mendelssohn, without waiting for inspiration and the right mood, we would also have nine symphonies by Glinka and dozens of quartets and operas by Dargomyzhsky or Musorgsky.

Above the bed in the bedroom hung a painting with the inscription, "Melancholy." The painting depicted night: over the sea, above whimsical clouds, one could see the moon, its silvery light extending like a quivering path along the water. . . . Tchaikovsky told me that he had received this picture in a peculiar fashion.

At his concert in Berlin, there was a performance of his famous *Sérénade mélancolique* for violin. The next day a modestly dressed lady shyly knocked at the door of Tchaikovsky's hotel room. She held in her hands a cylindrical object wrapped in paper. The composer invited her to enter. The lady's face was extremely expressive, but pale and tortured.

"I heard your serenade yesterday. . . . Take my 'Melancholy,' I have nothing else with which to express my gratitude to you for yesterday's concert." And with these words she offered him the painting. In embarrassment Tchaikovsky energetically refused to accept the gift, but the stranger begged him tearfully not to refuse. The composer was extremely touched and accepted the painting. He did not even manage to put it down on the table before the lady left, and he was never to find out who she was. In memory of this strange visitor, Tchaikovsky brought the painting back to Klin and hung it in his house. . . .

Tchaikovsky was a true beacon for Russian musicians. Among them he had no rivals or enemies. For musicians, the charm of his personality was so great that, when I happened to accompany him to an opera in Moscow, it was enough for Tchaikovsky to appear in a box at the theater for the orchestra and stage to be transformed. It was as if the monotonous and lazy performances of state-supported singers had never existed. The creative thought of the work being performed struck the orchestra like a bolt of lightning; it became a living and breathing being, crying and laughing, now rustling shyly, now wailing awesomely like the sea. Every musician became an actor, and every actor, supported and electrified by the orchestra, excelled himself.

I shall adduce a very curious fact illustrating how Tchaikovsky was able to assume the most unglamorous role in the interest of art, doing everything to achieve an ensemble.

Fifteen years ago, the Symphonic Concerts of the Russian Musical Society were run for a long time by the German conductor Max Erdsmanndörfer, and the leading roles in the orchestra were taken by Germans. Then Erdmannsdörfer left and, with Tchaikovsky's assistance, twelve different conductors were invited for twelve different Society concerts. While the conductors were being brought from Germany everything went well, but when it came the turn of Russian conductors and the concert programs changed in favor of Russian composers, the orchestra began to fail. There was not enough time for rehearsals, the musicians played inattentively, and the Russian conductors had to work five times as hard to achieve a passable ensemble. Finally, there came the concert under the direction of Nikolay Rimsky-Korsakov. . . . His *Spanish Capriccio* was on the program. In Rimsky-Korsakov's music, each instrument is given such an important role that one inattentive drummer can ruin everything. At the rehearsal, a heavy and sleepy German in the orchestra took up the castanets. He played them so lazily and out of rhythm that the lusty dances of Andalusia were utterly lost, and all of the color disappeared. Rimsky-Korsakov simply dropped his hands, and his face clouded over.

In the evening, they began the concert. During the intermission, before the *Spanish Capriccio*, I saw Tchaikovsky backstage. In great agitation he was trying to convince Rimsky-Korsakov of something. I approached.

"Listen, that was nothing like castanets; it was Bismarck chewing nuts. He'll ruin us! I'll play myself."

Tchaikovsky took the music and the castanets and stood at the back of the stage, behind the timpani. The capriccio began. The heavy German was nowhere to be seen. When the musicians saw that Tchaikovsky himself would be playing the castanets, they were dumbfounded. They began. It is impossible to describe the performance. Germans are, after all, excellent musicians and they were so shocked by this that they tried as hard as they could. Only a great artist can sacrifice his personality to art in such a manner.

In memory of this evening, Tchaikovsky gave me his copy of the music with Rimsky-Korsakov's autograph, and I still have it. . . . Pyotr Ilyich was a real supporter for all who were talented, young, and aspiring. Many now-famous musicians, singers, and composers owe their careers exclusively to him. Anyone who came to Tchaikovsky always found sympathy, advice, or generous help, and Pyotr Ilyich's kindness has left an indelible trace in the hearts of the thousands of people who knew him.

Tchaikovsky's magnanimity was inexhaustible. One of his Moscow friends, Count [Vladimir] Sh[ilovsky], with whom Tchaikovsky had been very close, but then parted ways in a radical fashion, and whom Tchaikovsky had not seen for many years, became seriously ill.

Count Sh[ilovsky] was a well-known and wealthy Moscow philanthropist. The doors of his mansion in a lane near the Conservatory were always wide open for musicians and artists. The Count loved music and had the reputation of being the leading expert on Russian popular songs. Shilovsky's luncheons gathered all artistic Moscow. But suddenly the Count fell ill and began to exhibit eccentric traits. He rented out his home with its coats of arms to a young seamstress, himself moving into the cellar, accessible only through the servants' quarters. Everyone abandoned him, and he was utterly alone. When Tchaikovsky learned that Sh[ilovsky] was in trouble and had fallen ill, he visited him and placed me by his side in order to acquaint him with new trends in music, in order to distract the patient a bit. I frequently visited him in his cellar, and we analyzed new compositions. The Count ardently loved to compose, but did not have a pennyworth of talent. He was consumed by pride, and now Tchaikovsky was advising him to take up the popularization of music by reworking pieces appropriate for the masses to be played on tavern barrel organs. At that time the people had no access to music outside taverns, and even now we have not progressed much beyond that. There was a barrel organ in every Moscow tavern. The Count grasped at this thought with enthusiasm and organized the project excellently. He commissioned music rolls with the pieces he had reworked and donated them to the taverns, which readily accepted new rolls for free. . . . But the composing bug did not leave him, and Sh[ilovsky] began to compose his own pieces, donating them in the form of music rolls to the taverns.

This success was too meager for him, and he tried to get Tchaikovsky to listen to his compositions. And, indeed, Pyotr Ilyich, busy with the staging of *The Queen of Spades* in Moscow, concerts, the Conservatory, and thousands of other things, consented to Sh[ilovsky]'s request. Once he invited me, and we set off together to a tavern near Sretensky Boulevard. The tavern was of average style, badly lit and thoroughly filled with Muscovite spirit. The waiter wound up the barrel organ with the Count's music rolls. And now imagine an utterly unique picture. The great Russian composer, whose glory shone beyond the borders of Europe, the Doctor of Music of Cambridge University, and the only Honorary Member of the Russian Music Society, was wasting his precious time in a filthy tavern listening to a barrel organ play the Count's music rolls, in order to do something nice for an ailing eccentric.

X

Death
(1893)

Tchaikovsky arrived in St. Petersburg on 10 October.[1] Planning to leave in a few days, in order to be present at a concert of the Russian Musical Society in Moscow, he put up temporarily at the apartment his brother, Modest Tchaikovsky, shared with their nephew Bob Davydov. This apartment, located on the corner of Malaya Morskaya and Gorokhovaya streets, had been rented just a few weeks before Tchaikovsky's arrival.

The entire first week of Tchaikovsky's stay in the capital was occupied by orchestra rehearsals, and his free time was taken up in helping his brother and nephew get settled in their new apartment. The days following the premiere were spent visiting relatives and friends, conducting business negotiations and correspondence, and attending theaters and restaurants.

On the night of 20 October, after returning from a late dinner at Leiner's restaurant—the one most frequented by the composer and his brother—Tchaikovsky experienced an upset stomach. By morning it had worsened, but it was taken for the composer's usual "indisposition," which as a rule passed quickly. But this time his condition continued to worsen and self-treatment failed to give any positive results. Toward evening Modest Tchaikovsky was obliged to summon a doctor, the family friend Vasily Bertenson. Without making a definite diagnosis, but convinced of his patient's extremely dangerous condition (with symptoms of constant diarrhea and vomiting, extreme weakness, chest and abdominal pains), the doctor turned for help to his more experienced elder brother, the renowned Petersburg physician Lev Bertenson.[2]

Upon his arrival, Lev Bertenson immediately diagnosed Asiatic cholera in its severe or algid stage. By this time (about 11 P.M.) the life of the patient was in immediate danger: he began to experience spasms, his head and extremities turned dark blue, and his temperature fell. Throughout the night, the doctor undertook the most energetic measures, such as the constant massaging of his patient's body by several persons at a time, as well as injections of musk, camphor and other stimulants recommended by medical knowledge of the day. By the morning of 22 October Tchaikovsky's condition had greatly improved. It was on this morning that the police were informed of the composer's illness. An official announcement of Tchaikovsky's infection with cholera appeared in St. Petersburg's newspapers on the following day.

Vasily Bertenson, who had been obliged to leave Petersburg and therefore participated no further in the treatment of Tchaikovsky, was replaced by two other doctors, Alexander Zander and Nikolay Mamonov.[3] They took turns at the bed of the patient between visits of the head physician, Lev Bertenson. The latter was concerned about the progression of the disease, as Tchaikovsky's kidneys had ceased to function, but hesitated to use the one treatment considered effective—immersion in a hot bath—because Tchaikovsky and his family shared a superstitious fear of this treatment stemming from the death of Tchaikovsky's mother from cholera precisely as she was immersed in such a bath.

All other treatments failed, and, although on 22 October Tchaikovsky still had hopes of survival, the following morning his emotional state deteriorated; he stopped believing in the possibility of recovery. The inactivity of his kidneys (uremia) resulted in the inevitable gradual poisoning of his blood. In addition, his intestines became paralyzed: the continuing diarrhea turned uncontrollable, and the patient felt weaker still. On 24 October his condition became so critical that the doctors finally resorted to giving Tchaikovsky a hot bath. But even this belated treatment did not have any cardinal effect.

Throughout the day, Tchaikovsky repeatedly lost consciousness and succumbed to delirium; toward evening, his pulse began to weaken and his breathing became labored. After 10 P.M., the patient's state was declared hopeless. Almost without regaining consciousness, as a result of edema of the lungs and a weakening of cardiac activity, the composer died at 3:15 A.M. on 25 October 1893. Present during his final minutes were his brothers Modest and Nikolay Tchaikovsky, his nephew Bob Davydov, and the doctor Nikolay Mamonov.

On 25 October, several morning newspapers printed short announcements of the composer's death. At the apartment where he died, with measures having been taken for disinfection, the body of the deceased lay in state. Throughout the day, the flow of visitors gradually increased, and two memorial services were held at the apartment. After nine o'clock, at the insistence of health officials, the coffin was closed and was not reopened for the following two days. During this time, hundreds of people came to bid farewell to the composer, dozens of wreaths were laid, and several more memorial services were held.

The papers published reports on Tchaikovsky's illness, interviews with doctors, relatives, and friends of the deceased, along with the texts of numerous condolence telegrams. On 25 October, Alexander III indicated that the funeral was to take place in Petersburg with all of the expenses attendant on the burial being covered by the Tsar's personal treasury. On 28 October, after a funeral service at Kazan Cathedral and a grand public procession down Nevsky Prospect, with the participation of dozens of delegations from various cities, organizations, and institutions, the composer's body was interred at the Tikhvin Cemetery of the St. Alexander Nevsky Monastery in St. Petersburg.

The strong public reaction to Tchaikovsky's death found its primary expression in accusations leveled against the doctors who had treated him. The fact that he had been taken ill with cholera in a city that at the time was one of the centers of a cholera epidemic did not elicit surprise, although this was rare for members of the privileged class. Moreover, the papers reported that the composer was generally susceptible to abdominal illnesses, that he had survived a case of cholerine (a mild form of cholera) that very summer, that in Petersburg he had often drunk unboiled water (the usual source of infection), and that on the morning of 21 October, as a form of self-treatment, he had unwisely taken a glass of Hunyadi alkaline water, which had only aided the proliferation of the disease-bearing bacillus.

The only question was where Tchaikovsky could have become infected, at Leiner's restaurant or at home, since according to various testimonies he had drunk unboiled water at both places. But this question turned out to be of secondary importance, even considering the growing criticism of restaurant procedures which permitted the use of unboiled water. The composer's recklessness was self-evident, and he was not alone in ignoring elementary hygienic measures.

The treatment of the patient was another matter entirely. Here, all responsibility lay in the hands of the team of doctors, and they inevitably became the targets of waves of outraged attacks over the sudden demise of the world celebrity. Lev Bertenson and his assistants were accused of incompetence (specifically of a lack of practical experience in treating cholera, the belated use of the hot bath, and general ignorance of modern treatments, etc.) as well as criminal arrogance (e.g., their reluctance to call for consultation with colleagues more experienced in treating cholera and their failure to move Tchaikovsky to a special cholera ward, etc.).

Modest Tchaikovsky came to the doctors' defense, publishing two letters reviewing the circumstances.[4] In the first, he described in great detail the progression of the illness; in the second he declared that everything possible had been done to save his brother and that the family of the deceased had no grievance whatsoever against those who had treated him. Moreover, Modest expressed profound gratitude for the doctors' "sincere and irreproachably thorough treatment" of his brother's illness.

A second wave of emotions arose over the repeat performance of the composer's Sixth Symphony at a memorial concert on 6 November 1893. Stunned by the recent tragedy, the public was especially sensitive to the "funereal" mood of several passages in the symphony. It is not surprising that many listeners (including some journalists writing about the concert for the press) gained the impression that Tchaikovsky had written a "requiem" for himself. Shortly after this, there appeared the first rumors of the composer's possible "self-poisoning," although they then existed only in oral form: at this time, and even much later, not a single hint of intentional poisoning is to be found in print.

Tchaikovsky's contemporaries were profoundly shocked by his death in the early morning of 25 October. The sorrow over the irreparable loss for Russian and world art was exacerbated by its untimeliness: Tchaikovsky went to his grave full of creative energy and plans for the future, at the height of his glory and artistic success. Naturally, the causes and circumstances of his death immediately became the subject of heightened public scrutiny. The details of the tragedy were closely reworked in the press and actively debated, as well as elaborated upon, in venues as varied as the royal family and merchants' clubs. Hearsay and gossip would blend with fact in later memoiristic literature.

Along with accurate information, there emerged a number of conflicting accounts, which prompted the appearance of ridiculous rumors and conjectures. Some of these became so deeply rooted that in time they began to aspire to the status of "truth in the final instance," which was allegedly being concealed by Tchaikovsky's relatives, the Tsarist regime, the Soviet government, etc. Recent studies, however, permit one to reconstruct the picture of Tchaikovsky's last days with a greater degree of accuracy and completeness, and also to show decisively both the origin and baselessness of various "sensational" conjectures concerning his end.

As the event itself receded in time, versions of the legend of the composer's voluntary departure from life became more persistent. Two main trends can be identified. According to one, the "concealed suicide" version, Tchaikovsky, tormented by unrequited love, deliberately courts death and drinks unboiled water in the hope of catching cholera; once having caught it, he delays summoning a doctor until he is certain that the disease has progressed so far that no chance of recovery remains.

According to the second, the "forced suicide" version, the composer, under the threat of public scandal (or even criminal trial) as a consequence of the imminent exposure of his homosexual contacts with a man from the highest royal circles, saves his own and his family's honor by taking slow-acting poison that mimics the characteristic symptoms of cholera, thus allowing his doctors and family to explain his sudden death as resulting from natural causes, from a fatal disease. One variant that has long enjoyed popularity is that the "order" for suicide stemmed from Alexander III himself.

In the 1980s, widespread attention was garnered by another variant of the "forced suicide" legend, according to which the composer fell victim to a "court of honor" conducted by his former classmates at the School of Jurisprudence, who sentenced him to death at his own hands (owing to the same presumed threat of "homosexual scandal"). This variant is essentially a new elaboration based on old oral legends, but it received sanction by a scholarly interpretation and was publicized in an English music journal.[5] The conclusions by the author of the article were in fact so provocative as to move the question of Tchaikovsky's death from the realm of kitchen gossip and literary fantasy to that of the scholarly and mainstream press, becoming a topic of sharp discussion and stimulating a series of special studies.[6]

Since the underlying theses of this new version coincided with traditional arguments for Tchaikovsky's suicide (the motive being a fear of his criminal habit being revealed, the medical proof being conflicting testimony on the progression of the composer's illness and the allegation that proper sanitary measures were ignored), scholars were obliged to analyze first and foremost the occasion for such supporting testimony. At the same time they undertook a review of the entire spectrum of questions and factual gaps reflected in all diverse legends about Tchaikovsky's death.[7]

Recent studies suggest that, in the context of Russian social attitudes, sexual mores, and criminal practice in the late nineteenth century, any scandal or repression with respect to Tchaikovsky was most unlikely, both on the strength of his elevated social standing and due to the generally tolerant attitude toward homosexuality obtaining in court circles and within the Imperial family. The idea of a poison that could mimic the symptoms of cholera also turns out to be imaginary: not a single toxic substance available at that time fulfills the necessary "requirements."[8]

The Soviet microbiologist Nikolay Blinov has thrown particular light on the medical aspect of the problem. Analyzing contemporary ideas about the nature, prevention, and treatment of cholera in Russia before 1893, Blinov establishes that Tchaikovsky's doctors acted strictly in accordance with the recommendations of the medical science of their day. They were actually able to save the patient from cholera itself on the first night, at a stage when, statistically, ninety percent of all fatalities occur. But the treatment was started late, for reasons beyond the doctors' control, and they were unable to save the patient from postcholeric complications (uremia, blood poisoning, etc.), which eventually led to his death. He could only have been saved by modern medical treatments.[9]

It is precisely because Tchaikovsky died not from cholera itself (which had been a possibility during the night of 21–22 October), but as a result of the disease's inescapable repercussions (ultimately, edema of the lungs and the cessation of cardiac activity), that the coffin of the deceased could be left open to the public (on 25 October), which did not contradict prevailing sanitary practices. It was held that the activity of the choleric bacilli had ceased two days before death. But in any case, throughout the course of the disease and obsequies in the presence of the composer's body (on 25–27 October), sanitary and disinfective precautions were continually being taken in the apartment. That none of the relatives, servants, or friends who had contact with Tchaikovsky became infected is but another proof of the efficacy of these measures.

With respect to the theoretical possibility of a "conspiracy" of the attending doctors, with the aim of concealing the composer's self-poisoning, Blinov undertook a detailed study of the biographies of the doctors who treated Tchaikovsky and of the laws governing contemporaneous medical practice and professional ethics, and concluded that such a conspiracy was unthinkable for these people.[10]

A close study of newspaper accounts and the series of memoirs relevant to Tchaikovsky's illness and death permits one to explain the apparent factual contradictions found in the testimony of eyewitnesses to the tragedy. Along with the purely objective factors (such as the differences in the doctors' and the family members' perceptions of Tchaikovsky's illness and the psychological differences between an immediate evaluation of events and a later reconstruction, etc.), one can also identify a series of subjective factors that abetted distrust in the official ("choleric") version at the time of the event.

In the first place, the media frenzy over the illness of the famous composer must be noted, the race for "hot" news, as a consequence of which the papers published inaccuracies, distorted information, and sheer disinformation (for example, the emotional statements of Tchaikovsky's friend, the singer Nikolay Figner, were reported as "the opinion of Dr. Bertenson," and an interview with Lev Bertenson himself was treated in such a way as to suggest that Tchaikovsky's death occurred on 24 October, etc.).[11]

Confusion was also abetted by the authors of memoirs written years after the event. In his 1912 memoir, Vasily Bertenson, who was absent from Petersburg after 22 October (and who did not send a condolence telegram from Moscow until 26 October), presented the whole affair as if he personally had been present at the dying man's bedside throughout his last days. This, despite the fact that in a letter of 11 January 1911 he had requested Modest Tchaikovsky to recount details of the event "to refresh my memory."[12]

The composer's nephew Yury Davydov (the younger brother of Bob) and the actor Yury Yuryev composed "cooperative" memoirs in the 1940s describing their presence at Leiner's restaurant with Tchaikovsky, embellished with lurid details of that "fateful supper" on 20 October, when in actuality neither had been present at all. In each case the psychological motivation for such "license" is simply explained: people close to the great composer found it permissible to distort the truth in order to enhance their own role as eyewitnesses.[13]

Yury Davydov, who was seventeen at the time of his uncle's death, has unfortunately played a unique role in the creation of recent myths. Although Davydov denied Tchaikovsky's suicide in his memoirs and public lectures, in private conversation he would sometimes hint that his uncle had, after all, taken poison, according to the testimony of several people who knew him closely. So great was the authority of the head curator of collections at Tchaikovsky's home-museum (1945–1962) and the last living near relative of Tchaikovsky, that such "hints" achieved instant credibility, which in turn enhanced oral rumor. Since Davydov's own recollections contain a series of demonstrable untruths, none of his statements can be believed without independent confirmation. However, it was precisely Yury Davydov who also provided in print a bold but psychologically plausible hypothesis that the very first rumors of Tchaikovsky's suicide might have appeared with the participation of Lev Bertenson's apologetic students, who chose this peculiar way to shield their mentor from criticism over his allegedly misguided treatment of the composer.[14]

The various rumors concerning "Imperial wrath" directed at Tchaikovsky also turn out, upon close analysis, to be nothing but lurid fiction. Alexander III revered the composer's talent, and members of the Imperial family frequently attended Tchaikovsky's operas and ballets, buying up new editions of Tchaikovsky's music to play at home. Tchaikovsky's outstanding merits as a citizen were also appreciated: he was awarded the Order of St. Vladimir and a lifetime pension, and was given a valuable ring as a personal gift from the Tsar. His death, according to Grand Duke Konstantin Konstantinovich's diary entry of 26 October 1893, "grieved the Tsar and Tsarina greatly." "How sorry I am for him and what a disappointment!" wrote the Tsar to the Minister of Court Illarion Vorontsov-Dashkov on 25 October after receiving the news of Tchaikovsky's demise. On that same day he issued a resolution concerning the organization of a state funeral for the composer at his own expense, and then he personally revised the plan of the memorial events submitted to him for review by Ivan Vsevolozhsky. It is impossible to imagine that such evidence of the Tsar's attention could be bestowed posthumously on a man who during his lifetime had fallen into royal disfavor.[15]

A series of documents found in recent years present firm evidence against the historical, psychological, and medical foundations of the various suicide theories, while no substantial evidence whatsoever in support of these theories has been discovered. The composer's death from cholera is attested in the official burial certificate from 28 October 1893, preserved in the archive of the St. Alexander Nevsky Monastery.[16] Tchaikovsky's brother Nikolay noted on a page together with a list of memorial wreaths: "Three doctors treated his cholera."[17] In 1898, Bob Davydov, in a letter to his uncle Modest (both were direct witnesses of Tchaikovsky's last days), recalled: "You know, Uncle Pyotr had terrible digestive problems, which by the time I knew him had evidently lessened, but which when aggravated could even serve in the end as the breeding-ground of his fatal disease."[18] Vasily Bertenson also wrote, concerning the onset of Tchaikovsky's illness: "He fell ill only as a consequence of faults in his diet and having drunk bitter-alkaline water on an empty stomach" (letter to Modest Tchaikovsky from 20 June 1905).[19] Modest himself, a day before his brother's death (on 24 October at 12:48), sent a telegram on the progress of the illness to Vasily Bertenson, who had left Petersburg: "The first period passed, full retention of urine, condition is grave."[20] On 25 October, Lev Bertenson wrote to Modest: "The dreadful disease that took the life of your unforgettable brother has brought me closer to him, yourself, and all to whom he was dear. I cannot recover from the terrible drama I have lived through, and I am utterly incapable of communicating to you all the torment I am experiencing!"[21] These testimonies alone from the archive of the Tchaikovsky Museum at Klin suffice to put an end to the old rumors and new fantasies generated by the proponents of an "unnatural" death theory.[22]

There remains the theoretical possibility of the composer's intentional self-infection with cholera, or so-called "Russian roulette." It is impossible to reject this theory completely insofar as no one can know with any precision what was concealed in the hidden depths of Tchaikovsky's soul in the autumn of 1893. But the abundance of creative, artistic, and practical plans which Tchaikovsky mentioned in personal letters and conversations, and the fact that he had already experienced a mild form of cholera in June of that year (the bacilli of which could have remained in his organism, under certain conditions, for up to several months), both support the view that Tchaikovsky's illness was not the result of intention, but rather a fateful combination of circumstances. Tchaikovsky's organism was predisposed to infection and could give a sensitive "reaction" at any moment to infected Petersburg water.

Following are recollections, diary entries, and interviews of various contemporaries pertaining to the composer's death. First is Modest Tchaikovsky's account of the composer's illness, the best so far, which was published at the time in St. Petersburg's newspapers and later on, with some minor variations, in his brother's biography.[23] Written five days after Tchaikovsky's death, it reflects the correct sequence of events, albeit vitiated by its author's desire to minimize the blame that could be placed on him for his preoccupation with his own affairs during the decisive first day of Tchaikovsky's illness (Modest spent most of it at the rehearsal of his new play at the Alexandrinsky Theater).[24]

Modest's narrative is followed by recollections of the younger son of the conductor Eduard Nápravník, Vladimir Nápravník (1869–1948), who spent some time with Tchaikovsky before his illness. This particular memoir was written by Nápravník in the 1920s for Igor Glebov's collection of memoirs and letters, but for some reason it was not included in the book, which was published in 1924. It has been preserved among Glebov's papers and is published here for the first time.[25] Nápravník's reminiscences seem generally reliable: one notes, for instance, that he does not include himself among those in attendance at the final dinner at Leiner's restaurant, whereas Tchaikovsky's nephew Yury Davydov (1876–1965) boldly and erroneously claimed to have been present. Excerpts from the latter's mostly fictional account are presented below as an example of unreliable memoirs.[26]

Tchaikovsky's physician Vasily Bertenson, in recollections penned in 1912,[27] speaks about the famous composer's cholera case, but in a carefully phrased way. He intentionally obscures his own incompetence (he could not have diagnosed cholera at the time when he implies that he did) as well as his absence after the first day of Tchaikovsky's illness.[28]

An interview with his brother, Dr. Lev Bertenson (1850–1929), about the course of the illness appeared in *Novoe vremia* on 27 October 1893. This, however, provided an incomplete picture of the composer's treatment and misled several generations of readers. In order to minimize this confusion, the interview is here reprinted with the inclusion of the reporter's questions to the doctor, which were omitted in the newspaper publication and which we have reconstructed.[29]

Another physician who treated Tchaikovsky, Nikolay Mamonov (1869–?), was also questioned by reporters, and his replies resulted in an interview published on 26 October in *Novosti i birzhevaia gazeta,* which adds significant information about the composer's treatment and fully supports the aforementioned accounts of Modest Tchaikovsky and Lev Bertenson.[30]

Short entries from Grand Duke Konstantin Konstantinovich's diary and newspaper accounts help to recreate the events surrounding Tchaikovsky's death much more reliably than any memoir.[31] These are followed by the moving account of Tchaikovsky's funeral from the pen of Yulian Poplavsky, who only a few weeks earlier had visited the composer at the latter's home in Klin, where he had found Tchaikovsky to be in vibrant good health.[32]

Modest Tchaikovsky

Pyotr Ilyich arrived in St. Petersburg on 10 October [1893]. As usual, our nephew and I met him, and I found him as hale and hearty as when I had last seen him in Moscow. He liked everything about our new apartment, and his good mood stayed with him, especially during the first few days, while his arrival was not yet known in the city and he could still dispose of his time freely.

Only one thing disturbed him: the musicians at the rehearsals were little impressed with his Sixth Symphony. Besides the fact that he valued their opinion, he was worried that their indifference might affect the actual performance of the piece. Pyotr Ilyich conducted well only those of his works which he knew the orchestra liked. In order to achieve subtlety of shading, overall harmony, it was essential for him to feel sympathy and pleasure from those around him. A cold expression, an indifferent gaze, the yawn of an orchestra member—all understandable when a piece is as yet unfamiliar—constrained and flustered him, and he paid scant attention to polishing up details, but tried to get the rehearsal over with as quickly as possible in order to release the musicians from their tedious chore. Thus, whenever he was conducting a new composition for the first time, his performance showed an uncertainty, even carelessness, in his communication of details—a lack of determination and strength in communicating the whole. That is why the Fifth Symphony and *Hamlet,* given such a pallid showing by their composer, had so hard a time winning a true appraisal, and also why the *Voivode* ballad perished.

We have seen . . . several times how easily Pyotr Ilyich could be swayed by others' opinions of his works, and how often under someone else's influence his attitude toward a work might shift from enthusiasm to disdain, or the reverse. This time he remained unshakable, and despite the coolness of the musicians continued to maintain that he "had never written and never would write anything better than this symphony." Nevertheless, he did not succeed in winning either the performers or the public to this view at the concert on 16 October. The symphony was well liked—the audience applauded, and the composer was called forth, but no more enthusiastically than after the performance of his other works, and it produced nothing approaching the powerful and thrilling impression it made so soon afterwards on 6 November under Nápravník, which has since been repeated in so many other cities.

Besides the Sixth Symphony, the program . . . of the concert directed by Pyotr Ilyich included [after the intermission] the Overture to Laroche's unfinished opera *Karmozina,* Tchaikovsky's own Piano Concerto in B-flat Minor, op. 23, the dances from Mozart's opera *Idomeneo,* and the piano solo from Liszt's *Spanish Rhapsody.* . . .

Coming down to morning tea next day, I found Pyotr Ilyich already long since up and with the score of the Sixth Symphony before him. He had agreed to send it to Jurgenson in Moscow that very day and could not decide what title to give it. He did not want to leave it with simply a number, and had abandoned his original intention of calling it the "Programme" Symphony. "Why *Programme* when I don't want to give out the programme!" I suggested calling it "Tragic." That did not please him either. I left the room with Pyotr Ilyich still undecided. Then suddenly the title *Pathétique* came into my head. I went back and, I remember as though it were yesterday, I stood in the doorway and pronounced this word. "Excellent, Modest, bravo, *Pathétique!*"—and as I watched, he wrote upon the score the title that has remained ever since.

In citing this incident, I do not relate it in order to connect my name with this work. . . . Probably I should never have mentioned it but for the fact that it serves to illustrate in a simple way how far the conjectures of the most enlightened commentators may wander from the truth. . . .[33]

Throughout his final days, Pyotr Ilyich was preoccupied with the thought of [the young composer] Georgy Conus' *Suite from Childhood [Siuita iz detskoi zhizni];*[34] several times he mentioned that he was eagerly looking forward to the pleasure he would derive from conducting the piece at the next symphony concert, and he praised it everywhere, calling its appearance an "event" in Russian music.

During these same days, he also spoke to me a great deal about the revisions of *The Oprichnik* and *The Maid of Orleans,* which he intended to work on in the near future. For this purpose, he borrowed the score of *The Oprichnik* from the library of the Imperial Theaters and acquired the complete works of [the Russian poet Vasily] Zhukovsky. He never told me his intentions concerning the first of these operas, but we did discuss the revision of the final scene in *The Maid of Orleans.* I urged him, since he had already made wide use of Schiller's scenario, to follow Schiller's ending as well.[35] This appeared to interest him, but he was not destined to come to a final decision.

His mood during these final days was not exclusively cheerful, yet neither was it at all depressed. In the company of the people closest to him he was content and jolly, but with strangers he was, as always, nervous and agitated, and afterward tired and listless. . . .

On Tuesday the nineteenth, at the request of the opera company which performed in the former Kononov Theater, [Pyotr Ilyich] attended a production of Anton Rubinstein's *Die Makkabäer.*

On Wednesday the twentieth, [Pyotr Ilyich] was perfectly healthy. Out on a stroll with one of our nephews, Count Alexander Litke, he told him many stories about [his eccentric friend Nikolay] Bochechkarov, about his oddities, sayings, and jokes, and spoke of how he missed him almost as much now as just after his death in 1876.

That day he dined with his old friend Vera Butakova, née Davydova. For the evening he had a box at the Alexandrinsky Theater, where Alexander Ostrovsky's *The Ardent Heart [Goriachee serdtse]* was being performed. During the intermission he and I visited Konstantin Varlamov in his dressing room. He had always appreciated the latter's amazing talent, and in the 1890s, having made his acquaintance, he grew fond of him as a person. The conversation turned to spiritualism. Varlamov, with his characteristic humor, impossible to convey on the page, expressed his distaste for all "that fakery," and for anything that reminded him of death in general. Nothing could have pleased Pyotr Ilyich better; he agreed with delight and laughed heartily at the original manner in which this had been said. "We shall yet make the acquaintance of that repulsive snub-nosed monster," he said, and then, as he was leaving, he turned back to Varlamov: "But you and I have a long way to go before then! I feel I shall live a long time."

From the theater, Pyotr Ilyich went with our nephews the Counts Litke, and Baron Rudolph Buxhövden, to Leiner's restaurant.[36] I was to join them there later, and when I arrived about an hour later I found all the above-mentioned persons in the company of Ivan Gorbunov, Alexander Glazunov, and Fyodor Mülbach.[37] They had all finished dining, but I learned that my brother had eaten macaroni and washed it down with his customary white wine and mineral water. The supper lasted only a short time, and soon after one o'clock the two of us returned home on foot. Pyotr Ilyich was quite healthy and calm.

Vladimir Nápravník

Pyotr Ilyich arrived in Petersburg on 10 October. Each time he came he would usually visit our home on the very day of his arrival, or else on the following day at about eleven o'clock, in time for Papa's breakfast. He could always depend on catching Papa at home at that time, since Papa usually left for rehearsal at twelve. At this time one of my sisters was sure to be practicing on the piano, but at the sound of the doorbell she would leave the hall while the front door was being opened. The entranceway opens directly into the hall. Pyotr Ilyich would hear various scales and exercises from the outside stairs, but upon entering the hall and not seeing anyone there, sometimes he sat down at the piano and continued those very scales or exercises by ear.

Papa and all of us were always terribly glad to see Pyotr Ilyich. He and Papa would usually embrace and kiss at their meeting, then they would sit down at the table in the hall and tell each other the news that had accumulated since their last meeting. At five minutes after eleven, they would usually go to the dining room to dine. Papa and Pyotr Ilyich used the familiar form of address, although only for about the two or three years following the dinner organized by Pyotr Ilyich after the debut performance of *The Queen of Spades*. Anton Rubinstein was also present at that dinner, among the very close circle of friends. Right at the start of the dinner, Pyotr Ilyich proposed to Papa that they drink a toast to *Brüderschaft*. . . .

That 11 October, I did not see Pyotr Ilyich, but met him for the first time on the thirteenth, on the street, on Police Bridge. Embracing and greeting each other, we set off together along Morskaya and Gorokhovaya toward his [brother's] home. I expressed to him my desire to attend the rehearsal of the symphonic concert on the next day, the fourteenth, to which Pyotr Ilyich replied: "No, it's better not to come. Yesterday at the first rehearsal I hardly managed to cover everything, and it's still going badly. It would be better if you came the day after tomorrow, and ask your Papa also not to come tomorrow."

Then we spoke of his nephew, who was seeking a position but had not yet found anything.[38] I knew that Tchaikovsky could not bear to walk around and petition for anyone. Still, I told him that it would be very good if he himself went to ask my university friend on behalf of his nephew. At the very mention of this, Pyotr Ilyich's face adopted a look of displeasure, an expression that badly suited his usually kind face.

"Well, I'm sorry, I cannot go to anyone. I don't know anyone and no one knows me. . . . Once in my life I wanted to petition regarding a matter that didn't even concern me personally, and all the Moscow actors of the Imperial Theaters asked me to. I was, so to speak, the petitioner for an entire corporation before the Ministry of the Court. Since then I will never again in my life petition for anyone."

I fell silent and changed the subject.

On Friday the fifteenth, I was with Papa at the dress rehearsal of the Symphonic Concert. Among other things Tchaikovsky's new Sixth Symphony was being performed. Any composer becomes inordinately shy at performances of his own works, and reticent about making too many comments to the performers. Pyotr Ilyich was especially distinguished by this trait and therefore, one must admit, usually his performances of his own works were not as good as they might have been. Once, after a rehearsal of one of Papa's pieces, at which Pyotr Ilyich had been present, he said to my mother: "A curious thing. Nápravník, who is infamous for his inexorable demands when others' works are being performed, becomes utterly unrecognizable when his own piece is being played. He is shy, reticent, and doesn't make the necessary comments. . . ."

On the sixteenth, the first Symphonic Concert [of the RMS] was held before a full hall. Tchaikovsky's entrance was met rapturously. Even before his entrance, I saw him walking nervously around the large greenroom. It was better not to approach him at this time, when there invariably turned out to be quite a few persons who, for some reason, considered themselves obliged to approach him and ask him about his music. It is difficult to imagine a more awkwardly chosen time for such conversations. Later, he told me that he was very glad that he had spent the entire intermission after the symphony in the box of Grand Duke Konstantin Konstantinovich, thereby avoiding any conversations about music in general, and about his symphony in particular.

Usually he became terribly agitated whenever he had to conduct. I remember him telling me once: "I am so tense, so agitated when conducting, that one day I shall explode at the podium. . . ."

As it happened, the audience [at the Symphonic Concert] received the new symphony without enthusiasm. After the concert Pyotr Ilyich dined at Palkin's restaurant in the company of Laroche, Glazunov, Verzhbilovich, Lavrov, Lyadov, Blumenfeld, Blok, and Sokolov.[39] Remaining until three o'clock, Pyotr Ilyich felt very fatigued and went home, while the rest of the company stayed on.

At twelve o'clock on the seventeenth I had lunch with Pyotr Ilyich, his brother Modest, Herman Laroche, and August Gerke.[40] The conversation, obviously, turned to the concert that had taken place the day before.

"It is strange that I don't like many of my own works," said Pyotr Ilyich, "but it is quite the opposite with this last symphony: I find it very successful and, to tell the truth, I like it. I do not care at all that the public received it with restraint, but I feel, and this I find most unfortunate, that the orchestra doesn't like it. . . ."

This conversation took place before lunch. And still before lunch he passed into my room and here, after arranging his attire, he asked me: "Vladimir, tell me honestly, do you like my symphony or not?"

In answer to my rapturous response he kissed me and said: "That terribly pleases and calms me."

Several times at lunch he repeated that he was frightfully pleased that I had praised his symphony. "After all, [Vladimir's] awfully severe. He curses me so often, says so many unpleasant things about me, that I appreciate his praise."

Although it is immodest of me, I present the entire conversation as it was. When conversation turned to his further musical plans he said: "I would like to take up opera again, but so far I haven't found a subject."

At parting, we agreed to meet for lunch on Tuesday at his apartment. On that day, the nineteenth, he was supposed to leave for Moscow, and my mother and sisters had promised to accompany him to the Nikolaevsky Railway [station] for the 9 P.M. train, as they often did. But that afternoon, he dropped by our house and, not finding anyone at home, left a note for mother with the doorman: "Dearest Olga Eduardovna! I *am not going* today. I kiss your hand. Pyotr Tchaikovsky."[41] This note was therefore written during his last visit to our house. Although he meant to come two days later, and even set off for our house, he was unable to make it. . . . In the note he left at our house the words "am not going" are underlined. Could he think that, by postponing his train from Petersburg, he would never leave it, not even when dead? This note will be preserved by our family like a holy of holies. By general agreement we agreed to glue it onto a folder, make an appropriate inscription below, and frame it.

At half past five on 19 October I was at his apartment, or rather at the apartment of Modest. . . . There remained half an hour before dinner, and we sat talking on the couch in the living room. Apart from members of the household and myself, the dinner guests included two nephews of Pyotr Ilyich, the counts Alexander and Konstantin Litke, the young Laroche, a student, and Baron Buxhövden. Above the couch hung a laurel lyre with a ribbon, presented to Pyotr Ilyich at the last symphonic concert. He very much wanted to know whom it was from, but he never did find out. Alexander Litke stood next to Pyotr Ilyich and was diligently combing Pyotr Ilyich's hair with his hands, at which the latter said with a satisfied smile: "I adore it when someone pulls at my hair, as long as it doesn't hurt."

At dinner Pyotr Ilyich was in very high spirits; he treated us to wine he had bought himself, inquiring how we liked it, and told a lot of stories about one of his old friends, now dead, a very original and eccentric man. Along with the stories, Pyotr Ilyich mimicked his friend's voice and gestures. We were all dying of laughter. In the evening we all set off to Kononov Hall for *Die Makkabäer,* which was being put on by the Russian Private Opera Company. Before we set out for the theater, conversation had turned to this opera and Pyotr Ilyich played on the piano a chorus from it that he especially liked. Pyotr Ilyich was in general very well disposed toward private opera companies, trying with all his might to support their grievous state in Russia.

His box-ticket for the evening had been sent to him ahead of time, and he was quite glad to go. We who surrounded him knew that his very presence would be a kind of moral support for the company. He listened attentively to the opera and energetically applauded the singers. During one of the intermissions he went on stage to thank whomever was responsible for kindly sending him the box-ticket. Upon his return he told us how nicely the singers had received him. "It is only here that stages are so unwelcoming, the dressing rooms so small, in general so crowded. . . ."

After the performance we dined at Leiner's restaurant, where Alexander Glazunov joined our table and spoke to Pyotr Ilyich about his most recent work, sketching several chords on a scrap of paper to show their resolution. Fascinated with the conversation, Pyotr Ilyich for his part also sketched several examples of especially interesting aural combinations. We left after one o'clock, and I accompanied Pyotr Ilyich and Modest to their house. Upon parting, Pyotr Ilyich invited me to dinner on Friday. It was here, at their doorway after 1 A.M., that I saw Pyotr Ilyich and kissed him for the last time in my life. If only I had known that then! . . .

Pyotr Ilyich decided to leave on Friday and promised to drop by to say goodbye to us on Thursday. But, as I have said, he did not make it to our house. . . . At dinner on Thursday, Papa asked me: "Has anything happened by chance to Pyotr Ilyich? He promised me he would be here." None of us, however, was concerned. Each thought that something had detained him and that he would definitely come the next day.

After five on Friday, as had been agreed, I ascended the staircase to Modest's apartment. To my surprise the door to the apartment was half-open, and on it was pinned a piece of paper with the words: "Please do not ring." My heart was wrenched, but I did not yet know anything. Only upon entering did I see on everyone's face that something unusual had happened there. Modest explained to me that Pyotr Ilyich had a most terrible, most serious case of cholera. "At the given moment he is a bit better, but the danger has not yet passed; only an hour ago he was experiencing tremors."

Having sat there for half an hour without seeing the patient, I ran home like a madman to tell the horrible news. Papa was terribly taken aback, as was our entire family, all of whom loved Pyotr Ilyich so warmly.

Unfortunately, I got no further opportunity to see Pyotr Ilyich. I myself fell ill and spent two days at home. We sent someone several times a day to inquire about Pyotr Ilyich's health, and each time we received more and more disconcerting news.

Reading on the morning of the twenty-fifth the terrible news of his death, I instantly went to Modest, who, by the way, said the following regarding his brother's death:

"He always preserved enough strength to turn himself over, lift his own leg, and cough with an effort. . . . It is my deep conviction that he preserved consciousness until the very last moment. A quarter of an hour before his death he opened his eyes, and I shall never forget the expression of his gaze. There appeared some indescribable expression of his clear consciousness of approaching death. His gaze stopped on his favorite nephew, who was standing by his side, and then it rose toward the sky. For several instants something lit up in his eyes, and then went out with his last gasp."

Yury Davydov

And so the fateful day of 20 October arrived. Free after classes, I went to visit my Uncle Modest and found out that Pyotr Ilyich was going to dinner at the home of Vera Butakova, my father's younger sister. Her son, Grigory, was my closest childhood friend, so I went over there. Uncle Pyotr arrived soon after me. He was in a very good mood: cheerful, hale and hearty. . . . The dinner was very intimate, with no strangers present, and it passed in a warm and friendly atmosphere, as Pyotr Ilyich always had interesting things to talk about. . . .

Suddenly [Pyotr Ilyich] looked at his watch, turned to me, and said, "Well, get ready, or we'll be late." When Mrs. Butakova asked where he was going, he told her that he had taken a box in the Alexandrinsky Theater to amuse us, his nephews. . . .

We arrived at the theater just as the curtain was raised. Some were already present in the box: my uncle Modest, my brother Bob, the two Litke brothers, Bob's friend Rudolf [Rudi] Buxhövden, and my cousin, Grigory Davydov. All of us left immediately after the brilliantly acted show with the exception of Uncle Modest, who stayed to talk with Mariya Savina [a famous actress]. He promised to catch up with us if we went by foot. At the moment of our exit we encountered the most talented comic actor, Ivan Gorbunov; we walked up Nevsky all together in a crowd, in the direction of the Admiralty. On the way . . . Pyotr Ilyich suggested that we should go to Leiner's restaurant, which we frequently went to, since it was one of the few that would let students like myself in through the back door—naturally, not without a bribe to the doorman. That evening there were quite a number of us who had no right to enter. My brother, Buxhövden, and Alexander Litke were army volunteers and dressed in military uniform, while Konstantin Litke and myself were cadets; legal entrance to the restaurant was therefore prohibited to all of us. Consequently, we all went to the courtyard and waited until Pyotr Ilyich negotiated the matter with the owner, at which point we were called in. We did not have to wait long. We were taken to a large separate room and were reunited with the others, now joined by Fyodor Mülbach, a great friend of the Tchaikovsky brothers. At the very moment of our arrival, Pyotr Ilyich was occupied with ordering supper for us. After completing his order, Pyotr Ilyich proceeded to ask the waiter to bring him a glass of water. A few minutes later the waiter came back and reported that they had run out of boiled water. Thereupon Pyotr Ilyich, not without a certain irritation in his voice, said: "Then bring me some unboiled water, and the coldest there is." Everyone tried to talk him out of drinking unboiled water, given the cholera epidemic in the city, but Pyotr Ilyich said that all this was a prejudice he didn't believe in. The waiter left to carry out his order. At this point the door opened, and Modest entered the room accompanied by the actor Yury Yuryev. Modest exclaimed, "Aha, I should have guessed! Passing by, I thought I might drop in and inquire whether by chance you were here."

"And where else could we be?" answered Pyotr Ilyich.

Close on Modest's heels, the waiter entered with a glass of water on a tray. Having learned what had transpired and about the substance of our continuing dispute with Pyotr Ilyich, Modest became truly angry with his brother and exclaimed, "I categorically forbid you to drink unboiled water!"

Laughing, Pyotr Ilyich jumped up and went to meet the waiter, and Modest rushed after him. But Pyotr Ilyich forestalled him and, pushing his brother aside with his elbow, succeeded in drinking in one gulp the fateful glass. Modest once again scolded him, and the merriment began. I say that merriment began, because in Pyotr Ilyich's presence it was always merry. He beamed merriment as the sun beams rays. One must, however, emphasize that this occurred only in the company of people who were close to him, that is to say, those toward whom he was not shy. A single stranger was enough to make his whole mood of merriment disappear.

Occupied in this way by lively chatter over a glass of wine or mug of beer, we stayed there until two in the morning. I accompanied my uncles and my brother to their apartment and went home in a bright and cheerful mood, recalling everything I had experienced during the last few hours, and little concerned with the problem of how I could creep into the dormitory unnoticed by the officer on duty.

Vasily Bertenson

During Pyotr Ilyich's first visits from Moscow, I found myself treating him almost constantly for his famous stomach upsets. In the end, he grew so accustomed to his continual ailment that he would treat himself according to the routine I had already prescribed, without resorting to my help, even when the attacks grew more acute. But on that unforgettable day of 21 October 1893, having arrived home around 8 P.M., I found on the table the following note from Modest Tchaikovsky: "Pyotr doesn't feel well. He has continuous nausea and diarrhea. For God's sake, come see what this means."

I went at once to see the patient.

One should know that Pyotr Ilyich's delicacy toward those around him knew no bounds. This was the main reason why Pyotr Ilyich, according to his brother, had so long refused to allow him to send for me.

When I entered Modest Ilyich's small apartment, where he lived with Pyotr Ilyich's favorite nephew—Bob Davydov—and where Pyotr Ilyich was staying, I found the patient in bed. It was half past eight in the evening. Pyotr Ilyich, despite the fact that the attacks of his dreadful illness were already troubling him incessantly, greeted me with words characteristic of his sincere kindness and his surprising delicacy.

"Poor Vasily," he said to me, "you're such a music lover and no doubt you were longing to go to the opera; and today they're even performing *Tannhäuser.* But instead you've had to come see me, boring, nasty Tchaikovsky, who's sick, and with such an uninteresting ailment. . . ."

Having heard about the onset of the illness and examined Tchaikovsky, I was to my dismay immediately convinced that he had something much worse than the upset stomach and bowels which Tchaikovsky himself and everyone else in the house thought he had.

At that time in St. Petersburg (October 1893), cholera had already made a secure little nest for itself, but the educated classes rarely encountered this disease. It was only the poor, as always, who died of it. I must confess that I myself had never had an opportunity before this time to witness an actual case. Nevertheless, on examination of the patient's excreta, I had no doubt that Tchaikovsky had classic cholera. When I went into the next room and explained the seriousness of the situation to Tchaikovsky's brother and nephews, and further explained that because of my sense of ethical responsibility I could not and would not take on treatment by myself alone, my good friends at first refused to believe me.

The most difficult part (knowing Tchaikovsky's dislike of doctors) was persuading him to agree to an [outside] consultation. Finally, we convinced the patient of the utter necessity of this. Tchaikovsky's preference was for my brother. After writing the necessary prescriptions, I immediately rushed off to get my brother.

The rapid progress of the cholera in Tchaikovsky's case is attributable to the fact that, given his chronic digestive problems, he had taken in the morning, on his own initiative, a glass of Hunyadi-Janos water [a mild cathartic] instead of castor oil. It is well known, of course, that alkaline liquids, because of their neutralizing action, are contraindicated in such a situation. The cholera bacillus multiplies all the more rapidly in an alkaline environment.

In addition to everything else, after drinking the alkaline water, Tchaikovsky turned around and drank a glass of unboiled water.

Despite the fact that all thoughtful Russians, and not only Russians but also Europeans, wounded by such a loss, read with intense interest about all the details of Tchaikovsky's last days (details written by his brother Modest and published in articles in *Novoe vremia* and *Novosti i birzhevaia gazeta*), despite the presence at the patient's bedside of four doctors—there were people even then, as there are today, who declared confidently that Tchaikovsky did not die from cholera at all, but perished from poison, taken with the intention of committing suicide!

Does it pay to speak about such an insinuation, particularly in light of the nasty innuendoes about the reason that provoked the suicide?!

Lev Bertenson

Inconsistencies in the evidence appearing in the press in connection with the illness of the late Pyotr Ilyich Tchaikovsky have compelled us to turn to Dr. Lev Bertenson, who was in charge of the treatment of the deceased composer.

At our urgent request, Dr. Bertenson told us the following:

[When did Tchaikovsky fall ill?]

"I was called in to see Pyotr Ilyich on the evening of Thursday, 21 October, by my brother, Dr. Vasily Bertenson, who was a close friend of Tchaikovsky's family and always treated all the members of the family. Arriving at Modest

Tchaikovsky's apartment, where Pyotr Ilyich was staying, at about ten in the evening, I found [him] in the so-called algid stage of cholera. The state of the illness was indisputably typical, and I immediately recognized a very serious case of cholera. We began employing all the scientific measures prescribed for such a situation. By 2 A.M. we had almost succeeded in stemming the spasms, which at the time of my arrival had become so violent that the patient had been crying out loud. The bouts of diarrhea and vomiting also became significantly less frequent and less severe. I departed in the middle of the night, leaving my brother with the patient. Toward dawn on Friday, during my absence, there was a further deterioration in Pyotr Ilyich's condition: the spasms returned and his heart activity fell so rapidly that my brother was forced to give Pyotr Ilyich an injection of musk and camphor. Early Friday morning my brother was replaced by my assistant, Dr. Mamonov, and I myself arrived at eleven o'clock. The patient's condition was such that I was convinced that the attacks that had threatened the patient's life during the night had passed.

"'How do you feel?' I asked Pyotr Ilyich.

"'Vastly improved,' he replied. 'Thank you: you have snatched me from the jaws of death.'. . . "

[Would you describe the course of Tchaikovsky's illness?]

"The convulsive stage of cholera could be considered over. Unfortunately, the second stage—the reaction—had not set in. I should mention that in cholera cases as serious as that which Pyotr Ilyich had, the kidneys usually cease to function. This is the result of their rapid deterioration. From the onset of Tchaikovsky's illness complete failure of the kidneys had been apparent. This is very dangerous, for it entails poisoning of the blood by the constituents of the urine. On Friday, however, there were no marked signs of such poisoning. All measures were taken to revive the action of the kidneys, but nothing was effective. Still, one measure—the [hot] bath—I did not resort to until Saturday, and the reason is this. The mother of the late Pyotr Ilyich had died of cholera— and indeed had died at the very moment she was placed in the bath. Pyotr Ilyich was aware of this fact, and it had instilled in him and in all his relatives a superstitious fear of the bath. On Saturday, the signs of uremic poisoning became evident, and at the same time the patient had a new and very significant increase in diarrhea, which now indicated the paralytic condition of the intestines. This diarrhea had a very dispiriting effect on Tchaikovsky, and he turned to me with the words: "'Let me go, don't torment yourself. It's all the same to me if I don't recover.'. . . "

[What happened on the final day?]

"I suggested to Pyotr Ilyich that we should give him the bath. He readily consented. When he had been placed in it, I asked: 'Do you find the bath unpleasant?'

"'On the contrary, it's quite pleasant,' he replied, but after a while, complaining of weakness, he started asking to be lifted out.

"The immediate effect of the bath was beneficial: a warm sweat appeared, and with it came the hope that the uremic poisoning might diminish and functioning of the kidneys be restored. By evening the hope [of improvement] was gone. Drowsiness set in and there was a sudden weakening of the heart action, so severe that my assistant Dr. Zander, who had remained with Pyotr Ilyich, gave the patient an injection of musk and sent for me. I found Pyotr Ilyich with a sharply weakened heartbeat and in a comatose state, from which he could only be roused for the very shortest periods. Thus, for example, when he was offered a drink, he accepted it with full consciousness, saying: 'That's enough,' 'more,' and so on. By half past ten that evening all hope for a possible favorable turn in the course of the illness completely disappeared. The drowsiness grew ever deeper, and despite repeated and frequent injections of stimulants, the pulse remained undetectable. At two in the morning the death throes began, and at three o'clock Pyotr Ilyich was no more."

Nikolay Mamonov

Wishing to know more about the course of the illness and the last moments of our departed composer, Pyotr Ilyich Tchaikovsky, we turned to the young Dr. N[ikolay] Mamonov, assistant to the famous physician-in-ordinary, L[ev] Bertenson, who remained the entire while by the patient, Pyotr Ilyich Tchaikovsky, and witnessed his demise.

"Pyotr Ilyich Tchaikovsky," Dr. Mamonov told us, "was susceptible to stomach ailments in general, and last summer he fell ill with cholerine. I should tell you that Pyotr Ilyich regarded the cholera epidemic with great skepticism, and this was one of the reasons for the illness which has taken him prematurely to his grave."

"When did Tchaikovsky fall ill?"

"On Wednesday morning he was already complaining of a loss of appetite and general indisposition, but ignored it. On Thursday, from nine in the morning, he began experiencing a severely upset stomach, which grew still worse after he drank two glasses of water. It was on this day that it became clear to us what a terrible illness had struck Pyotr Ilyich. By that evening the choleric spasms had commenced, along with retention of urine—which worried us most of all. His relatives began rubbing his body, and this somewhat eased the patient's condition. Thursday night passed fairly calmly for Pyotr Ilyich, and the spasms ceased. Saturday passed tolerably, but the absence of urine continued to worry us. On Sunday morning, very clear signs of poisoning from the urine were evident and a bath was administered, which produced a strong sweat.

After this the patient seemed to be better. At 8 P.M. uremia set in and by midnight he was in agony."

"Was Tchaikovsky unconscious during his final illness?"

"Not at all. Pyotr Ilyich was fully conscious, though of course very dispirited. He was often very drowsy, but one had only to ask him, 'Do you want a drink?' or something else, and he would acknowledge the speaker at once and express his wishes. He lost consciousness completely only some seven hours before his death."

"Was the dying man aware of the gravity of his condition?"

"Yes, he was. The day before he died, he said that he felt death approaching, and declared: 'I am not afraid to die, but I would still like to live a little longer.'"

"So, how was his death agony?"

"It was not too excruciating, but it lasted a very long time, from midnight to 3 A.M."

"Did you hear Pyotr Ilyich express any last wishes or say any last words?"

"He spoke little, and his consciousness was generally marginal."

"At what stage was artificial respiration applied?"

"Beginning at ten o'clock, and for the next two hours, we had to change the oxygen bags every five minutes, and during Tchaikovsky's illness fourteen cubic feet of oxygen were brought from the pharmacy. . . ."

Modest Tchaikovsky

When I came out of my bedroom on Thursday morning, 21 October, Pyotr Ilyich was not in the sitting room taking tea as usual but in his own room, and complained of having spent a bad night because of a stomach upset. This did not particularly disturb me, because he quite often had such upsets, which were always very acute but passed very quickly. At eleven o'clock he changed and headed out to visit Nápravník, but in half an hour he returned without having got there, and decided to take further measures in addition to the flannel that he had put on earlier. I suggested sending for Vasily Bertenson, his favorite doctor, but he flatly refused. I did not insist, knowing that he was accustomed to illnesses of this sort and that he always managed to get over them without anyone's help. Usually castor oil would help him in these cases. Assuming that he would resort to it this time as well and knowing that in any event it could do him no harm, I was quite unworried about his condition and, going about my own affairs, did not see him again until one in the afternoon. At lunchtime he had a business meeting with Fyodor Mülbach. In any event, during the period from eleven until one Pyotr Ilyich was in good enough shape that he managed to write two letters, though by the third he had no patience for writing a detailed letter and limited himself to a short note. During lunch he showed no aversion to food.

He sat with us but did not eat, though only, it seems, because he realized it might be harmful. It was then that he told us that instead of castor oil he had taken Hunyadi water. It seems to me that this lunch has a fateful significance, since it was right in the middle of our conversation about the medication that he had taken that he poured a glass of water and took a sip from it. The water was unboiled. We were all frightened: he alone was indifferent to it and told us not to worry. Of all illnesses, cholera was always the one he least feared. Immediately after this, he had to leave because he began to feel nauseated. He did not return to the sitting room, but lay down in his own room so that he might warm his stomach. All the same, neither he himself nor those of us around him were at all anxious. All this had happened often enough before. Although his indisposition grew worse, we attributed this to the action of the mineral water. I again suggested sending for Vasily Bertenson, but again was forbidden to do so; moreover, a little while later he felt better and, asking to be allowed to sleep, he remained alone in his room and, so I assumed, went to sleep. Satisfying myself that all was quiet in his bedroom, I went out on my own affairs and did not get back home until five o'clock.[42] When I returned, the illness had so worsened that, despite his protests, I sent for Vasily Bertenson. However, there were still no alarming signs of mortal illness.

Around six in the evening I again left Pyotr Ilyich, after placing a hot compress on his stomach. At eight o'clock, when I returned, my servant, Nazar Litrov, was tending him and had managed to move him from his small bedroom into the spacious drawing room, because during this time, that is, between 6 and 8 P.M., the vomiting and diarrhea had quickly become so severe that Litrov gave up waiting for the doctor and sent for the first one who could be found, but still nobody was thinking about cholera.

At quarter past eight, Vasily Bertenson arrived. The diarrhea and vomiting were becoming ever more frequent, but the patient was still strong enough to get up every time he needed to. As none of his excretions had been preserved, the doctor could not at first establish that it was cholera, but he was convinced at once of the extreme seriousness and gravity of the illness. Prescribing all that was necessary in such circumstances, the doctor immediately judged it essential to call in his brother, Lev Bertenson. The situation was growing more alarming. The excretions were becoming more frequent and very copious. The weakening so increased that the patient was now unable to move by himself. The vomiting was especially unbearable; while vomiting and for several moments afterward he would become quite frenzied and cry out at the top of his voice, never once complaining about the ache in his abdominal cavity, but only about the unbearably terrible state of his chest, and at one point he turned to me and said: "I think I'm dying. Farewell, Modest!" He later repeated these words several times. After every excretion he sank back onto the bed utterly exhausted. However, there was as yet no lividity or spasms.

Lev Bertenson arrived with his brother at 11 P.M. and, after examining the patient and his excretions, determined that it was cholera. They immediately sent for a medical attendant. Including the doctors, there were eight of us with the patient: the [two] Counts Litke,[43] our nephew Davydov, Nazar Litrov, the medical attendant, and myself. At midnight, Pyotr Ilyich began crying aloud and complaining of spasms. We began directing all our efforts to massaging him. The patient was fully conscious. The spasms appeared in various parts of his body at the same time, and the patient asked us to massage now this part of his body, now that. His head and extremities began to turn very blue and became completely cold. Not long before the appearance of the first spasms, Pyotr Ilyich asked me: "It's not cholera, is it?" However, I concealed the truth from him. But when he overheard the doctor giving instructions about precautionary measures against infection, he exclaimed: "So it is cholera!" The more important details of this phase of the illness are difficult to relate. Right up to five in the morning it was one uninterrupted struggle with his spasms and numbness, which, the longer these lasted, the less they yielded to our energetic rubbing and artificial warming of his body. There were several moments when it seemed that death had come, but an injection of musk and a tannin enema revived the patient.

By 5 A.M. the illness began to abate, and the patient became relatively calm, complaining only of depressed spirits. Up to this point the most frightening thing had been the moments when he had complained of the pain around his heart and of being unable to breathe; but now this ceased. Three quarters of an hour passed in complete quiet.[44] The vomiting and bowel movements lost their alarming appearance, though they recurred fairly frequently. The spasms reappeared whenever he tried to move. He grew thirsty, but said that drinking seemed more pleasant in his imagination than in reality. Scarcely would we give him a teaspoon of something to drink than he would turn away from it in revulsion, but a few minutes later he would ask for the same thing again.

But generally what disturbed him most was that the outward signs of his illness caused such anxiety in those around him. In the midst of the most serious attacks he tried to apologize for the trouble he was causing, fearful that some details would arouse disgust and retaining sufficient awareness to be able to joke a bit now and then. Thus, he turned to his favorite nephew, saying: "I'm afraid you'll lose all your respect for me after all this nasty business." He was continually urging everyone to go to bed and thanked us for the slightest service. Early in the morning, as soon as the patient no longer needed nursing, Vasily Bertenson sent me to notify the police verbally of what had happened.[45]

On Friday, 22 October, at 9 A.M., Vasily Bertenson, who had not left my brother for a moment, was replaced by Dr. Nikolay Mamonov. At this point there had been relative calm for about an hour. Vasily Bertenson recounted the case history to Dr. Mamonov and left without waiting for my brother to wake up.[46] By this time the lividity had passed, though there were black spots on his face, but these soon disappeared. There came the first period of relief. We all breathed more easily, but the attacks, though significantly less frequent, still continued, accompanied by spasms. In any event, he felt so much better that he considered himself saved. Thus, when Lev Bertenson arrived at about eleven o'clock he said: "Thank you. You have snatched me from the jaws of death. I feel immeasurably better than during the first night." He repeated these words more than once both that day and the next. The attacks and the accompanying spasms finally ceased around midday. At three that afternoon, Dr. Alexander Zander replaced Dr. Mamonov. The illness appeared to have yielded to the treatment, but by this time the doctors feared the second phase of cholera— inflammation of the kidneys and the typhoid stage—though at that point there were still no signs of either ailment. His only discomfort was an insatiable thirst. This condition continued until evening, but by that night it had improved to such an extent that Dr. Mamonov, who came to replace Dr. Zander, insisted that we all go to bed, since he foresaw no threatening symptoms that night. . . .

On the morning of Saturday the twenty-third there was no improvement in the patient's morale. He seemed in a more depressed state than the previous evening. His faith in recovery had vanished. "Leave me!" he told the doctors. "There's nothing you can do, I won't get better." A certain irritability began to show in his treatment of those around him. The previous evening he had still been joking with the doctors and arguing with them over his drink, but on this day he merely followed their orders submissively. The doctors began directing all their efforts to restoring the function of his kidneys, but it was all in vain. We all placed great hopes on the hot bath, which Lev Bertenson prepared to give him that evening. I should mention that our mother died of cholera in 1854 and that death took her the moment she was placed in the bath. My elder brother Nikolay and I involuntarily regarded this necessary measure with superstitious fear.[47] Our fear increased when we learned that Pyotr Ilyich, asked by the doctor whether he wished to have the bath, replied: "I'm very glad to wash, only I shall probably die like my mother when you put me in the bath." We had to forgo the bath that evening because his diarrhea again worsened, becoming uncontrollable, and the patient grew weak. Lev Bertenson left after 2 A.M., dissatisfied by the state of affairs. Nevertheless the night passed relatively well. After two enemas the diarrhea decreased significantly, but the kidneys still were not functioning.

By the morning of Sunday the twenty-fourth, the situation was not yet hopeless, but the anxiety of the physicians about the inactivity of the kidneys grew. Pyotr Ilyich felt quite bad. To all inquiries about his condition, he several times replied: "Rotten!" To Lev Bertenson he said: "How much kindness and patience you're wasting in vain! I can't be cured!" He slept more, but it was an uneasy, heavy sleep: he was slightly delirious and continually repeated the name of Nadezhda von Meck, reproaching her angrily. Then he would quiet down as if listening to something—now frowning intently, now seeming to smile. After he slept his consciousness seemed more sluggish than on the other days. Thus he did not immediately recognize his servant Sofronov, who arrived that morning from Klin, but all the same he was happy to see him. Up to 1 P.M. the situation appeared to those around him to remain unchanged. There was not a drop of urine, so we did not examine it even once. Lev Bertenson arrived at one o'clock and immediately judged it essential to resort to what seemed to us the extreme measure for prompting activity of the kidneys—the bath. At two o'clock the bath was ready. Pyotr Ilyich was in a half-conscious state while [the bath] was prepared in the same room. He had to be roused. He seemed not to grasp clearly at first what they wanted to do with him, but then he consented to the bath, and when he was lowered into it, he was fully aware of what was happening. When the doctor asked him whether he found the hot water unpleasant, he replied: "On the contrary, it's quite pleasant," but very soon he began asking to be lifted out, saying that he felt weak. And indeed, from the moment he was taken out of the bath his drowsiness and his sleep took on a certain peculiar character. The bath did not have the anticipated effect, though it produced a strong sweat; at the same time, according to the doctors, it reduced for a while the signs of blood poisoning from the urine. The perspiring continued, but at the same time the pulse, which up till then had been comparatively regular and strong, again weakened. It was again necessary to resort to an injection of musk to restore his failing strength. This was successful: despite the perspiration the pulse rose and the patient grew calm. Until eight o'clock it seemed to us that his condition was improving. Soon after Dr. Mamonov had left, at about a quarter past eight, his replacement, Dr. Zander, again noticed a sudden weakening of the pulse and became sufficiently alarmed to deem it necessary to inform Lev Bertenson immediately. According to the doctors, the patient was by this time in a comatose state, so that when I went into his room the doctor advised me not to leave him for a minute. His head was cold, his breathing labored and accompanied by moans, yet still the question "Do you want something to drink?" would bring him momentarily to consciousness. He would answer "Yes" or "Of course," then would say "That's enough," "I don't want any," or "I don't need it." Shortly after ten o'clock, Dr. Zander diagnosed the onset of edema of the lungs, and Lev Bertenson quickly arrived. At the request of [my brother] Nikolay, a priest was sent for from St.

Isaac's Cathedral. Only by increased injections to stimulate the action of the heart could the condition of the dying man be maintained. All hope of improvement vanished. The priest who came with the Holy Sacraments found it impossible to administer them to Pyotr Ilyich because of his unconscious state, and simply read loudly and clearly the prayers of the dying, not a single word of which seemed to reach my brother's consciousness. Soon after this, the fingers of the dying man moved strangely, as though he had an itch in various parts of his body.

The doctors continued tirelessly employing all possible measures to prolong the action of the heart, as if still hoping for a miraculous recovery. During this time the following people were by the dying man's bedside: the three doctors, the two Litke brothers, Buxhövden, Nikolay Figner, [Dmitry] Bzul,[48] Vladimir Davydov, my brother's servant [Alexey] Sofronov, [Nazar] Litrov and his wife, the medical attendant, my brother Nikolay, and myself. Lev [Bertenson] decided that there were too many people for the small room. The window was opened, and Figner and Bzul departed. Bertenson, judging all hope lost, left in extreme exhaustion, leaving Nikolay Mamonov to witness the final moments. His breathing grew more shallow, though he could still be brought to consciousness, it seemed, by asking him whether he wanted something to drink: he no longer responded with words, but only with affirmative or negative sounds. Suddenly his eyes, which up until then had been half-closed and glazed, opened wide. An indescribable expression of full consciousness appeared. He rested his gaze in turn on the three people who were standing near him, then lifted it toward the sky. For a few moments something in his eyes lit up and then faded with his final breath. It was a little after three in the morning.

Grand Duke Konstantin Konstantinovich

Thursday, 23 September
Tchaikovsky wrote to me that he has written a new symphony with which he is very satisfied. In it he has departed from the accepted rules and put an *Adagio* at the end. I have repeatedly suggested that he try his strength at an oratorio. He liked the idea but could not find the appropriate words. In my last letter I reminded him of Apukhtin's *Requiem*; this text is appropriate and one could write music for it in memory of the late author. Tchaikovsky answered me from Moscow that he doesn't have these words at hand and that the new symphony is similar in its content precisely to the mood of the *Requiem*. Returning to Klin he will read Apukhtin's text and see whether he can compose music to it. He is planning to stay with us in the middle of October, when he will come to conduct at a symphonic concert.

Friday, 1 October

Was in town with my wife, Olga, and Dmitry[49] in order to hear *Eugene Onegin* at the Maryinsky Theater. Olga had never seen it. Figner sang the part of Lensky, Yakovlev the part of Onegin, Baulina the part of Tatyana, and the performance was quite all right.

Saturday, 16 October

Lieutenant Count [Alexander] Litke came to ask for leave to visit Revel for two days. He told me that Pyotr Ilyich Tchaikovsky is the cousin of his mother, née Schobert. . . . Went to town for the first Symphonic Concert under Pyotr Ilyich Tchaikovsky's baton at the Assembly of the Nobility. . . . The concert began with Tchaikovsky's new Sixth Symphony in B-minor. I liked it very much. The first, introductory *Adagio* is very gloomy and mysterious and sounds delightful. It passes into an *Allegro,* which has some wonderful passages. The second movement *Allegro con grazia* is written in a 5/8 or 5/4 and is very clear and good. The third movement is a kind of *Scherzo* with a loud march at the end. And the finale is in *Adagio;* it has some places reminiscent of a memorial service. I saw Tchaikovsky during the intermission.

Saturday, 23 October

At the regiment I was told that Pyotr Ilyich Tchaikovsky has a serious case of Asiatic cholera that began on Thursday, and that he is dangerously ill. His nephew Davydov is a volunteer with privileged status in the fourth company. I am very concerned for Pyotr Ilyich.

Sunday, 24 October

I went with Dmitry . . .[50]

At this very moment I received a telegram from Modest Tchaikovsky: Pyotr Ilyich passed away at 3 A.M. My heart is painfully wrenched. I loved him and venerated him as a musician. We had a good, sincere relationship; I shall miss him.

I could not regain my senses for a long time after receiving the grievous news of Tchaikovsky's death. We have lost yet another man who was so dear to Russian art. I corresponded with him, I have quite a few of his letters.

Monday, 25 October

Yesterday morning I was not really myself.[51] I lamented the untimely death of Tchaikovsky. Everyone was struck by it. I tried to write a poem on Tchaikovsky's death, but nothing worked out. The Tsar and the Tsarina are upset by the death of Tchaikovsky.

Tuesday, 26 October

The Empress sent me the music of Tchaikovsky's last compositions, a series of pieces for the piano and several romances to words by Rathaus. I played two of them. We left Gatchina together with Niki. . . .[52] We didn't go to the memorial services for Tchaikovsky; at home they are afraid of the disease. I returned to Strelna around four o'clock.

Thursday, 28 October

Yesterday it was precisely one month since I received Tchaikovsky's last letter, and now he has already been buried. I went to town on purpose, in order to attend the funeral service and burial at Kazan Cathedral. The Emperor assumed the expenses of the funeral; it was arranged by the Directorate of the Imperial Theaters, which bathed it in great solemnity. At the cathedral His Eminence Nicandrus, the Bishop of Narva, performed the liturgy, and the chorus of the Russian Imperial Opera sang. Throughout the liturgy six students from the School of Jurisprudence stood by the coffin as alumni of the composer's alma mater. The church was full, only those with tickets were admitted. I have not seen such a solemn liturgy for a long time. They sang the "Credo" [*"Veruiu"*] and "We sing to Thee" [*"Tebe poem"*] from the late composer's liturgy. I felt like crying and thought that the dead man could not help but hear his own sounds, accompanying him into the other world. I did not get to see his face; the coffin was closed. It was both painful and sad, and solemn and good in Kazan Cathedral. From there the coffin was taken to the Alexander Nevsky Monastery, where he was buried in the graveyard.

My head ached badly.

Friday, 29 October

In the train I tried to compose a poem in Tchaikovsky's memory but, it seems, with no result.[53]

Monday, 1 November

I added another stanza to the poem in Tchaikovsky's memory; but I don't think it will go any further.

Saturday, 6 November

I heard a wonderful symphonic concert dedicated to the memory of Tchaikovsky and consisting exclusively of his compositions. A bust of the late composer, surrounded by palms, towered above the orchestra. The Sixth Symphony, the *Pathétique*, was played. It was indescribable to hear those sounds, just like a last testament, a farewell to life. Some excellent baritone, half

French and half American, superbly sang selections from *Onegin* and some of the romances in English.[54] Auer played the Violin Concerto, and then, for an encore, played the *Andante [Cantabile]* in transcription for violin and orchestra from the String Quartet [No. 1]. It was marvelous, it seems that many in the audience wept.

Yulian Poplavsky

How vividly I recall that sullen October morning ten years ago when I hurried from the Moscow Train Station along Nevsky Prospect toward the funeral procession of Pyotr Ilyich Tchaikovsky.

Deputations participating in the funeral procession were grouped in front of his apartment on Malaya Morskaya Street. There was a very small group of us Muscovites.

The streets were an extraordinary sight. Along the path of the procession, traffic was halted and the sidewalks were filled with people.

The procession began. The crowd grew larger from minute to minute. There was a short prayer service at the Maryinsky Theater, and we stood on the square before the Kazan Cathedral. Here was an entire sea of people, and it took incredible effort to get into the cathedral.

It was a solemn service. The choirs of the Court Chapel and the Imperial Opera, like a giant, living organ, filled the enormous church with waves of sound. And it was strange. One's reason told one that Tchaikovsky was dead, in his coffin; but the sounds of the liturgical hymns he had composed, being performed by the choirs, penetrated one's heart, and the heart felt that Tchaikovsky was alive in the sounds, that in the music he was beyond death. The service ended. The coffin swayed above the crowd, and we found ourselves at the portico of the church.

What a majestic and moving moment. As far as the eye could see there were people with their hats doffed in respect. One felt that at that instant all eyes were riveted on that simple coffin, and within it there lay he who left a quivering trace of his inspiration in each heart that is familiar with the sounds of his music.

To the sound of the ringing chords of the brass band's horns the procession moved forward.

Finally we arrived at the Alexander Nevsky Monastery. The autumn day was short and it was already getting dark.

"Memory Eternal," the clergy announced, "Memory Eternal," sang out thousands of voices all around, "Memory Eternal," responded the crowd, which had not all fit in the cemetery and had flowed over beyond the walls of the Monastery.

The coffin was sprinkled with dirt. The Russian earth had taken back "the Singer of Its Grief."

The crowd surged away, thinned, and began to disperse. Darkness had fallen.

I returned from the cemetery. Lights were coming on in the enormous city. The street roared with noise. The animation of evening was emerging. Several hours later I was sitting in the train carriage.

Dawn broke. The train rolled by the empty fields with a hollow clang. Clouds of steam like white phantoms ran past the windows and disappeared in the clouds which lazily crawled toward them.

Familiar places began to flash by. From beyond the bare trees peered out a high chimney and the roof of the house where Tchaikovsky had lived. We had passed Klin.

Not so long before, I had happened to spend many marvelous days in that house with Pyotr Ilyich. His image and all the kindness and light that surrounded this ideal man are impressed in my memory with definition and clarity. And now, ten years later, I still cannot forget the stinging nostalgia and profound grief that grasped my heart when, in the foggy distance of the dawn, that unassuming little house flashed by and disappeared, the house from which inspired sounds will never again pour in a mighty, broad wave.

ABBREVIATIONS

BTR	David Brown, *Tchaikovsky Remembered* (London, 1993)
d.	*delo* (file)
CZN	*P. I. Chaikovskii, zabytoe i novoe: vospominaniia sovremennikov, novye materialy i dokumenty [P. I. Tchaikovsky, forgotten and new: recollectons of contemporaries, new materials and documents]* (P. I. Chaikovskii—almanakh, vyp. 1), sostaviteli P. E. Vaidman, G. I. Belonovich (Moscow, 1995)
GARF	Gosudarstvennyi arkhiv Rossiiskoi Federatsii [State Archive of the Russian Federation], Moscow
GDMC	Gosudarstvennyi arkhiv doma-muzeia P. I. Chaikovskogo [Tchaikovsky State Archive and House Museum], Klin
f.	*fond* (collection)
l., ll.	*list, listy* (folio, folios)
no.	number
op.	*opis'* (inventory) or opus
PBC	N. O. Blinov, *Posledniaia bolezn' i smert' P. I. Chaikovskogo [Tchaikovsky's Last Illness and Death]* (Moscow, 1994)
PR	P. I. Chaikovskii, *Pis'ma k rodnym [Letters to relatives]* (Moscow, 1940)
PSS	P. I. Chaikovskii, *Polnoe sobranie sochinenii: Literaturnye proizvedeniia i pis'ma [Complete Collected Works: Literary Works and Correspondence]* (17 vols.; Moscow, 1953–81)
RGALI	Rossiiskii gosudarstvennyi arkhiv literatury i iskusstva [Russian State Archive of Literature and Art], Moscow
RGIA	Rossiiskii gosudarstvennyi istoricheskii arkhiv [Russian State Historical Archive]
TLD	Alexander Poznansky, *Tchaikovsky's Last Days* (Oxford, 1996)
TQM	Alexander Poznansky, *Tchaikovsky: The Quest for the Inner Man* (New York, 1991)

TsGIA SPb   Tsentralnyi gosudarstvennyi istoricheskii arkhiv Sankt-Peterburga [Central State Historical Archive of St. Petersburg]

UT   Alexander Poznansky, "Unknown Tchaikovsky: A Reconstruction of Previously Censored Letters to His Brothers (1875–1979)," in *Tchaikovsky and His World*, ed. Leslie Kearney (Princeton, 1998), 55–96.

VC   *Vospominaniia o P. I. Chaikovskom [Recollections of Tchaikovsky]* (Moscow, 1962); 4th ed. (Leningrad, 1980)

ZC   M. I. Chaikovskii, *Zhizn' P. I. Chaikovskogo [The life of P. I. Chaikovskii]* (3 vols.; Moscow, 1900–2)

NOTES

Introduction

1. *TLD*, 1–29.

2. *VC* (1962); *VC* (1973); *VC* (1979); *VC* (1980); *Piotr Tchaikovski: écrits, critiques, lettres, souvenirs de contemporains* (Moscow, 1985), 167–254.

3. David Brown in *BTR*, although professing caution in regard to the texts hitherto published in Russia, did not, contrary to his claim, move boldly away from the Soviet canon. Another problem with Brown's work is the apparent strategy he adopted in the arrangement of the memoirs he chose to present. In fact, he endeavored to excerpt and break up narratives of various lengths and orchestrate them in accordance with his particular perspective on Tchaikovsky's personality as well as his own polemical agenda. An example is Brown's omission of such a major source (despite its pecularities) as the recollections of Tchaikovsky's wife Antonina, which still stand in need of detailed commentary. The German edition *Tschaikowsky aus der Nähe: Kritische Würdigungen und Erinnerungen von Zeitgenossen,* compiled and edited by Ernst Kuhn (Berlin, 1994), is organized according to the métier of the contributors and their status vis-à-vis the composer: relatives, classmates, colleagues, pupils, journalists, critics, etc. This contrasts favorably with Brown's selection in terms of representation, occasionally reaching beyond the Soviet canon, but it does not provide the appropriate context and commentary.

4. *VC* (1962), 35.

5. Leopold Auer, *My Long Life in Music* (New York, 1923), 205.

6. *TLD,* 23.

7. The exceptions are chapters that deal with the composer's matrimonial fiasco and his last days. Owing to the crucial importance of these events for the study of Tchaikovsky's biography, the material they contain had to be scrutinized at greater length and in much closer detail.

I. The Schoolboy (1840–1863)

1. In an earlier draft of Modest's biography it was stated that Tchaikovsky "was born a weak baby, with a strange abscess on the left temple that was successfully lanced soon after his birth"; *P. I. Chaikovskii, gody detstva: materialy k biografii* (Izhevsk, 1983), 23. Hereafter quoted as *Gody detstva.*

2. On Tchaikovsky's genealogy see further: V. I. Proleeva, *K rodoslovnoi P. I. Chaikovskogo* (Izhevsk, 1990); Marina Kogan, "Rodoslovnaia," *Sovetskaia muzyka* 6 (1990): 83–90; also "Rod Chaikovskikh k 1894 godu," in *CZN,* 146–147; on Ilya Chaikovskii, see *Russkii biograficheskii slovar,* [vol. 22] (St. Petersburg, 1905) and his own unfinished memoir: "Zapiski kadeta Gornogo kadetskogo korpusa I. P. Ch[aikovskogo]," *CZN,* 148–150.

3. *ZC,* I: 11–12.

4. On Andrey Assier's career, see the attestation certificate (*Attestat [A. M. Assiera]*) issued to him upon his retirement in 1831, in *Gody detstva*, 102–106; *CZN*, 151–153.

5. "Recollections of the Famous Composer Tschaikowsky," *New York Times*, 12 November 1893; reprinted as "Tschaikowsky's Early Life," in *The Musical Standard* 46 (1894): 10. Friedrich Wilhelm Kalkbrenner (1784–1849), son of German pianist and composer Christian Kalkbrenner (1755–1806), studied at the Paris Conservatory, lived in London (1814–23), then moved to Paris, where he established himself as a renowned teacher, whose classes were attended by Chopin; he also composed chamber music and piano pieces.

6. That Tchaikovsky's family decided to enroll him in the School of Jurisprudence on the advice of Ilya Tchaikovsky's friend Modest Vakar is partially supported by archival material: there exist documents signed by Vakar as the family's representative, guaranteeing to pay the boy's tuition and to take responsibility should he be sent home by the school (TsGIA SPb, f. 355, d. 3390, l. 3–4).

7. Gavriil Lomakin (1812–1885), distinguished Russian choirmaster, conductor, music teacher, and composer.

8. *PSS*, 8: 434.

9. *New York Times*, 12 November 1893.

10. For more on Tchaikovsky's life and friendships in the School of Jurisprudence, see *TQM*, 18–49.

11. Interesting details on homosexual life in the Russian capital of that time are provided in the memoirs of the Petersburg bureaucrat Viktor Burnashev: "When various heterae in skirts emerged onto Nevsky Prospect [every evening] for their catch, there also appeared a multitude of heterae in trousers. These were all very pretty postilions (there aren't any nowadays, since four-horse carriages [with hooded tops] went out of style), cantonists, church singers of various choirs, apprentices of tidy workshops, mostly hairdressing, wallpaper, and tailors' workshops, and also unemployed shop boys, young clerks of the military and marine ministries, and even uniformed chancellery bureaucrats of various departments. Unlike the girls they did not offer their services. But as soon as you threw a glance at them, as they walked slowly and stopped at the gas lamps, in order to see them the better, they would smile, and if you answered their smile with another smile, then these male heterae would note you and start following you, walking close behind or beside you, until you caught a cab in order to avoid their following you, unless the man being followed was aroused pederastically. In this case the hetera-boy and the debauchee went together to some inn to rent a room, or else to *family* bath houses—of which you had a choice as many had separate rooms. Indeed, some enthusiasts even took the youths to their own apartments. Among young cabbies, especially drivers of smart cabs, there were quite a lot of young men occupied with this disgusting trade. It stands to reason that all of these subjects paid great attention to their looks and wore silken shirts. Some even took their heterism to the point that they wore powder and rouge. . . . The disposition toward homosexuality was so developed in Petersburg that the Nevsky Prospect prostitutes themselves began to sense a terrible neglect, and their mistresses experienced hard times. Thus the girls, strolling around in groups, began to attack the boys and often beat them quite severely, chasing them off Nevsky, which did not prevent the boys from forming their own bands. Then Nevsky was the site of battles between these Guelphs and Ghibellines, which sometimes reached the proportions of serious bloodletting" (A. I. Reitblat, "Letopisets slukhov: neopublikovannye vospominaniia V. P. Burnasheva," *Novoe literaturnoe obozrenie* 4 (1993): 167–168).

12. *New York Times*, 12 November 1893.

13. *VC* (1962), 389–394; partial translation into English, see *BTR*, 4–8.

14. In GDMC are preserved twelve letters from Fanny Dürbach to Tchaikovsky

(1892–93); partially published in *Chaikovskii i zarubezhnye muzykanty* (Leningrad, 1970), 127–134.

15. *PSS*, 16b: 215.

16. M. I. Chaikovskii, "M-elle Fanny Durbach," in *CZN*, 154–158; "Vospominaniia M-elle Fanny," in *Gody detstva*, 91–97; *ZC*, I: 21, 25–29, 44.

17. I. I. Chaikovskii, "Epizody iz moei zhizni," *Istoricheskii vestnik* 131 (1913): 73–74.

18. GDMC, B 1, no. 2 dop.; B 1, no. 50.

19. *ZC*, I: 96–98, 103, 121–123; *VC* (1962), 394–398; *VC* (1980), 27–32; partial translation into English, see *BTR*, 10–12, 13, 15. A. V. Mikhailov, "Iz proshlogo: vospominaniia pravoveda," *Russkaia shkola* 1 (1900): 30.

20. The photograph is reproduced in *TQM*, ill. 5.

21. For more on Modest Tchaikovsky, see Alexander Poznansky, "Modest Tchaikovsky: In His Brother's Shadow," in *Čajkovskij-Studien* (Mainz, 1995), I: 233–246.

22. Cf. Tchaikovsky younger brother Anatoly's letters to Modest from 12 December 1893 and 7 April 1894, where he discusses the strategy for publishing intimate passages from Tchaikovsky's correspondence (GDMC, B 10, no. 6263; no. 6265).

23. GDMC, B 2, no. 21; *VC* (1962), 399–405 (partial).

24. In 1993 Modest's *Autobiography* was announced for publication in Moscow, but so far has not yet appeared.

25. A[rkadii] R[aich], "K biografii A. N. Apukhtina," *Istoricheskii vestnik* 107 (1907): 580–582.

26. Besides four-year-old Tchaikovsky, Fanny Dürbach's pupils included his fourteen-year-old cousin Lidiya, daughter of Ilya Tchaikovsky's brother Vladimir, his six-year-old brother Nikolay, and Venedikt Alexeyev, son of a factory worker, who had just lost his mother. Zinaida was at this time at the Catherine Institute in St. Petersburg.

27. Sabine Casimir Amable Tastu (1798–1885), French poet, achieved success with her *Oiseaux du Sacre* (1825). Maria Edgeworth (1767–1849), British novelist and educator, collaborated with her father Richard Lovell Edgeworth in *Practical Education* (1798), based on recorded conversations of children with their elders to illustrate the child's reasoning. Ms. Dürbach used the French translation of Edgeworth's book *Family Education*, published in Paris in 1832–34 in 12 volumes.

28. Comte George Louis Leclerc de Buffon (1707–1788), French naturalist, author (with others) of *Histoire Naturelle* in 44 volumes (1749).

29. François Pierre Guillaume Guizot (1787–1874), French historian and statesman. Among his many works are *Histoire de la civilisation en Europe* (1828); Christof de Schmidt (1768–1854), German educator, author of books for children.

30. August-Michel Masson (1800–1883), French writer, wrote several books for children.

31. Achille Meissas et Michelot, *Petit atlas universel de géographie moderne* (Paris, 1840).

32. Johann Franz Ahn (1796–1865), German educator, known for his methods of teaching modern languages.

33. According to Modest, Fanny Dürbach "little relished the prospect of a musician's life for her favorite charge, and she was far more sympathetic to his literary efforts, playfully calling him 'le petit Pouchkine' along with other nicknames. The reason for this was not only that she herself did not particularly care for music and was ill-versed in it, but also that Fanny observed that music had such a powerful effect on the boy. . . . Now and then a Polish officer named Maszewski visited Votkinsk. He was a fine amateur pianist and was particularly noted for his playing of Chopin mazurkas. His visits were always a great occasion for our little musician. For one of these visits he even learned two mazurkas all by himself and played them so well that

Maszewski kissed him. 'I never saw Pierre,' says Fanny, 'so happy and content as that day'" (*ZC*, I: 44–45).

34. Elizaveta Schobert (née Assier) (1822–?), younger sister of Tchaikovsky's mother.

35. Modest reminisced about their mother later in his *Autobiography*: "My first memory is of sitting in a woman's arms, around me were bushes of yellow acacia, and down on the path a frog was leaping along. I held in my hands a silver cup. . . . I was only four years and 44 days old. I don't remember anything else, but I know that feeling of inexplicable love for the large, dark-haired woman, who was distinuished from all the others by the name of "mama." This one word concealed something sweet and tender that gave me a blessed feeling of joyful satisfaction and quietude, which singled out the being that bore the name from the ranks of all other people. Throughout my entire life I never ceased to yearn for her, to cry, to consider myself cruelly and unjustly insulted by her departure from our midst, to be jealous of the other inhabitants of the Smolensk Cemetery, and in my imagination to melt sweetly while kissing her arms and knees. In my old age, I dream of her more seldom than before, and now it is always with a feeling of hurt that she left us and with a feeling of jealousy toward those with whom she is now. I always missed her. I still miss her" (GDMC, B2, no. 21).

36. The beginning grade in the School of Jurisprudence was the seventh, graduating form—the first. Fyodor Belyavsky (1839–1870), Tchaikovsky's schoolmate, left the school before graduation on 21 March 1856 to became an army officer.

37. Tchaikovsky's schoolmate Gamaley did not stay in the school to graduate.

38. The student Khristianovich also did not graduate from the School of Jurisprudence.

39. Pyotr Yurenev graduated from the school a year earlier than Tchaikovsky.

40. Nikolay Seletsky (1839–1909), Tchaikovsky's classmate.

41. Mikhail Ertel (1838–1872) later became a barrister.

42. According to Modest, the diary *Everything* was accidentally burned by Tchaikovsky when he moved from St. Petersburg to Moscow in 1866 (*ZC*, I: 98).

43. Alexander Rutenberg (?–1855), Senior Inspector of the School of Jurisprudence from 1849 to 1855.

44. Enrico Tamberlik (1820–1889), a tenor at the Italian Opera in St. Petersburg (1860–1863) and also in Moscow (1870). Margarita Bernardi, soprano, and Achille De Bassini, baritone, at the Italian Opera. On the Italian Opera in Russia and its impact on musical life in both Russian capitals, see Richard Taruskin's excellent essay "Ital'yanshchina," in *Defining Russia Musically: Historical and Hermeneutical Essays* (Princeton, 1997), 186–235.

45. Gerard's portrayal of Tchaikovsky as a poor civil servant is not supported by archival documents. While working at the Ministry of Justice Tchaikovsky received several commendations from his superior (TsGIA SPb, f. 1405, op. 63, no. 23350, ll. 21, 26).

46. "Zalivkina" was a boarding school for young women.

47. The Lyceum in Tsarskoe Selo near St. Petersburg was a famous educational institution for young men from noble families, founded by Alexander I in 1810.

48. Henry Charles Litolff (1818–1891), French pianist and composer.

49. Matvey Bernard (1794–1871), owner of a music publishing house and shop in St. Petersburg, where musicians often gave recitals. In 1840 he and his son Nikolay founded the journal *The Nuvellist,* in which Tchaikovsky published in 1876 his piano cycle *The Seasons [Vremena goda].*

50. In his biography of Tchaikovsky, Modest casts doubt on the lessons allegedly given by Kündinger's brother August (*ZC*, I: 122).

51. In a letter of 14/26 January 1886 to the French publisher Félix Mackar, Tchaikovsky refers thus to his lessons with Rudolph Kündinger: "I am indebted to this

outstanding artist for the fact that I came to realize that music was my true vocation; it was he who brought me to the classics" (*PSS*, 13: 245).

52. Emma Lagrua, soprano, sang at the Italian Opera in St. Petersburg, 1859–1862.

53. Tchaikovsky's part in this affair has been established by F. N. Malinin in his unpublished paper "Chaikovskii i Apukhtin" (GDMC, B2, f. 22, l. 65).

54. Ippolit Tchaikovsky in his unpublished notes remembers that "among Pyotr's eccentricities were his absentmindedness and a penchant, from his adolescence, for ballet performances and dances, which he enacted beautifully, imitating ballerinas" (GDMC, B 1, no. 2, dop. and B 1, 50).

55. Vladimir Adamov (1838–1877), Tchaikovsky's classmate from the School of Jurisprudence and one of his closest friends; after graduation, they worked together in the Ministry of Justice; Pyotr Meshchersky, Vladimir Tevyashev, and Slatvinsky were Tchaikovsky's acquaintances in St. Petersburg.

56. Amaliya Schobert (1841–1915), daughter of Elizaveta Schobert, cousin of Tchaikovsky; she later married Count Litke.

57. For more on Tchaikovsky and the theater, see *Teatr v zhizni i tvorchestve P. I. Chaikovskogo* (Izhevsk, 1985).

58. Adelaida Ristori (1822–1906), Italian actress.

59. Amalia Ferraris (1830–1904), Italian ballerina; in 1858–1859 she appeared with great success in St. Petersburg.

60. The effect of Mozart's *Don Giovanni* on the young Tchaikovsky was enormous. In a letter to his patroness Nadezhda von Meck on 1 September 1880, Tchaikovsky wrote: "I was sixteen when I first heard Mozart's *Don Giovanni*. Before that I had only heard Italian opera. People of my generation, brought up on a diet of contemporary music from childhood onwards, made the acquaintance of Mozart only after they had got used to Chopin, for instance, in whom the Byronic spirit of despair and disillusionment is still to be seen so clearly reflected. It was my good fortune that fate brought me up in a not very musical family, and in consequence I did not suffer in childhood from that poison into which music stepped after Beethoven. It was that same fate which nudged me toward Mozart when I was still young and through him opened up to me unknown musical horizons of unbounded beauty, and this youthful impression will never leave me" (*PSS*, 9: 255).

61. Ekaterina Alekseyeva (née Assier) (1805–1882?), Tchaikovsky's mother's older sister.

62. Karl van Ark (1842–1902), pianist and professor at the St. Petersburg Conservatory.

63. The Golov dacha was a rented summer house in the suburbs of St. Petersburg.

64. Further in his *Autobiography*, Modest mentions the story that once Kireyev boasted that he could do anything to Tchaikovsky, even smack him in the face. When he did so Tchaikovsky bore it silently. For more about Sergey Kireyev, see *TQM*, 47–48.

65. Modest also informs us in his *Autobiography* that "Pyotr's other passion at this time was one Frederick, a young Frenchman of great beauty, whose family name even Pyotr himself probably did not know. He prized his portrait and placed it everywhere somewhat conspicuously." At the present time this portrait hangs on the wall of Tchaikovsky's living room at his House-Museum in Klin.

66. Tchaikovsky's contemporary describes homosexual meeting places in St Petersburg: "In winter the aunties [contemptuous slang for homosexuals, modeled on the French *tantes*] meet: on Wednesday at the ballet, on Saturday at the circus and at the Mikhailovsky and Maly theaters, on Monday at *cafés chantants*, whence they invariably set off for dinner at hotels, of which one restaurant is chosen and considered a kind of club for the aunties. Here they enjoy great respect as profitable guests and even have at their constant disposal a lackey, who brings young soldiers and boys into private rooms

for the partying aunties" (Konstantin Rotikov, "Epizod iz zhizni 'golubogo' Peterburga," *Nevskii arkhiv: istoriko-kraevedcheskii sbornik* (St. Petersburg, 1997), III: 454).

67. Probably at the home of the composer Nikolay Khristianovich, also a graduate of the School of Jurisprudence.

68. Nikolay Nekrasov (1821–1878), Russian poet. Tchaikovsky drew on his verses for the song "Forgive" [*"Prosti"*], op. 60, no. 8 (1887), and for a cantata in celebration of the golden jubilee of the Russian singer Osip Petrov (1875). Nikolay Shcherbina (1821–1869), also a Russian poet. Tchaikovsky used the latter's poem for the song "Reconciliation" [*"Primirenye"*], op. 25, no. 1 (1875); Ivan Gorbunov (1831–1896) and Vasily Vasilyev were actors with the Alexandrinsky Theater in St. Petersburg.

69. Prince Shakhovskoy, Tchaikovsky's society friend.

70. Grand Duke Nikolay Aleksandrovich (1843–1865), elder son of Alexander II.

II. The Music Student (1863–1865)

1. The work was published posthumously by Mitrofan Belyayev as op. 76 (1896).

2. Strauss probably obtained the music of the *Dances* through his friend August Leibrock, the owner of a music shop in St. Petersburg, since Leibrock's daughter was in the same class as Tchaikovsky at the Conservatory.

3. Apparently it was not Tchaikovsky's choice, but Rubinstein's.

4. TsGIA SPb, f. 361, op. 11, ed. kh. 370.

5. Modest Tchaikovsky, *The Life and Letters of Peter Ilyich Tchaikovsky,* edited from Russian, with an introduction, by Rosa Newmarch (London, 1906), 45–55.

6. *ZC,* III: 331–332; ibid., 591–592.

7. Tchaikovsky himself later recalled that "during my final year I had the opportunity of hearing Rubinstein—and not only of *hearing* him, but *seeing* him play and conduct. I lay stress upon the first *visual impression,* because it is my profound conviction that Rubinstein's renown is based not only upon his rare talent, but also upon an irresistible charm which emanates from his entire person, so that it is not sufficient to hear him in order to gain a full impression—one must see him too. I heard and saw him. Like everyone else I fell under the spell of his charm" (*PSS,* 16b: 104).

8. V. V. Bessel, "Iz moikh vospominanii o P. I. Chaikovskom," *Ezhegodnik Imperatorskikh teatrov, 1896/1897,* appendix 1, 19–43; *VC* (1962), 406–410 (partial).

9. G. A. Larosh, "Vospominaniia o P. I. Chaikovskom," *Novosti i birzhevaia gazeta,* 23 November 1893; "Iz moikh vospominanii o P. I. Chaikovskom," *Severnyi vestnik* 2 (1894): 175–186; also in *VC* (1962), 11–23, 26–41; *BTR,* 19–25 (partial).

10. I. A. Klimenko, *Moi vospominaniia o Petre Il'iche Chaikovskom* (Riazan, 1908), 5–6, 30–31; *CZN,* 68. For more on Klimenko, see ibid., 64–67.

11. A. Spasskaia, "Tovarishcheskie vospominaniia o P. I. Chaikovskom," *Russkaia muzykal'naia gazeta* 44 (1899): 1113–1118; partial in *VC* (1962), 410–412.

12. A. I. Rubets, "Vospominaniia prof[essora] A. I. Rubtsa o pervykh godakh Peterburgskoi konservatorii," *Novoe vremia,* 27 Aug. 1912; 3 September 1912; partial in *VC* (1962), 412.

13. Iosif Gunke (1801–1883), Czech violinist, composer, and professor at the St. Petersburg Conservatory; Constantin Decker- Schenk (1810–1876), Austrian pianist and music scholar, taught at the St. Petersburg Conservatory; Heinrich Stiehl (1829–1886), German organist and composer, played in St. Peter's Kirche in St. Petersburg, founded the *Singacademie,* was professor at the St. Petersburg Conservatory.

14. Adolf Bernard Marx (1795–1866), German theorist and composer, cofounder of the Berlin Conservatory.

15. Ivan Rybasov (1841–1875), pianist and conductor, later taught at the St. Peters-

burg Conservatory; Gustav Kross (1831–1885), pianist and composer, the first performer of Tchaikovsky's First Piano Concerto in St. Petersburg in 1875.

16. Pyotr Mosolov (1830–1905) later became a jurist.

17. Henryk Wieniawski (1835–1880), Polish violinist and composer, taught at the St. Petersburg Conservatory, 1862–1868, and the Brussels Conservatory, 1875–1878.

18. Anton Gerke (1812–1870), pianist, cofounder of the Russian Symphonic Society, father of Tchaikovsky's schoolmate August Gerke, who was also a pianist.

19. Cesare Ciardi (1817–1877), Italian flutist, who from 1853 played in the orchestra of the Italian Opera in St. Petersburg; professor at the St. Petersburg Conservatory.

20. Viktor Tolstov (1848–1908), pianist, professor at the St. Petersburg Conservatory, 1878–1908; Louis Homilius (1845–1908), conductor, professor at the St. Petersburg Conservatory.

21. Porfiry Konev (1847–188?), pianist, professor at the Moscow Conservatory, 1872–1882.

22. Karl van Ark (1842–1902), pianist and composer, professor at the St. Petersburg Conservatory from 1876.

23. "Là ci darem la mano," the duet of Don Giovanni and Zerlina in the first act of Mozart's *Don Giovanni.*

24. Clara Schumann toured in Russia in 1844 and in 1863–1864.

25. Cesare Pugni (1802–1870), Italian composer of ballets at the St. Petersburg theaters, 1853–1870.

26. Friedrich Kuhlau (1786–1832), Danish composer and pianist of German birth. Although he did not play the flute, he composed many works for this instrument. His *Großes Quartett für vier Flöten,* op. 103, was finished in 1826.

27. The Mikhailovsky was the only theater in St. Petersburg where plays were performed in French.

28. Otto Jahn (1813–1869), German classical philologist, archeologist, and music scholar.

29. Before the Conservatory opened, Tchaikovsky and Spasskaia attended the classes offered by the Russian Musical Society.

30. Johann Bellermann (1832–1903), German composer and author of a historical exposition on mensural music (1858), a treatise on counterpoint (1862), and other theoretical works.

III. The Conservatory Professor (1866–1876)

1. The opera *The Voyevoda* was based on Ostrovsky's play *A Dream on the Volga [Son na Volge].*

2. Friedrich de la Motte-Fouqué's tale had long been popular in Russia in the version by Vasily Zhukovsky.

3. P. I. Chaikovskii, *Dnevniki P. I. Chaikovskogo (1873–1891)* (Moscow-Petrograd, 1923), 176–177.

4. The composer's third opera, *The Oprichnik,* was adapted from the tragedy by the historical novelist Ivan Lazhechnikov and set during the reign of Ivan the Terrible in the sixteenth century.

5. Quoted in *TQM,* 159.

6. *PSS,* 5: 353.

7. *PSS,* 7: 64–65.

8. *PSS,* 6: 80.

9. R. V. Genika, "Iz konservatorskikh vospominanii," *Russkaia muzykal'naia gazeta* 36–37 (1916): 637–638; 40 (1916): 938–943; partial in *VC* (1962), 147–153, and *BTR,* 31–32.

10. *PR*, 686–687; GDMC, M 2, no. 40, f. 4, ll. 2–4.

11. *VC* (1962), 154–156; partial in *BTR*, 33–34.

12. *VC* (1962), 157–158; partial in *BTR*, 34–35.

13. V. A., "Iz vospominanii o N. G. Rubinshteine i Moskovskoi Konservatorii," *Russkii arkhiv* 3 (1897): 463, 469- 470.

14. On Tchaikovsky and Klimenko, see *TQM*, 138–140; *CZN*, 64–67.

15. Finally published in post-Soviet Russia in 1995, see *CZN*, 64–92.

16. Siegfried Wilhelm Dehn (1799–1858), German music scholar, well known for his works in harmony. Mikhail Glinka and Anton Rubinstein were among his students. Johann Georg Albrechtsberger (1736–1809), Austrian musicologist and composer. François-Joseph Fétis (1784–1871), Belgian music scholar. Baron François Auguste Gevaert (1828–1908), Belgian composer and musicologist. Tchaikovsky translated into Russian the latter's textbook on harmony.

17. Nikolay Klenovsky (1853–1915), Russian composer and conductor.

18. Glikeriya Fedotova, Lyubov Nikulina, Evlaliya Kadmina, Ivan Samarin, and Mikhail Reshimov were actors with the Moscow Maly Theater.

19. About Litvinov's financial support by Tchaikovsky see *PSS*, 7: 15.

20. Dimitry Usatov (1847–1913), tenor at the Bolshoy Theater, later taught at the Moscow Conservatory; Fyodor Shalyapin was one of his students.

21. Klimenko's own footnotes are included in the main text in parentheses, immediately after the corresponding sentence.

22. The program of *Fatum,* as told by Klimenko, most certainly has to do with Tchaikovsky's homosexuality.

23. Sergey Rachinsky (1836–1902), professor of botany, society friend and admirer of Tchaikovsky's music, who wrote the libretto for the composer's unfinished opera *Mandragora.* Tchaikovsky dedicated to him the first String Quartet, in D Major, op. 11.

24. Konstantin Batyushkov (1787–1855), Russian poet.

25. Pyotr Jurgenson (1836–1903), founder and owner of a major music publishing house in Russia; first publisher of Tchaikovsky's works, and personal friend of the composer, who dedicated to him the song "A tear trembles" [*"Sleza drozhit"*], op. 6.

26. Ivan Turgenev (1818–1883), Russian writer.

27. Vladimir Kashperov (1827–1894), professor of voice at the Moscow Conservatory.

28. Elizaveta Lavrovskaya (1845–1919), singer (contralto); sang at the Maryinsky Theater, 1868–1872, 1879–1880, and at the Bolshoy Theater in Moscow, 1890–1891, worked as a teacher at the Moscow Conservatory, performed the vocal part in Tchaikovsky's cantata *Moscow* at its premiere in May 1883. Tchaikovsky dedicated to her six songs, op. 27 (1875), and the vocal quartet "Night" [Noch'] (1893).

29. Nikolay Bugaev (1837–1903), professor of mathematics at Moscow University, father of the writer Andrey Belyi.

30. Part of Tchaikovsky's name—"Tchai" in Russian means "tea," but the name actually originated from the word "chaika," i.e., "seagull."

31. Johann Wenzel (Jan Václav) Kalliwoda (1801–1866), Czech composer and violinist.

32. *Yeralash* is a card game.

33. Vladimir Stasov (1824–1906) critic, a champion of Russian nationalism in arts, especially music. Coined the phrase "Mighty Handful," which was later applied to Russian nationalist composers known as "The Five."

34. Cui's opera *William Ratcliff* (1869).

35. 'Tip-cat' is a popular Russian children song, "Chizhik- pyzhik."

36. Prov Sadovsky (1818–1872), actor with the Maly Theater in Moscow from 1839.

37. Vasily Zhivokini (1805–1874), actor with the Maly Theater in Moscow from 1825.

IV. The Socialite (1866–1876)

1. *ZC*, I: 259.

2. Ibid.

3. *TLD*, 1–29.

4. Alexander Poznansky, "Tchaikovsky's Suicide: Myth and Reality," *19th Century Music* 11 (1988): 202–206; idem, *Samoubiistvo Chaikovskogo: mif i real'nost'* (Moscow, 1993), 25- 41. A recently discovered document in the Russian archives on the status of homosexuality at the end of the 1880s in St. Petersburg, written by an anonymous contemporary exposer of debauchery in the Russian society, fully supports my conclusions. He admits that "the vice of homosexuality has existed for several years, but never has it assumed such proportions as of late, when, one might say, there is not a single class in the population of Petersburg among which there are not many of its practitioners." The author concludes his consideration of the "malefaction that has put down deep roots in the capital" with the following words: "[society] has become convinced that legal penalties are of no use in this respect, for, despite its strict condemnation . . . , the malefaction has not only not stopped its growth, but has become even stronger." Konstantin Rotikov, who published extensive excerpts from this document, agrees: "The epic tone of our unnamed informer creates the impression both of the widespread nature of the [homosexual] mores . . . and of the essentially neutral social opinion: of a healthy tolerance with respect to certain psychological characteristics that do not present a social hazard" (Rotikov, "Epizod iz zhizni 'golubogo' Peterburga," 451–452, 465–466); also in his book *Drugoi Peterburg* (St. Petersburg, 1998).

5. *TQM*, 463–485; Rotikov, "Epizod iz zhizni 'golubogo' Peterburga," 449–466.

6. *PSS*, 5: 145.

7. *PSS*, 5: 149–150.

8. *ZC*, I: 306–307.

9. *PR*, 677.

10. *PSS*, 5: 155.

11. *PSS*, 6: 49–50 (partial); *CZN*, 127–128; *UT*, 61–63..

12. K. de Lazari, "Vospominaniia o Petre Il'iche Chaikovskom," *Rossiia*, 25 May, 31 May, 12 June, 18 July 1900. De Lazari's memoirs were never reproduced during the Soviet era, except for a few short excerpts; see *PR*, 677–680.

13. A. Sokolova, "Komicheskii sluchai s P. I. Chaikovskim," *Istoricheskii vestnik* 119 (1900): 557–571; A. Sokolova, "Vstrechi i znakomstva," ibid., 127 (1912): 536–538.

14. *VC* (1980), 81–82; partial translation in *BTR*, 38.

15. His penchant for imitating female dancers and for using feminine names in reference to himself or other male homosexuals was quite pronounced, see *TQM*, 131–150.

16. Ibid., 118.

17. Iosif Setov (1826–1894), tenor at the Bolshoy Theater in Moscow, taught at the Moscow Conservatory, later manager of the Kiev Opera.

18. Ivan Gorbunov was the same actor that Tchaikovsky met earlier in St. Petersburg; at this time he was playing at the Maly Theater in Moscow.

19. Pauline Lucca (1841–1908), Austrian soprano; Adelina Patti (1843–1919), Italian soprano; Angiolina Bosio (1830–1859), Italian soprano.

20. Tchaikovsky dedicated to Artôt his Romance in F minor for piano, op. 5 (1868), and Six Songs, op. 65, only. Here de Lazari was certainly referring to the piano Romance, op. 5.

21. The name of an Armenian man who courted Artôt is provided by Alexandra Sokolova; see A. I. Sokolova, "Vstrechi i znakomstva," *Istoricheskii vestnik* 127 (1912): 908.

22. Christine Nilsson (1843–1921), Swedish soprano; Jean-Baptiste Fauré (1830–

1914), French baritone; *Hamlet,* opera by Ambroise Thomas (1811–1896), French composer.

23. Daniel François Auber (1782–1871), French composer.

24. Prince Vladimir Odoevsky (1804–1869), Russian writer and music critic.

25. At the end of this story the memoirist is preoccupied less with Tchaikovsky than with Vladimir Begichev, who flirted with young actresses and then confided his annoyance with his wife to a person dressed as a witch, whom he took to be Tchaikovsky, but who was in reality Begichev's own wife. A scandal ensued, to the embarrassment of the whole family.

V. Marriage (1877)

1. GDMC, A 3, no. 1464; *PSS,* 6: 66 (with omissions); *CZN,* 121.

2. GDMC, A 3, no. 1465; *PSS,* 6: 69 (with omissions); *UT,* 64.

3. GDMC, A 3, no. 1490; *PSS,* 7: 263 (with omissions); *CZN,* 122.

4. GDMC, A 3, no. 1467; *PSS,* 6: 76 (with omissions); *TLD,* 13; *CZN,* 121.

5. GDMC, A 3, no. 1467; *PSS,* 6: 76 (with omissions); *PR,* 260; *UT,* 66; *CZN,* 121.

6. Ibid.

7. Later Tchaikovsky fullfilled this request by composing his *Valse-Scherzo,* op. 34.

8. GDMC, A 3, no. 1470; *PSS,* 6: 110–111 (with omissions); *CZN,* 129–131 *UT,* 66–69.

9. GDMC, A 3, no. 1471; *PSS,* 6: 130 (with omissions); *CZN,* 123 *UT,* 70.

10. All surviving letters of Antonina Milyukova to Tchaikovsky have been published in full, see V. Sokolov, *Antonina Chaikovskaia: istoriia zabytoi zhizni* (Moscow, 1994), 219–251.

11. Ibid., 13–15.

12. Ibid., 16–18.

13. The letter has not been preserved; its date has been established on the basis of circumstantial data; see Sokolov, *Antonina Chaikovskaia,* 19–20.

14. Ibid., 19–24.

15. Ibid., 29–32.

16. Ibid., 33–34.

17. GDMC, A 3, no. 1473; *PSS,* 6: 139; *CZN,* 123; *UT,* 72–73.

18. Sokolov, *Antonina Chaikovskaia,* 34.

19. *TQM,* 211; Sokolov, *Antonina Chaikovskaia,* 31.

20. Sokolov's attempt to prove on the basis of circumstantial evidence that their marriage was consummated is by no means convincing; see Sokolov, *Antonina Chaikovskaia,* 35; cf. *UT,* 69–85.

21. For more on Tchaikovsky's marriage, see *TQM,* 204–230; *TLD,* 12–19; Sokolov, *Antonina Chaikovskaia,* 35–56.

22. Sokolov, *Antonina Chaikovskaia,* 40–47.

23. *PR,* 310; *PSS,* 6: 227.

24. N. D. Kashkin, "Iz vospominanii o P. I. Chaikovskom," in *Proshloe russkoi muzyki: materialy i issledovaniia, P. I. Chaikovskii* (Peterburg, 1920), I: 129–131.

25. *TQM,* 195–249; Sokolov, *Antonina Chaikovskaia.* Sokolov's admirable archival study of Milyukova's life creates an idealized image of the composer's wife. Sokolov failed, however, to comprehend the complexities of Tchaikovsky's psychosexuality, which inevitably led him to misinterpret the composer's motives in marrying her and his behavior during the events that followed.

26. In a program of one of the Conservatory's student concerts (preserved in RGALI), Antonina Milyukova is listed as performing one of Dussek's sonatas for piano, which testifies to quite an advanced level of technical mastery; see Sokolov, *Antonina Chaikovskaia,* 188.

27. Claiming Shlykov's children as legitimate would mean that they would have received the surname of their legal father, i.e., Tchaikovsky, which could have caused significant complications for the composer's future life.

28. In the letter to Count Illarion Vorontsov-Dashkov, the Minister of the Imperial Court, of 8 December 1893; Sokolov, *Antonina Chaikovskaia*, 254.

29. A detailed medical history of Antonina's mental illness has survived, from which one learns that her paranoia had considerably weakened by May 1902, when the question of her release was raised. But her illness then worsened again and took quite severe forms until 1907, after which the main symptoms of her condition (delirium, hallucinations, etc.) practically disappeared, according to her medical records, which I was able to study in TsGIA SPb (f. 216, op. 2, no. 365; f. 389, op. 1, no. 2980).

30. Sokolov, *Antonina Chaikovskaia*, 57–143.

31. "U vdovy P. I. Chaikovskogo," *Peterburgskaia gazeta*, 5 December 1893.

32. "Iz vospominanii vdovy P. I. Chaikovskogo," *Peterburgskaia gazeta*, 3 April 1894; reprinted in *Russkaia muzykal'naia gazeta* 42 (1913): 915–927 and in Sokolov's book.

33. Kashkin, "Iz vospominanii o P. I. Chaikovskom," 99–132. Partially translated into English in Alexandra Orlova, *Tchaikovsky: A Self-Portrait* (Oxford, 1990), 73; *BTR*, 50–63.

34. Orlova, *Tchaikovsky*, vi, 411; David Brown, *Tchaikovsky: A Biographical and Critical Study*, 4 vols. (London, 1978–1991); *BTR*, xv, 49–50.

35. *TQM*, 233; Sokolov, *Antonina Chaikovskaia*, 41, 197.

36. *TQM*, 211.

37. *PSS*, 6: 194.

38. For more on this episode, see *TLD*, 21–212.

39. Alexander Milyukov died in 1885.

40. Ekaterina Khvostova (née Sushkova) (1812–1868), became famous for her affair with the poet Mikhail Lermontov. She presided over a salon in St. Petersburg frequented by Glinka and Borodin. Her husband, Alexander Khvostov, was the Russian consul in Genoa (Italy).

41. Vladimir Khvostov entered the School of Jurisprudence in 1857 but did not graduate.

42. Tchaikovsky graduated from the School of Jurisprudence in 1859.

43. The first meeting of Tchaikovsky and Antonina took place in May 1872 at her sister-in-law's apartment.

44. Antonina entered the Conservatory in 1873.

45. Sokolov suggests that the letter was written on 26 March; see Sokolov, *Antonina Chaikovskaia*, 19–20.

46. Tchaikovsky's letter was received by Antonina on 19 May; the composer came to visit her the next day, 20 May.

47. Here Antonina almost repeats a phrase from her letter to Tchaikovsky of 15–18 May 1877: "I am dying of longing and burn with desire to see you, to sit and talk to you." See Sokolov, *Antonina Chaikovskaia*, 221.

48. Tchaikovsky's next visit to Milyukova took place not the following day but two days later, on 23 May.

49. An obvious mistake, since she is still talking about the same day, 23 May.

50. Tchaikovsky probably visited Milyukova a few times during his stay in Moscow at a Conservatory student examination session before his departure in the beginning of June for Shilovsky's estate, Glebovo.

51. Iosif Kotek died on 24 December 1885 in Davos (Switzerland).

52. On 6 July, Tchaikovsky and his wife took the 6:30 P.M. train from Moscow to Petersburg. For more on their stay there, see *UT*, 75–83.

53. The wedding took place on 6 July; Tchaikovsky actually left his wife on 24 September, not in November 1877.

54. In fact, upon his return from his sister's estate, Kamenka, in Ukraine, Tchaikovsky lived together with Antonina only 12 days, from 12–24 September.

55. The visit to the photographer Ivan Diyagovchenko at his Kuznetsky Bridge shop took place on Sunday, 24 July 1877.

56. In her letter to Count Illarion Vorontsov-Dashkov of 8 December 1893 asking for financial assistance, Antonina admitted that she married Tchaikovsky in 1877 "from a powerful feeling of love. With his enormous genius he was extremely intelligent and had a heart of gold. Thus I was endlessly happy. His emotional qualities were so high that his own sister would say: 'If only his personality was free of certain minor faults he would be perfect.' I loved him as a superior creation and viewed him as a god" (Sokolov, *Antonina Chaikovskaia,* 253).

57. The same arguments were made by Tchaikovsky's friends during his infatuation with Désirée Artôt. Antonina also stressed these arguments in her letter to Vorontsov-Dashkov of 8 December 1893: "But our bliss was not fated to last long. Two months had not passed before his friends began persistently to ask him to leave me, saying that geniuses should not marry lest their genius be wasted; that they belong not to themselves but to art and society, and that they supposedly should not even dare to think of their personal happiness. At first he did not pay attention to such talk. But, knowing his weak-willed nature, they repeated it to him unceasingly in my absence and, finally, achieved what they desired" (ibid., 253).

58. This time, at the composer's request, his brother Anatoly sent him from Petersburg a fictitious telegram from conductor Eduard Nápravník about the necessity of Tchaikovsky's urgent presence at the Imperial Theaters.

59. Some more interesting details of Tchaikovsky's last day with Antonina are found in her letter to Vorontsov-Dashkov: "They decided ahead of time upon their plan for arranging it. Once my husband told me that he had just received a telegram at the Conservatory and that he was being urgently summoned to Petersburg for three days in connection with his works. I believed him. His things were packed immediately and I accompanied him to the mail train. Upon arriving at the station I was struck by his confused, helpless state of mind. He shook, his step became uneven, and before the first bell he had a spasm in his throat and hurried off to drink some soda water. On his way he tripped up several times. But I still did not suspect the real situation" (ibid., 253).

60. In a letter to Vorontsov-Dashkov, Antonina describes those moments slightly differently: "We entered the carriage, and after the second bell he embraced me firmly, pressed me strongly with his lips and gave me a long kiss. Then he said somewhat breathlessly: 'Now, go on.' The train departed, and he never returned to me. Three days later other people were already telling me that he would never return. And since then I have been fated to a pitiful, unbearably difficult, lonely existence" (ibid., 253–254).

61. In a letter to Vorontsov-Dashkov, Antonina provides some information about herself after the separation: "I wrote to him many times, pleading on my knees for him to return, but all was in vain. Twice I was able to catch him. I sobbed, begging him to come back to me. He was tender and promised to come, but again he was dissuaded. Since then my life has been full of grief and unbearable emotional suffering. Immediately after my marriage I became the object of universal attention, but as soon as my husband left everything changed. I became the object of ridicule, insult, and malicious rumor. All this has broken me to such an extent that I have begun to fear people, to hide, and I have taken recourse in prayer" (ibid., 254).

62. Nikolay Bochechkarov (d. 1879), Tchaikovsky's close friend from the 1870s. For more on Bochechkarov, see *TQM,* 133–135.

63. Tchaikovsky indeed dedicated this song, op. 6, no. 6 (1869), to Alina Khvostova.

64. Milyukova is talking here about Tchaikovsky's First Piano Concerto, composed at the end of 1874.

65. Hans von Bülow played the First Piano Concerto for the first time on 25 October 1875 in Boston.

66. Karl Albrecht (1836–1893), inspector at the Moscow Conservatory.

67. Ivan Balinsky (1827–1902), Russian psychiatrist. Tchaikovsky's brother Anatoly, in his unpublished notes about this event, mentioned another doctor, Kwicinski; see Sokolov, *Antonina Chaikovskaia*, 198.

68. As new archival documents reveal, Tchaikovsky and his brothers actually faked his illness in order to provide valid reasons for his separation from his wife. Kashkin's doubts actually make sense here, see Sokolov, *Antonina Chaikovskaia*, 42–43.

69. Tchaikovsky's conversation with Lavrovskaya took place 13 May 1877; Kashkin's *Reminiscences* was published in Moscow in 1896.

70. Tchaikovsky started working on the new opera at Shilovsky's estate, Glebovo, after 29 May.

71. Tchaikovsky actually received Antonina's second letter at the end of April, see Sokolov, *Antonina Chaikovskaia*, 21.

72. On the relationship of Tchaikovsky and Nadezhda von Meck see next chapter and *TQM*, 195–203, 250–271.

VI. The Composer (1878–1892)

1. Leopold Auer (1845–1930), Hungarian violinist and teacher, studied in Budapest and Vienna, taught at the St. Petersburg Conservatory.

2. Adolf Brodsky (1851–1929), Russian violinist, studied in Vienna and Moscow, later professor at the Moscow Conservatory.

3. Eduard Hanslick (1825–1904), Austrian music critic and writer. His first work, *Vom Musikalisch-Schönen: ein Beitrag zur Revision der Aesthetik der Tonkunst* (Leipzig, 1854), brought him worldwide fame.

4. Sergey Taneyev (1856–1915), composer and pianist, Tchaikovsky's pupil, opponent of the nationalist school, premiered the Second and Third Piano Concertos; Ivan Hřimaly (1844–1915), violinist and professor at the Moscow Conservatory; Wilhelm Fitzenhagen (1848–1890), cellist and professor at the Moscow Conservatory.

5. *PSS*, 11: 216.

6. *PSS*, 13: 33.

7. Ippolit Shpazhinsky (1844–1917), Russian playwright, adapted his play *The Sorceress* as a libretto for Tchaikovsky's opera.

8. Max von Erdsmannsdörfer (1848–1905), German conductor and composer.

9. Mikhail Ippolitov-Ivanov (1859–1935), composer and professor at the Moscow and Tiflis conservatories.

10. Léo Delibes (1836–1891), French composer, especially of operettas and ballets, including *Sylvia ou la Nymphe de Diane* (1876) and *Lakmé* (1883); Ambroise Thomas (1811–1896), French composer, among his operas *Mignon* (1866) and *Hamlet* (1868); Gabriel Fauré (1845–1924), French composer, author of songs, piano pieces, chamber music, sonatas, concertos, and incidental music for various plays, such as *Pelléas et Mélisande*.

11. Nikolay Rimsky-Korsakov (1844–1908), Russian composer, member of the Mighty Handful; Alexander Glazunov (1865–1936), Russian composer of symphonies and ballet music; Anatoly Lyadov (1855–1914), Russian composer and musicologist.

12. Nikolay Kondratyev (1837–1887), a wealthy landowner, graduate of the School of Jurisprudence, one of Tchaikovsky's circle of homosexual friends. On their relationship, see *TQM*, 140–144, 361–363, 476–478.

13. Marius Petipa (1818–1910), dancer and choreographer, born in France. In 1847

he went to Russia, where he became ballet master at the Maryinsky Theater in St. Petersburg.

14. *PSS,* 15b: 107.

15. *PSS,* 15b: 237.

16. Alexander Siloti (1863–1945), Russian pianist and conductor.

17. A. K. Glazunov, "P. I. Chaikovskii v vospominaniiakh," *Birzhevye vedomosti,* 24 October 1913.

18. Eduard Nápravník, "P. I. Chaikovskii i 'Onegin'," *Solntse Rossii* 44 (1913): 36.

19. Igor Glebov is the pseudonym of Boris Asafyev (1884- 1949), Russian composer and musicologist.

20. *Chaikovskii: vospominaniia i pis'ma,* ed. Igor Glebov (Petrograd, 1924), 13–88; *VC* (1980), 151–199, partial in *BTR,* 72- 74, 166–167.

21. Romain Rolland, "Le cloitre de la rue d'Ulm," *Cahiers Romain Rolland* 4 (Paris, 1952): 190–191.

22. *The Sunday Times,* 24 March 1888.

23. Julius H. Block, *Mortals and Immortals: Edison, Nikisch, Tchaikofsky, Tolstoy* (Bermuda, 1965), 26–28.

24. Varvara Tsekhovskaia, "Pervaia postanovka 'Pikovoi damy,'" *Solntse Rossii* 44 (1913): 13–14.

25. Alexander Adlerberg was an official in the Directorate of the Imperial Russian Theaters in St. Petersburg.

26. Ivan Vsevolozhsky (1835–1909), Director of the Imperial Theaters in St. Petersburg (1881–99).

27. Platon Domershchikov (1850–1900), stage designer at the Maryinsky Theater.

28. Gennady Kondratyev (1834–1905), baritone and director of the Maryinsky Theater.

29. Emiliya Pavlovskaya (1853–1935), soprano at the Maryinsky Theater; created the roles of Maryia and Kuma in Tchaikovsky's operas *Mazepa* and *The Sorceress;* for more on, see her own recollections on Tchaikovsky, *VC* (1980), 148–150; for partial translation into English, see *BTR,* 147.

30. Pavel Pchelnikov (1851–1913), head of the Moscow branch of the Imperial Theaters; Anton Barzal (1847–1927), tenor at the Bolshoy Theater in Moscow.

31. Konstantin Galler (1845–1888), composer and music critic, collector of Russian folk songs; Grigory Lishin (1854–1888), composer and translator of librettos, also graduate of the School of Jurisprudence.

32. Leonid Yakovlev (1858–1919), baritone at the Maryinsky Theater, created the roles of Yeletsky and Robert in Tchaikovsky's *The Queen of Spades* and *Iolanta* respectively.

33. Tchaikovsky's diary of 1884 contains much of interest concerning the card game *vint* and his feelings about it; see *TQM,* 436–440.

34. By this time Tchaikovsky already had a few drafts of *The Sleeping Beauty,* which he began to compose in December 1888. In January 1889 Tchaikovsky finished four scenes and the entire ballet was completed between 19–26 May 1889.

35. Riccardo Drigo (1846–1930), ballet conductor and composer at the Maryinsky Theater.

36. Carlotta Brianza (1867–c. 1933), Italian ballerina.

37. Mariya Anderson (1870–1944), ballerina at the Imperial Theaters, author of reminiscences about her meetings with Tchaikovsky, see *VC* (1980), 202–203, partial translation into English, *BTR,* 81–82. The ballet *Cinderella* was composed by Boris Vietinghoff-Schell. His own recollections on Tchaikovsky are in the next chapter.

38. Nikolay Klenovsky (1853–1915), Russian composer and conductor, wrote ballet music and cantatas.

39. As is well known, Tchaikovsky borrowed this song from André-Ernest-Modeste Grétry's opera *Richard Coeur-de-lion* (1784).

40. Pavel Kamensky (1858–?), sculptor at the Imperial Theaters, creator of Tchaikovsky's grave monument (1897).

41. The embankment of the Arno River in Florence.

42. Nikolay Figner (1857–1918), tenor at the Maryinsky Theater, created the roles of Herman and Vaudemont in Tchaikovsky's operas *The Queen of Spades* and *Iolanta* respectively.

43. Pogozhev's note: Later, after leaving my duties at the Directorate, I read an interview in one of the Petersburg papers, in which Figner gratefully recalled my timely intercession on his behalf.

44. Konstantin Ivanov (1853–1916), chief designer at the Imperial Theaters.

45. Martin-Pierre-Josef Marsick (1848–1924), Belgian violinist and composer.

46. Vasily Safonov (1852–1918), Russian pianist, conductor, professor at the Moscow Conservatory, and its director 1885–1905.

47. Anatoly Brandukov (1856–1930), cellist, Tchaikovsky's former pupil at the Moscow Conservatory.

48. Ippolit Pryanishnikov (1847–1921), baritone, created the role of Lionel in Tchaikovsky's *The Maid of Orleans* (1880) and sang Mazepa in 1884. In Kiev he organized his own Opera Company.

49. Lev Kupernik (1845–1904), writer, critic, and member of the Russian Music Society.

50. Josef Přibyk (1855–1937), Czech composer, conductor, and teacher; from 1878 lived in Russia.

51. Mikhail Medvedev (1856–1925), tenor at the Bolshoy Theater in Moscow, invited for this production by Pryanishnikov to Kiev, later professor at the Moscow and Kiev conservatories.

VII. The Man (1878–1892)

1. *PR*, 374; see my discussion in *TQM*, 184–185.

2. *PSS*, 8:138–139 (partial); *PR*, 547–549 (partial); Pyotr Ilyich Tchaikovsky, *Letters to his Family: an Autobiography* (New York, 1981), 221–222 (partial); GDMC, A 3, no. 1541; *CZN*, 132–134; *TLD*, 21 (partial); *UT*, 88–91.

3. *CZN*, 121; *TLD*, 9–22.

4. De Lazari, "Vospominaniia," *Rossiia*, 18 July 1900.

5. *PSS*, 9: 89.

6. The Grand Duke published his poetry under the initials "K. R."—Konstantin Romanov. For more on the Grand Duke, see L. I. Kuz'mina, *Avgusteishii poet* (St. Petersburg, 1995).

7. Dnevnik Velikogo Kniazia Konstantina Konstantinovicha; GARF, f. 660, op. 1, d. 17.

8. Also known in another transcription as Fitingof-Shel'.

9. Baron B. A. Fitingof-Shel', "Al'bom avtografov: Petr Il'ich Chaikovskii," *Moskovskie vedomosti*, 5 January 1889.

10. V. D. Korganov, *Chaikovskii na Kavkaze* (Erevan, 1940), 43–52; *CZN*, 96–99.

11. V. B. Bertenson, "Za tridsat' let: listki iz vospominanii," *Istoricheskii vestnik* 128 (1912): 807–812; also, in V. B. Bertenson, *Za 30 let: listki iz vospominanii* (St. Petersburg, 1914), 90–97; on Vasily Bertenson, see *PBC*, 15–16.

12. K. A. Varlamov, "P. I. Chaikovskii—chelovek vydaiushcheisia dushevnoi krasoty," *Solntse Rossii* 44 (1913): 2.

13. Nazar Litrov, Dnevnik, GDMC, f. 15, op. 1, ll. 1–101.

14. Vera Butakova (née Davydova) (1843–1923), sister of Tchaikovsky's brother-in-law, Lev Davydov.

15. Alexey Apukhtin, Tchaikovsky's friend from the School of Jurisprudence; Prince Vladimir Shcherbatov, a friend of the Grand Duke.

16. In March of 1880 Tchaikovsky was almost forty years old.

17. This is inaccurate. Tchaikovsky completed the opera The Maid of Orleans in February 1879; the score was published in August 1880, and the first performance took place on 13 February 1881.

18. Konstantin Nilov, naval officer.

19. This project was never realized.

20. The Grand Duke wrote a song to the words of Russian poet Alexey Tolstoy (1812–1875).

21. The wife of the Chairman of the Tiflis Chambers of Justice, Sergey Goncharov.

22. Ivan Verinovsky, young officer from Tiflis, who after failing the miliary school examination committed suicide in 1886.

23. Georg Wilhelm Friedrich Hegel (1770–1831), German philosopher; Pierre Joseph Proudhon (1809–1865), French journalist and politician, regarded as the father of anarchism; Hippolyte Adolphe Taine (1828–1893), French philosopher and critic; Antoine Élisée Cherbuliez (1797–1869), Swiss economist; Herman von Helmholtz (1821–1894), German physicist, anatomist, and physiologist.

24. Alexander Litke (1868–1918), the second son of Tchaikovsky's first cousin Amaliya Litke (née Schobert), often called one of Tchaikovsky's nephews.

25. Reinhold Engel, German violinist and and conductor.

26. Bertenson is mistaken. The first performance of the Third Suite took place on 12 January 1885. On 8 July 1892 the Nutcracker Suite was performed at the Aquarium.

27. Feklusha is the wife of Tchaikovsky's manservant Alexey Sofronov.

VIII. The Celebrity (1891–1892)

1. New York Daily Tribune, 27 April 1891.

2. New York Herald, 6 May 1891.

3. P. I. Chaikovskii, Dnevniki, 273.

4. Ibid., 274.

5. New York World, 8 May 1891.

6. New York Times, 12 November 1893.

7. Chaikovskii, Dnevniki, 284.

8. Musical Courier, 13 May, 20 May 1891.

9. Walter Damrosch (1862–1950), American conductor, pianist, and composer, who was in charge of the celebration for the opening of Carnegie Hall in New York. It was his idea to invite Tchaikovsky to the Music Festival.

10. Rafael Joseffy (1853–1915), Hungarian pianist.

11. Most likely the reporter misunderstood the name "Vsevolozhsky."

12. In fact, Tchaikovsky dedicated his First Piano Concerto to Sergey Taneyev, and later, to Hans von Bülow as a token of gratitude for the latter's performance of it in Boston on 13/25 October 1875.

13. For the song "None but the lonely heart," Tchaikovsky used Lev Mey's Russian translation of "Nur wer die Sehnsucht kennt," Mignon's song from Goethe's Wilhelm Meister.

14. This project never materialized.

15. Dmitry Bortnyansky (1751–1825), Russian composer, pupil of Galuppi. Director of the Imperial Court Chapel, which he reformed and brought to a high state of efficiency.

16. Tchaikovsky mentions here several Russian composers of the eighteenth century: Stepan Davydov (1777–1825), Stepan Degtyarev (1766–1813), Maxim Berezovsky (1745–1777), Pyotr Turchaninov (1779–1856), and Artemy Vedel (1772–1808).

17. Apparently a misunderstanding on the part of the reporter, since the composer mentions only composers of the eighteenth century.

18. This refers to the lawsuit initiated in 1879 against Tchaikovsky's music publisher Pyotr Jurgenson by Nikolay Bakhmetyev, Head of the Imperial Court Chapel, who protested the publication of the composer's *Divine Liturgy of St. Chrysostom*, op. 41, without Bakhmetyev's approval. The suit lasted for several years with a series of reversals, but was finally adjucated by the Holy Synod in Jurgenson's favor.

19. Tchaikovsky liked Pryanishnikov's private Opera Company based in Kiev and had agreed to appear as conductor for his own *Eugene Onegin*, Rubinstein's *The Demon*, and Gounod's *Faust* during the company's Moscow concerts.

20. In the letter to pianist Alexander Siloti a week earlier, Tchaikovsky had also spoken of his latest idea: "I am already considering a new large composition, that is a symphony with a *secret* program" (*PSS*, 16b: 70). The project in question, the forerunner of his Sixth Symphony, was the abortive symphony in E-flat Major. The opera *Iolanta* is mistakenly called by the reporter *Iontala*.

21. Vasily Nemirovich-Danchenko (1844–1936), Russian writer and the brother of famous theater director Vladimir Nemirovich-Danchenko. The project was never undertaken.

22. Those travel plans were never realized.

23. Edouard Colonne (1838–1910), French conductor.

24. *Cavalleria rusticana,* opera by Pietro Mascagni.

25. Tchaikovsky spent 27 October to 12 December 1892 in St. Petersburg.

26. The play was published in *Russkii vestnik* in February 1883.

27. Moritz Moszkowski (1854–1925), Polish pianist and composer, lived in Berlin until 1897, then moved to Paris.

28. Johan Severin Svendsen (1840–1911), Norwegian composer, violinist, and conductor.

29. Zdenek Fibich (1850–1900), Karel Bendl (1838–1897), Karel Kovarovic (1862–1920), and Joseph Bohuslav Foerster (1859–1951), Czech composers.

30. Tchaikovsky has in mind Anton Rubinstein's book *Muzyka i iya predstaviteli [Musik and its representatives]*, published in Moscow in 1891.

31. Here Tchaikovsky is recalling his work in the 1870s in the Moscow newspaper *Russkie vedomosti*.

32. Alexander Sumarokov (1717–1777) and Vasily Tredyakovsky (1703–1769), Russian poets; Zoilus, name of the most renowned detractor of Homer.

33. Anton Arensky (1861–1906), Russian composer; in the newspaper's text Sergey Rakhmaninov's name was mispelled as "Rakhmanov." Anyway, the 19-year-old Rakhmaninov was very pleased, as he wrote in his letter of 14 December 1892 to singer Mikhail Slonov (S. V. Rachmaninov, *Pis'ma* (Moscow, 1955), 81).

34. Mamont Dalsky (1865–1918), actor with the Alexandrinsky Theater in St. Petersburg.

IX. The National Treasure (1892–1893)

1. Sophie Menter (1846–1918), German pianist and teacher.

2. *PSS*, 16b: 213.

3. V. L. Sapel'nikov, "Iz vospominanii o P. I. Chaikovskom," *Teatr* 539 (1909): 12–13.

4. Iu. Poplavskii, "Poslednii den' P. I. Chaikovskogo v Klinu," *Artist* 42 (1894): 116–120; reprinted in *VC* (1962), 365–374; translated in English, *TLD*, 32–39; *BTR*, 199–

203 (partial). Some new details on their relationship can be found in Poplavsky's article "Iz zhizni P. I. Chaikovskogo: zapiski sovremennika," *Vozrozhdenie* 56 (1956): 5–13.

5. L. Sabaneev, "Moi vstrechi s P. I. Chaikovskim," *Russkaia mysl'*, 3 October 1963. A slightly different version of Sabaneyev's first meeting with Tchaikovsky appeared in his book *S. I. Taneev: mysli o tvorchestve i vospominaniia o zhizni* (Paris, 1930), 80–82.

6. Mikhail Bukinik,"Vospominaniia o P. I. Chaikovskom," *Novyi zhurnal* 28 (1952): 239–243.

7. Anton Door, "Tschaikowski Erinnerungen," *Neue Freie Presse*, 30 März 1901.

8. I. E. Bukinik, "Kontserty P. I. Chaikovskogo v Kharkove (po lichnym vospo-minaniiam)," *VC* (1962), 213–228; *BTR*, 30–134 (partial).

9. A. Kaufman, "Vstrechi s Chaikovskim (iz lichnykh vospominanii)," *Solntse Rossii* 44 (1913): 15–17.

10. K. M. Dumchev, "Vstrechi," *Znamia kommuny* (Novocherkassk), 6 May 1940; *VC* (1962), 211–213; *BTR*, 97 (partial).

11. I. A. Klimenko, Moi vospominaniia, 39–51; *CZN*, 78–81.

12. Iulian Poplavskii, "Pamiati P. I. Chaikovskogo," *Pravda* 1 (1904): 257–263.

13. This is untrue. Tchaikovsky did not change a single note in this concerto after Rubinstein's harsh criticism.

14. Sabaneyev is wrong again. Ferdinand Laub died three years before the violin concerto was written.

15. The first performance of the Fifth Symphony in St. Petersburg on 5 November 1888, with Tchaikovsky conducting, was very successful.

16. In reality, Sergey Taneyev liked the Fifth Symphony. Tchaikovsky wrote to Modest 7 September 1888 from Frolovskoe: "Imagine my joy—my new symphony, according to all my Moscow friends, has caused a sensation, and Taneyev (this is most important) is completely enthusiastic. And I imagined that it was no good at all, and was afraid that they might be trying to keep it from me that I had composed something too awful for words" (*PSS*, 14: 524).

17. This meeting at Block's apartment took place 27 September 1892.

18. Tchaikovsky conducted two concerts of Rubinstein's music for the maestro's jubilee, on 19 and 20 November 1889.

19. Nikolay Solovyov (1846–1916), Russian composer, music critic, and teacher; Tchaikovsky wrote to Mrs. von Meck about this incident on 22 November 1889 (*PSS*, 15a: 212).

20. Apparently untrue. Tchaikovsky's first public appearance as a conductor since 1877 took place on 19 January 1887 at the first performance of his opera *Cherevichki* at the Bolshoy Theater in Moscow, but he actually began conducting at the first rehearsal of this opera on 4 December 1886. In his interview with the *New York Times*, Tchaikovsky remembered this occasion: "Up to the age of forty-six, I regarded myself as hardly able to direct an orchestra. I suffered from stage fright, and couldn't think of conducting without fear or trembling. I twice tried to wield the baton, but was covered with shame and confusion. However, during the preparation for the production of [*Cherevichki*] at Moscow, the conductor [Ippolit Altani] was taken sick, and I had to fill his place. This time I was more successful, and I continued to conduct Altani's rehearsals and finally mastered the stage fright" (*New York Times*, 12 November 1893).

21. It is hard to tell whether the anecdote was really told by Tchaikovsky or whether the memoirist borrowed it from Leopold Auer's recollections, *My Long Life in Music*, 204–205; the Russian edition: *Sredi muzykantov* (Moscow, 1927), 106.

22. Alexander III actually permitted Tchaikovsky to compose *The Captain's Daughter* (see Pogozhev's recollections in chapter 6); Tchaikovsky discussed the idea of compos-ing an opera on the subject of Ivan Turgenev's *On the Eve* with schoolteacher Pavel Pereletsky on 21 April 1885 (*PSS*, 13: 71).

23. According to the earlier memoirist, it was *Rigoletto*.

24. Sergey Kondratyev was the younger brother of Tchaikovsky's society friend Nikolay Kondratyev, who died in 1887 in Aachen.

25. Inaccurate information. Tchaikovsky received the degree *honoris causa* not from the London Academy but from Cambridge University.

26. Sapelnikov's memoir was written after Tchaikovsky's death and publication of Modest's biography. For this reason Sapelnikov retrospectively read into their last meeting signs of Tchaikovsky's impending doom (such as the glass of water which later figured prominently as a possible source of Tchaikovsky's contracting cholera and his presentiment of his imminent death). It does not mean that all this necessarily took place. For more on these reminiscences, see Poznansky, *Samoubiistvo Chaikovskogo*, 66- 67.

X. Death (1893)

1. For more on Tchaikovsky's final stay in St. Petersburg, see *TLD*, 49–191.

2. Lev Bertenson (1850–1929), court physician from 1897, who practiced in St. Petersburg high society; for further information about Bertenson, see *PBC*, 11–15.

3. Alexander Zander (1857–1914), physician, from 1896 personal doctor of the Grand Duke Mikhail Nikolayevich, also court physician from 1887; Nikolay Mamonov (1869–?), specialist in internal medicine, later became personal physician to Anatoly Tchaikovsky; for more on both doctors, see *PBC*, 18–20.

4. The first account of the composer's illness was published in *Novoe vremia* and *Novosti i birzhevaia gazeta* on 1 November 1893; the second appeared in *Novoe vremia* on 7 November.

5. Alexandra Orlova, "Tchaikovsky: The Last Chapter," *Music & Letters* 62 (1981): 125–145, and her book *Tchaikovsky*, 406–414.

6. Poznansky, "Tchaikovsky's Suicide: Myth and Reality," 199–220; idem, *Samoubiistvo Chaikovskogo*; Brown, *Tchaikovsky*; *BTR*, 207–226; V. Sokolov, "Do i posle tragedii: smert' P. I. Chaikovskogo v dokumentakh," *Znamia* 11 (1993): 144–169; Richard Taruskin, "Pathetic Symphonist," *New Republic*, 6 February 1995, 26–40; *PBC*; *TLD*; Alexander Poznansky, *Tschaikowskys Tod* (Mainz, 1998).

7. *PBC*; *TLD*.

8. Poznansky, "Tchaikovsky's Suicide," 199–220.

9. *PBC*, 31–34.

10. Ibid., 10–28.

11. *TLD*, 94–95, 117–118.

12. GDMC, B 10, no. 8, 471.

13. *TLD*, 76–78; *PBC*, 89–90, note; Poznansky, "Tchaikovsky: The Man Behind the Myth," *Musical Times* 4 (1995), 182. Like Yury Davydov, another of Tchaikovsky's contemporaries, Sergey Diaghilev (1872–1929) yielded to the temptation to exaggerate his own role in the events in his later memoirs, when he "recalled" meeting Tchaikovsky (whom he never met in real life) in the Alexandrinsky Theater and personally handling the body of the dead composer together with Rimsky-Korsakov and Nikolay Figner; see Richard Buckle, *Diaghilev* (London, 1969), 23–24, and *TLD*, 134, 139.

14. *PBC*, 166.

15. *TLD*, 125–126, 137.

16. Ibid., 162.

17. *PBC*, 190–191.

18. Ibid., 191–192.

19. GDMC, B 10, no. 467; *PBC*, 183.

20. *TLD*, 108.

21. Ibid., 132.

22. The most recent fantasies on this subject can be found in Anthony Holden, *Tchaikovsky* (London, 1995), 373–400.

23. *Novoe vremia*, 1 November 1893; *ZC*, 3: 642–654; *BTR*, 210–212, 215–219.

24. For a detailed analysis of Modest's account see Poznansky, "Tchaikovsky's Suicide," 208; *TQM*, 579–589.

25. RGALI, f. 2658, op. 1. ed. kh. 844, ll. 1–13. There are two more versions of Nápravník's recollections, which differ in emphasis and details: the first was published in *VC* (1962), 359- 360; the second in V. Nápravník, *Eduard Frantsevich Napravnik i ego sovremenniki* (Leningrad, 1991), 314–315.

26. I. L. Davydov, "Poslednie dni zhizni P. I. Chaikovskogo,"*VC* (1980), 332–333; *BTR*, 209–210 (partial).

27. Bertenson, "Za tridsat' let," 813–814.

28. *TLD*, 94–95, 100.

29. *Novoe vremia*, 27 October 1893; *BTR*, 213–215; for a detailed analysis of Bertenson's interview, see *TLD*, 94–95.

30. *Novosti i birzhevaia gazeta*, 26 October 1893.

31. GARF, f. 660; *PBC*, 77–81.

32. Poplavskii, "Pamiati P. I. Chaikovskogo," 255–257.

33. Actually, Modest invented this story. An unpublished letter from his publisher Pyotr Jurgenson from 20 September makes it clear that Tchaikovsky came up with the title *Pathétique* for his new symphony toward the end of August or the beginning of September 1893; see *TLD*, 28, note.

34. Georgy Conus (1862–1933), Russian violinist and composer.

35. Schiller's lyric drama, translated by Vasily Zhukovsky, has Joan of Arc dying from wounds on the battlefield instead of being burned at the stake in Rouen.

36. Baron Rudolph Buxhövden, (1870–?), friend of Bob Davydov, Tchaikovsky's nephew.

37. Fyodor Mülbach, piano manufacturer, friend of Tchaikovsky's brothers.

38. Probably Tchaikovsky was looking for a permanent position for his nephew Bob Davydov.

39. Alexander Verzhbilovich (1850–1911), Russian cellist and professor at the St. Petersburg Conservatory; Nikolay Lavrov (1861–1927), pianist, professor at the St. Petersburg Conservatory; Felix Blumenfeld (1863–1931), composer, pianist, and conductor, professor at the St. Petersburg Conservatory; Nikolay Sokolov (1859–1922), composer, critic, and professor at the St. Petersburg Conservatory.

40. August Gerke (1841–1902), senator, Tchaikovsky's schoolmate, member of the Russian Music Society.

41. Tchaikovsky's alleged note to Nápravník's mother, which was also mentioned in previously published versions of the memoir, has caused some scholarly controversy. It has been pointed out that Nápravník's statement that Tchaikovsky visited their home contradicts Modest's assertion in his book that he returned home when halfway there because of the onset of stomach spasms. Furthermore, it has been suggested that the note referred to by Nápravník and addressed to his mother may in fact have been written three years earlier, in November 1890, when the composer wrote a very similar note to the same person (*PBC*, 93–94). Elsewhere I concurred with the view that this was possible (*TLD*, 81). The discovery, however, of the present version of Nápravník's memoir, with its detailed and reliable account, makes it clear that Tchaikovsky's visit to the Nápravníks, during which he presumably wrote the note in question, took place on 19 October while Modest, mistakenly, applied this information to 21 October—the day when the composer fell ill (it must be observed that the earlier, newspaper version of Modest's narrative does not mention the note at all). As it appears in the present version, Nápravník's chronology is entirely plausible and leaves no cause to doubt the authenticity of the note.

42. Modest passes over the fact that he spent most of the day in the theater at the rehearsal of his new play, which delayed the call for medical help and and contributed to the fatal nature of Tchaikovsky's condition.

43. In the original—"three counts Litke," which is obviously a mistake, since only two were present on the occasion: Alexander and his brother Konstantin.

44. This phrase is missing in Modest's account published in *ZC*.

45. As a result of this Tchaikovsky was included in the daily bulletin of people who contracted cholera in St. Petersburg between 12 A.M. of 22 October and noon on 23 October. See *Viedomosti Sankt Peterburgskogo gradonachalstva i stolichnoi politsii*, 24 October 1893; *Peterburgsii listok*, 24 October 1893.

46. The unpublished correspondence between Modest and Bertenson shows that Vasily Bertenson in fact left the city on Saturday, 23 October, traveling to the Smolensk region to visit another patient. GDMC, f. B 10, no. 466. For more about Lev Bertenson's assistants, Nikolay Mamonov and Alexander Zander, who participated in Tchaikovsky's treatment, see *PBC*, 18–20.

47. This is the first mention of Nikolay's presence at the patient's bedside, which indicates that he arrived no later than 23 October and would know about the events of previous days from his relatives.

48. Dmitry Bzul' (1867–1894), cellist, professor at the St. Petersburg Conservatory.

49. Dmitry was the younger brother of Konstantin Konstantinovich.

50. As usual, the Grand Duke wrote his diary entry for the previous day on the morning of the next day and this entry was made on the morning of 25 October. Obviously, at the moment he wrote the phrase "I went with Dmitry," the Grand Duke must have received the telegram about Tchaikovsky's death.

51. This entry was recorded by the Grand Duke on the morning of 26 October.

52. Niki was the future Russian Tsar, Nicholas II (1868–1918).

53. Konstantin Konstantinovich did not finish his poem devoted to Tchaikovsky's memory.

54. Eugène Oudin, English singer, who sang *Eugene Onegin* at its English premiere.

INDEX

ALEXANDER POZNANSKY is a Russian scholar and a librarian at Yale. His extensive publications on Tchaikovsky include *Tchaikovsky's Last Days: A Documentary Study.*

ROBERT BIRD, Assistant Professor of Russian at Dickinson College, has published studies and translations of Russian philosophy and modernist literature.

RALPH C. BURR, JR. is a freelance editor and translator.